····································

FOOD · WINE · BURGUNDY

····································

FOOD

WINE

BURGUNDY

{ BY }

DAVID DOWNIE

PHOTOGRAPHS BY ALISON HARRIS

A Terroir Guide

THE LITTLE BOOKROOM

© 2010 David Downie
Photographs © 2010 Alison Harris

Book Design: *a*DESKTOP.
based on a series design by Louise Fili Ltd
Maps: Adrian Kitzinger

Library of Congress Cataloging-in-Publication Data

Downie, David.
Food wine Burgundy / by David Downie ; photographs by Alison
Harris.
p. cm.
Includes indexes.
ISBN 978-1-892145-75-8 (alk. paper)
1. Restaurants--France--Burgundy--Guidebooks.
2. Grocery trade--France--Burgundy--Guidebooks.
3. Wine and wine making--France--Burgundy--Guidebooks.
I. Title.
TX907.5.F72D78 2009
647.9544'41--dc22
2009010263

Published by The Little Bookroom
435 Hudson Street, 3rd Floor
New York, NY 10014
editorial@littlebookroom.com
www.littlebookroom.com

DEDICATION AND THANKS

This book is dedicated to Burgundy's scores of butchers, bakers,
and beeswax-candlestick makers, pastry-chefs, market gardeners,
jam or honey-makers, cooks, cattle and poultry farmers, cheese-
makers, chocolatiers, winegrowers, winesellers, restaurateurs,
and the many other unsung *artisans de la bouche* who, against
the odds and in the face of rampant standardization, continue to
source locally and responsibly, buy or sell only the highest-quality
goods, make or serve excellent, one-of-a-kind foods and wines,
and shun large-scale production methods, catering to clients
directly in their shops, on their farms, and in their wineries

The author and photographer wish to express special thanks
to David Malone for his encouragement and hospitality, and to
Angela Hederman, Tamar Elster, Linda Hollick, Adrian Kitzinger,
Tim Harris, A.J.B. and Catherine Healey, Mia Monasterli, Kathryn
Dwyer, Cécile Mathiaud of B.I.V.B., Claude Guinchard of CRT
Bourgogne, and Ghislain Moureaux of CDT Saône et Loire.

TABLE OF CONTENTS

....

AUTHOR'S FOREWORD

. . . .

THE AIM OF THE *TERROIR* GUIDES IS NOT SIMPLY TO AID READERS IN THE PURSUIT of hedonistic pleasure, but rather to encourage their appreciation of a slower, more meditative lifestyle based on respect for the soil, the seasons, and deeply rooted cultures capable of producing not only great food and wine, but also a saner and more tolerant world view and way of life.

In the year 2000, José Bové, the controversial spokesman for France's Confédération Paysanne, a small, independent

farmers' union, told this correspondent that, "The real challenge is to face down the prospect of industrial agriculture's
triumph, with a little niche market for tourists . . . we still
have a heritage that we can save in France, but we've got to
radically change agricultural policy."

Confédération Paysanne co-founder François Dufour
showed cautious optimism, pointing to France's struggle
against the European Union to preserve traditional French
chocolate made with only pure cocoa butter and sugar, or

France's and the EU's victory over the World Trade Organization concerning raw-milk cheeses (had a US-sponsored initiative won, the Burgundians would have been forced to stop making Chaource, Époisses, Langres, Soumaintrain, and many other raw-milk cheeses with centuries-old pedigrees). "I think we're stemming the tide," noted Dufour. "We're reversing things. It's not just the peasants, it's local people in various parts of France who're aware of the problems and willing to stand up and fight."

Nearly ten years after that encounter, the battles continue against standardized, adulterated food, factory farming, growth hormones, fresh raw milk versus UHT milk, GMOs, vegetable fats in chocolate, trans-fats, and many other related issues, including the spread of hyper-markets and big-box discounters. Hope comes in the form of the country's symbol, a rooster; the feistiness of French farmers and consumers is the best guarantee French food and French cooking, and that of Burgundy in particular, will continue to strive for excellence in decades to come.

—David Downie

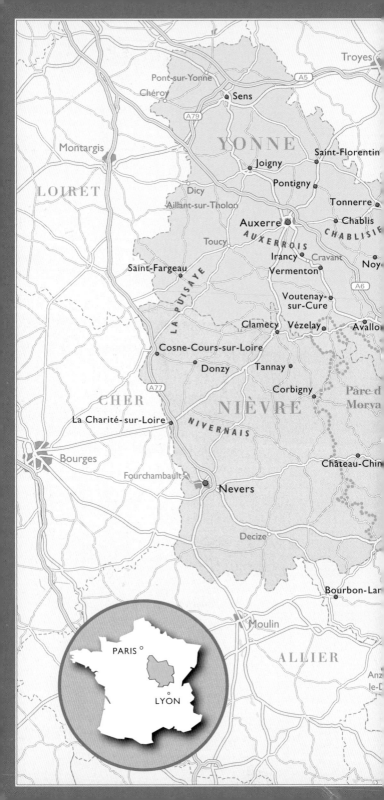

BURGUNDY

KILOMETERS

0 — 25 — 50

MILES

0 — 25 — 50

Parc de la
Forêt d'Orient

AUBE

HAUTE-MARNE

Laignes

Châtillon-sur-Seine

Ancy-
le-Franc

Fontenay

Aignay-
le-Duc

Montbard

CÔTE-D'OR

HAUTE-
SAÔNE

Semur-en-Auxois

Saint-Seine-l'Abbaye

A31

AUXOIS

Vitteaux

DIJON

aulieu

A68

VALLÉE DE L'OUCHE

Gevrey-
Chambertin

Genlis

A39

Auxonne

VAL DE SAÔNE

RVAN

CÔTE DE NUITS

Nuits-
Saint-Georges

Dole

Aloxe-Corton

Beaune

A36

AUTUNOIS

CÔTE DE BEAUNE

Pommard

Seurre

Autun

Meursault

Pierre-
de-Bresse

Santenay

Couches

BRESSE

JURA

Torcy

BOURGUIGNONNE

Givry

Chalon-sur-Saône

Dole

SAÔNE-ET-LOIRE

Buxy

Lons-le-Saunier

Louhans

A39

Tournus

A6

CLUNYSOIS

Charolles

Cluny

ay-
Monial

Igé

AIN

CHAROLLAIS

MÂCONNAIS

Tramayes

nur-en-
ionnais

La Clayette

Mâcon

Bourg-en-
Bresse

Chauffailles

Romanèche-
Thorins

RHÔNE

INTRODUCING BURGUNDY,
ITS FOOD AND WINE

....

VAST, VARIED, AND SCENIC, BURGUNDY—*LA BOURGOGNE* IN FRENCH—COVERS MUCH OF Eastern-central France. Taken clockwise, it abuts the Ile-de-France (and greater Paris), Champagne-Ardenne, Franche-Comté/Jura, Rhône-Alpes, Auvergne, and Centre-Loire regions. Green yearround, the territory has been shaped by four major rivers, the Saône, Yonne, Seine, and Loire. More Romanesque churches, abbeys, and monasteries dot Burgundy than the rest of the country combined. Scores of picture-postcard medieval villages such as Vézelay, Châteauneuf-en-Auxois, Flavigny-sur-Ozerain, Rully, or Solutré nestle in valleys, or perch on mountainsides and vine-groomed limestone escarpments—*les côtes*—their glazed-tile roofs glistening and foundations set deep.

Depth is the key to understanding Burgundy: each of its many sub-regions has a distinctive *terroir*, history, and character, arising from feudal times or as far back as the Bronze Age. Burgundy was the heartland of ancient Gaul. Some locals continue to bemoan Julius Caesar's conquest in 52 BC, which was played out in Bibracte and Alésia, now archeological sites. In Late Antiquity, as the Roman Empire imploded, the Burgonds, from Bornholm Island (Denmark), arrived circa 442 AD, took over the Saône and Rhône Valleys, and created Burgundia. The demise of the Duchy of Burgundy (1342 to 1477), or the region's division during the French Revolution of 1789 into four administrative *départements*, seem recent by Burgundian standards.

Those *départements*, taken clockwise, are Yonne, Côte-d'Or, Saône et Loire, and Nièvre. Two of them—Côte d'Or and Saône et Loire—dwarf several entire French regions. Burgundy is over 200 miles north to south, and 125 miles wide. Yet the population—1.6 million—could fit easily into the first seventeen of Paris's twenty arrondissements. The population density of Burgundy as a whole is low; in remote or mountainous areas such as Le Morvan, it is as low as that of the Himalayas. Once outside the populous river valleys, and beyond the industrial parks or winegrowing slopes, Burgundy is almost entirely rural. The economic mainstays are farming, cattle ranching, forestry, and tourism. Cattle outnumber humans. Tractors from the 1950s still rattle down looping two-lane roads. Crumbling châteaux signal stone-built villages where time lazes by. This is what Frenchmen affectionately call *la France profonde*—deep, rural France.

Burgundians are proud of their heritage and peculiarities. This manifests itself in everything from the region's characteristic singsong accent and rolling Rs, to the almost obsessive way food and wine are revered. At worst, Burgundians' reverence means kitsch folklore, sound-and-light shows, waxwork dummies, winemakers and peasants in costumes, and restaurants, museums, and wineries that feel like theme parks. At best, it reflects Burgundy's culinary and cultural wealth, and the region's role in shaping French winemaking and cuisine from the Middle Ages through the nineteenth century. Many of the twentieth century's legendary chefs—Alexandre Dumaine, Jean Ducloux, and Bernard Loiseau—ran gastronomic pilgrimage sites along the Paris-to-Lyon highways that traverse Burgundy. Today, dozens of luxurious starred restaurants and hundreds of simple auberges devoted to *terroir* cuisine dot the region.

From a winegrower's perspective, Burgundy is the bridge linking Champagne and the Jura to the Beaujolais and Loire Valley. Administratively, the northern edge of the Beaujolais is part of Burgundy; so is the eastern Centre-Loire (Pouilly sur Loire). Some of the world's most expensive, hard-to-find wines grown today come from Domaine de la Romanée-Conti (DRC), in Vosne-Romanée, on the Côte de Nuits, between Dijon and Nuits Saint Georges. Wines from many other Côte de Nuits estates also fetch colossal sums—hundreds of dollars a bottle. At the same time, some of France's most underrated, affordably priced, outstanding whites are grown in the Côte Chalonnaise and southern Mâconnais, both in the Saône et Loire *département*. Excellent-value regional whites and reds bearing the generic Bourgogne AOC label are made in much of the region.

Pinot Noir for red, and Chardonnay for white, account for nearly all of the wine made here. These varieties are rarely blended, and never in top wines (exceptions include regional appellations from Northern Burgundy, which allow inclusion of heirloom grapes, Passetoutgrain, and Grand-Ordinaire). Yet, because of the complexity of the region's soil and climate, and the way wines are made and aged, though mono-varietals, both Chardonnay and Pinot Noir have an exceptionally wide range. To employ a musical metaphor, drinking a white Burgundy is akin to listening to a solo violin that somehow metamorphoses into a violin duo or trio. A red Burgundy is not symphonic like a Bordeaux—it's Beethoven for four hands, played on two pianos.

✤ THE NUMBERS ✤

Surface area: 31,500 sq. km (12,162 sq. miles)

Population: 1.62 million

Population density: 51 inhabitants per sq. km

Working population: 617,000

Head of cattle: 1.4 to 1.8 million

Farmland: 60 percent of land area

Forests: 34 percent of land area

Vineyards: 2 percent of land area

Wineries: 4,000

Regional capital: Dijon

***Départemental* capitals:** Auxerre (Yonne); Dijon (Côte d'Or); Mâcon (Saône et Loire); Nevers (Nièvre)

....

Sources: INSEE, CRT, BIVB

PRACTICALITIES

....

RESIDENTS AND BUREAUCRATS OFTEN REFER TO BURGUNDY'S ADMINISTRATIVE *départements* by using their official departmental numbers: Yonne = 89, Côte d'Or = 21, Saône et Loire = 71, Nièvre = 54. The Yonne corresponds to Northern Burgundy; Côte d'Or is Eastern Burgundy; and Saône et Loire is Southern Burgundy. Western Burgundy is shared by the Nièvre and Yonne. Central Burgundy is shared by all four *départements*, and is covered almost in its entirety by Le Morvan, a mountainous multi-use park.

Normal retail business hours are Monday through Saturday 8/8:30am to 12/12:30pm and 2:30/3:30pm to 7/7:30pm; few retail businesses stay open during lunchtime.

Opening hours for bakeries vary widely, sometimes starting early in the morning (6/6:30am). Wine shops and wine bars often open late (10/11am) and close late (8/8:30pm). Cafés open early (7am), and remain open through lunchtime, closing at 7/8pm. Restaurants seat guests for lunch from noon/12:30 to 2/2:30pm; dinner is from 7/7:30pm to 9/10:30pm.

Important: Nine in ten businesses are closed Sunday afternoons and a half day or full day once a week, usually Monday, sometimes Wednesday. Most businesses close for vacation for several weeks or a month, usually in fall/winter, and again in July/August, particularly around July 14th (Bastille Day) and August 15th (Assumption). Off-season opening days are often more limited than spring/summer hours, particularly in Le Morvan and resort areas. Wineries are often closed in July and/or August. Unusual opening or closing hours of businesses are noted in guidebook entries.

French addresses often include a comma following the street number, and a lower case letter in rue, place, avenue, boulevard, and so forth (i.e., 17, place Bonaparte). For the sake of clarity, the addresses in this guidebook are given without the comma, using upper case letters (17 Place Bonaparte). Particularly in villages and hamlets, there are often no street numbers. Common addresses are "Bourg" (the center of the village), "Grande Rue" (main street) or the highway or rural route running through the village (i.e., D789 or Route de Dijon).

All landline telephone numbers in Burgundy begin with "03." Mobile phones begin with "06" everywhere in France. Pay-per-minute and toll-free numbers begin with either "08" or "09." Wherever you are in France, always dial all 10 digits of a phone number.

The French are hyphen-mad, and while official rules surely exist, they are not applied systematically. You will often find village names (or those of vineyards or wine appellations) spelled both with and without a hyphen (i.e., Saint-Véran and Saint Véran). Many vineyards (and wines) are also given both as singular and plural (i.e., Grenouilles Grand Cru and Grenouille Grand Cru). Likewise, wines, cheeses, and some other products, especially those whose name is also the name of a village or area, can be spelled either with upper or lower case; if upper case, the accent, where present, on the first letter, is optional. The most common instances regard wines such as Pernand-verge-lesses (or Pernand-Vergelesses, or Pernand vergelesses, or Pernand Vergelesses), originally a village and a vineyard; and Nuits Saint Georges (or Nuits-Saint-Georges, or Nuits saint georges, etc.), originally the name of a town and a wine appellation. Cheeses such as époisses (or Époisses or Epoisses) begin, in theory, in lower case (the village always has an upper case first letter). In practice, confusion reigns. For clarity, all wines, cheeses, and village +

vineyard combinations are given with initial upper case letters and accents: Pernand Vergelesses, Nuits Saint Georges, Époisses. Hyphens are omitted. However, where a specific brand or winery or village spells their product differently, or uses hyphens, their spelling is reproduced in this guidebook.

Tourism boards:

The Comité Regional du Tourisme (CRT), based in Dijon, has a very useful website: www.bourgogne-tourisme.com.
   Each *département* has a website:
   Yonne = www.tourisme-yonne.com
   Côte d'Or = www.cotedor-tourisme.com
   Saône et Loire = www.bourgogne-du-sud.com
   Nièvre = www.nievre-tourisme.com.
   The Parc du Morvan's site is www.parcdumorvan.org.

How to use this guidebook:

The five divisions in this guidebook reflect the geographical, cultural, historic, and/or administrative divisions of the Burgundy region. For ease of use, they are listed clockwise, from north to center, east, south, and west. Because of their size, several of the five divisions are sub-divided into sub-regions.
   Listings within each of the sub-divisions are alphabetical; an alphabetical index of place names can be found at the back of the book.

Prices for a three-course meal, per person, without beverages:

Very Inexpensive = under 20 euros; Inexpensive = 20 to 30 euros; Moderate = 30 to 40 euros; Expensive = 40 to 55 euros; Very Expensive = 55 to 75 euros; Astronomically Expensive = over 75 euros.

Important: Every attempt has been made to verify the accuracy of the information included in this guide but businesses close and change hours of operation. To avoid disappointment, call ahead and confirm that an establishment is open.

FOOD

THOSE BENT ON HARD-SELLING BURGUNDY INSIST THAT CULINARY TRADITIONS REIGN SUPREME. That's only part of the story. Certainly, you can eat very well in traditional restaurants and auberges, and particularly at farmhouses and *table d'hôtes* serving fresh, homegrown, local foods. Many perennials are as delicious as ever. Burgundy's gougère—a puff whose dough is studded with cheese which melts when baked—is still found widely. Typical jambon persillé—chunky cured ham in a parsley aspic—is made by hundreds of butchers and *charcutiers*. Escargots are still baked in the snail shell with garlicky parsley-butter. Frog's legs get much the same treatment, though they're usually sautéed. Oeufs en meurette are the region's classic poached eggs in a red-wine reduction sauce with bacon and onions. Crayfish continue to be used in soups, or swim in creamy butter sauce. Pike, *sandre* (a cross of pike and perch), perch, eel, char (*Salvelinus alpinus*), and other freshwater fish are stewed or sautéed as they have been for centuries, sometimes with rough Aligoté white wine or Pinot Noir. Bresse Bourguignonne chicken—the country's most prestigious poultry—is often simply roasted in its own juices or sautéed with heavy cream. Roasted veal or sautéed rabbit come with traditional, creamy mustard sauce. Long-simmered lièvre à la royale is hare in a rich blood-and-wine reduction sauce. Thick-sliced, bone-in baked ham is a favorite of Le Morvan and Chablisienne areas, and can usually be found unmolested. The region's excellent Charolais beef, mutton, and lamb are slow-stewed, grilled, or pan-fried with butter by traditionalists. Wild mushrooms and Burgundy truffles (*tuber uncinatum*) appear in a dozen classic recipes, and so far have escaped the near extinction of better-known Périgord black truffles.

Moreover, the region boasts France's largest concentration of goats, particularly numerous in the south; chèvre cheeses come in many shapes and sizes, from fresh to rock hard or blue. One of France's most luscious and pungent cow's-milk cheeses is Époisses, from the northern village of the same name, while mild Abbaye de la Pierre Qui Vire and Cîteaux are still handmade by monks at their respective medieval abbeys.

Traditional desserts range from rich millefeuilles and seasonal fruit tarts or chocolate pastries, to sugar-sprinkled pets-de-nonne fritters, honey-sweet gingerbread, and round, honey-flavored nonnettes, originally from Flanders (via Dijon).

However, *terroir* traditions, farming, and winegrowing face radical challenges from globalizing trends, factory farming, fast food, European Union health and safety rules, supermarkets, and rural abandonment. A few examples: in Charolles, cradle of the prized Charolais breed of cattle, only one butcher remains; supermarkets have driven others out of business. Much of Burgundy is depopulated, with few local businesses: swaths of Le Morvan have no groceries, butchers, or cheese shops, and are served by roving bakery trucks that also sell UHT milk and a few staples.

A recent and insidious menace is gentrification. Hyper-markets, with convenient, free parking, colonize blighted outskirts, as historic center-city neighborhoods in Beaune, Cluny, Tournus, and a dozen other towns are progressively "beautified" and pedestrianized, keeping cars and customers out—and killing off mom-and-pop shops.

Burgundian ingredients are also embattled: nearly all snails are imported from Poland or Turkey or raised on snail farms; most are not of the indigenous *Helix Pomatia* variety. Frog's legs and crayfish come from Eastern Europe, America, Turkey, or Switzerland. Raw-milk cheeses are ever rarer, as industrialized cheese-making spreads.

Pressure from Paris—a talent magnet drawing Burgundy's youth—to modernize, lighten, and aestheticize homely-yet-delicious Burgundian *terroir* cooking is stronger than ever. The trend began several decades ago, and shows no sign of abating.

The region's best-known culinary innovator of the recent past was the late Bernard Loiseau, of La Côte d'Or restaurant in Saulieu. Loiseau perfected what critics initially derided as *cuisine à l'eau*—water-based, low-fat cooking. It proved flavorful and healthful, and has been widely imitated. Jean-Michel Lorain, another three-star Michelin chef, based in Joigny, is outspokenly suspicious of *terroir*. He has spawned many followers.

Change is also coming from young Burgundian practitioners. They tour France on the marquee chef circuit, apprenticing themselves to (or taking crash courses from) star chefs. This helps budding talents improve their skills and professionalize their kitchens; it also attracts inspectors from guidebooks whose ratings can make or break a business. Burgundian chefs also travel to Asia, and countries long considered Barbarian—England, Germany, the United States. They return with notions about contemporary world-food and décor. Haute cuisine, neo-fusion, pseudo-scientific *cuisine moléculaire*, creative *cuisine d'auteur*, and so-called *bistronomie*—*gastronomique* bistro food—copied from fashionable restaurants, have shoved traditional dishes off many menus. Haute can be delicious; often it's fussy, rootless, and confused. In Burgundy, at least, such gift-wrapped, Eiffel-engineered food also seems to arrive cold at table much of the time, because so much effort goes into the styling.

The truth is, Burgundy, like the whole of France, is suffering from a loss of authentic, traditional, peasant food and *cuisine bourgeoise* (*terroir* food for the middle classes), and an excess of creativity. One aspect of this trend is the mania to *épater le bourgeois*. Borrowed from Baudelaire et al, the expression means "to thrill, shock, or entertain the middle classes." Said differently, dining is the bread and circuses of modernity. The expression might be updated to read *épater le bourgeois Bohème*—thrilling the bobos. Many trendy Burgundian chefs catering to migratory bobos now pay lip service to *terroir* while creating travesties of it. Perhaps that should not come as a surprise; in French, *farce* means both stuffing and nonsense.

Updating recipes and remodeling restaurants is one thing; indulging in play-with-your-food improvisation, with interiors to match, is another. One former Michelin inspector confessed to this correspondent that he thought most starred restaurants in France were "hideous," one place in particular bringing to mind "a high-class brothel," while a celebrated restaurant critic, no enemy of the multiple-star brigade, said she found several to be "temples of bad taste" and "theme parks of gastronomy." Currently, plastic bucket seats, garish, clashing colors, and blinding spotlights are the rage.

It must be added, however, that, while lamenting the loss of traditional food served in traditional settings, many Burgundians welcome a degree of healthy evolution. The danger is that top talents, focused on chasing Michelin stars, are losing touch with their *terroir*.

Perhaps even more important, many chefs now buy the bulk of ingredients not at local markets or from regional producers. Rather they patronize giant cash-and-carry outlets reserved for the trade. One chain in particular has colonized the nation and is radically altering the foodways of France: Metro. Originally German, it was bought in 2008 by UK giant Tesco. Stocked yearround are thousands of items from across the world, including many ready-to-serve dishes; in Burgundy, these include snails, jambon persillé, coq au vin, and boeuf bourguignon. Chefs no longer need prepare everything from scratch; they needn't cook anything at all, and some do not, choosing instead to reheat and garnish what they've purchased. Your tastebuds will tell you whether this is a good or a bad thing.

The above are only some of the reasons why classic Burgundian recipes now appear in novel ways, made with everything from African root vegetables to Middle Eastern spices or Asian and South American sauces. The universal fad among Burgundian chefs is seafood—trucked in hundreds of miles—often merged with beef or snails. Mediocre olive oil is replacing delicious butter and cream in many kitchens.

It's worth noting that this guidebook wherever possible lists restaurants whose chefs still work from scratch, using fresh, locally sourced, high-quality ingredients, serving traditional or updated regional fare and *cuisine bourgeoise* that captures the spirit—if not always the letter—of *terroir*.

SNAILS (*escargots*)

The snail is the symbol of Burgundy. Hundreds of millions of them are consumed annually. Each *terroir* restaurant in the region serves an average 40,000 per year. Burgundy's ancient Gauls and Romans devoured snails. According to legend, in 437 AD, the Burgonds, transplanted from Denmark, when fighting Attila the

Hun near what's now Châtillon sur Seine, banged snail shells on their shields and chanted warlike taunts. What they ate were escargots of the sub-species *Helix Pomatia*, the only one legally recognized as Escargots de Bourgogne and entitled to bear that label. They are pale, with coiling, striped shells, and can weigh as much as fifty grams. Once plentiful, in the 1970s they nearly went extinct from over-gathering, pesticides, and habitat loss. Harvesting of wild snails has been regulated since 1979. *Helix Pomatia* do not readily breed in captivity, and are not widely farmed. If you're lucky enough to eat one, it has probably come from Poland, where it also occurs in the wild. *Helix Aspersa* and variants are commonly known as the European brown snail. They're farmed in Burgundy, the Jura, and other parts of Europe, are prized, and make up about twelve percent of so-called Burgundy snails eaten in France. *Helix Aspersa maxima*, a plump sub-species, are *Gros Gris* (Big Gray) in French. Most snails eaten today in Burgundy are wild or farmed *Helix Lucorum*, from Turkey, Greece, and the Balkans.

Many traditional chefs and home cooks claim that the trick to making delicious snails is to add Pernod to the court-bouillon and garlicky stuffing. Fresh snail season runs from spring through summer. Farmed snails are fed grass and clover, and sometimes cabbage and radishes, purged (or starved) for several weeks, boiled, and cleaned. They are then ready to be cooked again. The classic recipe is for snails baked in the shell with butter, salt, garlic, and parsley. Snails have a distinctive flavor; they do not lend themselves to globalized, creative cooking, of which they are now the victim. Mixed with ground beef—so-called Escarboeuf—or paired with everything from calf's head to raw fish, they are distinctly unappetizing.

Snail caviar is produced by a few hatcheries, has a powerful, earthy, fishy flavor, is extremely expensive, and enjoys limited popularity.

FROG'S LEGS *(cuisses de grenouille)*

Like snails, frog's legs are eaten by the million, are no longer Burgundian, and rarely French. Frogs are a protected species. Frozen frog's legs come primarily from Indonesia. Live frogs from Turkey are flown in young and "Frenchified" for six weeks in purpose-built holding ponds in the Saône and Rhône River Valleys, before being slaughtered, de-legged, and shipped to gourmet restaurants. Frog's legs are nearly always prepared using the same ingredients as for snails, and are sautéed. They, too, have fallen victim to creative genius. Ground frog's legs mixed with everything from ground snails to beef or fish now show up on menus.

CHAROLAIS BEEF AND BOEUF BOURGUIGNON

Burgundians are serious meat eaters. At its best, Southern Burgundy's Charolais is some of the most flavorful, evenly marbled,

juicy, and tender beef anywhere. The Charolais breed is large and uniformly white. It thrives throughout Europe and North America but comes from the Charollais, a sub-region on Burgundy's southern edge. Confusingly, the cattle gets one "L," the region is spelled with two "L"s, like the town of Charolles for which it is named. You can eat Charolais beef in Paris, New York, or Sydney. Most beef experts agree, however, that the best Charolais is exclusive to the Charollais.

Charolais were long used as draught animals. They're unfazed by rain, heat, drought, or subzero conditions, and are unusual for their stature and heft. Prize-winning bulls top 3,500 pounds and stand six feet tall at the shoulder. Ranchers refer to them as "Schwarzenegger bulls." Cows commonly weigh a ton. Charolais, bred for meat, are comparable in quality to Angus, Chianina, and French Salers, Normandy, Limousin, Aquitaine, and Aubrac. However, Charolais was the first beef, and among the first foods, to earn France's Label Rouge (red label) for flavor. Label Rouge Charolais are range-raised ten months of the year, naturally fed and fattened, and guaranteed free of growth hormones or antibiotics (equally true of Agriculture Biologique AB organic-label Charolais).

As with wine, when it comes to beef, ripeness is all: animals must be old enough, and once slaughtered, must be dry-hung long enough, to develop full flavor potential. A fourth element is cooking. To judge the texture, juiciness, and flavor, eat a simple grilled or pan-fried steak, preferably thick entrecôte rib steak, with the ideal amount of fat, and a firm texture. Charolais steaks should be seared outside, rare inside. The rare meat of properly dry-aged beef is dark blood-red.

Boeuf bourguignon stew is made from off-cuts and/or shanks, and, usually, carrots, onions, and bacon and/or salt pork, and, thickened with flour, must simmer slowly for up to three hours. Ideally, it should marinate with herbs in Pinot Noir for forty-eight hours before being cooked, and be made ahead and reheated before being served. The recipe is similar to that for coq au vin and oeufs en meurette.

LAMB AND MUTTON (*agneau and mouton*)

Up to a million head of Charolais sheep roam the region. However, in recent decades, Charolais lamb has been replaced on dinner tables by lamb from New Zealand, which is cheaper. The Charolais breed is now seen primarily in the form of mutton, and often sold to butchers serving France's Muslim community, or exported to North Africa. Slow-stewed, grilled, or pan-fried, Charolais lamb and mutton are delicious and flavorful.

HAM AND PORK PRODUCTS (*porc* and *charcuterie*)

The ancient Gauls raised pigs. Thick-sliced, bone-in, baked ham is a specialty of many parts of Burgundy to this day, but is at its best in the Chablisienne and Le Morvan. Chunky cured ham and parsley in aspic are the components of Burgundy's succulent jambon persillé, found everywhere. Air-dried, raw Jambon du Morvan and pork terrines are especially good in Central Burgundy.

POULTRY AND COQ AU VIN

France's most prestigious poultry comes from Bresse, a region abutting southeastern Burgundy, and in part shared with it. The

Bresse Bourguignonne (a.k.a. Le Louhanais) is the source of outstanding, range-raised poultry bearing the prestigious Appellation d'Origine Contrôlée (AOC) label, awarded in 1957; some Bresse poultry now also bears the new European Union AOP (Appellation d'Origine Protegée) label. All Bresse poultry is of the Gauloise de Bresse breed, is fed only local corn, wheat, cereals, and milk by-products from Bresse, and range-raised. They weigh upwards of 1.2 kilos (2.7 pounds) when slaughtered at three to eight months. To add flavor and tenderize their flesh, Bresse poultry is humanely cage-fattened for four weeks. Only certified, high-quality butchers may sell it. For info: www.pouletdebresse.fr.

Bresse and other Burgundian poultry is delicious simply roasted, sautéed with cream, truffled and steamed, or simmered in a white-wine (or Vin Jaune) sauce with morel mushrooms.

In Bresse, a *poularde* is a female chicken that has never laid eggs, and is at least five months old. A *chapon* is a capon (castrated male), at least eight months old. *Poulet*, chicken, is a generic term (male or female). *Poule* is hen, and is usually cooked *au pot* (simmered whole in broth with a whole onion, carrots, turnips, and other root vegetables).

The best coq au vin is made with Bresse chicken; the classic recipe is very much like that for boeuf bourguignon, and calls for at least one liter of wine, preferably a red Burgundy, onions, carrots, herbs, seasonings, and bacon or lard. Coq au vin should be simmered for two to three hours.

CHEESE (*fromage*)

The region boasts some thirty cheese types (depending on how you count them). Burgundy's chèvre goat's-milk cheeses, sometime admixed with cow's milk, come in every imaginable form, shade, and firmness; thousands of tons of chèvre are made yearly. AOC Mâconnais is always pure chèvre, is pecan-sized but plug-shaped, and costs more than many other chèvres because it's made with fresh, raw milk and aged for at least ten days; only fifteen tons of it is produced annually. Charollais, also pure chèvre and a premium cheese, looks like a three-inch-high wine barrel stood on end. Local variants include Saint Biquet (about half the size of a Charollais), Cabrilou (smaller), Boutons de culottes (half-dollar-sized), Briquettes (flat and long), Crottines (round, low, small), Crottins de Chavignol (like Cabrilou, but from the Nivernais), soft or runny fresh chèvre frais and fromage blanc en faisselle (or faisselles), and pungent, powerful, spreadable fromage fort. Even more than cow's-milk cheese, chèvre is highly seasonal, the best of it made from spring through mid November; the milk for winter chèvre is obtained by "de-seasoning" she-goats with light treatments and/or hormones.

Northern, Central, and Eastern Burgundy make the most flavorful cow's-milk cheeses: AOC Époisses (1,047 tons per year), AOC Langres (434 tons), mild Soumaintrain, Saint-Florentin, Cîteaux, and Abbaye de la Pierre Qui Vire, and thick, rich AOC Chaource (2,245 tons). Also mild, Ami du Chambertin, Plaisir au Chablis, and Délice de Pommard are specialties of the Côte d'Or.

Currently, battles are raging over the use of raw or pasteurized/ Ultra Heat Treated UHT milk, especially in cow's-milk cheeses. Large cheese-makers that truck in milk from far and wide favor UHT milk, which lasts longer and, they claim, is less likely to lead to bacterial contamination. The argument, promoted by industry lobbies, is not backed by scientific evidence. Many small cheese-makers, especially those with their own goats or cows, still use raw milk; their cheeses are universally more flavorful, and, as millennia of experience suggests, wholesome. With cheeses, think—and buy—small, local, and raw.

HONEY (*miel*)

Burgundy's honey is about as good as honey gets. The region has many beekeepers and honey-makers, the best of which

are in uncontaminated areas far from vineyards and industrial-agricultural lands, where pesticides and hybrid crops pose dangers. Particularly prized are honeys from Le Morvan (specifically, those of pioneering organic Les Ruchers du Morvan), and Southern Burgundy's cattle and forest lands (organic L'Abeille de Guye is outstanding). Small honey-makers also bake the best gingerbread and nonnettes. Note that *miel de sapins* (*melat* or *miellat*), is made from the sticky juices and excrement of aphids that feed off fir, pine, and other coniferous trees. It is rare, exquisite, and expensive. All honey-makers listed in this book make cold-extracted, untreated, unfiltered, natural honey.

MUSTARD (*moutarde*)

A condiment related to mustard was made by the ancient Romans in Burgundy and elsewhere. By the late 1300s, the

Burgundians had developed their own mustard, similar to mustard made today. In the 1800s, there were thirty-three mustard factories in Beaune, 150 in Burgundy. By the end of World War II, sixty operated in France. Of today's six, four are in Burgundy, and two are revivals: Moutarderie Fallot (Beaune), Téméraire (Couchey), La Reine de Dijon (Fleurey sur Ouche), and Maille-Amora (Dijon—owned by multinational Unilever). A handful of artisans make garage mustards, usually sold direct or at outdoor markets. Of the mustard seed used for Gray Poupon, i.e. Moutarde de Dijon, and other Burgundian mustards, only two percent is grown in France. The rest comes from Canada and Poland. Why? Misdirected French government farm subsidies. In the 1950s, mustard plantations were replaced by rapeseed (*colza*); officials deemed rapeseed "strategic." Of the two percent of mustard seed grown in Burgundy, all is bought by family-owned Moutarderie Fallot in Beaune, the region's premium maker. *Verjus*, the astringent, sour juice of unripe grapes, was formerly considered an essential ingredient in most Burgundian mustard, but not that of Dijon. It has been replaced by water, salt, vinegar, and/or white wine. Traditionally, Moutarde de Dijon has a smooth texture, and is made with acidic white wine (Aligoté or a blend of varieties). Little Burgundy white wine is used nowadays in mustard-making; it is too expensive.

FRESHWATER FISH

The Bresse Bourguignonne, and the town of Verdun-sur-le-Doubs, are the heartland of pocheuse, a stew of mixed freshwater fish. The earliest known recipe for it dates to the 1500s and includes garlic, eel, carp, pike, perch, and Aligoté, which is flambéed. These same fish, plus the crossbred pike-perch and recently introduced torpedo fish, are found in a similar stew known as matelote, or are sautéed, often with Aligoté or Pinot Noir, or simply grilled. Gentrified versions of pocheuse and matelote are generally made with farmed salmon and cream sauce.

Wild crayfish, now practically extinct in France, often come from Lac Leman in Switzerland, are prepared in soups, or served with creamy butter sauce. Wild trout are rare, found only in Le Morvan; many fish farms in Le Morvan supply the region with good trout. Wild salmon, once abundant, are no longer found in France; however, char, *omble chevalier* in French (*Salvelinus alpinus*), of the salmon family, still occurs, and is highly prized.

GINGERBREAD (*pain d'épices*)

Called pain d'épices (spice bread, a better name), Burgundian gingerbread is rarely hard or shaped like a cookie, as it is in

America. It comes in loaves or rounds, and usually is flavored with some or, rarely, all of the following: aniseed, nutmeg, cinnamon, allspice, ginger, orange zest. There are two basic types. One is firm and dry, eaten as is, spread with butter or with other sweet or savory foods, and used as an ingredient in cooking. This type is baked in large loaves, and contains honey, sugar, and other sweeteners; it is made artisanally and industrially. The second, more luscious type, is moist, tender, and fluffy, and is eaten as is, as a snack or for dessert; it is sweetened exclusively with honey—thirty-five to eighty percent. Honey-makers generally bake pain d'épices of the second type. In the late 1300s, Duchess Marguerite of Flanders, wife of Burgundian Duke Philippe le Hardi, brought a type of gingerbread to the region. Local bakers modified the recipe, which is now specific to Burgundy.

TRUFFLES (*truffes*)

Tuber uncinatum, the Burgundy truffle, is actually found in many places in France. These dark brown nubs ripen earlier

than black *melanosporum* Périgord truffles, have an earthy, nutty, sweet flavor sometimes reminiscent of mushrooms, moss, or even raspberries, are more subtle in flavor than black, and cost one third as much. Burgundy truffles were extremely popular throughout France from the 1400s to the mid-twentieth century, when *melanosporum* gained the upper hand. Burgundy's wet climate, and these truffles' relative obscurity, has spared them the fate of over-harvested *melanosporum*, also a victim of drought and climate change; an estimated eighty percent of Burgundy's truffle country is unexploited.

For information on truffle-hunting, truffle-growers, and truffle retailers: **ADT Yonne** (1–2 Quai de la République, Auxerre, Tel: 03 86 72 92 10, www.tourisme-yonne.com); **ODT** (2 Allée Jean Moulin, Is-sur-Tille, Tel: 03 80 95 24 03, www.covati.fr); **L'Or des Valois** (97 Rue Paquier d'Aupré, Saint-Appollinaire, Tel: 03 80 73 46 20, www.truffedebourgogne.fr); **Le Cos-Piguet** (Cortevaix, Tel: 03 85 59 99 72, devevre@yahoo.com); **Armelle and Bertrand Rion** (8 RN74, Tel: 03 80 61 05 31, www.domainerion.fr, armelle@domainerion.fr).

WINE

THE NOTION OF *TERROIR* AS FIRST APPLIED TO WINEGROWING—TAKEN TO MEAN BOTH THE CULtivation of grapes and the making of wine—may very well have been born in Burgundy. Nowhere else will you find comparable diversity: currently there are one hundred Burgundy appellations (AOCs), some of them *monopoles* covered by a single, small plot. Even more narrowly focused and difficult to grasp is the so-called Climat, which designates a micro-environment, micro-climate, and micro-*terroir*. Indeed, the Climat is the quintessence of *terroir*.

You might find more than one Climat within a *monopole*, and you will find many Climats in some AOCs. Climats share top-soil type, exposure, slope, quantity of stone, clay or limestone, PH of topsoil and subsoil, weather, humidity, topology, and depth of subsoil. Climats can embrace a few rows of vines here, another few rows there, separated by another Climat or even another AOC. Not all the names of Climats appear on labels; traditionally, only in the prestigious Grand Cru and 1er Cru growing areas do winegrowers specify them. However, an increasing number of wineries in the Côte Chalonnaise or Mâconnais are now doing so, unofficially. A good example is La Soufrandière—Bret Brothers, which specifies a dozen Climats, including Les Quarts, which might be considered a 1er Cru or even Grand Cru were it in the highly touted Côte d'Or and not in Vinzelles, near Mâcon.

Wine was first grown in Burgundy in antiquity, possibly by Gauls, certainly by invading Romans after Julius Caesar's conquest (58 to 52 BC). Often quoted is an edict by Emperor Domitian in 92 AD calling for half the vineyards in Gaul to be uprooted, because Gallic wines competed too favorably with those of Italy. Even more thrilling to Burgundians is Rector Eumenus' speech to Emperor Constantine at Autun in 312 AD, during which he extolled the vineyards of Belenos (Beaune).

In the Middle Ages, a handful of royal vineyards produced excellent wines, including today's Corton-Charlemagne. However, Burgundy's winemaking traditions, its complex system of appellations and rankings, reflect the last 1,000 years or so of

✦ BURGUNDY WINE AT A GLANCE ✦
THE NUMBERS

- Burgundy has 100 Appellations d'Origine Contrôlée (AOC) and four *vins de table* (vdt) (Coteaux
de l'Auxois, Coteaux du Brionnais, Vignoble de
Riousse, Coteaux du Charitois).

- Vineyards cover approximately 67,500 acres.

- There are approximately 4,000 wineries, each
averaging five to ten acres.

- Total wine production is approximately 204 million bottles (0.5 percent of world wine production;
3.3 percent of French wine production). About 51
percent is exported.

- The grape varieties grown, by surface area
planted, are:
  — Chardonnay: 46 percent
  — Pinot Noir: 36 percent
  — Gamay: 11 percent
  — Aligoté: 6 percent
  — Other (Sauvignon Blanc, Pinot Blanc, Pinot
  Beurot/Gris, Sacy, César): 1 percent

- Burgundy's wine country is divided into five
main districts, each called a *vignoble*, all near
the Yonne, Seine, and Saône rivers, most with
sub-districts. From north to south they are:
  — Yonne (Chablis + Grand Auxerrois, Auxerrois,
  Jovinien, Vézelien, Tonnerrois, Châtillonais)
  — Côte de Nuits + Hautes Côtes de Nuits
  — Côte de Beaune + Hautes Côtes de Beaune
  — Côte Chalonnaise + Couchois
  — Mâconnais

- A sixth wine district is on the Loire River in the
Nivernais of western Burgundy and includes:

Vignoble de Riousse (vdt); Coteaux du Charitois
(vdt); Pouilly Fumé and Pouilly-sur-Loire AOCs;
Coteaux du Giennois AOC.

- Vineyards break down into four Crus—literally
  "growths." Cru rank is determined by soil quality,
  exposure, tradition (historical and cultural
  intangibles).

- The Cru pyramid, from top down:
  — **Grand Cru:** found in thirty-three of
    Burgundy's 100 AOCs, 1.5 percent of total
    production (1 percent of white wines and 2.5
    percent of reds). Confusingly, in the Côte d'Or,
    Grands Crus are identical to Climats. Grand
    Crus are found only in Côte d'Or (thirty-two)
    and Chablis (one Grand Cru with seven
    Climats within it). The total number of
    Grands Crus Climats is therefore thirty-nine.
  — **1er Cru:** found in forty-four AOCs, 13.5
    percent of total production. 1er Crus are also
    identified by their Climat, of which there are
    (officially) 562.
  — **AOC Communale (also known as Villages):**
    forty-four villages = 34 percent of total
    production.
  — **AOC Régionale (aka Bourgogne, regional):**
    twenty-three AOCs = 51 percent of total
    production.

Important note: Grands Crus, 1er Crus, and Crus
Communales/Villages may each bear the name of
the village the wine comes from.

- In Burgundy, wine accounts for 2 percent of agricultural land, 3 percent of GDP, fills 20,000 direct
  jobs and 100,000 indirect jobs (bottle-making,
  barrel-making, transportation, etc.).

....

Source: BIVB/Hospices de Beaune

winegrowing. Its history really begins with the monks of Cluny Abbey in what is now southern Burgundy's Mâconnais. That is when the best parcels and their corresponding grape varieties, with local variants, were identified. Growing out of them is the mind-boggling classification of Crus and Climats.

During the French Revolution, church properties were confiscated and sold off, giving rise to the thousands of vineyards and some 4,000 wineries currently on the books. By New World standards, most Burgundy estates are tiny, ranging from five to ten acres. The general rule established centuries ago is that each hectare (1,000 square meters, or 2.5 acres) grows 10,000 vines, producing 10,000 bottles (one vine per square meter, one bottle per vine).

Even if only ten percent of the region's wineries were worth visiting, it would be impossible to include all of them in this book. Hundreds are worthy of your attention; scores are outstanding. For reasons of practicality, a limited selection of those accessible to the public is listed. Independent winegrowers—meaning the 1,300 winemakers who grow their own grapes, and make, age, and bottle their own wines—account for the bulk of those listed. However, some of the region's co-ops make remarkably good-value wines and are included. Co-ops are easily accessible: visitors are not expected to make a purchase, and the choice is wide.

GRAPE VARIETIES

Pinot Noir has been the red grape of the best wines of Burgundy since Duke Philippe le Hardi banned Gamay. Gamay still crops up, particularly in granitic areas, accounting for eleven percent of red wines (and some rosé and sparkling Crémant de Bourgogne). It's used in the unfashionable Bourgogne Ordinaire and Grand Ordinaire reds and rosés of the Yonne, and in Mâconnais Rouge.

Burgundy makes twice as much white as red wine, almost all of it with Chardonnay. Chardonnay is also employed in most Crémant (eight percent of total wine production). However, Crémant can equally be made with a blend of Chardonnay and Aligoté (blanc de blancs), or these blended with white-fleshed Gamay and Pinot Noir; though rare, a pure Pinot Noir Crémant also exists (the white flesh and juice are not allowed to touch the skins, except in the case of Crémant rosé, or the very rare Crémant noir de noirs red). The village of Rully on the Côte Chalonnaise is considered one of the best growing areas for Crémant from Chardonnay and Aligoté.

Burgundy's second white wine, Aligoté, is tart. A component in Bourgogne Ordinaire, Grand Ordinaire, or Crémant, it is commonly stirred into Crème de Cassis, a black currant liqueur, and rebaptized Kir. The most prized Aligoté comes from the village of Bouzeron, also on the Côte Chalonnaise.

Minute quantities of heirloom varieties are grown in the Yonne. César, an indigenous red grape, brings body to thin northern reds; so too Sacy, an heirloom white, blended into northern whites. In the Auxerrois sub-region, white Sauvignon is grown around Saint-Bris-le-Vineux. Pinot Gris is found around Joigny. Melon de Bourgogne (Muscat) is also grown in northern-central areas.

In western Burgundy's Nivernais, on the Loire, about eighty acres of Chasselas are still grown to make Pouilly-sur-Loire AOC wines (www.pouilly-fume.com).

It's often said that Burgundy's best whites come from the Côte de Beaune, reds from the Côte de Nuits—both in Côte d'Or. A ditty can help you remember this: *Bone white, dark as night.* Bone as in Beaune, for whites; Nuits, meaning nights, for red (dark). However, Beaune grows many excellent reds, and Nuits exceptional whites; the claim itself is suspect.

PHYLLOXERA AND GRAPEVINE CLONES

With a handful of exceptions, grapevines in Europe are grown from American rootstock resistant to *Phylloxera Daktulosphaira vitifoliae*, a button-sized pest of the aphid family that resembles a tick when born. It saps the life from grapevines, causing them to die after ten or twelve years. Unwittingly shipped in the 1850s with plant samples from the East Coast of America to England, it crossed the Channel to France, Italy, Spain, Germany, and Eastern Europe, devastating vineyards in a matter of decades. Nine in ten European winegrowing areas were affected. Despite modern treatments (pesticides and ultra-heat-treating of soil with steam), phylloxera thrives. That explains the continuing need for American rootstock, which phylloxera abhors. A convincing argument could be made that phylloxera was a blessing in disguise. Countless marginal winegrowing areas were abandoned, and overproduction of mostly bad wines ceased (it returned in the postwar era, when factory farming methods were applied to wine).

Clones are vine seedlings descended from specific vine stock, selected for specific characteristics and health. Initially, typical Burgundian local clones were grafted onto American rootstock. In recent decades, "improved" clones have replaced local ones, particularly those considered inferior. Overall, this has increased the quality of wine, but has also led to loss of genetic diversity, standardizing grapes and hence wines. As with everything from chalk to cheese and real estate, one man's "improvement" is another's destruction.

In 2008, the Bureau Interprofessional des Vins de Bourgogne (BIVB) and Burgundy Regional Government created a study center (CRITT) in Dijon to protect local clones of Pinot Noir and Chardonnay from extinction. It includes a conservatory, currently being planted, in Époisses (of cheese fame). In greenhouses and vineyard plots, some 2,000 to 3,000 different clones are grown, among them, about 200 heirloom lines of Pinot Noir. That such steps are being taken indicates how serious is the threat to Burgundy's rich viticultural heritage.

THE MAKING OF BURGUNDY WINE

Producing great wine anywhere is difficult. In Burgundy it is particularly challenging. Centuries of intensive winegrowing—and half a century of chemical poisoning—has eroded and impoverished the topsoil. The climate is tricky, with severe, long

winters and short summers. Small, often steep vineyards mean that grape-growing is labor intensive. This partly explains the low yields and premium prices. The reputation, quality, and increasing worldwide demand for Burgundy explain the rest. It's now almost a truism that, while many European wine regions are struggling to survive, Burgundy cannot make enough wine. Investors are extending vineyards into formerly unexploited territory, in the Hautes Côtes de Nuits or Hautes Côtes de Beaune, or reclaiming abandoned areas. Much acreage was lost in the nineteenth and twentieth centuries to phylloxera, notably in the

Yonne and Châtillonnais (Côte d'Or). Ironically, global warming is helping make replanting possible. The longterm effect on Burgundy's reputation of reviving what were often marginal vineyards is debatable.

Just as globalized haute cuisine is influencing Burgundy's cooking, the selection of clones, oaking, and technical manipulation of wines is affecting traditional winegrowing. The large oak barrels and oak or cement vats and tanks of yesteryear are still in use. However, many wineries employ increasing numbers of generously toasted, new-oak barrels and casks, imparting New World flavors to wines, particularly those for export to the UK, US, and Northern Europe, or to hide defects.

Nowadays, Burgundian red wines are commonly low-temperature macerated—meaning, the partially crushed grapes are allowed to sit, often with skins and sometimes with stems and seeds—for days or weeks, to extract color and tannins. Only afterwards does alcoholic fermentation (in open vats) begin. As in traditional bakeries using a sourdough sponge, indigenous yeasts on grape-skins, in the air, and on winery walls, should ensure proper grape fermentation. Yet many winemakers, like anxious bakers, stir in selected yeasts to turbo-charge fermentation, theoretically to guarantee predictable products; this challenges the nature of wine, a living beverage which differs from vintage to vintage and place to place.

Once alcoholic fermentation is complete, reds go into tanks, vats, or barrels, where the malolactic fermentation and aging occur. For whites, the grapes are gently crushed upon arrival, macerated for several hours, and the pressed juice allowed to settle overnight. The juice is then filtered before going into tanks, vats, or oak barrels, often with the addition of selected yeasts, for alcoholic, followed by malolactic, in-barrel fermentation.

With both reds and whites, each winemaker has his recipe. Varying widely are the degree of crushing or fracturing of grapes; the length of maceration and settling; the inclusion of stems, skins, and seeds; the use of selected or indigenous yeasts; the stirring and filtering of the must; and many other processes, right up to the choice of stopper: cork for traditionalists who favor micro-oxygenation and natural aging, screwcaps for the avant garde.

Happily, the soil and relatively cool, wet, semi-continental climate—though changing—mean that most Burgundy wines are unlikely to develop the flab of their New World counterparts.

✦ OAK AND FIG LEAVES ✦

Traditionalist Burgundians refer
to over-oaking as a *cache-misère*—a fig leaf.
In this case, the leaf is used to cover defects, or to
sex-up uninteresting wines. The darker the toasting,
the newer the barrel, and the longer the wine stays
in it, the more the oak and tannins are captured.
Many Burgundies benefit from judicious oaking, and
have traditionally been fermented and aged in oak,
whether in small, medium or large barrels or vats, of
varying ages. Apologists of oaking often claim that
their ancestors the ancient Gauls were skilled barrel-
makers, which is true. Whether these barrels were
used for winemaking is uncertain: until the arrival
of Caesar, the Gauls were drinkers of beer, which
they called *cervoise*. Whether winemaking began in
Gaul before the Romans, or was widely known, is
controversial. In either case, it's a poor defense for
over-oaking wines today.

As a rule of thumb, the fatter the wine, the better
it stands up to oak; big Burgundies are improved. It's
difficult to imagine a vintage Grand Cru Clos des
Lambrays or Clos-de-Tart, a Bâtard-Montrachet or
Meursault, made without new oak barrels. However,
most Chablis and Mâconnais white wines are delicate, highly complex, and etched by minerals, and
are not necessarily improved, but often deadened, by
oak; those that attempt to resemble Meursaults or
other big wines usually fail miserably. Many Bourgogne AOC regional wines should also be spared:
they are pleasant when made in stainless steel.
Burgundies with vanilla overlays and high alcohol
content made with oenological wizardry—selected
yeasts, extended maceration or sugaring—are often
designed for fledgling, foreign palates, particularly
those that favor flab.

. . . .

The global market-chasing mania of fruit-forward, quick-and-easy bottlings has not entirely taken root, especially among independent winegrowers. In fact, that trend appears to be reversing. Most Burgundian Pinot Noirs are still subtle, complex, and lightly tannic, with an intense, many-layered violet or blackcurrant nose, and a relatively light red color. Chardonnays range from the nervy, lean, mineral-rich to the fat and subtly honeyed. The best Burgundy whites and reds take time to develop, some lasting twenty or thirty years.

Overall, Burgundy wines are better-made today than they have been in much of the preceding postwar era.

NÉGOCIANTS, INDÉPENDANTS, AND CO-OPS

Traditionally, a *négociant* (also *négociant-eleveur*) is a wine merchant or wholesaler who does not make wine, but ages and bottles others' wines. From one hundred to just a few years ago, the number of *négociants* has risen to 250 today. However, the statistics are confusing: scores of winegrowers are also *négociants*; they buy grapes from other vineyards, because vineyard property has become too expensive to purchase; they also make, age, and bottle their own wines.

Of the region's 4,000 winegrowers, approximately 1,300 grow their own grapes, and make, age, and bottle their own wines using their own labels; 2,700 others sell their grapes or wines to co-ops and *négociants*. The biggest *négociants* (or *maisons de négoce*) are corporate-owned and continue to cherry-pick prestigious, independent family-run properties.

Many of Burgundy's co-operative wineries are huge, representing hundreds of grape-growers and winemakers. Until recently, most co-ops did not embrace respectful vineyard practices, using pesticides and herbicides, and routinely machine-picking grapes. Many are improving. The number and size of co-ops is rising; independents find it hard to compete with them in a global marketplace.

INDEPENDENT WINEGROWERS' ASSOCIATIONS

Increasingly embattled, many small, independent winegrowers have banded together by *département*. For a complete listing of them: **Vignerons Indépendants de France** (4 Place Félix Eboué, 75012 Paris, Tel: 01 53 02 05 10, www.vigneron-independant .com).

ORGANIC AND BIODYNAMIC WINE

After decades of mechanical ploughing and pruning, causing soil-compaction; destruction of vineyard grasses and weeds; and intense use of vineyard fertilizers, pesticides, fungicides, and herbicides; suddenly Burgundy (and other French regions) is going green. More accurately, it is attempting to appear to be greening itself.

It comes as a surprise to many winelovers that there is no such thing as "organic wine" in France. Organic grapes exist, organic wine does not. However, as shorthand, wines made from grapes grown using approved organic methods—*agriculture biologique*, labeled AB—are broadly referred to as *vins biologiques* or *bio*. Over 100 wineries in Burgundy are certified AB. Biodynamic wines—*vins biodynamiques*—are organic and additionally follow methods

codified by Austrian scientist-philosopher Rudolf Steiner in the 1920s; the certifying organism in France is not recognized by the French government. Biodynamism focuses on natural defenses and respect for lunar cycles. For information: **Biobourgogne SEDARB** (19 Avenue Pierre Larousse, Auxerre, Tel: 03 86 72 92 20, www.biobourgogne.fr). Like traditional wines, nearly all *bio* and *biodynamique* wines are sulfured.

A halfway house is *agriculture raisonnée* or *lutte raisonnée*, with limited treatments; it's backed by agro-chemical companies, who see trouble on the horizon. Their acolytes commonly claim that organic grape-growing results in grape-loss of up to fifty percent (to mold, disease, and pests). Therefore, they argue, only eccentrics, the rich, or the long-established can afford *bio*. This is nonsense. As organic methods spread, and grape-growers reap rewards, the green movement gains respectability.

Enherbement—letting grass grow—is gaining ground across the board: it reduces erosion, fosters competition, and appears to enhance, not weaken, the vigor of grapes. (It also gives wildlife a chance.)

Raisonné, organic, and even biodynamic wines are experiencing a boom, particularly in the Mâconnais and Côte d'Or. Domaine des Comtes Lafon, Anne Leflaive, and Domaine Lalou Bize-Leroy are three prestigious organic or biodynamic properties. Other celebrated wineries, including Domaine de la Romanée Conti, shunned chemical fertilizers and treatments from the outset, but preferred not to identify themselves as organic, long considered marginal.

In the postwar era, the Mâconnais engendered the first self-declared French organic grape growers. The earliest certified-organic vineyard in France (1954) belongs to the Guillot family; its members still make fine wine in the village of Cruzille-en-Mâconnais.

WINE ROUTES

Each *vignoble* and many sub-regions have a wine route—usually marked "Route des Vins." Dozens of wineries on these routes are open to the public. They range from fledglings up. Organic wine-growers have their own route (www.biobourgogne.fr). However, Burgundy is not the Napa Valley. Many premium wineries sell out far ahead and are accessible only to professionals.

For up-to-date wine and winery statistics and info, an exhaustive list of AOCs, Crus and Climats, and hundreds of wineries open to the public on wine routes, visit www.bivb.com.

WINERY ETIQUETTE

Before visiting, it's always best to phone a winery and make contact, especially at prestigious, independent, small, family-run properties, even if they are theoretically open without appointment. The reason: winegrowers are in their vineyards part of each day; they also deliver their wines, participate in fairs, and sell at open markets. At small, independent wineries it is also good practice to make a purchase, even a small one, after a tasting. Important: Winery hours vary widely; few if any are open from noon to 2pm or on Sunday; summertime closings are common. Unusual opening or closing hours are noted in guidebook entries.

WINERY NAMES

To avoid confusion, every effort has been made to provide the full name of the winery, starting with Château or Domaine or EARL. Many winemaking families share the same last name; in a single village you're likely to come across half a dozen *domaines* (estates) named Bouzereau, Chapelle, Cornu, Dufouleur, Leflaive, and so forth. Some wineries simply bear the owner's or founder's name, nothing else.

LES CHEVALIERS DU TASTEVIN'S LIST

A brotherhood of wine professionals, formed in 1932 to promote the region's wines, and based since 1944 at Château du Clos

de Vougeot in Vosne-Romanée, les Chevaliers du Tastevin do bi-yearly blind tastings of hundreds of Burgundy bottlings. Knights are asked the simple question: would you be proud to serve this wine to a friend? On average, one third of wines submitted get the thumbs-up. In 2008, the list ran to over 1,497 different bottlings, of which 518 were approved. The list may be viewed at www.tastevin-bourgogne.com.

❧ FAVORITE WINERIES ❧
OF TOP BURGUNDIAN WINESELLERS

MANY LOCAL WINESELLERS ARE EXPERTS on the wines and wineries of Burgundy and their sub-region. They stock bottlings which you would not find elsewhere, and might never be able to buy at the winery (most top wineries are not accessible; many reserve their best wines for winesellers, restaurateurs, and regular customers). Some *cavistes* stock rare, old vintages. All these are reasons to patronize winesellers, even if it means spending more than you would by going directly to a winery, In the long run, they can save you time and money. Yet another reason to patronize them is they often organize wine tastings. Guided tastings can be instructive and enjoyable. Finally, at wine shops, you choose among many bottlings, and are not pressured to make a purchase.

The following are short lists of top winesellers' *coups de coeur*—their favorite wineries or winemakers. Many of these wineries are not open to the public. The winesellers are listed clockwise from north to center, east, south, and west; the wineries are listed in alphabetical order, not in order of preference (with occasional comments from the winesellers).

• **Le Cellier des Agapes** (13 Rue de Preuilly, Auxerre, Tel: 03 86 52 15 22, ragaine.marc@wanadoo.fr). Caviste: Marc Regaine.

—**Domaine Jean Hugues et Ghislaine Goisot**, Saint Bris, Yonne.
—**Domaine Olivier Morin**, Chitry, Yonne.
—**Xavier Bernier**, Saint Julien, Beaujolais.
—**Domaine Chantal Lescure**, Nuits Saint Georges.
—**Jean Louis Trapet**, Domaine Trapet, Gevrey Chambertin.
—**Raveneau**, Chablis.
—**Benoît et Jean-Paul Droin**, Chablis.
—**Pascal Roblet-Monnot**, Curil, Bligny-les-Beaune.
—**Les Champs de l'Abbaye**, Aluze, Couchois.
—**Christiane et Jean-Claude Oudin**, Chablis.

• **Le Saint Vincent** (28 Rue Saint Etienne, Vézelay, Tel: 03 86 33 27 79, www.bourgogne-vin.com). Cavistes: Roger and Jocelyne Blanco.

RED WINES
—**Domaine Philippe Charlopin**, Gevrey Chambertin. *Best wine:* Gevrey Chambertin Vieilles Vignes, a full-bodied, silky, softly tannic wine; wait five years to drink it.
—**Domaine Gentet-Pansiot**, Gevrey Chambertin. *Best wine:* Marsannay Champs Perdrix, fruity, with blackberry and cherry aromas; wait five years to drink it.
—**Domaine R. et S. Groffier**, Morey St Denis. *Best wine:* Chambolle Musigny 1er Cru Les Sentiers, a velvety wine with fresh fruit aromas; wait five to ten years to drink it.
—**Domaine Meo-Camuzet Frère & Soeur**, Fixin. *Best wine:* Fixin 1er Cru Clos du Chapitre, delicately oaked and silky; wait five years to drink it.
—**Domaine Denis Mortet**, Gevrey Chambertin. *Best wine:* Gevrey Chambertin Vieilles Vignes, densely colored, lightly smoky and oaky, as good as a 1er Cru. Drink within ten years.

—**Domaine Jacques Frédéric Mugnier**, Nuits Saint Georges, Nuits Saint Georges 1er Cru Clos de la Maréchal, a powerful wine smelling of cherries, stiff backbone. Drink within ten years.

WHITE WINES

—**Domaine Hubert Lignier**, Morey St Denis. *Best wine:* Saint Romain Sous le Château, pure, clean and straight mineral qualities; its acidity stimulates the taste buds. Drink in two to five years.

—**Domaine Ponsot**, Morey-Saint-Denis. *Best wine:* Morey-Saint-Denis 1er Cru Les Monts Luisants, made from Aligoté from vines seventy years old or more. As good as Burgundy's great whites. Astonishingly fresh. Keeps for well over ten years.

—**Domaine des Héritiers du Comte Lafon**, Milly Lamartine, Mâconnais. *Best wine:* Mâcon Clos de la Crochette, lively, pleasantly mineral, with citrus aromas, to drink any time of day. Drink young.

—**Domaine Vincent Dauvissat**, Chablis. *Best wine:* Petit Chablis, a big wine from a humble AOC. Drink within five years.

—**Domaine Jean Hugues et Ghislaine Goisot**, Saint Bris (Yonne). *Best wine:* Saint Bris Cuvée Corps de Garde, a fine Sauvignon full of freshness and delicacy. Drink in two to five years.

• **La Carte des Vins** (1 Rue Musette, Dijon, Tel: 03 80 30 45 01, www.lacartedesvins.com). Cavistes: Jean-Luc Roblin, Adrien Tirelli.

—**Alain Coche Bizouard**, Meursault.
—**Alain Michelot**, Nuits Saint Georges.
—**Bernard Moreau**, Chassagne-Montrachet.
—**David Duban**, Hautes-Côtes-de-Nuits.
—**Dujac**, Morey-Saint-Denis.
—**Dupont-Tisserandot**, Gevrey-Chambertin.
—**Étienne Sauzet**, Puligny-Montrachet
—**Rapet Père et Fils**, Pernand Vergelesses.

—**Robert Arnoux/Pascale Lachaux**, Vosne-Romanée.
—**Robert-Denogent**, Pouilly-Fuissé.

• **La Vinothèque** (4 Rue Pasumot, Beaune, Tel: 03 80 22 86 35, www.bourgogne-vinotheque.com). Caviste: Jérôme Filliatre.

—**David Duband**, Hautes-Côtes-de-Nuits. All his Côtes-de-Nuits wines.
—**Domaine Alain Coche Bizouard**, Meursault. Fabien Coche makes excellent wines, from the Aligoté to the Meursault Goutte d'Or.
—**Domaine Boillot**, Gevrey-Chambertin. Lucien Boillot's Volnay and Puligny-Montrachet.
—**Domaine Diconne**, Auxey Duresses. Christophe Diconne's Auxey Duresses red and 1er cru are very fine.
—**Domaine Joillot**, Pommard. Jean Luc Joillot, maker of fine wines from Pommard, Beaune and Beaune 1er Crus.
—**Domaine Manière**, Vosne Romanée. Richard Manière's Vosne Romanée and 1er cru Suchots and Echezeaux.
—**Domaine Nudant**, Ladoix-Serrigny. Jean René Nudant's Hautes-Côtes-de-Nuits and Ladoix.
—**Domaine Olivier**, Santenay. Antoine and Rachel Olivier's Santenay white is remarkable and rare for this AOC.
—**Domaine Poulleau**, Volnay. Thierry Poulleau winemaker, coming into his own since 2006 vintage.
—**Domaine Rapet**. Vincent Rapet makes wines to be discovered, among them Pernand Vergelesses.

• **Cellier Saint Vincent** (14 Place Saint Vincent, Chalon-sur-Saône, Tel: 03 85 48 78 25, www.bourgognepassion.fr). Caviste: Pascal Laville.

CÔTE CHALONNAISE:
—**Domaine Joblot**, Givry. Jean Marc and Vincent Joblot. *Best wine:* Givry red.
—**François Lumpp**, Givry. *Best wines:* Givry red and white.

- **Manu Tupinier-Bautistat**, Mercurey. *Best wines:* Mercurey white and red.
- **Vincent Dureuil-Jantial**, Rully. *Best wines:* Rully white and red, and Rully 1er Cru Margotée (superb).

CÔTE DE BEAUNE:
- **Domaine Regis Rossignol**, Volnay, a humble but great and wise winegrower.
- **Domaine Tollot**, Fine Corton, Chorey-lès-Beaune, Savigny-lès-Beaune.

CÔTE DE NUITS:
- **Christian Gouges**, Nuits Saint Georges.
- **Domaine du Clos-de-Tart**, Morey-Saint-Denis. Manager Sylvain Pitio, a straight-shooter able to make moving wines without huffing and puffing.
- **Jacques Fréderic Mugnier**, Chambolle-Musigny. Burgundy's most enlightened winegrower.
- **Nicolas Meo Camuset**, Vosne Romanée. Maker of extremely fine wines.

• **La Cave des Cordeliers** (59 Grande Rue, Louhans, Tel: 03 85 75 36 69, cbuatois@club-internet.fr). Cavistes: Christine and Eric Buatois.

CATEGORY: "MOST RESPECTFUL OF TERROIR"
- **Domaine Chataigneraie Laborier**, Vergisson. *Best wine:* Pouilly Fuissé La Roche.
- **Domaine Luc Brintet**, Mercurey. *Best wine:* Mercurey 1er Cru Champs Martins.
- **Domaine Lucien Muzard**, Santenay. *Best wine:* Santenay Champs Claude Vieilles Vignes.

CATEGORY: "MOST PROMISING"
- **Domaine Chevrot**, Cheilly les Maranges. *Best wine:* Cuvée d'exception Gamay Pivoine.
- **Domaine Prunier Bonheur**, Meursault. *Best wine:* Saint Romain red Sous le Château.
- **Domaine Nicolas Ragot**, Givry. *Best wine:* Givry 1er cru "clos jus" 2005.

—**Domaine Guillaume Tardy**, Vosne Romanée. *Best wine:* Fixin 2006.

CATEGORY: "BEST IN THEIR AOC"
—**Domaine Stéphane Aladame**, Montagny lès Buxy. *Best wine:* Montagny 1er Cru Les Coères.
—**Domaine Paul Jacqueson**, Rully. *Best wine:* Rully 1er Cru Gresigny.
—**Domaine Rémi Jobard**, Meursault. *Best wine:* Meursault 1er cru Les Genevrières.
—**Domaine Michel Lafarge**, Volnay. *Best wine:* Volnay 1er Cru Clos du Château des Ducs.
—**Domaine Alain Michelot**, Nuits Saint Georges. *Best wine:* Nuits Saint Georges Aux Champs Perdrix.

CATEGORY: "MAJOR WINERY"
—**Maison Champy**, Beaune. *Best wine:* Bourgogne Blanc Chardonnay Signature.

CATEGORY: "BEST BIG WINES"
—**Domaine Marc Colin et Fils**, Saint Aubin. *Best wine:* Montrachet.
—**Domaine Sérafin Père et Fils**, Gevrey Chambertin. *Best wine:* Charmes Chambertin Grand Cru.
—**Domaine Thenard**, Givry. *Best wine:* Grand Echezeaux.

• **Le Cellier de l'Abbaye** (13 Rue Municipale and Rue du 11 Aôut, Cluny, Tel: 03 85 59 04 00, www.cellier-abbaye.com). Cavistes: Alice Brinton, Sonia Blondeau.

—**La Soufrandière • Bret Brothers**, Vinzelles, Mâconnais.
—**Clos Salomon • Gardin et Fabrice Perrotto**, Givry, Côte Chalonnaise.
—**David Duband**, Nuit Saint Georges, Côte de Nuits.
—**Château de Monthelie • Eric de Suremain**, Monthelie, Côte de Beaune.
—**Domaine des Hautes Cornières, PH Chapelle & Fils**, Santenay, Côte de Beaune.

- —**Domaine Perraud · Jean-Christophe Perraud**, La Roche Vineuse, Mâconnais.
- —**Domaine de Montille**, Volnay, Côte de Beaune.
- —**Domaine Michel Lafarge**, Volnay, Côte de Beaune.
- —**Jacques et Natalie Saumaize**, Vergisson, Mâconnais.
- —**Stephane Aladame**, Montagny, Côte Chalonnaise.

- • **Le Vin** (7 Place des Pêcheurs, La Charité sur Loire, Tel: 03 86 70 21 30). Caviste: Jean-Paul Quenault.

  - —**Domaine Anne Leflaive**, Côte d'Or.
  - —**Domaine de la Vernière**, La Vernière, Chasnay.
  - —**Domaine des Pénitents · Alphonse Mellot**, Organic Chardonnay and Pinot Noir, Nièvre.
  - —**Domaine du Clos-de-Tart**, Morey-Saint-Denis.
  - —**Domaine du Puits de Compostelle · Emmanuel Rouquette**, Mauvrain, La Celle sur Nièvre.
  - —**Jean-Claude Châtelain**, Les Berthiers, Pouilly-sur-Loire.
  - —**Domaine Joblot**, Givry, Côte Chalonnaise.
  - —**Domaine Marc Colin**, Saint-Aubin.
  - —**Serge Dagueneau & Filles**, Les Berthiers, Pouilly-sur-Loire. Rich Pinot Beurrot (Pinot Gris), hand-picked. Montées de Saint-Lay red.
  - —**Vincent Dauvissat**, Chablis.

  . . . .

☙ LE SAINT-VINCENT-TOURNANTE ☙ WINE FESTIVAL

BURGUNDY'S SAINT-VINCENT-TOURNANTE is a modern Bacchanalia. Similar celebrations have been popular throughout Europe since antiquity. This fête's origin, however, is recent. In the 1800s, Burgundian winemakers banded together in mutual-aid societies called "Saint-Vincents." Member families helped others temporarily unable to harvest grapes or make wine. Each village held its own festival. With nationwide Social Security in the 1930s in France, the societies and corresponding festivals faced extinction. In 1938, the recently founded Chevaliers du Tastevin invented the Saint-Vincent-Tournante. Since then its *tournées*— rotating from village to village—have covered all of Burgundy. Some towns or winegrowing areas also hold independent Saint-Vincents.

Saint Vincent was a martyr from Saragossa, Spain. He died in 304 AD and was adopted in France as the protector of winemakers, because his name begins with *vin*. His feast day is January 22nd; the Saint-Vincent-Tournante usually honors him the weekend closest to that date. Nowadays, the festival has little to do with religion. Locals say that the saint's real miracle is to bring together hundreds of independent-minded *vignerons*, giving the region a sense of community.

It's widely held that "You can count on Saint Vincent for great weather." Burgundian skies usually are clear in late January, and the air is cold. Luckily, the food stands, cafés, and restaurants which set up in each host village serve mulled wine and hot specialties, from gougères and snails, to peppery andouillette sausage or long-cooked coq au vin and beef bourguignon. The real excitement begins when the cellars are opened mid-morning. Partygoers are issued an engraved wineglass on a strap; it entitles them to drink unlimited quantities of Cuvée Saint-Vincent. This is often assembled from wineries' second pressings or unsold stock, and dispensed at participating cellars during the Saint-Vincent weekend. Temperatures are often such that the wine's qualities can't be judged; few merrymakers appear to mind, and that's certainly for the best.

....

LIQUEURS

BURGUNDY MAKES MORE THAN WINE. DOZENS OF DISTILLERIES PRODUCE ABOUT A HUNDRED different fruit liqueurs, eaux de vie, Marcs de Bourgogne and, above all, Crème de Cassis. The region is the cradle of Crème de Cassis—distilled from blackcurrants—and grows tons of the tiny, pungent berries, particularly in the Hautes Côtes de Nuits. Burgundy makes four in five bottles of the Cassis produced in France—about 17 million liters. Nine in ten bottles exported from France come from Burgundy. The best industrial-sized producer is Vedrenne; the best medium-sized family-owned distillery is Cartron (both are in Nuits Saint Georges). The most highly regarded artisanal producers are the two rival branches of the Joannet family (in Arcenant), Fruirouge (in Concoeur), and Chantal and Jean-Michel Jacob in Échevronne. All are within a twenty-minute drive of Nuits Saint Georges. In central Dijon, near Place Wilson, you'll find top-flight artisanal Cassis-maker and distiller Edmond Briottet; he only sells semi-wholesale at the distillery, but you may purchase his wares at Mulot & Petitjean gingerbread-and-gourmet food outlets in the region. Odd-man-out distiller is remarkable Domaine Michel Langlois (see page 429) in Pougny, on Burgundy's western edge; he makes award-winning Cassis and other fruit or berry liqueurs. Cassis is the essential ingredient—with Aligoté white wine—in the region's traditional aperitif, Kir.

CHAPTER 1

NORTHERN BURGUNDY

Département: Yonne.

Population: 341,000.

Population density: 46 inhabitants/sq. km.

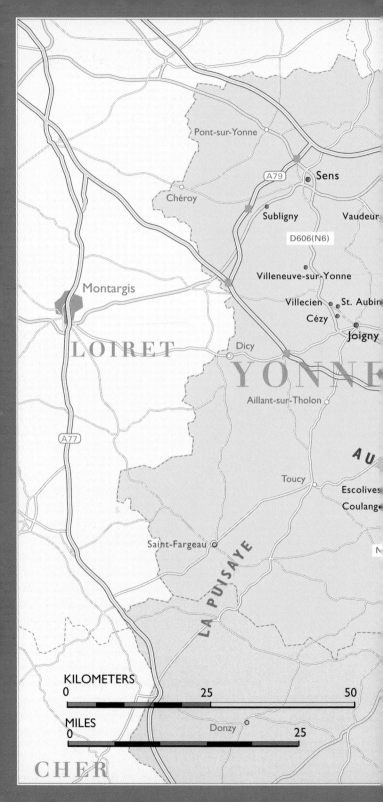

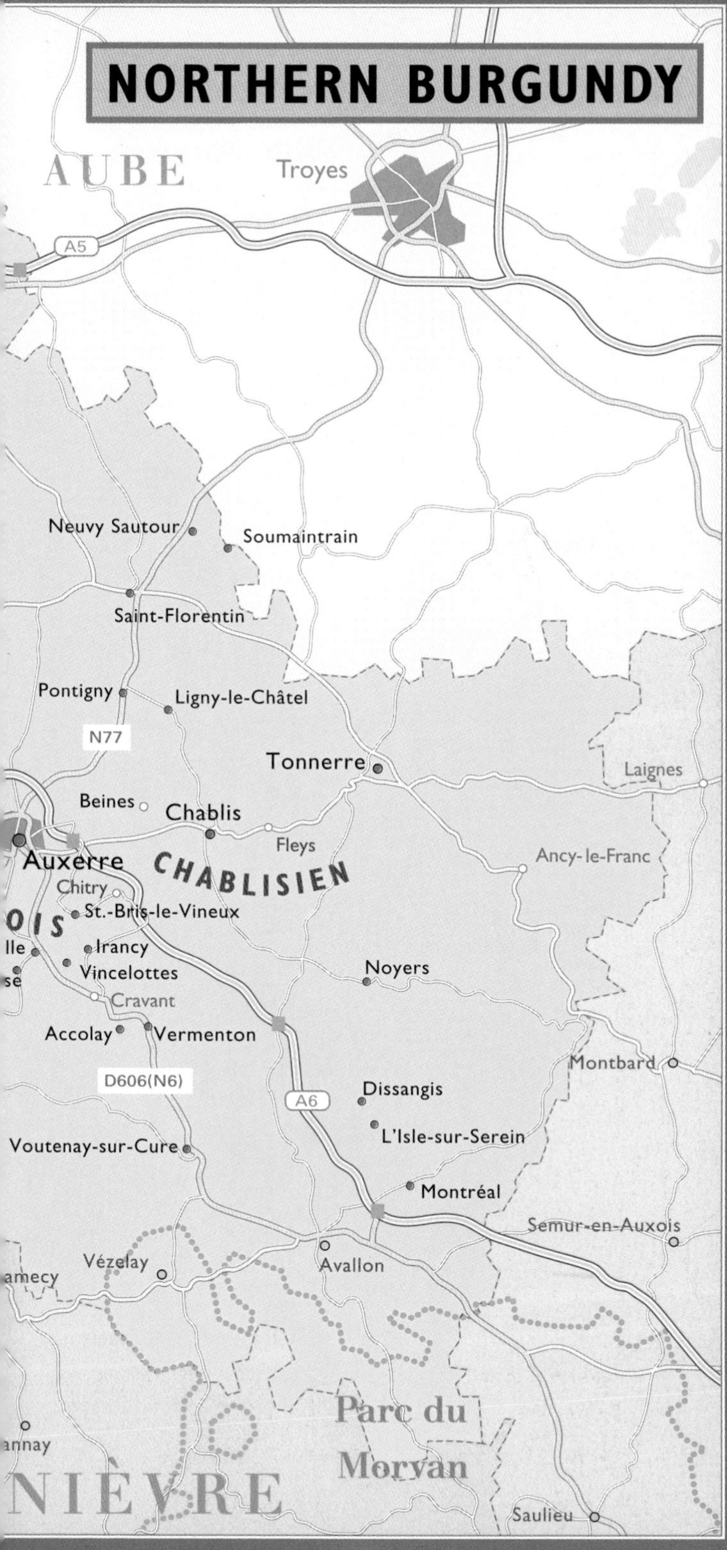

NORTHERN BURGUNDY

AUBE

Troyes

A5

Neuvy Sautour

Soumaintrain

Saint-Florentin

Pontigny

Ligny-le-Châtel

N77

Tonnerre

Laignes

Beines

Chablis

Fleys

Auxerre

CHABLISIEN

Ancy-le-Franc

Chitry

St.-Bris-le-Vineux

OIS

Irancy

lle

Vincelottes

Noyers

se

Cravant

Accolay

Vermenton

Montbard

D606(N6)

A6

Dissangis

L'Isle-sur-Serein

Voutenay-sur-Cure

Montréal

Semur-en-Auxois

amecy

Vézelay

Avallon

Parc du

annay

Morvan

NIÈVRE

Saulieu

AUXERRE and AUXERROIS, JOIGNY, SENS

....

Includes: Accolay, Auxerre, Cézy, Coulanges-la-Vineuse,
Irancy, Joigny, Neuvy Sautour, Saint Aubin sur Yonne,
Saint-Bris-le-Vineux, Saint-Florentin, Sens,
Soumaintrain, Subligny, Vaudeurs, Vermenton, Villecien,
Villeneuve-sur-Yonne, Vincelottes, Voutenay

STRETCHING SOUTH FROM THE ILE-DE-FRANCE REGION, PARIS'S BACKYARD, AND BORDERED TO the east by Champagne, it comes as no surprise that northernmost Burgundy feels like an extension of both. Many of its towns, villages, and small cities including Sens and Joigny lead a double life as bedroom communities, many residents commuting to Paris and Troyes.

There is as much apple cider made here—primarily in the Othe Valley west of Villeneuve-sur-Yonne—as wine. The fledgling vineyards of the Côte Saint-Jacques, also known as Le Jovinien, around the riverside town of Joigny, were revived in the 1980s and '90s, largely thanks to the initiative of chef Michel Lorain. His Michelin-starred temple of gastronomy is the Joigny district's main tourism attraction. Hearty Pinot Gris was long the traditional grape; when replanted, Pinot Noir and Chardonnay were added, with mixed results. The wines are pleasant when quaffed on site, and are getting better by the year.

Many industrial-scale wheat, corn, and rapeseed farms are to be found here, many owned by the so-called "grain barons" of the Beauce. Some small family-run farms still thrive, set amid pastures, fields, and river valleys. The cheeses are primarily derived from cow's milk, and include mild Soumaintrain and Saint-Florentin, named after a village and town, respectively. Some goat's-milk cheese is also made. The cider can be as good as that of Normandy. Game, tripe sausage (from Troyes and Chablis), variety meats, and the pan-regional Burgundian repertoire—snails, coq au vin, boeuf bourguignon—are what you'll find on traditional menus.

A compact city of 40,000, Auxerre (pronounced *Ausserre*) has modern suburbs, shopping malls, highways, overpasses, a ring of busy boulevards and low-cost housing projects, and a convenient commuter train station—it's only ninety minutes to Paris. Hard-driven, the ancient fortress-city of Autessiodurum, of Imperial Rome, on the Via Agrippa consular highway, Auxerre perches on a rise above the Yonne River. It's an endearing place, and has been discovered by riverboat and canal-cruise vacationers. Currently undergoing a systematic refit, with flower beds galore, and restored half-timbered houses, Auxerre is attempting to revitalize and attract tourists. Streets have been pedestrianized. In some areas the result feels like the malls that have caused many inner-city businesses to fold. The remake has only begun.

Around Auxerre spreads the Auxerrois, a land of fertile, rolling countryside watered by the Yonne and Cure Rivers. The territory extends as far south as Le Morvan, north to Joigny, west to the Puisaye, and east to Chablis and Tonnerre.

Auxerrois wine country is experiencing a renaissance. New AOCs were created in the last decade. The fruity reds of Irancy and white Sauvignons of Saint-Bris-le-Vineux in particular are currently the focus of widespread attention.

ACCOLAY

Halfway between Auxerre and Avallon, in the Cure River Valley near Vermenton, this handsome village on the river's left bank is a few miles from the Reigny Abbey. On the road leading to it, find **Hostellerie de la Fontaine** (16 Rue Reigny, Tel: 03 86 81 54 02, closed Tuesday lunch and Monday, Sunday from October to March, and late November to mid February, moderate to expensive), an old-fashioned inn with cozy rooms. More important is the pleasant restaurant serving *terroir* food, both in a vaulted cellar dining room, or on a garden terrace. Don't expect culinary fireworks, and resist the temptation to order scallops or monkfish millefeuille with raw ham. Stick to delicious snails served with warm lentil salad (typical of the nearby Morvan) with mild, creamy garlic sauce, oeufs en meurette, or thick, peppery Charolais steak flambéed with Marc de Bourgogne (or with a dauntingly rich foie gras sauce). Even more flavorful is rib steak pan-fried and topped with Époisses. Lighter is fresh trout with clarified butter and baby vegetables. There are many cheeses, and traditional desserts (pears poached in red wine with spices, gingerbread, and caramel ice cream). The wine list includes good-value bottlings from the Auxerrois and Chablis.

AUXERRE

In recent years, the Saint-Etienne cathedral has been sandblasted to a blinding shade of white. But even in the handsome historic part of town around it, gentrification hasn't quite taken off: the square fronting immense Saint-Etienne is a parking lot. So is the town's other main square, Place des Cordeliers.

Auxerre's lively outdoor clothing market, organic farmers market, and underground food mart at Place de l'Arquebuse, abutting the ring-road on the town's western edge, is among the best in Northern Burgundy (open Tuesdays and Fridays). Unfortunately, it's housed in a 1970s eyesore, and there's no easy, free parking, which might explain why many customers patronize suburban malls instead.

Auxerre's most attractive neighborhood lies between Place des Cordeliers, the cathedral, the Saint-Germain Abbey (a must-see for those interested in crypts and local history), and the Yonne River. It's here, on the riverside drive, near the tourism office (1–2 Quai de la République, Tel: 03 86 52 06 19, www.ot-auxerre.fr) that you'll find Michelin-starred **Jean-Luc Barnabet** (14 Quai de la République, Tel: 03 86 51 68 88, www.jbarnabet.com, closed Monday, Sunday dinner, Tuesday lunch, and late December to mid January, moderate to extremely expensive). In a historic townhouse with a garden terrace and spacious dining rooms where uniformed waiters glide silently, *terroir* cooking isn't what Marie and Jean Luc Barnabet's gastonomic temple is about. However, they're among the region's top Burgundy truffle specialists; from October to mid January you'll find excellent, light dishes flavored with *tuber uncinatum.* You'll also discover earthy fricasséed snails, and veal sweetbreads finished in the oven and flanked by sautéed potatoes, not to mention local pike-perch with onions, or long-stewed heirloom pork. The desserts are complicated and sumptuous, the wine list long and deep. Note: the entry-level prix fixe menu is a bargain.

A few hundred yards away, on the sloping street from the cathedral to the church of Saint Pierre, watch for **La P'tite Beursaude** (55 Rue Joubert, Tel: 03 86 51 10 21, auberge.beursaudiere@ wanadoo.fr, closed Tuesday, Wednesday, end June to early July, end August to early September, and end December to mid January, inexpensive to expensive). It faces Auxerre's municipal theater. With an unmistakable blue, half-timbered façade and geraniums, this traditional, studiously rustic bistro is the second address of La Beursaude in Nitry (a village south of Chablis). At the kitsch mothership, the staff wear Burgundian costumes of yore, the ladies in long, lace-topped dresses, the men in Ye Olde Farmer outfits. Luckily, only the ladies are so dressed in Auxerre, making it easier to enjoy the food. The menu states that you'll eat *cuisine traditionnelle*; you will, seated at wooden tables, surrounded by timbers and knickknacks, with a view into the open-plan kitchen. The tartines spread with Époisses, served with baked potatoes and salad, are delicious; the snails, too, and the simple roast chicken with honey is homey. Gutsy tripe sausage with creamy mustard sauce, calf's head with gribiche sauce, and pan-fried Charolais steak with red-wine reduction sauce are very good. Don't miss the gratin of strawberries. There are pitchers or glasses of Aligoté (from Morin in Chitry-le-Fort), *chopines* (half a liter) of Irancy and Bourgogne Epineuil; the short wine list features Yonne bottlings from Richoux (Irancy) and Goisot (Saint-Bris-le-Vineaux). Note: you'll also find artisanal apple cider from sixth-generation producers Louisette and Serge Frottier of Les Brissots.

Two simple bistro-style places in the Quartier de Paris, along Rue de Paris, are fine for a light meal: **Le Grandgousier** (#45, Tel: 03 86 51 04 80, closed Sunday) is small, cheek-by-jowl, and a favorite among local white collars. Cavernous and frequented by hipsters and intrepid tourists, **Le Bistrot du Palais** (#65, Tel: 03 86 51 47 02, closed Sunday and Monday) is in a reconverted movie theater, with bentwood chairs, banquettes, and tables outside on three terraces. Both are very inexpensive to moderate, and serve *terroir* specialties, plus sauerkraut, pig's ears and trotters, and blanquette de veau.

Up the scale, on the riverside drive, a pair of restaurants favored by the rivercruise-set are pleasant in good weather, when the terraces are open. The menus include a choice of please-all French and authentic, gutsy regional specialties. **Le Maxime** (4 Quai de la Marine, Tel: 03 86 52 04 41, www.lemaxime.fr, closed Saturday lunch and Sunday, inexpensive to moderate) has faux Louis XIII chairs inside and is the more luxurious. It's independent from, and shouldn't be confused with Le Maxime Hôtel (at #4). **Le Bounty** (3 Quai de la République, Tel: 03 86 51 69 86, open daily, inexpensive to moderate) has nothing to do with mutineers, though the rustic décor vaguely suggests a galleon, with storm lanterns and brass fittings. Le Bounty does a good job with snails, beef bourguignon, and guinea fowl cooked in the style of coq au vin (but made instead with white wine from Chablis).

The favorite local café has decent coffee but is otherwise banal: **Le Biarritz** (15 Place des Cordeliers, Tel: 03 86 51 36 38, closed

Sunday in low season, open daily 8am to 8pm the rest of the year). The terrace faces parked cars.

Happily, there are many fine gourmet food shops, making a stroll through Auxerre a voyage of discovery. Award-winning **Charcuterie Robert Hattier** (30 Rue du Temple, Tel: 03 86 52 02 24, www.boucherie-hattier.com, closed Sunday, Monday, and Wednesday) is a third-generation butcher-deli, now run by Hattier's daughters, Catherine, Sophie, and Valérie. An upscale operation, on the main road, between Place Charles Surugue and the marketplace, the women offer remarkable terrines, headcheese, and jambon persillé. Note that Hattier also sells at the market on Tuesday and Friday mornings.

At the end of this same main street, on a square lined by handsome half-timbered buildings, outstanding chocolates and pastries are found at **Pascal Jarry** (3 Place Charles Surugue, Tel: 03 86 52 04 25, closed Sunday and Monday). In addition to classic filled chocolates, bars, and chocolate pastries, among the nearly fifty house specialties you'll want to try chocolate snails, Bourquinettes, truffles with liqueur-soaked raisins, Florentins, chocolate-dipped candied orange peel and other candied fruit, elaborate fruit cream-filled tartelettes, and irresistible macarons.

Equally excellent is **Chocolatier-Pâtissier Claude et Michèle** (88 Rue de Paris, Tel: 03 86 52 11 64, www.chocolat-claude-michele.com, closed Sunday afternoon and Monday), in the Quartier de Paris, near Le Bistrot du Palais. Owned and run by pastry chefs Claude and Michèle Guillet and their family, this compact boutique also roasts fresh coffee (the Arabica monovarietals and blends are excellent). House specialities include the seemingly un-PC Bamboula and Negro, both invented in 1919 in homage to the Senegalese troops who fought in World War I, and were cared for at the Auxerre military hospital. The first is a simple chocolate cookie, the second a chocolate-coated gingerbread cookie filled with hazelnut praline. You'll also find Kirsch-filled, chocolate-coated cherries grown in Saint-Bris-le-Vineux, and Soissons d'Auxerre, which look like white broadbeans but are made with toasted candied hazelnuts dipped in dark chocolate and then dipped again in white chocolate. Among other specialties are crunchy Croquignoles Auxerrois biscuits made with almonds and hazelnuts and flavored with coffee, aniseed, Marc de Bourgogne, and other delights.

On the same street as restaurant La P'tite Beursaude, near the cathedral, inticing window displays draw eyes to cheesemonger **Pâquerette Soufflard** (23 Rue Joubert, Tel: 03 86 52 07 07, closed Sunday and Monday). She sells only the best, from L'Ami du

Chambertin to raw-milk Soumaintrain (from Ferme Leclère), Plaisir au Chablis to Pouligny-Saint-Pierre, Saint-Florentin, Époisses, Brillat-Savarin, L'Aisy Cendré, L'Abbaye de la Pierre-Qui-Vire—all of them handmade, farmstead curds. She also runs a stand at the Auxerre market.

Further along the street is **Boulangerie Haybrard** (53 Rue Joubert, Tel: 03 86 52 24 44, closed Monday and Tuesday). Baker Jean-Claude Haybrard has a wood-burning oven; his crusty, old-fashioned loaves are scented by it.

Look for the carved polychrome statue of Saint Nicolas in a wall-niche on the square of the same name, off the riverside road on the north side of Auxerre, and you'll also find gourmet food boutique **Au Fin Palais** (3 Place Saint Nicolas, Tel: 03 86 51 14 03, open daily nonstop 9am to 7:30pm from mid March to mid October, closed Monday and at lunchtime the rest of the year). In addition to Fallot mustard from Beaune, liqueurs (Ratafia, Marc de Bourgogne), jams from La Trinquilinette in the Morvan, gingerbreads, honeys, cookies, candies, and more, on sale are the micro-brewery beers of Sens, from the far north of Burgundy, and a number of fine regional wines.

Wine is still grown and made within the city limits (at Clos de la Chaînette, a very old vineyard on the northern edge of town), but to call Auxerre a Mecca for wine-lovers would be exaggerated. Unless you're talking about its *caviste*. In the southeastern outskirts, near the sports stadium is **Le Cellier des Agapes** (13 Rue de Preuilly, Tel: 03 86 52 15 22, ragaine .marc@wanadoo.fr, closed Sunday and Monday). Self-effacing owner Marc Ragaine is youthful but was voted the World's Best

Independent Wineseller in 2003 (the award was created by the French Federation of Independent Winesellers, FNCI). You'll find everything from $5 bottlings and bag-in-box, to three- and four-figure wines from the top estates of France and the world. Some 450 wineries are represented. There are also liqueurs, Armagnac and Cognac, eaux de vie, wine accessories and gift items, plus cookies, mustards, jams, and other gourmet treats.

Note: unless you like soccer crowds and traffic, the neighborhood should be avoided when Auxerre's team is playing.

Next door, in a reconverted garage that fits the neighborhood's edge, is a simple but trendy restaurant favored by savvy locals (no one else but soccer fans drive out this far): **Le Bourgogne** (15 Rue de Preuilly, Tel: 03 86 51 57 50, closed Sunday, Monday, and Thursday dinner, holidays, three weeks in August, Christmastide through New Year's, and other holidays, moderate). Ambitious young Eric Gallet took over recently, having spent time on Ile de la Reunion (and at Bernard Loiseau, and Le Crillon in Paris). He returned with spices on the brain, but luckily has not tossed out the Burgundian baby with the bathwater. The menu changes seasonally. Expect to find updated Burgundian classics (calf's head, kidneys with mustard, snail spring rolls), chalked up on the blackboard. Food is made from scratch with high-quality ingredients. The wine list includes a hundred Burgundies, a roster of the Yonne's wineries. There's a summer terrace and big dining room. Both are fully booked most of the time; reserve ahead.

Across the street, find **Germinal Auxerre** (22 Rue de Preuilly, Tel: 03 86 72 90 50, closed Monday morning and Sunday), an organic market with a wide variety of local and regional organic produce and gourmet foods, from honeys and jams to cookies and wines.

CÉZY

Halfway between Villeneuve and Joigny, on highway D184, in the hamlet of Thèmes, part of Cézy, seek out **Hôtel Le P'tit Claridge** (2 Route de Joigny, Thèmes, Tel: 03 86 63 10 92, closed Sunday dinner, Monday, and from mid January to mid February, inexpensive to very expensive). Locals mix with migratory Parisians. You'll eat in a comfortable dining room with country-style décor, or on a deck in the landscaped garden. The food is updated regional, and leans toward creativity and complication—foie gras added to the delicious free-range chicken breast with mushroom sauce, for instance, or creamy freshwater fish stew with, for some reason, snails in the mix. The desserts follow suit. Stick to the daily seasonal menu, which is affordable and simpler. The service is professional, the wine list strong on regional bottlings.

COULANGES-LA-VINEUSE

In Auxerrois wine country, about ten miles due south of Auxerre, Coulanges-la-Vineuse is set among rolling hills which, until recent decades, were planted with cherries, apples, and other fruit trees. It is the seat of a museum of wine, **Musée de la Vigne et du Vieux Pressoir** (55bis Rue André-Vildieu, Tel: 03 86 42 20 59, open afternoons only 3pm to 6pm, closed Wednesday and Sunday, guided visits available). Here you'll see a vast assembly of vineyard tools, and a 500-year-old wine press weighing tons, capable of crushing about a metric ton of grapes in one go. You'll also learn how phylloxera spelled the end to viable commercial winemaking in the Auxerrois by the 1930s (the press was last used in 1924), and how there's been a revival since the postwar period, which has taken off recently.

The best wines of the Auxerrois can be very good. Most come from neighboring Irancy and Saint-Bris-le-Vineux. However, you can visit several wineries in the Coulanges area, among them **Domaine du Clos du Roi** (17 Rue André Vildieu, Place de l'Église, Tel: 03 86 42 25 72, open daily 8am to 7pm without appointment, Sunday afternoon by appointment only) and **Domaine Maltoff** (20 Rue d'Aguesseau, Tel: 03 86 42 32 48, phone ahead), which is also a B&B.

A few miles away in equally vinous and even more ancient Escolives-Sainte-Camille, known for its pocketsized Imperial Roman archeological site on the Via Agrippa, and its excellent fruit (cherries and apples), is **Domaine Borgnat** (Le Colombier, 1 Rue de l'Église, Tel: 03 86 53 35 28, www.domaineborgnat .com, phone ahead). This friendly family-run winery and B&B with comfortable rooms, offering rustic, tasty *table d'hôtes* meals to overnight guests, makes very good Coulanges-la-Vineuse wines with Pinot Noir (and César). It has won medals for its good-value bottlings, and for hospitality. *Best wines:* Coulanges Rosé Pinot Noir, Coulanges Tradition (red), Coulanges Tête de Cuvée (red), Coulanges Blanc.

IRANCY

About thirty reputable wineries now operate in the Irancy area. This is one of Burgundy's most recent AOCs, awarded in 2000, but the remarkable red wines from here have been appreciated by insiders for decades. The village is doubly blessed, because it's among the area's most attractive, nestled in a deep fold of the chalky hills, and dotted with handsome old houses. Before leaving, drive to the panoramic point above town for sweeping views of vines, villages, and the Yonne River Valley. While nearly all the grapes grown here are Pinot Noir, a few estates continue to plant César (locally called Romain), almost always as a blending wine used to add tannins and character.

JOIGNY

Joigny is on the Yonne River, exactly ninety miles south of Paris, with an elaborately sculpted city gate, and many historic, handsome, half-timbered houses. For gourmets, it is synonymous with the Lorain family and their luxury hotel-restaurant **La Côte Saint-Jacques** (14 Faubourg Paris, Tel: 03 86 62 09 70, www .cotesaintjacques.com, closed Monday and Tuesday in winter, and January, astronomically expensive). This is one of Burgundy's temples of eno-gastronomy (and a palatial Relais et Châteaux hotel, on the riverbank). Native son Jean-Michel Lorain took over from his father Michel, becoming the country's youngest chef to get three Michelin stars. The Lorains' relationship with tradition is uneasy. Clearly, the younger chef's passion is the global maelstrom. You'll find snails on the market-based, creative menu; they might come sautéed and dressed with parsley-cream and garlic, or with a mushroom emulsion. The frog's legs come with gazpacho jelly and sun-dried tomatoes. The veal kidneys are rolled in gingerbread crumbs before being sautéed and flanked by chard spring rolls with citrus chutney. Even the heirloom dishes (called "*plats de mémoire*") show impatience with simplicity (seabass smoked and served with caviar; macaroni stuffed with foie gras to accompany not local Charolais but Hereford standing rib roast). Lorain runs a cooking school and organizes local wine tours, starting with his father's twenty-three-acre *domaine*. The service is flawless, the wine list many inches thick, the prices truly astronomical.

Across the street, in his winery-retail boutique, **Michel Lorain SCEV** (Tel: 03 86 62 06 70, www.bourgogne-michel -lorain.com, closed Saturday afternoon, Sunday, and Wednesday), the elder, flanked by oenologist Kyriakos Kynigopoulos, produces some true-to-type wines from Pinot Gris, Pinot Noir, and Chardonnay. Of them, the "premium" Cuvée ML Pinot Noir and Chardonnay are oaked for over a year, and are less *terroir*-sensitive than those made with little or no oaking.

❧ WINERIES ❧
IN OR NEAR IRANCY

Domaine Benoît Cantin (35 Chemin des Fossés, Tel: 03 86 42 21 96). *Best wine:* Irancy Cuvée Emiline.

Domaine Anita, Stéphanie et Jean-Pierre Colinot (1 Rue des Chariats, Tel: 03 86 42 33 25). *Best wine:* Irancy Les Mazelots.

Domaine Lucien Joudelat (10 Chemin des Fossés, Tel: 03 86 42 31 46). *Best wine:* Irancy Les Mazelots.

Domaine Renaud (11 Chemin des Fossés, Tel: 03 86 42 27 39, by appointment). *Best wine:* Irancy Lot 0104 (Vieilles Vignes, with 5 percent César).

Thierry Richoux (73 Rue Soufflot, Tel: 03 86 42 41 60, by appointment). *Best wine:* Irancy Lot 02108, Lot 02248, and Veaupessiot.

Domaine Saint Germain (7 Chemin des Fossés, Tel: 03 86 42 33 43, by appointment). *Best wine:* Irancy.

....

Lorain's wines are available at the family's restaurant or across the river at their second hotel-restaurant, pleasantly traditional yet upscale **Rive Gauche** (Chemin du Port-au-Bois, Tel: 03 86 91 46 66, www.hotel-le-rive-gauche.fr, closed dinner Sunday, inexpensive to expensive). In the oldest part of town, the property affords views over the vineyards. On the menu are snails (in the form of a potato-pancake), housemade terrines, pan-fried filet of beef with a luscious potato gratin with Époisses, simmered beef jowl with red-wine sauce, seafood, local cheeses, and traditional desserts. The wine list here also features regional and local bottlings, but at a reasonable mark-up.

Those who prefer a casual atmosphere, and local clientele, should consider travelers' hotel-restaurant **Le Paris-Nice** (Rond-Point de la Résistance, Tel: 03 86 62 06 72, parisnice@wanadoo .fr, closed dinner Sunday, Monday, the second half of August, and three weeks in February, very inexpensive to moderate). The cooking is solid, with both authentic regional and updated dishes, and a wide selection of desserts, many built around chocolate themes.

NEUVY SAUTOUR

Some people drive the five miles northeast of Saint Florentin to see Neuvy Sautour's remarkable Renaissance church. Others come for cheese. Ewe's milk cheeses have practically disappeared from Burgundy, though in preindustrial days they were popular. You'll find them in small rounds at dairy farm and cheese factory **GAEC de Neuvy Sautour** (10 Chemin des Nozins, Tel: 03 86 56 31 07 or 06 30 54 28 58, open late afternoon from Monday through Saturday or by appointment). Sheep farmer Patrice Ferrand runs about 150 head on his big, 900-acre ranch, which is about halfway between Auxerre and Troyes on major highway RN 77, not far from Lasson. Ferrand's flavorful round tomes are also sold at the Saturday market in Saint Florentin.

SAINT AUBIN SUR YONNE

Just over a mile from Joigny's train station, on the old main highway to Paris, honey-makers Christophe and Sylvie Dosnon of **Les Ruchers Dosnon** (6 Route de Paris, Tel: 03 86 62 43 01, closed Sunday), in the same family for over a century, produce excellent gingerbreads in many flavors (plain, figs, chocolate, almonds, walnuts, raspberries, prunes), honey cookies, and half a dozen varieties of honey. They also sell at the Saturday morning market in Joigny, and the Auxerre market on Tuesday and Friday mornings.

SAINT-BRIS-LE-VINEUX

Since 2001, this long-unsung, ancient winegrowing village south-east of Auxerre has its very own AOC, for white Sauvignon, not Chardonnay. It also grows Pinot Noir, and some Chardonnay (for Crémant). Wine is the main but not the only attraction. A handsome place in rolling hills bisected by highway D956, Saint-Bris-le-Vineux has a Romanesque church upon whose site, supposedly, occurred the martyrdom of Saint Prix (the name was later deformed). More appetizingly, on the main street there's an authentic auberge with regional fare, **Le Saint-Bris** (13 Rue du Docteur-Tardieu, Tel: 03 86 53 84 56, closed Sunday and Monday dinner and Wednesday, inexpensive). For good baked goods, including crisp Croquets de Saint-Bris nut cookies, don't miss **Boulangerie-Pâtisserie Michel Depardieu** (27 Rue Bienvenu Martin, Tel: 03 86 53 32 04, closed Sunday afternoon and Monday).

Dozens of wineries are scattered around the village and its surroundings. Directly behind the church, **Domaine Bersan et Fils/ Domaine Saint-Prix** (20 Rue du Dr. Tardieux, Tel: 03 86 53 33 73, www.bourgognes-bersan.com, open without appointment, closed afternoons on Sunday and holidays) would be worth a visit for the medieval architecture alone. Happily, this multi-generational winery now run by Jean-François and Jean-Louis Bersan also makes very good wines, the best of which is actually an Irancy Cuvée Louis Bersan, as well as a Sauvignon Saint-Bris Domaine Saint-Prix.

If you visit only one winery, however, make it **Domaine Jean-Hughues et Ghislaine Goisot** (30 Rue Bienvenu Martin, Tel: 03 86 53 35 15, www.goisot.com, by appointment only, closed Sunday). Not only are the cellars medieval. This is also a certified-organic winery, and several of its bottlings are widely recognized as among the best in their AOC. The Côtes d'Auxerre Gondonne, Gueules de Loup, and Corps de Garde, all white wines, receive judicious oaking, and are about as good as a Burgundian Sauvignon gets. Ditto the Aligoté, which has an almost medicinal, wild, herby yet pleasant quality to it. The Les Mazelots Irancy is full of fruit and flowers, and big enough to last many years. Idealistic but also down to earth, the Goisots are moving into bio-dynamic winegrowing to "regenerate" the soil.

On the edge of town, heading toward Champs, get one-stop information, do tastings, and purchase wine from up to thirty-five wineries in the Yonne winegrowing districts of Épineuil, Irancy, and Auxerrois, but not Chablis, at **La Maison du Vignoble Auxerrois** (14 Route de Champs, Tel: 03 86 53 66 76, www

.maisonduvignoble.com, closed Sunday and Wednesday). On Thursdays in summer the maison hosts Les Jeudis du Goût, during which you taste wine and local farm products or specialty foods.

For a taste of slick corporate gigantism, head south a few miles to the D362 on the Yonne's banks and visit **Caves Bailly-Lapierre** (Quai de l'Yonne, Bailly, Tel: 03 86 53 77 77, www.bailly-lapierre.fr, open daily, closed Christmas and New Year's). This subterranean maze of cellars in a former quarry covers ten acres and is filled with millions of bottles of sparkling Crémant (the annual production figures here are three million bottles), and a handful of other local wines (Irancy and Saint-Bris). The quality is high—this is the area's premier Crémant-maker—and the walls are adorned metaphorically with many gold, silver, and bronze medals. If you like kitsch, you'll love the life-sized sculptures carved from living rock. At Christmastide, Bailly-Lapierre hosts a Christmas Market, with truffles, foie gras, chocolate, cheese, baubles, and wines.

Follow signs out of town to nearby **Ferme de Chèrevie** (Tel: 03 86 53 79 02, open Friday from 5pm to 7pm and Saturday 10am to noon, closed four weeks in January, by reservation only). Farmers Jean-Michel and Barbara Bahr not only raise free-range poultry until they're fully grown and flavorful—from five to six months. They also make and/or sell artisanal rapeseed oil, nearly fifty different flavored vinegars, terrines of guinea fowl and chicken, and a bewildering range of housemade liqueurs and aperitifs, using everything from poppies and beer to grapefruit or acacia flowers. Phone ahead to arrange a visit and tasting.

SAINT FLORENTIN

The Romans built a fortress at the confluence of the Armance and Armançon rivers, which became an ecclesiastical stronghold in the Middle Ages, after its namesake saint was martyred here in the third century AD. Though some of the charm of yesteryear lingers, the Hundred Years' War, Wars of Religion, World War II, and real estate speculation have altered much. There's a lively Saturday morning market, with many local farmers, honey- and, especially, cheese-makers: Saint Florentin is also a mild round cow's-milk cheese, crafted here since the days of the unlucky saint. Soumaintrain, a village about six miles away, makes a similar curd, also sold here.

Market-based, regional cooking and a landmark setting in a reconverted convent from the 1600s are good reasons to choose **Les Tilleuls** (3 Rue Decourtive, Tel: 03 86 35 09 09, www.hotel-les -tilleuls.com, open daily from mid June to mid September, closed

❧ OTHER WINERIES ❧
IN OR NEAR SAINT-BRIS-LE-VINEUX

Domaine du Château du Val de Mercy (8 Promenade du Tertre, Chitry, Tel: 03 86 41 48 00, by appointment). *Best wine:* Chablis 1er Cru Beauregard.

Domaine Philippe Defrance (5 Rue du Four, Tel: 03 86 53 39 04, by appointment). *Best wine:* Sauvignon.

Domaine Félix et Fils (17 Rue de Paris, Tel: 03 86 53 33 87, domaine.felix@wanadoo.fr, open without appointment, closed Sunday). *Best wine:* Sauvignon.

Domaine Anne et Arnaud Goisot (4bis Route de Champs, Tel: 03 86 53 32 15). *Best wine:* Côtes d'Auxerre red, Chablis.

Domaine des Remparts (6 Route de Champs, Tel: 03 86 53 33 59). *Best wine:* Irancy Les Cailles (with trace amounts of César).

Domaine Philippe Sorin (12 Rue de Paris, Tel: 03 86 53 60 76, open daily without appointment 8am to 8pm). In a historic former coaching inn. *Best wine:* Sauvignon.

Domaine Verret (7 Route de Champs, Tel: 03 86 53 31 81). *Best wines:* Irancy Palotte, Irancy L'Âme du Domaine.

. . . .

Sunday dinner and Monday the rest of the year, inexpensive to moderate). There's a handsome dining room, with timbers, contemporary colors, and comfortable furniture, and an even more pleasant terrace shaded by an antique linden (which gives the place its name). Note: the chef also indulges in creative cuisine.

SENS

Sixty miles southwest of Paris, with 27,000 inhabitants, Sens is a sizeable town, which most visitors to Burgundy pass by. It's neither handsome nor glamorous, boasts no vineyards, and the autoroute has drained away the traffic that flowed through on the Route Nationale. It does have good food, however, and anyone remotely interested in history and ecclesiastical architecture will want to consider visiting the Saint-Étienne cathedral and abutting **Musée du Trésor** (Place de la Cathédrale, Tel: 03 86 64 46 22, hours vary widely), which has a vast and impressive collection of artworks.

Michelin-starred **La Madeleine** (1 Rue Alsace Lorraine, Tel: 03 86 65 09 31, www.restaurant-lamadeleine.fr, very expensive to astronomically expensive) is the city's *gastronomique* restaurant, where chef Patrick Gauthier regales guests with post-neoclassical French cooking. If chintz upholstered armchairs and flowing peach drapes tempt you, settle in for coddling. The most satisfying *terroir* dishes are prepared in the restaurant's rotisserie annex: **Au Crieur de Vin** (same address and website, Tel: 03 86 65 92 80, closed Sunday and Monday, and lunch Tuesday, two weeks in June, two weeks in August, and Christmastide, inexpensive to moderate). Step down the socio-economic ladder to where the hired help once gathered. You'll find locals parked on the bentwood chairs, surrounded by timbers, massive uprights, and copper pots, a rotisserie turning in the background. Daily blackboard specials (snails and bacon on a skewer, saddle of rabbit seasoned with thyme, roasted quail with parsnips) flank perennials (variety meats, grilled tripe sausage, spit-roasted poultry, beef and lamb, simple fruit tarts and rustic apple croustade). Affordable wines come from Irancy, Chablis, and Saint-Bris-le-Vineux.

More authentic, **Hôtel de la Poste** (97 Rue de la République, Tel: 03 86 65 17 43, www.hotel-paris-poste.com, closed for dinner on Friday and Sunday, Monday, and the first week in January, moderate to expensive) is a Second Empire coaching inn, with slate roofs and gables, a courtyard with summer service, a comfortable dining room, and *terroir* cooking. Classic oeufs en meurette are always available; alas, the snails come with Chaource cheese; the roasted guinea fowl breast is good and, if you enjoy pig's trotters, you'll like the shepherd's pie made with them. The clientele is mostly local—tourists are few in Sens—and the wine list is strong on regional bottlings.

Your other *terroir* option is **Auberge de la Vanne** (176 Avenue de Sénigalia, Tel: 03 86 65 13 63, aubergedelavanne@hotmail.fr, closed for dinner Sunday to Wednesday, all day Monday, and the first half of January, inexpensive to expensive). It's on the main road heading out of town to Auxerre, near the Vanne River. Look for the low, half-timbered building on the roadside. *Traditionnelle* is writ large. There are caned chairs, wall sconces, exposed timbers, and cooking to match, from egg to apple. In summer, you can dine on a shaded terrace.

Of Sens's gourmet shops, **Fromagerie Parret** (1 Rue Vieilles Etuves, Tel: 03 86 65 11 54, closed Monday) stands out. You'll find the region's best curds displayed, and a small selection of specialty foods.

For a wide range of gourmet items, on Sens's main street seek out **Depreux Epicerie Fine** (115 Grande Rue, Tel: 03 86 65 10 40, closed Tuesday morning and Sunday). On offer are cookies, candies (log-shaped Bûchettes Sénonaises), jams, honeys, oils and vinegars, micro-brewery beer from Sens, gingerbread, and more (skip the Belgian chocolates and balsamic vinegar in a spray bottle).

To buy freshly roasted, high-quality Arabicas, follow your nose to long-established, pintsized **Jacques Verzi—Le Caféier** (13 Rue du Général-Allix, Tel: 03 86 65 49 19, closed Sunday and Tuesday), near Rue Abélard, one block in from the ring road on the south side of town. The Italian espresso packs a punch. You can also buy monovarietal Moka or Maragogype, and Santo-Domingo, Colombian, Guatemalan, Brazilian Santos, and coffee accessories.

Buy your picnic on the main east-west road at **Charcuterie Thierry Morin** (85 Grande-Rue, Tel: 03 86 65 17 91, closed Sunday), where the terrines and jambon persillé are particularly delicious.

Of the many pastry and chocolate shops, locals agree it's a toss-up between **Le Bon Sens du Pain** (44 Rue de la République, Tel: 03 86 64 91 01, www.lebonsensdupain.fr, closed Sunday afternoon), on the main north-south street, where jolly chocolatier Francis Pautrat makes wonderful classic chocolates in an old bakery setting, and upscale **Eric Gaufillier** (53 Rue de la République, Tel: 03 86 65 12 99, closed Sunday and Monday), on the same street. A veteran of Lenôtre in Paris, Eric and his wife Carine turn out classic and innovative filled chocolates, cookies and pastries, and Bûchettes Sénonaises, plus chocolate-coated caramelized almond clusters which he calls Rochers de Sens.

Wine is not the forte here; beer has been made since the Gauls perfected cervoise. Revival micro-brewery **Brasserie Larché** (89 Rue Bellocier, Tel: 03 86 65 19 89 or 06 89 10 31 17, contact@ brasserie-larche.fr, www.brasserie-larche.fr, phone ahead to arrange a brewery tour with tasting), on the northwest side of town, near the Sablons industrial park, makes excellent artisanal beers under the Thomas Becket label: classic blond, unfiltered blanche, malted amber with local honey, and brune de Bourgogne, a dark beer (plus Christmas beer, in season).

SOUMAINTRAIN

Soumaintrain, the place, about six miles east of Saint Florentin, is not remarkable; Soumaintrain, the cheese, is delicious, if mild. Some of the most flavorful around is made from raw cow's milk and comes from long-established **Ferme Leclère-La Jonchère** (4 Rue de la Jonchère, Tel: 03 86 56 31 06, phone ahead), due west a quarter mile from the village. Another top local cheesemaker of Soumaintrain, Saint Florentin, and fresh, creamy fromage blanc is **Ferme Patrick Lorne** (8 Rue de l'Etang, open daily except holidays by appointment). Aim for Ervy-le-Châtel, and, on the southeastern edge of the municipal area, turn onto D61, following signs to the farm.

SUBLIGNY

Six miles west of Sens on highway RN 60, a reliable, long-established place to fuel up on regional *cuisine bourgeoise* is **La Haie Fleurie** (30 Route de Courtenay, La Haie-Pélerine, Tel: 03 86 88 84 44, moderate to expensive, closed dinner Sunday and Wednesday, Thursday, Christmastide, and ten days in July). With the fireplace lit in chill weather—much of the year, it seems—the timbers, light mustard-yellow walls, framed motel art of a higher variety, and miniature living room–style shaded lamps on each handsomely dressed table, give a cozy feel to this favorite of well-to-do locals and travelers.

VAUDEURS

Between main highway RN60 and smaller D905, near Cerisiers, on the putative Route du Cidre et des Pressoirs du Pays d'Othe (watch for the rare signs), there's one good reason (in addition to seeing orchards and the scenery) to drive to Vaudeurs: apple cider. Louisette and Serge Frottier are the sixth generation of cider-makers at **Cidre Frottier** (8 Les Brissots, Tel: 03 86 96 25 37, www.cidrefrottier.com, cidrefrottier@wanadoo.fr). They still use the family's original, 200-year-old press, part of a mini-museum of cider (open 3pm to 6pm from March to November). You can taste and buy the Frottiers' lightly sweet *cidre bouché*, fresh apple juice, and Ratafia, a liqueur, made from cider, plus apple eaux de vie, and Marc de Pommes.

VERMENTON

On a curve in the RN6 expressway in the handsome Cure River Valley, halfway between Auxerre and Avallon, Vermenton resembles Voutenay and several other spots in this beautiful valley, only slightly blighted by the highway. Its real appeal derives from its location near wine country and the Morvan, and its regional roadside restaurant, **Auberge de l'Espérance** (3 Rue du Générale de Gaulle/RN6, Tel: 03 86 81 50 42, closed Monday year-round, and Sunday, Monday and Thursday dinner from October to March, and January, inexpensive to moderate). This is not the luxurious, celebrated Espérance run by superchef Marc Meneau. For some reason, giant prawns are the chef's hobby horse, but his simple *terroir* dishes—snail salad with wild mushrooms, frog's legs with creamy garlic sauce, long-cooked stews—are tasty, and generously served. The wine list includes local wines by the glass.

Across the river valley on the quiet side, but still within Vermenton's municipal limits, is the historic **Abbaye de Reigny** (Tel: 03 86 81 59 30, www.abbayedereigny.com, business hours vary widely), no longer a religious institution. The medieval refectory and tower, plus the startlingly eighteenth-century abbey complex built by visionary architect Claude-Nicolas Ledoux, are open for guided tours; you can also book a room at the abbey's luxurious B&B, whose rooms are in a reconverted monks' dormitory from the 1300s.

VILLECIEN

Minutes north of Joigny, on the old main highway to Paris, the modest roadside hotel-restaurant **Domaine des Grandes Vignes** (23 Route de Paris, Tel: 03 86 63 11 74, closed Friday and dinner Saturday, and from Christmas to early February, very inexpensive to inexpensive) is a favorite of locals and back-road travelers. This is a good place to stop for a simple, warming *terroir* meal, from classic snails to tripe sausage à la Chablisienne, steaks, stews and poultry. There's a small selection of regional cheeses, and homey seasonal fruit pies, rich cakes, and old-fashioned pears poached in Pinot Noir from Irancy.

VILLENEUVE-SUR-YONNE

About halfway—twelve miles—between Sens and Joigny, Villeneuve is a large, handsome town of medieval foundation on the banks of the Yonne, with a hulking thirteenth-century tower, and two fortified city gates. Surprisingly, given its 5,000 inhabitants, remarkable food and drink are scarce. It boasts good but interchangeable bakeries and *charcuteries*, and one extremely simple bar-pizzeria-lunch spot on the main drag favored by locals, **Le Parisien** (32 Rue Carnot, Tel: 03 86 87 14 55, lunch only, closed Sunday, extremely inexpensive), indicative of the town's loyalties. This is a fallback, and serves decent salads, tripe sausages, and generous portions of stew and suchlike, depending on the season, in basic surroundings.

Romance and charm, and updated *terroir*, too: **La Lucarne aux Chouettes** (Quai Bretoche, Tel: 03 86 87 18 26, www .lesliecaron-auberge.com, closed Monday and dinner Sunday except in July and August, and January, inexpensive to expensive) is on the river's north side, in a series of historic buildings lovingly restored. The area's celebrated bide-a-wee, the canopy or four-poster beds await in love-nest rooms, and there's an airy dining room whose tables and chairs are swaddled in linen and lit by curlicue chandeliers (plus a lovely riverside terrace). Actress Leslie Caron owns this chic hostelry favored by Parisians and newlyweds. Japanese chef Daisuke Inagaki does the creative, precise, market-based Franco-Japanese cooking. Beyond the yakitori, Inagaki gives a new spin to regional food. The pike-perch with wild mushrooms is delicious, and so are the veal kidneys cooked in an Irancy Pinot Noir reduction sauce. Desserts range from chocolate soufflé with pistachio sauce to fresh exotic fruit skewers. The service is casual but polished. On the wine list, fine local and regional bottlings.

VINCELOTTES

A few miles west of Irancy, this village is in the heart of Auxerrois wine country. On the banks of the Yonne River you'll find **Auberge des Tilleuls** (12 Quai de l'Yonne, Tel: 03 86 42 22 13, www.auberge-les-tilleuls.com, closed Tuesday and Wednesday, Thursday from October to Easter, and late December to late February, moderate to expensive). Take a table on the shady riverside terrace or in one of the two cozy dining rooms—timbers, stones, comfortable seating—and enjoy the classic French country fare, which follows the seasons, and includes everything from oeufs en meurette and coq au vin to the inevitable foie gras, scallops, or lobster, jugged hare to game and wild mushrooms. Everything chef Alain Renaudin serves is fresh and housemade, including the fruit tarts, Baba au rhum, and rich spoon sweets. The service is professional, the wine list boasts local bottlings at reasonable prices, and the clientele merges locals and travelers.

VOUTENAY

The train station is a shed, facing the Cure River, and the handful of passengers on this secondary trunk line are usually pilgrims en route to Vézelay. Somehow this small village set between the river and the rumbling RN6 superhighway preserves a modicum of charm, despite the traffic. Slow down and put on your turn signal. On the highway you'll find **Auberge Le Voutenay** (8 RN6, Tel: 03 86 33 51 92, http://monsite.wanadoo.fr/auberge.voutenay, closed Sunday dinner, Monday, Tuesday, one week in the second half of June and three weeks in January, moderate to expensive). In a centuries-old manor transformed into a coaching inn, the building is charming, the terrace wide and shaded by big trees, the grounds running most of the way to the tracks and riverbanks. The dining room has a fireplace, and the food you'll eat is rustic, from the crapiaud crêpes of Le Morvan to the pan-fried rabbit or chicken with wild mushrooms. Take a stroll in the grounds; if you spend the night, make sure to get a room in the middle, facing the park. Trains pass infrequently, whereas the road traffic can wake the dead.

CHABLIS and CHABLISIEN

*Includes: Chablis, Dissangis,
L'Isle-sur-Serein, Ligny-le-Châtel, Montréal,
Noyers, Pontigny, Tonnerre*

CHABLIS

Chablis is an attractive town of 2,500 set in a wide valley crossed by
the Serein River. Marsannay be damned, it's also nicknamed the
Porte d'Or—Golden Gate—of Burgundy. Chablis claims Roman
roots: vines were planted here in the third century. Chablis was
destroyed several times and rebuilt in the sixteenth century. After
phylloxera, rural abandonment, a climate celebrated for frost, and
a devastating Nazi aerial bombardment during World War II,
Chablis has gradually pulled itself together. The introduction of
smudge pots in the 1960s and '70s—environmentally unfriendly
but essential for keeping buds above freezing—underlies the
area's renaissance. Global warming is further reducing the fre-
quency of frost. The prosperity found nowadays is rarely matched
elsewhere in Burgundy. Thoroughly restored and tidy, Chablis's
streets are lined by stone or half-timbered buildings, with many
restaurants, comfortable places to lodge, and a handful of gourmet food artisans and boutiques.

Officially part of the Auxerrois, Chablis feels like it should be
on the Côte d'Or. Locals even refer to the Chardonnay grape as
Beaunois, and many major Beaune-based wineries own vineyards

or wineries here. Though much smaller than Beaune, and less self-consciously important, it's nonetheless the proud, independent wine capital of Northern Burgundy. As in Beaune, scores of excellent wineries are found in and around town. Many produce limited quantities, sell out regularly, and are not easily accessible.

Chablis boasts an astonishing seven Grand Cru Climats totaling 250 acres, all on a single hill overlooking town, La Colline des Grands Crus, with due-southern exposure (and a panoramic point up top). They are Blanchot, Bougros, Les Clos, Grenouille, Preuses, Valmur, and Vaudésir. Confusingly, sometimes they're spelled in the singular, sometimes in the plural, and within them are found individual vineyard parcels with their own names (La Moutonne monopole, for instance). At fifty acres, Les Clos is the most extensive Climat. On this hill the fossilized oysters and sea creatures that make up Chablis's prized Kimmeridgian soil lie particularly deep. There are also many 1er Cru vineyards hedging town. Lesser vineyards lie progressively farther out, where the soil, exposure, and micro-climate are not as favorable. All told, the Chablisien—the district surrounding Chablis, comprising about twenty villages—currently covers about 12,500 acres owned by 300 winegrowers.

Only trace quantities of Aligoté, Sauvignon, and Pinot Noir are grown. Chardonnay is the mainstay. Chablis wines are nervy and lean, the best of them complex enough to also be honeyed and fat. Typically, entry-level Petit Chablis AOC and Chablis AOC wines are made in stainless steel; they have a clean, floral bouquet and an initial flavor suggesting green apples, and are best drunk young. Grand and 1er Cru bottlings are often oaked for considerable periods, developing an elegant nose and richer flavors, and can last decades. Here as elsewhere, connoisseurs and oenologists are locked in an unwinnable ideological and gustatory war over oak, the use of selected yeasts, and the timing, temperature, and percentage of malolactic fermentation. Many claim the Chablisien is a special case. Whereas judicious use of lightly or medium-toasted barrels and casks can enrich muscular Meursaults and Puligny-Montrachets, even light oaking can mask the natural qualities of Chablis, a subtle beverage with rare mineral qualities.

"Chablisien" is also what a local inhabitant is called. Collectively they seem inclined to industriousness and self-promotion. Anyone familiar with vintage photographs of nineteenth-century French cities will feel at home on Chablis's main street: signage beckons from sidewalk sandwich-boards and every nook and cranny. Many of these advertisements shout their claims, vying for the title of "oldest"—often the oldest date of edification, establishment, or invention, whether it be for a cellar, tower, moat, stone, process, or recipe. Of the latter, tripe sausage is the city's culinary claim to fame: *andouillette à la chablisienne* or *andouillette au Chablis* are seemingly interminable lengths of tripe heavily peppered and seasoned with onions or shallots, salt, parsley, Chablis wine or Marc de Bourgogne, and then rolled, bound, and cut to short lengths to make sausages, or otherwise transmogrified into terrine. Two of the region's premier tripe experts are on the main drag, next door to each other. Each has received the coveted "5A" rating from the Association Amicale Amateurs d'Andouillette Authentique. Each has its regular customers, who disdain the other. **Charcutier Marc Colin** (3 Place Charles-de-Gaulle, Tel: 03 86 42 10 62, closed Sunday afternoon and Monday), who's as famous for his terrines, bone-in hams, and jambon persillé as for his andouillette à la chablisienne tripe, is held by many to be the authentic tripe-sausage and tripe-terrine master, revered throughout Burgundy. He also has a stand at the Auxerre market (open Tuesday and Friday mornings). No ham-bone himself, the vigorous, cheerful Colin gets up at dawn to make his product entirely by hand. Despite what you might think of tripe and the Burgundian obsession for it, his passion is contagious. A traditional shop run by the friendly Colin family, it also stocks a small selection of fine gourmet products, and is an excellent source for picnic supplies.

Bellied up next door is the luxurious, button-bright boutique of rival Laurent Camus, who took over the business from the godhead of tripe, **Michel Soulié** (3bis Place Charles-de-Gaulle,

Tel: 03 86 42 12 82, closed Sunday afternoon). Camus claims a pedigree reaching back to 1886, via Soulié, but to many locals he's a newcomer. Watch out: his tripe sausage should be called andouillette de Chablis and not andouillette à la chablisienne. The stylish, smiling shop attendants also sell terrines and hams, beautifully displayed local cheeses, Fallot mustard, cookies, and chocolates—in other words, this a one-stop food extravaganza, favored by itinerant bobos.

Chablis hosts a particularly good outdoor market, Le Marché Bourguignon (Tourism Office, Tel: 03 86 42 80 80, www.chablis .net), on Sunday morning. It fills Rue Auxerrois, the main street, and sometimes spills into adjoining streets. You'll find gourmet foods, kitchen tools, and clothing, not to mention tripe and wine. Speaking of which, the Fête des vins de Chablis is on the fourth weekend in November; the Saint-Vincent-Tournante wine festival takes place each end-January or early February in a different village in the Chablisien district (see page 63). Both are an excuse to eat, drink, and make merry. Also worth noting is the Marché des Vins de l'Yonne featuring wines from everywhere in the *département*, held the first Saturday in May.

Places to eat and drink

....

The most entertaining place to eat, drink, and lodge in town is trendy **Laroche Wine Bar/Hôtel du Vieux Moulin** (18 Rue des Moulins, Tel: 03 86 42 47 30, www.larochewines.com and www .larochehotel.fr, hotel open daily, restaurant closed Sunday and dinner Monday to Wednesday, moderate to expensive). Housed in a tastefully reconverted mill bridging the Serein River in the heart of town, water cascades below decks and jazz plays on the sound system. The colorful, quirky décor in the restaurant and luxury B&B upstairs, and even some of the furnishings, were designed by protean winemaker-hotelier Michel Laroche, flanked by his fashionable wife, Gwénaël. The wine tasting possibilities (by the glass or bottle) take in the range of Domaine Laroche's properties scattered across the world. Clearly, the most worthwhile ones to taste showcase Chablis's *terroir*. They range from quaffable, affordable Petit Chablis via Chablis Saint Martin and buttery 1er Cru Les Vaudevey, to the giant Grand Cru Les Blanchots and Grand Cru Réserve de L'Obédience. All told, the house serves Laroche's nine Chablis wines, plus eleven others from its estates in Southern France, Chile, and South Africa. When it comes to the food, *terroir* is not the focus. The mini-appetizer you're served

unbidden on a large plate is an exquisite flake of smoked trout with caramelized cabbage, and is a bellwether. Talented young chef Philippe Legrand's heart lies in the land of culinary arabesques: he worked at L'Espérance and with trendy chef David Zuddas in Dijon. Nonetheless, Legrand has concocted a delicious, innovative *terroir* menu featuring oeufs en meurette, snails, spicy tripe sausage, pike-perch, and a host of updated classics. His tricks include fluffing the eggs in the meurette, and serving them with fresh wild mushrooms in a creamy Chablis sauce, flanked by crispy bacon. The shelled snails—enormous servings—are cooked in a classic meurette, with a red wine–reduction sauce, pearl onions, and bacon. The pike-perch gets a Pinot Noir reduction sauce, the tripe a dusting of minced chives and an emulsion of Chablis and seasonings. Some of the local cheeses come from Pascal Le Roux (in nearby Brion). The desserts are complicated but luscious. Though casual, the service is professional, courteous, and efficient. Expect to be surrounded by upscale travelers, businessmen, local merchants and winemakers. See wineries, below, for more on Domain Laroche.

As the tale of two tripe masters reveals, rivalry also appears to be a trait of Chablisiens. It's not surprising that, given the success of Laroche Wine Bar, another multi-talented winemaker, Daniel-Etienne Defaix, has leapt into the business of being a trendy restaurateur. Already owner of the traditional Hôtel-Restaurant Aux Lys de Chablis, his new eatery, with cutting-edge décor, is **La Cuisine au Vin** (16 Rue Auxerrois, Tel: 03 86 18 98 52, www .lacuisineauvin.fr, closed Sunday dinner, Monday and Tuesday). The dining-area cellars are from the tenth to twelfth centuries; they're painted white, with white marble floors, and are brilliantly lit by wrought iron wall sconces made to look like torches. The tabletops are glass, the seats green transparent plastic resembling bentwood. When in them, if you're not dazed and blinded, you can savor chef Patrick Bouloton's handsomely served andouillettes au Chablis, snails cooked in Chablis, oeufs en meurette with Chablis sauce and truffle shavings, pike-perch slabs cooked on the skin, and other hearty food whose earthy qualities seem strange given the surroundings. The wines are from Defaix's Domaine du Vieux Château. The Chablis Vieilles Vignes is the best deal. The seating at street level, in Defaix's wine and gourmet food boutique and tasting area, next door to the restaurant, **Cave Le Monde du Vin** (#14, Tel: 03 86 42 14 14, www.chablisdefaix.com, open daily), consists of even more challenging, multicolored, transparent plastic perches. They contrast sharply with the stone walls and thick old timbers. However, this shock-the-bourgeois and challenge-the-backbone approach to eno-gastronomy appears to work: business is booming.

For a different, more traditional dining experience, seek out Michel Vignaud, chef-proprietor of luxurious, Michelin-starred **Hostellerie des Clos** (18 Rue Jules-Rathier, Tel: 03 86 42 10 63, www.hostellerie-des-clos.fr, open for dinner daily, closed for lunch Monday to Thursday, and mid December to late January, expensive to very expensive), a Chablis institution. Vignaud is from Le Morvan. Despite the artistic presentation and lightening of recipes, the authentic rusticity still surfaces in his traditional dishes. Among them are oeufs en meurette made with Irancy red wine, the house signature dish of chicken liver terrine macerated with Chablis, delicate steamed omble chevalier, sautéed sweetbreads with crunchy celery, veal kidneys browned in their own fat and then cooked in and drizzled with Chablis, and Charolais thin-sliced and matched to sautéed wild mushrooms. Like most marquee practitioners, however, he also serves variations on the theme of foie gras and seafood, including the inevitable lobster and roasted prawns (drizzled, perhaps, with hazelnut oil). Both restaurant and hotel have a classic country feel, with comfortable overstuffed armchairs and floral patterned décor. Bay windows overlook the back garden. The wine list is strong on Chablis— dozens of the best bottlings—and other local and regional wines. By request, Vignaud's sommeliers will guide guests through Chablis wine tastings in the cellar.

Vignaud's more affordable, casual, pleasant baby bistro, a few doors down, past the William Fevre winery, is called **Le Bistrot des Grands Crus** (8–10 Rue Jules-Rathier, Tel: 03 86 42 19 41, open daily for lunch and dinner, same website and vacation closing as above, inexpensive to moderate). You'll eat cheek-by-jowl, surrounded by locals and tourists, choosing your typical, well-made *terroir* dish off the blackboard or menu, from tripe or snails to beef bourguignon, and accompanying it with a local or regional wine. Everything is housemade, including the refreshingly classic desserts. There's a pleasant back terrace for summer dining. The service is friendly and swift.

The best low-end, local, and likeable eatery in town is **La Feuillette** 132 (8 Rue des Moulins, Tel: 03 86 18 91 67, open daily in summer, closed Sunday and Wednesday dinner in low season, and two weeks mid to end December, inexpensive). The first thing everyone asks is, what does the name mean? The moniker says much about the oaken décor, winey atmosphere, hearty food and chummy service—all unpretentious. In local parlance, a *feuillette* is an oak cask holding precisely 132 liters of wine. This is a good place to try traditional ham cooked with Chablis, jambon persillé, oeufs en meurette, stews, steaks, and more. There are wines from fifty local domaines, sold with a reasonable mark-up.

Gourmet shops and food artisans

Gourmet food is sold everywhere in Chablis, at tripe shops, restaurants, wineries and wine bars, bakeries, greengrocer shops, and specialized boutiques. **Au Cep Gourmand** (15 Rue Auxerrois, Tel: 03 86 18 97 83, open daily in summer, closed Sunday afternoon and Monday the rest of the year, and January) is across

the street from Cuisine au Vin and kitty corner to the Laroche
wine boutique. Crammed onto shelves are hundreds of inviting
jars, cans, vases, and baskets full of mustard, gingerbread, cookies,
liqueurs and whatnot, plus wine and Burgundian micro-brewery
beers (flavored with ginger, Marc de Bourgogne, and blackcurrant liqueur).

Continue down the main street and watch it change names
twice. Kitty corner to the town's chocolate and pastry shop you'll
find **Les Jardins Européens** (11 Rue Mal Delattre de Tassigny,
Tel: 03 86 42 43 57, closed Sunday afternoon and Monday), a
greengrocer's shop hung with baskets, and stuffed with top-
quality fruit and vegetables, gourmet foods and cheeses (Abbey
de la Pierre-Qui-Vire, Soumaintrain, chèvres, Époisses, Alain
Hess's Delice de Pommard). You'll find authentic *patatière* potato
baskets and *hottes* for grape-pickers. Run by Nadette Martinez
and her daughter Adelaïde, this shop has been in business since
1994. The family also runs a stand at the Auxerre market (on
Tuesday and Friday mornings).

Le Pilier de Chablis (6 Rue Mal Delattre de Tassigny, Tel: 03
86 42 10 28, closed Sunday afternoon and Wednesday) is the fief
of master chocolate-maker and pastry chef Pascal Sébillotte and
family. The house specialty, *Le Pilier*—a tiny Roman column—
is filled with a candied-toasted-hazelnut ganache flavored with
raisins macerated in Marc de Bourgogne or Ratafia, and comes
in dark, milk, or white chocolate. Among the pastries: Frou-frou
(chocolate-caramel mousse layered into translucent hazelnut-
praline dough mounted on a chocolate biscuit) and Citron Fram-
boise (lemon mousse with raspberry jam mounted on a biscuit
bottom made with crushed almonds). The housemade ice creams
are equally outstanding.

If you're less than wild about the scent of boiled tripe, but
would like to buy outstanding terrines (especially chicken liver
terrine with truffles, or snail terrine with Chablis), ham cooked
in a winey Chablis sauce, salamis, and suchlike, head to excellent
butcher-deli **Éric Porte** (7 Rue Auxerrois, Tel: 03 86 42 11 51, www
.ericporte-chablis.com, closed Sunday afternoon and Monday).

Wine shop and wineries

L'Avenue des Grands Crus (10 Rue Mal Delattre de Tassigny,
Tel: 03 86 51 32 94, www.grandscrusonline.com, closed Mon-
day), on the main street, opened in 2008 and is run by Hocine
Ladjadj. A wine expert from left field, Ladjadj represents five

BILINGUAL CHABLIS-BASED WINE EXPERT **Marc Chretien** (Tel: 06 11 47 82 98, 03 86 42 84 54, chablis.vititours@orange.fr, www.chablis-vititours.fr) takes visitors on guided tours of local wineries and vineyards, leaving from the Chablis tourist office, or with pick-ups at hotels, B&Bs, riverboats, and vacation rentals. Tours last from fifty minutes to half a day, and can include tastings. You'll learn more than you ever thought you'd want to know about Burgundian winemaking, and that of Chablis in particular. He'll take as few as two, and as many as eight clients. Chretien's minivan is a good way to see the area. You won't waste time, and you won't have to worry about designated drivers.

. . . .

OF CORKSCREWS, TASTING CUPS, AND WAX-WORK VINTNERS

ANYONE WHO'S OBSESSED WITH CORK-screws, tasting cups, funnels, spray cans, wine presses, vats, spigots, and a dizzying array of several thousand other vineyard tools won't want to miss **Le Musée de la Vigne et du Tire-Bouchon at Domaine Alain Geoffroy** (4 Rue de l'Équerre, Beines, Tel: 03 86 42 43 76, www.chablis-geoffroy .com, open weekdays 8am to noon and 2pm to 5pm, Saturday by appointment, closed Sunday). It's in the outlying village of Beines, five miles west of Chablis, and though it looks and feels like the archetypal kitsch tourist trap, and features those waxwork dolls the French love, it's actually fascinating. Best of all, the wines Alain Geoffroy makes are good: Petit Chablis, Chablis (Domaine le Verger), and Chablis Grand Cru Les Clos.

. . . .

independent, small Chablisien winegrowers who don't have their own retail outlets. He does a brisk business on the Internet, but is more than a clearing house. He sells eight wines from Bernard Defaix (a cousin of the more famous Daniel-Etienne Defaix, see below), from an affordable Petit Chablis to a Grand Cru Bougros; Patrick Piuze, Chablis, 1er Cru Montmains, and Grand Cru Vaudésir. Four wines from organic winegrower Domaine de Bois d'Yver include two 1er Crus (Montmain and Beauregard) and two Grand Crus (Blanchots and Valmur). Last but not least, Daniel Dampt, who's based in Milly, showcases his 1er Crus Fourchaume and Beauroy. You'll also find excellent wines from other parts of Burgundy, and unusual "ice cider" from Quebec.

The cellars of **Domaine Laroche** (22 Rue Louis Bro, Tel: 03 86 42 89 00, www.larochewines.com, by appointment) face the town's main church, Saint Martin, in sections of a townhouse and monastery dating to the ninth century. (The saint's relics were kept in the base of the tower now faced by Laroche's oak barrels). On display is a thirteenth-century wine press weighing ten tons (the building was erected around it.) It still works and is used each September. The actual winery is a modern facility in the outskirts, on the road to Auxerre. Overnight guests at Hôtel du Vieux Moulin (see page 96) can arrange a tour and tasting; for others, it's more practical to taste the estate's wines at the wine bar–restaurant or with bilingual wine expert Severine Bresson at the **Laroche** wine boutique on Chablis' main street (10 Rue Auxerroise, Tel: 03 86 42 89 28, open daily). Laroche is a compelling case study: it points to the future of Chablis and Burgundy. Current scion of the Laroche dynasty, oenologist Michel Laroche took over his father's fifteen-acre estate and with hard work, charm, and good luck expanded to 250 acres. Then he bought wineries and vineyards in the south of France, created or bought estates in Chile and South Africa, and watched his fortunes rise, as New World tastes became the global norm. Michel shocked premium winegrowers by embracing screwcap technology; he was the first in France to use a screwcap on a Grand Cru. The company makes forty-two wines, including ten Chablis (from easy-drinking Tête de Cuvée Bourgogne Chardonnay and Petit Chablis to three Grand Crus). Selected yeasts are used throughout. At twelve percent alcohol, the crisp Chablis Saint Martin is fermented for two weeks in stainless steel and then spends six months in stainless steel before being filtered and bottled under low pressure. The Grand

Cru Réserve de L'Obédience instead ferments for three weeks, seventy percent of it on oak. The same percentage then spends nine months on oak, the remaining thirty percent in stainless steel. The two are assembled, filtered and low-pressure bottled. All wines are balanced, a few are outstanding. The best: 1er Cru Fourchaume Vieilles Vignes, Grand Cru Les Clos, Grand Cru Blanchots Réserve de L'Obédience.

Don't overlook cooperative winery **La Chablisienne** (8 Boulevard Pasteur, Tel: 03 86 42 89 89, www.chablisienne.com, tasting and exhibition rooms open daily except holidays, vineyard and winery visits by appointment). Founded in 1923 and stronger than ever, it's among Burgundy's biggest and best, making fine Petit Chablis, Chablis, Chablis 1er Cru, and Grand Cru. The best of each type is made from Vieilles Vignes (some antebellum vines). About 300 grapegrowers and winemakers belong. Among the holdings—2,750 acres, a quarter of the entire Chablis acreage—is the coveted Château Grenouille parcel in the biggest Grand Cru Climat, La Grenouille. From the tasting room, where the Petit Chablis, Chablis, and some 1er Crus are available, you gaze into the cellar, stacked with casks. Happily, they are used judiciously.

Outside town, seek out **Domaine Philippe Goulley** (11bis Vallée des Rosiers, La Chapelle Vaupelteigne, Tel: 03 86 42 40 85, www.goulley.fr, by appointment only). This small, independent winery has been producing remarkable organic wines since 1991. Goulley hand-picks, selects the best grapes, discarding the rest, and uses temperature-controlled stainless steel tanks, and low-pressure presses and bottling equipment. The wines' natural mineral qualities shine through. Though he also makes two ambitious 1er Cru Chablis, his best are the straightforward and affordable Petit Chablis and Chablis.

DISSANGIS

A hamlet ten miles southeast of Avallon, seven miles northwest of Noyers, Dissangis is home to **Ferme-Auberge de l'Huilerie** (6 Rue du Moulin, Tel: 03 86 33 95 56, open for weekday lunch from spring to fall, by arrangement only and only for groups in late fall and winter, inexpensive). Housed in a former oil mill—once used for making walnut, hazelnut, and seed oils—and owned and operated by a family of cattle farmers, the handsome dining room is too vast to be cozy, but attractive, with a fireplace, solid wooden tables and chairs, heavy timbers and stone walls. The house specialty, unsurprisingly, is beef: boeuf bourguignon, thick Charolais pavé steak, and milkfed veal. The housemade fruit tarts

❧ OTHER WINERIES ❧
IN OR NEAR CHABLIS AND TONNERRE

Maison Jean-Claude Bessin (18 Rue de Chitry, Tel:
03 86 42 46 77, by appointment only). Family-run
and medium-sized. *Best wines:* Chablis Grand Cru
Valmur, Grand Cru Blanchot.

Domaine Alain Besson (Rue de Valvan, Tel: 03 86
42 40 88, domaine-besson@wanadoor.fr, open daily
without appointment). Family-run and medium-
sized. *Best wines:* Chablis 1er Cru Montmains, 1er
Cru Mont de Milieu, Grand Cru Vaudésir.

Pascal Bouchard (Parc des Lys, Tel: 03 86 42 18
64, www.pascalbouchard.com, open daily, except
Sunday afternoon, without appointment). This

excellent organic, family-owned winery has about 1.5 acres of Grand Cru Les Clos, and other choice Grand Cru parcels. *Best wines:* Chablis Grande Réserve Vieilles Vignes, 1er Cru Fourchaume, Grand Cru Blanchot.

Domaine du Chardonnay (Moulin du Patis, Tel: 03 86 42 48 03, www.domaine-du-chardonnay. fr, open daily without appointment most of the year, closed Sunday afternoons April to January, Tuesdays and Wednesdays in August, and holidays year-round). Owned by a trio of dynamic young winegrowers. *Best wines:* Chablis 1er Cru Mont de Milieu, Chablis.

Domaine Jean Collet et Fils (15 Avenue de la Liberté, Tel: 03 86 42 11 93, www.domaine-collet .fr, open without appointment Monday to Saturday, closed Saturday afternoon, Sunday, and holidays). Family-run and medium-sized. *Best wines:* Chablis Vieilles Vignes, 1er Cru Montée de Tonnerre.

La Cave du Connaisseur (6 Rue des Moulins, Tel: 03 86 42 87 15, open daily without appointment). *Best wine:* Petit Chablis.

Domaine Jean-Paul & Benoît Droin (14bis Rue Jean-Jaurès, Tel: 03 86 42 16 78, www.jeanpaul -droin.fr, open weekdays without appointment, closed weekends and August). This is an outstanding, family-run winery, established in Chablis since the 1400s. *Best wines:* Grand Cru Grenouille, Grand Cru Les Clos, Grand Cru Blanchot.

Caves Jean et Sébastien Dauvissat (3 Rue de Chichée, Tel: 03 86 42 14 62, jean.dauvissat@wanadoo. fr, open daily, except Sunday, without appointment). Family-run and medium-sized. *Best wine:* Chablis 1er Cru Séchet.

Domaine René & Vincent Dauvissat (8 Rue Emile Zola, Tel: 03 86 42 11 58, by appointment only). Family-run and medium-sized. *Best wines:* Chablis 1er Crus Séchet and La Forest.

Maison Bernard Defaix (17 Rue du Château, Milly, Tel: 03 86 42 40 75, by appointment only). Bernard is a cousin of the more famous Daniel-Etienne Defaix. This is a small, high-quality, family-owned winery. Note: you can taste his wines at wine shop L'Avenue des Grands Crus in Chablis. *Best wines:* Chablis, 1er Cru Les Lys, Grand Cru Bougros.

Domaine William Fèvre (10 Rue Jules Rathier, Tel: 03 86 42 12 06, www.williamfevre.com, open daily without appointment March to December). This large, premium winery is now owned by prestigious Reims-based Champagne-maker Henriot. *Best wines:* Chablis, 1er Cru Mont de Milieu, Grand Cru Grenouilles, Grand Cru Valmur.

Domaine Raoul Gautherin et Fils (6 Boulevard Lamarque, Tel: 03 86 42 11 86, www.chablis -gautherin.com, open daily without appointment). Family-run and medium-sized. *Best wine:* Chablis 1er Cru Vaillons.

Domaine Alain et Cyril Gautheron (18 Rue des Prégirots, Fleys, Tel: 03 86 42 44 34, www .chablisgautheron.com, open Monday to Saturday without appointment, Sunday by appointment only). Family-run and medium-sized. *Best wine:* Chablis, 1er Cru Les Fourneaux.

Domaine Millet Père et Fils (Ferme de Marcault, Route de Viviers, Tonnerre, Tel: 03 86 75 92 56, baudoin.millet@wanadoo.fr, by appointment). *Best wine:* Chablis.

Domaine Long-Depaquit (45 Rue Auxerroise, Tel: 03 86 42 11 13, www.albertbichot.com, closed Sunday and holidays, and from Christmas Eve to January 2). A feather in the cap of major wine merchant Albert Bichot of Beaune, this winery in handsome 1700s premises owns, among other prestige parcels in its 175-acre portfolio, La Moutonne Grand Cru monopole. *Best wines:* 1er Cru Les Vaucoupins, 1er Cru Vaillons, Grand Cru Les Blanchots.

Domaine Régnard (28 Boulevard du Dr Tacussel, Tel: 03 86 42 10 45, open daily without appointment, open mornings only Sundays and holidays April to October). This 150-year-old winery has been owned for the last quarter century by Baron Patrick de Ladoucette, a major player in the Loire and Champagne regions. *Best wines:* Chablis Grand Crus Valmur and Vaudésir.

Domaine Servin • Maison François Servin (20-22 Avenue d'Oberwesel, Tel: 03 86 18 90 00, www .servin.info, open Monday to Saturday without appointment, closed Sundays and holidays). Family-run and medium-sized. *Best wines:* Petit Chablis, Chablis.

Maison Simonnet-Febvre (30 Route de Saint-Bris, Chitry-le-Fort, Tel: 03 86 98 99 00, www.simmonet -febvre.com, open Tuesday through Saturday without appointment). This 170-year-old winery was taken over in 2003 by Beaune giant Louis Latour. *Best wines:* Chablis, 1er Crus Montmains and Vaillons, Grand Cru Blanchot.

Domaine Testut (38 Rue des Moulins, Tel: 03 86 42 17 50, by appointment only). Family-run and medium-sized. *Best wine:* Chablis Grand Cru Grenouille.

Domaine Gerard Tremblay (12 Rue de Poinchy, Tel: 03 86 42 40 98, www.chablis-tremblay.com, open daily, except Sunday, without appointment, closed August). Family-run and medium-sized. *Best wine:* Domaine des Îles, Chablis 1er Cru Côte de Léchet.

Domaine Vocoret et Fils (40 Route d'Auxerre, Tel: 03 86 42 12 53, www.vocoret.com, open daily, except Sunday, without appointment). Housed in Chablis former dairy. *Best wines:* Grand Cru Blanchot, 1er Cru Montée de Tonnerre.

....

are delicious. Expect to dine in the company of savvy locals and retirees on the farm circuit.

L'ISLE-SUR-SEREIN

Handsome and off the tourist beat, you might drive through this riverside village between Chablis, Montréal, and Époisses. If so, eat at cozy **Auberge du Pot d'Étain** (24 Rue Bouchardat, Tel: 03 86 33 88 10, www.potdetain.com, closed Sunday dinner, Monday, Tuesday lunch, two weeks in February, and the second half of October, moderate to expensive). Stick to traditional dishes— oxtails slow-cooked in Irancy wine, duck breast with vinegary wine sauce—unless you enjoy risky culinary adventurism (seemingly gift-wrapped giant prawns with marinated salmon "tartare," a flagrantly rich savory custard of foie gras with a bouillon of green asparagus tips and suchlike). The cherry crumble with a scoop of cheesecake ice-cream is memorable. There's a back terrace for fine-weather dining. The service is professional, the clientele merges regulars and off-the-highway travelers. The wine list is one of the region's longest, with 1,400 different bottlings, many from Burgundy, especially the Yonne (nearly fifty different Chablis). The rooms are also cozy and comfy.

LIGNY-LE-CHÂTEL

In a medieval village three miles from the Pontigny Abbey, modest hotel-restaurant **Le Relais Saint-Vincent** (14 Grande Rue, Tel: 03 86 47 53 38, relais.saint.vincent@libertysurf.fr, closed mid December to early January, very inexpensive to moderate) is where locals head for authentic, housemade *terroir* food at bargain prices (and seasonal specials). The house specialty: veal kidneys in a creamy sauce flambéed with Marc de Bourgogne. The dining room of this 1600s half-timbered townhouse is darkish; there's also a quiet, sunny, flower-filled inner courtyard for summer dining.

On the road to Chablis, behind the church and along the riverbanks of the Serein at a tuneful weir, **L'Auberge du Bief** (2 Avenue de Chablis, Tel: 03 86 47 43 42, open for lunch daily and dinner Saturday night year-round, dinner Wednesday, Thursday, Friday in summer, closed Monday, the second half of August, holidays, and Christmastide, moderate to very expensive) is an upscale restaurant favored by well-heeled locals and migratory Parisians. The décor, tablecloths, cutlery, presentation of dishes, and hence the atmosphere emanate bourgeois comfort and confidence. Everything is housemade and the pâtés, jambon, terrines,

Charolais or pike-perch in red wine sauce, and seasonal vegetables are tasty. The service is polished, the wine list strong on Chablis, Irancy, and other Yonne bottlings.

MONTRÉAL

Every blue-blooded Quebecois and many other North Americans feel they must make a pilgrimage to this medieval hilltop hamlet on highway D957, which once guarded the Serein River Valley. It now watches over gently rolling farmland six miles northeast of the A6 autoroute, in the neighborhood of Époisses and L'Isle-sur-Serein. The centuries-old houses march uphill to the fortified crow's nest, where towers and turrets and a remarkable church await. Inside you'll find exceptional woodwork and a sculpted alabaster choir from the 1400s, a minor masterpiece.

The unregenerate will want to creep back down to the main road, where they'll find local café-eatery **Au Quinze** (15 Place du Prieuré, Tel: 03 86 32 16 49, closed Monday, two weeks in September and two weeks in February, inexpensive). Have a jolt of tarry coffee, a sandwich, snack or a light meal of the traditional, unsurprising but satisfying variety, and marvel at how such a natty place can survive in the back of beyond.

NOYERS

The town's official name is Noyers-sur-Serein, because the river snakes by it. Be sure to pronounce the "r"—*nwa yeahr*—or you'll

sound like the droves of snooty Parisians who've colonized this handsome, restored, and charming medieval town due south of Tonnerre about fifteen miles. Lovers of self-styled artists or *artisans d'art* (and naïf art) will be thrilled. There are galleries galore, and a skippable municipal museum, but the view from the château on a rise outside the village is pleasing. Happily, Noyers has bakeries, grocery stores, and cafés, several eateries, and an open market on the small main square (on Wednesday morning). Here you'll see itinerant stands selling fruits, clothing, meat, fish, and whatnot, plus local farmers with their organic apples or produce, a poultry farmer with a rotisserie, and hot food prepared and sold by Noyers' celebrated butcher-restaurateur, **Denis Paillot**. His *charcuterie* shop is around the corner in the smaller square (14 Place Hôtel de Ville, Tel: 03 86 82 82 16, closed Sunday afternoon and Monday). In cold weather, Denis might tempt you with blood sausage, or slices of his Époisses savory tart, or an unusual braised trout topped with Époisses sauce. He also makes excellent jambon persillé, rosette salami, pâtés and terrines, and sells fine cheeses, Fallot mustard, and Burgundian micro-brewery beers, plus delicious pastries (including a wildly good blackcurrant tartelette). This is a great place to buy a picnic. If you'd rather savor Paillot's food at table, step through a connecting door to **Le Bistro** (aka **Le Petit Millésime**, same address and tel#, inexpensive to moderate, open daily for lunch, dinner Thursday to Saturday only), or sit on the rear terrace. The bistro setting is simple (the upstairs room is handsome), the service casual, the atmosphere relaxed. Local workers, farmers, and tourists crowd in for the lunch specials (Chernobyl-sized gougères, classic snails, crayfish terrine, veal scallops with creamy Chaource cheese sauce, jambon à la Chablisienne, breaded, pan-fried hamhocks, fricasséed chicken with mild spices, a fine cheese platter, and wonderful desserts). The wines are Petit Chablis or Irancy by the glass or bottle, plus a local curiosity: bottlings from Bardet et Fils, a winery on the road to Avallon.

Across the alley behind the deli and bistro is Paillot's upscale gourmet restaurant, **Les Millésimes** (8 Rue du Poids du Roy, Tel:

03 86 82 82 16, open daily, moderate to expensive). The ceiling is high, there's a heavy, upholstered screen to keep prying eyes out, the tables are big, well-spaced, and grandly laid, and the look and feel evoke a French bourgeois home. Friendly, the service is somewhat stylized. The menu is seasonal, based on "noble" ingredients (including inevitables with nothing to do with Burgundy), and the presentation and preparation are more elaborate yet less convincing than at the humbler address.

Noyers was wine country centuries ago, and perhaps global warming and sheer determination will revive its fortunes. In the meantime, if you tasted the local tipple at one of Denis Paillot's restaurants, and want to visit those responsible, head to **Domaine La Borde–Bardet et Fils** (3 Route d'Avallon, Tel: 03 86 82 83 93, phone ahead).

PONTIGNY

Even if you're not interested in church history (i.e., Thomas Beckett, and Edmond Rich, aka Saint Edme, buried here) or medieval architecture (one of the "sister" abbeys of Cîteaux, built starting 1114, with later modifications), the sheer majesty and magical atmosphere of **Pontigny Abbey** will induce you to drive out of your way, or apply the brakes, for a visit (open daily, Tel: 03 86 47 54 99, www.abbayedepontigny.eu). Should you be more than spiritually hungry, a restaurant-wine shop in a vintage millhouse bridging the river near the abbey and tourism office will provide earthly, earthy nourishment: **Le Moulin de Pontigny** (RN77, Tel: 03 86 47 44 98, closed Monday, Tuesday, Wednesday and January, very inexpensive to moderate). Aim for the weeping willow, take a table on the terrace, or in the cozy dining room, and dig into the Burgundian classics, from shelled snails with parsleyed cream sauce or classic oeufs en meurette, to jambon à l'Aligoté, beef or poultry in winey sauces, and pike-perch sautéed with Chablis, and wind up with good cheeses and rich spoon sweets or fruit desserts. Family run, the service at this favorite of tourists is relaxed. The wine list has bottlings from Chablis, Épineuil, and Irancy; at the wine shop on the same premises, you can taste and buy wines to go.

TONNERRE

The Tintin comic books of decades past are peppered with the exclamation "*Tonnerre de Tonnerre!* " By Thunder! This soulful, antique town—Gallo-Roman, naturally—with its fortress-like Saint-Pierre church poised on a hill, is east of Chablis eleven miles. The setting—vinous hills, the Armançon River Valley, and Canal de Bourgogne—is lovely, the town of 6,000 inhabitants itself full of landmarks, including the mysterious Fosse Dionne, a circular, natural-rock fountain of remarkable depth. To gaze into its gushing waters, and contemplate the tunnel that leads hundreds of feet down and then across, under the cliffs behind, would alone make a detour here worth your while. All the more reason to wonder how, in the second half of the twentieth-century, Tonnerre was allowed to implode. Seemingly half of the houses in the upper city are abandoned, many in ruins. Drive downhill to the main highway to see the people and businesses, in new tract home developments and a mega-shopping mall.

With much effort, inner-city Tonnerre will rebound. Pioneers in this struggle are **La Ferme de la Fosse Dionne** (11 Rue de la Fosse Dionne, Tel: 03 86 54 82 62, www.fermefossedionne.fr and www.bourgogne-terroir.fr, open daily, restaurant inexpensive and by reservation), an unusual B&B-bistro-café-gourmet foods-boutique-flea market. Not a farm, it occupies a restored, half-timbered house fronting the Fosse Dionne, with an outdoor terrace, inner patio, and cavernous dining room. You eat surrounded by vintage clothing, prints, antique cake molds, statuettes, and, above all, gramophones. Playing scratchily might be *Dans les plaines du Far West*—a saga of Prairie Schooners. You'll eat snails in puff pastry, boeuf bourguignon, coq au vin, and filet of pike-perch with sautéed shallots. The desserts are simple, the wines local, served by the glass or bottle. Sold are Fallot mustard, poppy-flavored liqueur from the Ferme Chèrevie in Saint-Bris-le-Vineux, jams from Yvette Rabuat, and more.

Central Tonnerre's traditional restaurant, on the main road into town from the highway, is **Le Saint-Père** (2 Rue Georges Pompidou, Tel: 03 86 55 12 84, www.le-saint-pere.fr, closed Sunday dinner, Wednesday, Tuesday dinner from October to July, and three weeks in January, very inexpensive to expensive). This ivy-clad auberge has a rustic, comfortable interior full of old coffee grinders, and a bright patio. On the perennial menu: jambon persillé, bone-in ham à la Chablisienne, pork jowls braised in red wine, Charolais filet flambéed with Marc de Bourgogne, potato gratin with pungent Époisses; good regional cheeses go with the quaffable local wines.

Tonnerre has one fine pastry shop on its main square, aptly named **La Tentation** (51 Rue de L'Hôpital, Tel: 03 86 55 02 05, closed Sunday afternoon and Monday). Sip a cup of coffee or tea, and don't miss the Chaource, a powdery white confection with Kirsch-flavored pastry cream and sponge cake, so called because it resembles Chaource cheese. The chocolates are also delicious, and the cheesy gougères, too.

CHAPTER 2

CENTRAL BURGUNDY

Départements: Yonne, Côte d'Or,
Nièvre, Saône et Loire.

Population (approximate): 37,000.

Population density (approximate):
11 inhabitants/sq. km. (Le Morvan only)

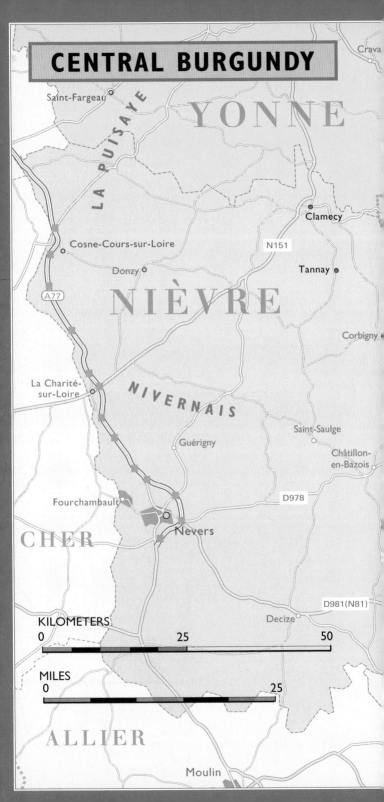

CENTRAL BURGUNDY

Crava

Saint-Fargeau

YONNE

LA PUISAYE

Clamecy

Cosne-Cours-sur-Loire

N151

Donzy

Tannay

A77

NIÈVRE

Corbigny

La Charité-
sur-Loire

NIVERNAIS

Saint-Saulge

Guérigny

Châtillon-
en-Bazois

D978

Fourchambault

CHER

Nevers

D981(N81)

KILOMETERS

Decize

0   25   50

MILES

0   25

ALLIER

Moulin

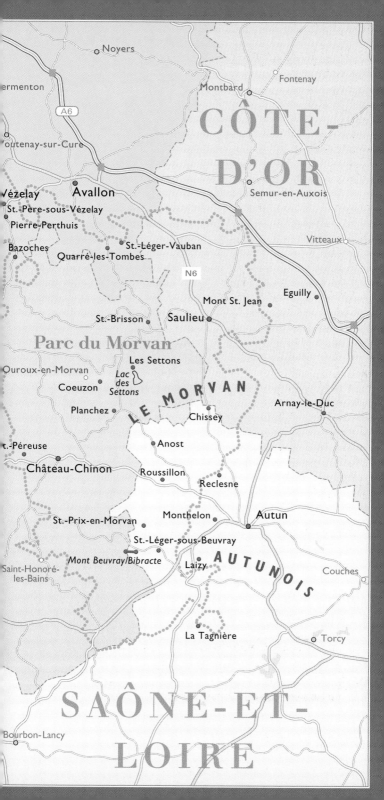

AUTUN and AUTUNOIS,
LE MORVAN, VÉZELAY

....

Includes: Anost, Arnay-le-Duc, Autun,
Avallon, Bazoches-en-Morvan, Bibracte—Mont Beuvray,
Château-Chinon, Chissey-en-Morvan, Clamecy,
Coeuzon, Eguilly—La Rente d'Eguilly,
Laizy, Mont Saint Jean, Monthelon, Pierre-Perthuis,
Planchez, Quarré-les-Tombes, Reclesne,
Roussillon-en-Morvan, Saint Brisson,
Saint-Léger-sous-Beuvray, Saint-Léger-Vauban,
Saint-Père-sous-Vézelay, Saint-Péreuse,
Saint-Prix-en-Morvan, Saulieu,
Les Settons-Lac des Settons, La Tagnière,
Tannay, Vézelay

SHARED BY ALL BURGUNDY'S ADMINISTRATIVE
DÉPARTEMENTS, THE MOUNTAINOUS CENTER OF
Burgundy stretches from Vézelay, Avallon, and Clamecy
in the north, via Saulieu and Château-Chinon on the east and
west, to Autun and Luzy in the south. Sophisticated and world-
famous, Vézelay, a pilgrimage site, draws over one million visitors a year. Autun was founded by Augustus Caesar, and boasts
one of the country's great cathedrals; the rolling hills around
Autun are known as the Autunois and merge with eastern and
southern Burgundy.

Much of this region is covered by Le Morvan, a vast park
with multi-use forests and reservoirs, and dozens of scattered
hamlets. Geologically, the Morvan is a granite plateau stretching from Vézelay forty-five miles south to Mont Beuvray, site of
the Gauls' "lost city" of Bibracte, where Julius Caesar dictated
The Conquest of Gaul. At under 3,000 feet the Morvan's peaks
aren't exactly the Alps. However, they frown over gorges, providing drama. This is where Paris' drinking water originates:
the Yonne and Cure rivers rise here, flowing into the Seine.
Lakes and streams abound. Snow closes many mountain roads;
this wettest, greenest, and prettiest part of Burgundy is recom-
mended for moss and lichen-lovers. Despite centuries of over-
logging, timber remains an important resource. The Morvan

has always been remote, impoverished, and sparsely populated, and retains a resilient identity not found elsewhere.

Les Morvandiaux, as locals are called, are reclusive. Their ancestors fought the Romans, the church, and the Burgundian dukes and French kings. The Wars of Religion left many villages in ruins. During World War II, the Résistance was active, and, again, many villages were destroyed by Nazis. Many Morvandiaux claim, partly in jest, descent from Dumnorix, the local Gallic chieftain; others are urbane. Most spend their professional lives in Paris, returning here to retire. Note: many remote villages have no restaurants, hotels, bakeries, or grocery stores, and the region goes dormant from late fall to spring.

ANOST

Anost is celebrated for its Galvachers—Wild West–style ox drivers who dragged timber into the Morvan's rivers, streams, and flumes (visit the Maison des Galvachers in the town hall, www.anost.com, impossible opening hours) and Résistance heroes. It's surprisingly civilized, with a post office, two grocery stores, **Le Sherlock Holmes Café** (no joke; coffee and drinks only), two decent restaurants, **La Galvache** and **Café Restaurant de la Poste** (Tel: 03 85 82 71 11 and 03 85 82 78 09 respectively; La Galvache is closed December to Easter), and a comfortable hotel (**Hôtel Fortin**, same telephone numbers). They're all on the main street (none of the streets in Anost have names), and owned by Catherine and René Fortin or their offspring, who appear to own everything in town. Like the décor, the food at La Galvache and de la Poste is archly traditional, from terrines and cold cuts to goat's-cheese salads, steaks, and stews. Sumptuous, the Morvan bone-in ham comes with heavy cream. You'll always find somewhere to eat: when La Galvache closes, de la Poste is open, and vice-versa.

ARNAY-LE-DUC

Halfway between the Côte de Nuits and the Morvan, it's easy to roll through Arnay-le-Duc without stopping: the unappealing N81 and N6 highways meet here in a cloud of fumes. But don't pass Arnay by; you'd miss gourmet food sources, an interesting food-related museum, and one of the most traditional hotel-restaurants of the district, **Chez Camille** (1 Place Herriot, Tel: 03 80 90 01 38, www.chez-camille.fr, open daily). Set on the highway at the foot of the hard-driven medieval hummock in the center of old Arnay, this Titanic-era coaching inn has been run for decades by chef Armand Poinsot and his team of premodernists, dressed in country-gentry uniforms. Before dining, you are invited to sink into a large armchair in the lobby—*le salon*—and feed upon housemade gougères and jambon persillé with your aperitif, while you study the menu. Whence you are conveyed into the rhomboid dining room, a kind of winter garden under an antique glass roof. Surrounded by leafy plants behind which lurk voracious regulars and tourists, seated in wicker chairs, you will be subjected to generous portions of *terroir* food. Some dishes—snails and breaded, fried frog's legs or fricasséed Bresse chicken thighs, duck pâté, thick pan-fried Charolais steaks—are always available. Others follow the market and seasons: oven-roasted spring lamb chops, stuffed squab à la royale in a pastry crust, or crayfish-tail parfait with watercress and saffron-perfumed cream sauce. There's a fine cheese platter; for dessert, housemade Cointreau soufflé, fruit sorbets in many flavors (passion fruit, herbs), fruit salad, almond *tuile* cookies, gingerbread and chocolates, creamy raspberry gratin. The wine list is long and deep. The Titanic sails on.

Also in Arnay, a hundred feet north of Chez Camille, is the one-of-a-kind **Maison Régionale des Arts de la Table** (15 Rue Saint-Jacques, Tel: 03 80 90 11 59, open daily April 1 to mid November, www.arnay-le-duc.com). Housed in a 1600s mansion with a garden, you'll find temporary shows with subjects related to food, cooking, dining, and entertaining. Don't miss the restored kitchen. There's a boutique with honeys, liqueurs, jams, terrines, foie gras. and cookies. The local tourism office is here (Tel: 03 80 90 07 55). At Christmastide, the grounds host a gourmet market.

Climb steep Rue Saint-Jacques to the medieval town, in the throes of floundering gentrification. On Place Craquelin, at #7, find **Boulanger-Pâtissier-Chocolatier Armelle Pranville** (Tel:

08 80 90 19 58, closed Monday), a compact shop with fine house-made chocolates, pastries, bread, and the specialty treat, Noisettes, a hazelnut-shaped and filled candy, plus Craquelines (named for the shop's address), which are, in essence, baked Rice Crispies with a variety of flavorings.

Farther up, past the landmark Renaissance corner building, and across the main square, is the town's other pastry shop, **Pâtisserie d'Arnay** (1bis Rue Jean Maire, Tel: 08 80 90 12 09, closed Monday). It has irresistible pastries and chocolates, plus house-made ice creams, and meringues with almonds and hazelnuts called Alumettes d'Arnay.

Fifty yards south, around the corner at 12 Rue Saint-Honoré, is Arnay's only remaining wine and gourmet-foods shop, **Le Caveau** (Tel: 08 80 90 28 57, closed Monday and Sunday morning in summer). Joëlle Gagnepain stocks many good local and regional specialties, and a fair selection of wines.

Back on the main square, **Café du Nord** is for sale but hopefully will not be gone by the time you visit Arnay. This historic café has been in business since the late 1500s, when then-princeling Henri de Navarre came to town. Much of the décor—brass-framed mirrors, iron columns, coffered ceiling, brass chandeliers—is from the 1700s and 1800s. The owner is retiring. With luck, those who follow will polish but not alter the interior.

Speaking of Henri IV, Arnay is home to the Confrérie de la Poule au Pot, one of those typically French clubs of self-styled gastronomes, ostensibly dedicated to good eating (in particular, of chicken braised in its own juices in a Dutch oven). When he was still known as Prince de Navarre, in 1570, Henri and his gallant Protestant men ransacked Roman Catholic Arnay, and why his memory should be celebrated is a mystery. A mystery until you realize Henri was later known as Le Vert Gallant—the evergreen galavanting geezer. A French pun and nudge-nudge, wink-wink sexual innuendo hides beneath the poultry pot's lid. If you're in Arnay on Thursday morning, visit the outdoor market in town center. Every first Thursday the market is even bigger. In July and August, Thursday nights until ten o'clock you'll see some of the same daytime market stands—plus musicians, craftspeople, and snack stands—at Arnay's Nocturnes Estivales, a hayseed shopping festival.

AUTUN

Modern-day Autun—founded by Augustus Caesar, originally named Augustodunum—has 17,000 inhabitants, fewer than in

antiquity, yet is still the largest municipality in Central Burgundy. A handsome Emerald City studded with belltowers and spires, surrounded by impressive ramparts, it straddles a ridge on Le Morvan's southern edge. The ramparts, primarily medieval, sit atop Caesar's bulwark, itself poised on earlier foundations. Autun is divided in two: an upper section with centuries-old buildings and narrow, twisting streets, and a lower, ostensibly more recent section with straight avenues, squares, municipal buildings, and a train station. The upper city is more attractive, but ancient monuments such as Roman city gates, temples, and an amphitheater are scattered around the lower part of town and immediate surroundings.

Autun's Roman amphitheater faces a lake on the city's southeast side. When built it was Gaul's biggest, with 12,000 seats. Each August it hosts entertainingly kitsch Gallo-Roman extravaganzas—La Semaine Gallo-Romaine—featuring cardboard shields, plastic swords, warriors in papier-maché helmets, chariots, and tinny trumpets (Tourism Office, Tel: 03 85 86 80 38, www.autun-tourisme.com). The Temple of Janus, across town on the floodplain of the Arroux River, is a pockmarked pile, in proximity to the former Roman road to Saulieu, Chalon-sur-Saône, Beaune, and Mâcon (known during the Empire as Cavillonum, Belenos, Matisco, and Sidolocum).

Saint Lazare cathedral rises over upper Autun, its majestic Gothic towers visible for miles around. The main tympanum is a masterpiece of Romanesque art, and the sculpted capitals in the Lapidary Room upstairs are among France's most impressive. The Musée Rolin (5 Rue des Bancs, Tel: 03 85 52 09 76, www.autun.com, hours vary widely), in a medieval-Renaissance townhouse, bursts with sarcophagi, statuary, and artworks. Don't miss the high-relief of Eve, from the 1100s, or carved wooden Virgin with Christ in her belly. The museum is also headquarters of the Société Eduenne, learned locals who keep alive the flame of their ancient forebears, the Aedui, forced by Caesar to relocate to Autun from Bibracte 2,000 years ago.

Autun has remarkable open and covered markets, among the region's best, held each Wednesday and Friday morning (8am to 1pm) on the main square, Place du Champ de Mars, and in the covered market flanking city hall. Cheese specialists include Marie-France and Georges Dodane of La Fouchale Crèmerie-Fromagerie in Saulieu; outstanding local butcher-*charcutier* Serge Henriot has a stand. Also, don't miss the covered shopping gallery, built 1742 to 1746, and remodeled 1835 to 1848, linking the square to Rue aux Cordiers.

Places to eat and drink

Dozens of cafés and restaurants stud Autun. When it comes to *terroir* food the scene is limited, with multi-generational **Le Chalet Bleu** (3 Rue Jeannin, Tel: 03 85 86 95 36, www.lechaletbleu .com, closed Monday dinner, Tuesday, and 15 days in February, inexpensive to very expensive) topping the list. It's fifty yards from the market. The Bouché family turn out handsomely plated *terroir* and bourgeois cuisine (oeufs en meurette, snails with garlicky croûtons, a deep-dish soupière of snails with mild garlic and wild mushrooms, a pocheuse-style fish stew of pike-perch, and frog's legs with caramelized pearl onions and mild garlic, thick Charolais steaks finished in wine sauce, rustic crapiaud crêpes with bacon, or Bresse chicken slow-cooked with heavy cream and morel mushrooms). Skip the creative offerings. Of the desserts, the apricot gratiné with gingerbread is excellent. The deep, quiet dining room has pastel-hued murals, well-spaced tables, and comfortable chairs. The wine list is also long.

Locals—farmers, shopkeepers, pen-pushers from city hall across the street—fill **Le Châteaubriant** (14 Rue Jeannin, Tel: 03 85 52 21 58, www.lechateaubriant.com, closed Sunday and Wednesday dinner, Tuesday, two weeks in February and three weeks in July, inexpensive to moderate). This is Autun's insider address, run by young Éric (*maître d'hôtel*) and Richard (chef) Brown, grandsons of an Englishman, but as native as an Aedui chieftain. The grilled Charolais rib-eye steak is delicious, with parsley and butter, period. The pike-perch filet, rolled in gingerbread crumbs before being pan fried, is slightly sweet and spicy. *Terroir* classics range from snails and frog's legs on up. Avoid hazardous territory where ingredients are scrambled: the puff pastries with snails and de-boned, ground frog's legs are not memorable. Desserts include fresh strawberry pie, chocolate mousse, crème brûlée, or a crumble of seasonal fruit. The wine list runs from easy local bottlings at low prices to ludicrously expensive Romanée-Conti La Tache at about 800 euros.

Other good-value local hangouts with *terroir* and classic French food are **Bar-Restaurant Hôtel de France** (18 Avenue de la République, Tel: 03 85 52 14 00, www.hotel-de-france -autun.fr, closed Sunday dinner and three weeks in February, very inexpensive to inexpensive), near the train station; **Restaurant des Remparts** (17 Rue Mazagran, Tel: 03 85 52 54 02, closed Monday, very inexpensive to moderate), on the northeast side of central Autun; and, more scenically sited, **Le Petit Rolin**

(12 Place Saint-Louis, Tel: 03 85 86 15 55, always open), a café-
crêperie-restaurant with tables facing the cathedral. It has an
inner court, and a yawning medieval cellar–dining room with
tree-trunk timbers, columns, and thick walls. Never mind the
motel art. The food is good (classics, including creamy veal with
mushrooms), served with flair. This is a good place to try the
roborative, unsightly Morvan specialty, crapiaud, a rustic crêpe
stuffed with just about everything imaginable (its apt name
sounds in French like "toad").

Gourmet shops and food artisans

Autun has a fine coffee roaster, **La Pause Café** (9 Rue aux Cordiers,
Tel: 03 85 86 34 60, www.lapausecafe.fr, closed Sunday and Mon-

day), on the pedestrianized
street south of the main
square, as you walk uphill
toward the cathedral. Of
the eighteen monovarietal
or pure-Arabica blends
toasted four times a week,
the most flavorful is Talleyrand, made with medium-
roasted beans from South
and Central America and
Africa. The café's owners
Agnes Sabbadini and Bruno
Lagarde drew inspiration
from a letter by Charles
Maurice de Talleyrand. On
December 26, 1825, the savvy statesman declared, "Coffee must
be as Black as the Devil, as Hot as Hell, as Pure as an Angel, and
as Sweet as Love." The capitalization is his. Enjoy this devilishly
good brew at a sidewalk table or in the rather chilling back salon,
or sip a cup of tea (there are ninety to choose from), and nibble a
sweet snack or chocolate from Cluizel (in Paris). Also sold are
cookies, condiments, jams, spices, and oils.

Nearby on Rue Saint-Saulge find outstanding **Au Cygne de
Montjeu** (#12, Tel: 03 85 52 29 61, www.autun-chocolat.com,
closed Monday), Autun's top pastry and chocolate shop, run since
1990 by Natalie and Alain Theuret. Compact yet dazzling, the shop
displays macarons, blueberry pies, walnut tarts, and plumcakes,
plus about fifty different handmade chocolates (flavored with

spices or herbal essences—lime, lavander, jasmin) and nougat. The Croquets du Morvan are shortbread sablés with almonds.

Across the street is **Isabelle Laly Produits du Terroir** (#5, Tel: 03 85 52 00 94, open daily in summer, closed mornings Sunday and Monday the rest of the year). Mademoiselle Laly is reserved, jealous of her suppliers, and sells excellent products. Fallot or Collignon et Fils mustards, Mulot & Petitjean gingerbread, terrines (rabbit, guinea fowl, and chicken) from Domaine des Richards, and delicacies made especially for the shop, are displayed.

Two butcher shop–delis stand out. **Keiffer** (14 Rue de Lattre de Tassigny, Tel: 03 85 52 06 58, closed Thursday afternoon, Monday, and mid September) borders the open market's clothing stalls. Patrice Keiffer, an old-fashioned butcher, chooses his beef on the hoof; the steaks and roasts are of exceptional quality. Of the good pork products sold only the jambon persillé and salami are housemade.

On the same street, which changes name as it heads north, seek out **Serge Henriot** (29 Rue Guérin, Tel: 03 85 52 28 56, www .charcuteriehenriot.fr, closed Sunday afternoon, Monday, and the second half of June). His 1800s shopfront is a delight. Henriot took over in 1985. A deli-man by training, his dry-aged hams, terrines and pâtés, salami and jambon persillé, are outstanding. Tireless, Henriot also runs a stand at the covered market on Friday mornings.

Wine shop

Autun's best independent wineseller is **Le Cellier de Benoît Laly** (14 Rue de la Grange Vertu, Tel: 03 85 52 24 83, www.vins-laly .com, open daily). Vast, a mini-museum of winegrowing tools and equipment, Laly stocks 5,000 bottles. From the stainless steel tanks in a back room Laly dispenses bulk wines of high quality, from Aligoté and Givry to Maranges 1er Cru La Fussière, an underrated red. Scores of Burgundy wineries are represented, from Meursault's Alain Coche Bizouard to Domaine de la Romanée Conti (3,500 to 5,000 euros a bottle, reserved years ahead). Wine tastings are held periodically. Phone or check the website for dates and details.

AVALLON

A sunny hilltown of considerable charm, Avallon rises over the Cousin River Valley, on Le Morvan's northeastern edge. Either blessed by Apollo, or the apple of the region's ancient Gallic eye, the town's name is said to derive from *aballo*, a Celtic word for apple. The etymology derives from Saxon terminology, however. The presence of apple orchards, and the tradition of making apple cider and pies, feed this origin-myth.

The tourism office and even the best guidebooks fail to mention that Avallon was home to Carolingian knight Gengulphus of Burgundy. Murdered by one of his unfaithful wife's many, many, many lovers, Gengoux, as the French refer to him, was sainted in 760 AD, becoming the country's first protector of jilted lovers, cuckolds, separated spouses, and those trapped in "difficult" marriages. Avallon shuns poor Gengulphus; he's celebrated in the less persnickety town of Saint-Gengoux-le-National, near Cluny and Chalon-sur-Saône.

Delicious local apples, and other produce, cheeses, wines, and gourmet items, are sold at the Saturday morning market, on Avallon's main square and esplanade, Promenade des Terreaux Vauban, and Place Vauban. You'll also find two cafés with terraces, and a trio of fine chocolate shops. Tiny **Maurissat-Confiserie Vauban** (8 Place Vauban, Tel: 03 86 34 06 25, closed Sunday, Monday, and from July 14 to August 15, open 7/7 in December) specializes in handmade chocolates, among them Délices de Vauban, a filled confection with blackberry-flavored ganache, plus Nougeottes (chocolate-coated toasted and sugared hazelnuts), Bourguignons with raisins soaked in Marc de Bourgogne, butter-caramels and exquisite rolled, dried fruit pastes and candied fruit.

A few shopfronts away, find **Stéphanie & Christophe Gauthier** (18 Place Vauban, Tel: 03 86 34 10 58, closed Sunday afternoon and Monday), Avallon's top pastry makers. The modest façade hides considerable talent. On offer are many French classics, from apple tarts and turnovers to lemon custard pies, chocolates and elaborate pastry confections, and house specialties (Chardons du Morvan and Mylors).

On the other side of the sprawling square, cornering Rue de Paris, is rival chocolate and gourmet foods boutique **Au Regal Bourguignon** (1 Rue des Odeberts, Tel: 03 86 34 23 93, closed Monday morning and Sunday) sells Belgian chocolates, candies, liqueurs (including Jacqoulot Marc de Bourgogne), over a hundred teas, excellent pure-Arabica coffees, gingerbread, wines, Champagne, canned foie gras, and terrines.

The ancient Via Agrippa consular highway ran through Avallon, which in, Roman times, was a fortress-city. During the Middle Ages it may have been home to King Arthur and the Knights of the Round Table, if certain conspiracy theorists are to be believed. Later, in the 1400s, it was a stronghold of the Dukes of Burgundy. In various guises, shedding and growing new walls, it remained a fortress until the twentieth century. The last great wall-builder of Avallon was Vauban (see Saint-Légér-Vauban). Stroll along his tree-lined, Louis XIV-period ramparts and follow by exploring the historic center of town with its drafty church, charming local history museum **Musée de l'Avallonnais** (5 Rue du Collège, Tel: 03 86 34 03 19, hours vary widely), and Tour de l'Horloge, a fifteenth-century clocktower.

In the tower's shadow you'll discover the pleasant restaurant—café—tea salon—gourmet food boutique **Dame Jeanne** (59 Grande

Rue, Tel: 03 86 34 58 71, open Monday to Saturday 10:30am to 6pm, closed Sunday and mid January to mid February, inexpensive). With chic décor blending cozy antiques, parquet floors, and contemporary furniture, service provided by trendy staffers in black, and a shady cobbled courtyard, this is a fine spot for a coffee, tea, light lunch, or snack. Stick to the daily specials—rabbit cooked with apple cider and prunes, for instance—or quiches and salads, and regional cheese platters. The house specialty is a weighty trio of giant gougères filled and topped with Époisses cream sauce. The seasonal fresh fruit tarts are outstanding; the good artisanal ice creams aren't housemade.

Avallon's best breads (and simple pastries) come from homely **Pélissier** (12 Rue de Paris, Tel: 03 86 34 14 53, open Tuesday to Sunday 6am to 8pm, closed Monday and three weeks in September), on the downhill, unfashionable side of the main square.

Two upscale butcher shops on the central pedestrian road (Grand Rue Aristide Briand) and small shopping square (Place du Générale de Gaulle) are known for their quality meat; the best *charcuterie* and picnic supplies in town come from a modest, compact shop 200 yards east of Place Vauban: **La Fine Gueule Traiteur Charcuterie** (8 Rue de Lyon, Tel: 03 86 34 19 52, closed Sunday). Affable Monsieur and Madame Anière handmake without preservatives, colorings, or nitrates outstandingly delicious rosette salami, baked ham, smoked sausages, spicy chorizo, jambon persillé, terrines, and many classics.

Next door is restaurant **Le Gourmillon** (8 Rue de Lyon, Tel: 03 86 31 62 01, open daily in high season, closed Sunday dinner, Thursday in low season, and January, inexpensive), a good fallback address, with regional specialties.

Le Relais des Gourmets (47 Rue de Paris, Tel: 03 86 34 18 90, www.relaisdesgourmets.com, closed Sunday dinner, Monday in low season, and January, inexpensive to moderate) serves the best *terroir* food in town. In lower, less attractive Avallon, this old-fashioned restaurant's façade, hung with geraniums, is easy to spot. The cozy dining room (stones and timbers), and outside seating fit with the tasty Burgundian dishes—oeufs en meurette, snails, jambon persillé, braised ham, thick Charolais cheesesteak, or whole roasted squab. The service is professional, the wine list adequate.

Another good-value address is **Hôtel-Restaurant Les Capucins** (6 Avenue Président Doumer/Avenue de la Gare, Tel: 03 86 34 06 52, www.avallonlescapucins.com, open daily, inexpensive to moderate), also in the unfashionable part of town, near the train station.

The premises are flower-filled, traditional and comfortable, the patio pleasant in warm weather. The nicely presented regional and French specialties, lightened and in some cases updated, follow the seasons. Everything is housemade, from the gougères up; the ingredients are high quality. The Charolais cheesesteak is satisfying, the desserts memorable (seasonal apple tarts or beggar's purses with apples macerated in Marc de Bourgogne).

In the outskirts, about three miles from town, are four restaurants (three of them with guest rooms) serving classic Burgundian and updated *cuisine bourgeoise*. **Hostellerie du Moulin des Ruats** (Vallée du Cousin, Tel: 03 86 34 97 00, www.moulindesruats.com, dinner only Tuesday to Saturday, closed Monday and mid November to mid February, moderate to very expensive) has atmosphere and a quiet setting. Founded in 1921 and going strong, this tony establishment in an old watermill complex on the Cousin River, at the foot of hills south of Avallon, is in a lush, lovely spot. Chef Jean-Pierre Rossi will make you garlicky snails, duck breast with morel mushrooms, fresh trout with citrus butter, and rich desserts.

The scenery and feel are very different—a coaching inn on the busy main highway due east of town—at **Le Relais Fleuri** (1 La Cerce, RN6, Sauvigny-le-Bois, Tel: 03 86 34 02 85, www.relais-fleuri.com, open daily, inexpensive to expensive). But the studiously folksy dining room is comfortable, and the updated regional cuisine (warm veal pâté en croûte with wild mushrooms, baked pike-perch, Charolais with morel mushrooms, chocolate-caramel pastry) whipped up by Richard Doit is remarkably good. The wine list includes fine Burgundian bottlings.

Also on the main highway, but on the west side, at Valloux, is popular, attractive **Auberge des Chenêts** (10 RN6, Valloux, Tel: 03 86 34 23 34, closed Sunday dinner and Monday year-round, and Tuesday in low season, end February to mid March, end June to early July, and the second half of November, moderate to expensive). The masses of hanging geraniums, red shutters, and handsome façade, catch the eye, compensating for the thundering truck traffic. Inside, the cozy dining room, with a crackling fire lit in cold weather, is a refuge. Owners Michèle and Bernard Gillot start at dawn, making everything from scratch. Tradition and modernity meet: the oeufs en meurette come with flavorful croutons and bacon, there are classic jambon persillé and coq au vin, but the veal sweetbreads are braised with Noilly Prat, the squab is cooked in two ways (the breast roasted in its own juices, the thigh slow-cooked on the stove top), and the thick Charolais steak has a peppery paprika sauce. Seasonal fruit tarts, crumbles, and a soufflé with wild plum liqueur, are scrumptious. On the short wine list are fine bottlings from Yonne organic winemakers Ghislaine and Jean-Hugues Goisot, and Jean-Louis Houblin, Alain Vignot, and La Chablisienne.

Also to the west of Avallon, in Pontaubert, on the D957 highway to Vézelay, similarly attractive, flowery, and upscale **Les Fleurs** (69 route de Vézelay, Tel: 03 86 34 13 81, www.hotel -lesfleurs.com, closed Wednesday year-round, Thursday from mid September to end July, and late December to end January, moderate to expensive) is run by Claire and Régis Tatraux and their children. There's a pleasant rear patio. The chef specializes in freshwater fish. Alongside meaty classics of the region, you'll find local trout with toasted hazelnuts and fresh spinach, and other light, delicious fish often topped with a lemony meunière butter sauce. The salmon is smoked in-house, the foie gras is also housemade. Everything except the bread and ice cream is, and is very good. Smiling service, fine wines, and the company of savvy travelers, make dining here pleasant.

BAZOCHES-EN-MORVAN

Six miles southeast of Vézelay, on the edge of the village, stands the triangular **Château de Bazoches** (Tel: 03 86 22 10 22, www .chateau-bazoches.com, open daily except at lunchtime from late March to mid November; in July and August, open nonstop, daily, until 6pm), where military engineer Sébastien Le Prestre de Vauban, Louis XIV's right-hand man, lived for decades. Don't miss visiting, whether you're interested in fortress-building or not. The architecture, maps, and family trees are astonishing. Across the way at a farmstead known as Domaine de Rousseau you'll find **Ferme-Auberge de Bazoches** (Tel: 03 86 22 16 30, www.auberge-bazoches.com, fermeauberge.bazoches@wanadoo .fr, closed Sunday dinner, seasonal closings vary, inexpensive, reserve ahead). Farmers Nadine and Philippe Perrier raise poultry, porkers, and Charolais beef, and serve delicious meals in their long, low nineteenth-century farmstead, which is also a B&B. Beyond the local produce and cheeses, and housemade seasonal fruit tarts, the specialties are hearty pork filet with Morvan honey, pork roast with creamy Époisses sauce, and old-fashioned estouffade de boeuf à l'ancienne—bourguignon by another name. You'll also savor good terrines and thick savory tourtes.

In the village proper, grab a snack, coffee, glass of wine, or a simple daily special at recently revived **La Grignotte** (Tel: 03 86

22 15 38, closed Sunday evening and Monday, except in summer, extremely inexpensive).

BIBRACTE–MONT BEUVRAY

Site of Bibracte, the "lost city" of the ancient Gauls, found in the late 1800s, this mountain on the Morvan's southern edge affords sweeping views over the patchwork countryside; an archeological site; and many lovely woodland paths. At the base of what was the Gauls' fortified roost, you'll find the **Musée de la Civilisation Celtique** (Mont Beuvray, Saint Léger sous Beuvray, Tel: 03 85 86 52 35, www.bibracte.fr, open daily mid March to mid November). Of interest to archeological-food lovers is **Le Chaudron de Bibracte** (Tel: 03 85 86 52 40, open daily for lunch in July and August; by arrangement, for groups, the rest of the year; always reserve ahead, very inexpensive). It's out front in an annex. Seated at rustic picnic-style tables, surrounded by amphorae, and equipped with terracotta dishes and wooden implements, tunic-wearing youths will serve you philologically accurate, surprisingly good Gallo-Roman food. The experience runs literally from egg to apple, with dessert, coffee, and wine—or cervoise, the Gallic beer—included. To describe the fare would be to spoil the effect; rest assured that nothing is repellent. For a more comfortable, if less scientific Gallo-Roman dining experience, you opt for Hôtel du Morvan, four miles south, in Saint Léger sous Beuvray.

CHÂTEAU-CHINON

Splayed on a ridge, Château-Chinon was the fief of former French president François Mitterrand, where he built and maintained his pedigree as a Résistance fighter. The museum dedicated to the gifts he received during his fourteen-year reign is here: **Musée du Septennat** (6 Rue du Château, Tel: 03 86 85 19 23, closed Tuesday and from January to late February). It contains some of the most absurd and kitsch items known to man, including crystal tables with legs in the shape of wild animals, stuffed or ceramic leopards, gilded elephant tusks, and suchlike—don't miss it. Mitterrand was a regular at the best hotel-restaurant in town: **Le Vieux Morvan** (8 Place Gudin, Tel: 03 86 85 05 01, www.auvieuxmorvan.com, open daily in July and August, closed Sunday dinner and Monday the rest of the year, and from mid December to mid January). Picture windows, a pleasant terrace, and good regional cooking—stewed snails with garlicky purée, chicken breasts sautéed with hazelnuts and Morvan honey, slow-cooked lamb shanks, Charolais with wild mushrooms—make this the only choice.

About four miles northeast in the hamlet of Château-Chinon Campagne, on a ridge above highway D37, on the way to Lac des Settons, is **Les Ruchers du Morvan** (Port-de-l'Homme, Tel: 03 86 78 02 43, www.achat-nivernais-morvan.com, closed Sunday in winter). Organic beekeepers and honey-makers Dominique and Jean-Jacques Coppin, gastronomic pioneers, launched a return of food artisans and economic activity to the Morvan starting in 1976. Now they have 1,000 hives and have won dozens of medals for their honeys. Small, intense, with sky-blue eyes, Jean-Jacques produces what are probably the best honeys in Burgundy, among the best in France: perfumed, flavorful, and of perfect consistency. Especially fine are the Fleurs Sauvages—guaranteed from wild flowers, and the honey equivalent of a Meursault Grand Cru—and Sapin—*miellat*, from aphids that feed on conifers. The linden or chestnut blossom honeys are also wildly good, with intense herbal, almost medicinal flavors. The Coppins will show you around, and tell you their story and that of beekeeping in France, if you ask, before guiding you through a tasting. The exceptionally delicious gingerbreads—made with a whopping seventy percent honey—might just be the most moist and flavorful anywhere, period. In the boutique you'll find a dozen other excellent Morvan food products made by fellow artisans, from Fruirouge jams to terrines from **La Blonde de Séguret** (Savigny Poil Fol, Tel: 03 86 30 83 59, www.la-blonde -de-seguret.fr) or apple cider jelly from Alexandre Lepoivre of Le Petit Montigny, and extra-virgin canola oil from **Patrick Ravery** (Le Magny, Souilly La Tour, Tel: 03 86 26 32 28).

CHISSEY-EN-MORVAN

A handsome pocketsized château lurks in the center of this village on the east side of the Morvan, strung along the two-lane highway, and so does handsome **L'Auberge Fleurie** (Tel: 03 85 82 62 05, always open). This classic, comfortable little coaching inn of centuries past has a cozy dining room with elegantly dressed tables, candlesticks, a chandelier, antique timbers, and a crackling fireplace for cool-weather dining (and a terrace open in summer). Elegant, professional proprietor Madame Bessière speaks softly and carries a big tray, upon which you'll spot nicely plated terrines, classic snails, beef filets, regional cheeses, and simple, housemade desserts. The wine list is more than adequate, the clientele, locals out for a special occasion, or mature travelers off the beaten path.

CLAMECY

Clamecy is on the upper Yonne River, at the northwestern edge of the Morvan, due west of Vézelay, in the Nièvre *département*. For centuries the wood-floaters of the Morvan roped their timbers together here and rode them downstream to Auxerre and Paris. Sizeable at about 4,500 inhabitants, and somewhat soulful, famous for its tripe sausages, Clamecy is still rough-and-ready, though in the process of gentrification, particularly along the Yonne's banks. The ancient upper city is hard-driven, and it's here, facing the church tower, in a half-timbered corner building, that you'll find what might be the best restaurant in town: **L'Angelus** (11 Place Saint Jean, Tel: 03 86 27 33 98, langelus@ cegetel.net, closed Wednesday and dinner Tuesday and Sunday, two weeks in February and Christmastide, inexpensive to moderate). Take a table on the terrace, or in the small but cozy dining room, and enjoy the updated regional fare, from gougères to chicken liver salad, jambon persillé to flavorful pork stewed with sage, served with friendly flair.

Bigger, farther up the scale, with starched tablecloths, polished service, and a long wine list, located a hundred yards from the riverbank, is **Hostellerie de la Poste** (9 Place Émile Zola, Tel: 03 86 27 01 55, www.hostelleriedelaposte.fr, inexpensive to moderate). Hardworking, serious proprietors Carla and Denis Guenot offer a *terroir* menu that's good value, from egg to apple, including the local tripe sausage, though their hearts lie in the land of *gastronomique* arabesques on oversized plates. There's a spacious terrace for fine weather dining.

The Saturday-morning market enlivens the lower part of Clamecy around Place du 19 Août; the third Saturday of the month a big fair is held along Avenue de la République.

Though famous for it, tripe sausage isn't the only delicacy made at **Charcuterie Guillien** (30 Rue Marié Davy, Tel: 03 86 27 19 18, closed Sunday afternoon and Monday), kitty corner to Hostellerie de la Poste. Every imaginable Morvan and Burgundian specialty involving meat—terrines, pâtés, jambon persillé, Morvan ham—plus salads and more, is made here daily by dedicated husband-and-wife team Patricia and Pascal Guillien. Other delis in town are fancier, but Guillien can't be beat.

On the pedestrian street that curls and zigzags up to the church, keep your eyes open for chocolate factory, pastry shop, ice creamery, and tearoom **Portal** (22 Rue de la Monnaie, Tel: 03 86 27 04 19, closed Sunday afternoon and Monday). In addition to thirty-five classic chocolates, marzipan fruits, luscious ice creams, and a dozen types of pastry (the almond croissants are delicious), Emmanuel and Angelique Portal make several trademark specialties, among them the poetically named Les Chi-dans-l'iau, which indeed look like little chocolate turds (though it's impossible to tell they're floating in water, as the dialect name claims). They contain hazelnut nougatine, candied orange peel, and pistachio cream, and are addictive. Other treats are made to look like logs, and the house pastry is a meringue cake filled with cream.

Up the same street is organic grocery **La Graineterie** (2 Rue de la Monnaie, Tel: 03 86 27 93 64, closed Sunday and Monday), where you'll find fair-trade, certified organic jams, cheeses, wines, honeys, and more.

COEUZON

Officially in Ouroux-en-Morvan, this hamlet is about eight miles from the lakes of Les Settons and Pannecière, in Le Morvan. The "Flo" at **Ferme-Auberge de Coeuzon "Chez Flo"** (Tel: 03 86 78 21 87, florence.berlo@wanadoo.fr, closed Monday, and Sunday in July and August, reserve at least two days ahead, inexpensive) is owner Florence Berio. She keeps this 1870s farmstead tidy, not to say blinding white. Cheek by jowl, you dine with famished seniors on the farm-tourism circuit, families and regulars, in a yawning room with stone walls grouted white, a fire roaring in the corner. On offer: housemade gougères, cold cuts and ham, coq au vin with a gratin of potatoes clotted with fresh cream, or chicken in fresh cream sauce, farmstead cheeses, fruit tarts or mousses and other homey desserts, and wine from both sides of Burgundy—Nièvre and les Côtes. This is a working farm; everything from the butter or milk to the eggs, pork, poultry, or Charolais is grown on site.

If you haven't reserved and can't eat at the *ferme-auberge*, in the village of Ouroux itself, facing the church, seek out the pint-sized hotel-restaurant serving Morvan foods. Also in the village, there's a private "museum" of wine and barrel-making, **Atelier Musée de la Tonnellerie-Caves Barbotte** (Tel: 03 86 78 24 01, www.ouroux-en-morvan.com, closed Thursday, and weekend afternoons), neither of which continues nowadays. The Barbottes are winesellers by trade. There's a farmers market on the main square Sunday mornings.

EGUILLY—LA RENTE D'EGUILLY

Eguilly and its château belong to greater Pouilly-en-Auxois, on the east side of autoroute A6. But Eguilly is sliced in half; the château's grounds are ruined by the freeway. Happily, the farmhouse that once kept the aristos of Eguilly in food is on a forested hillside, miles west of the autoroute, of Eguilly itself, and of the outlying village of Blancey, on Le Morvan's eastern edge. Reach it on one-lane roads, from Pouilly or Chailly-sur-Armançon. **Ferme de la Rente d'Eguilly** (Tel: 03 80 90 83 48, closed mid September to late October, inexpensive, reserve ahead) is a working farm; the tireless owners are "retired." The farm occupies a fortified, 1400s compound. Spend the night and you may dine on delicious, wholesome, housemade everything, sharing your table with affable Chantal and Michel Rance. The comfortable rooms are done up with country antiques (one is in a reconverted bakery). In winter you eat in a dining room with knickknacks, at a table twenty feet long. In mild weather, you dine in the courtyard. Michel grows the lettuces, potatoes, herbs, and vegetables which Chantal transforms into rustic ratatouille or casseroles with cream and cheese. The chickens (and eggs) are further afield, out of olfactory range; the eggs go into giant, luscious omelettes or classic, to-die-for oeufs en meurette with wild black trompettes de la mort mushrooms (gathered in the woods). The chickens are cooked with cream, or wine. The beef and pork come from a neighbor's farm (Michel was a cattle rancher, and knows his beef). Chantal's terrines from said pork are like dreamy meat loaf, each slice with a plump chicken liver in the middle. Even the pickles are homemade. The cow's milk, butter, cream, and fresh cheese come from a neighbor—and are delicious beyond description. For

dessert, fruit tarts or French classics, from scratch. The water is pure springwater. Be warned: the homemade aperitif—raspberry juice, sugar, white wine—will weaken your knees. Wine flows free, included in the price (it's from the local co-op). For breakfast, five housemade jams from homegrown fruit (cherries, blackcurrants, raspberries, apricots, figs), and more bread and wondrous butter than anyone could possibly devour. How the owners—he in his mid 70s, she retirement age—can survive this daily treatment is a question worth asking. "Work preserves," quips Michel, deadpan. The pair have been at it, with courtesy, grace and frankness, since 1982. Amazing.

LAIZY

Though officially in Laizy, in the Arroux River Valley, you have to drive into the hills on the extreme southern edge of the Morvan, close to Boudede or Saint-Léger-sous-Beuvray, to find the comfortable, attractive working farm and *chambre d'hôtes–table d'hôtes* **Ferme de la Chassagne** (Tel: 03 85 82 39 47, francoise. gorlier@wanadoo.fr, dinner not served on Sunday night, reserve ahead). It's worth seeking out, because Françoise Gorlier is not only a charming hostess, she's also a talented home cook. At her huge, square table set before a roaring fire you might just enjoy one of the best farmstead meals anywhere, period (for overnight guests only). At this forty-acre farm from the 1600s, Françoise and husband Jacques raise, grow, and handmake everything, from the goat's-milk cheeses, to the milk-fed veal, chicken and ducks, pâtés and ham, to seasonal fruit tarts; the butter and jams served with the exceptionally delicious breakfast too. Burgundians, the Gorliers are professionals from farm families, and have spent a decade recreating this premodern paradise, with all the modern comforts. It's both authentic and a revival, without being kitsch. Don't miss it.

MONT SAINT JEAN

Enjoy sweeping views and good food in this perched village edging the eastern Morvan, ten miles east of Saulieu (on highway D977bis and twisting D117). **Le Médiéval** (Place de la Halle, Tel: 03 80 84 34 68, www.restaurant-lemedieval.com, closed Monday year-round, also closed dinner Tuesday, Wednesday, and Thursday from October to June, inexpensive to moderate), a chic restaurant, serves regional classics and updated *cuisine bourgeoise*. Two linden trees shade a stone-paved terrace, where metal chairs and tables are backed by geraniums and petunias. Inside, white tablecloths sit atop well-spaced tables with red-upholstered armchairs. The fireplace and timbers provide an antique, if not medieval, touch. The bread is made in-house. The *terroir* menu features: oeufs en meurette with garlicky croûtons, or a dozen Burgundy snails bedded on mashers with creamy garlic; thick Charolais steak with Époisses, or pike-perch sauced with crayfish coulis. Two bites of cheese follow; dessert is either classic pears poached in red wine or frozen vacherin—not the cheese—with blackcurrants and cassis. A la carte, beware the curve-ball originals. Wines are from Domaine Roux—Aligoté to Rully, Saint-Aubin, and Meursault—or Domaine Fleurot-Larose, plus Bourgogne Pinot Noir from Flavigny-Alesia. The service is casual. The urbane clientele reflects the chic surroundings.

Walk around the corner and up Rue Glanot, where you'll see an espaliered grapevine and discover ye olde honey-maker. Down the road is **Le Château des Roches** (Rue Glanot, Tel: 03 80 84 32 71, www.lesroches-burgundy.com, meals moderate), a "private country residence," meaning a somewhat self-consciously wonderful, luxurious B&B in a manor with six guest rooms, views, and a garden. For wine lovers, your refined hosts offer regional *table d'hôtes* dinners Thursday and Saturday, during which felicitous pairings of food and wine are sought.

MONTHELON

Hankering for a farmstead feed? Five miles west of Autun, on a hillside amid pastures and forests, between highways D978 and D981, the Bethouart family run **Ferme-Auberge Les Cheminots** (Tel: 03 85 52 17 42, inexpensive, open for dinner on weekends from May to mid October and Sunday lunch by reservation only).

This poultry and dairy farm has thirty Holstein cows; from them come the milk François and Véronique transform into fresh cheeses and heavy cream (they also sell to a co-op milk producer in Beaune). Savor them at the rustic *table d'hôtes* in their house, but only after enjoying garden-grown salad, homemade pickles from homegrown cucumbers, local ham, omelettes with wild mushrooms and chives, roast chicken, chicken slow-cooked in heavy cream, or coq au vin. The sacrificial rooster has enjoyed one full year of happy life, and simmers for two hours in two bottles' worth of good red wine, with bay leaves, thyme, carrots, and bacon. On the side, homegrown Charlotte potato gratin, cooked with that incredible cream and cheese. Following the curds, you'll sample homey fruit tarts. The cozy dining room has dark, smoke-tinted timbers, an old tile floor, wooden tables and cane chairs, and an antique grandfather clock. Think Van Gogh, with happy potato eaters. The Bethouarts started in 1987; the pacing is professional. To drink: quaffable Haute-Côtes-de-Beaune from Guy and Jean-Luc Fouquerand of La Rochepot. You'll dine with intrepid French travelers, and groups of retirees on the *ferme-auberge* circuit.

PIERRE-PERTHUIS

Known for a natural stone arch and eighteenth-century bridge over the Cure River, this charming hamlet four miles south of Vézelay is home to hotel-restaurant-café **Les Deux Ponts** (D958, Tel: 03 86 32 31 31, http://lesdeuxponts.free.fr, restaurant closed Tuesday and Wednesday in February, at Eastertide and in summer, hotel closed early December to late February, inexpensive to moderate). Philippe and Marianne Bariteau—he Southern French, she Dutch—tastefully remodeled a roadside inn. The open-plan dining area's tables are well spaced and hemmed by live plants, and the many-paned windows in the carriage doors let in light. There's white china on the white tablecloths, and quality silverware, candles—and a fire burning in the lounge area—adding romance. On your plate: artful yet unfussy lightened classics. Philippe did time with marquee chefs, but doesn't do narcissistic *cuisine d'auteur*. The rustic terrine has wild mushrooms, the crayfish cream comes with baby vegetables, the filet mignon of pork is slow-roasted and flanked by delicate parsnip purée. Philippe buys his ingredients locally, including the duck, which he cooks exquisitely *à l'orange*. The cheeses are local and very good, the wine from excellent Yonne winemakers Alain Vignot, Elise Villiers, Jean Montanet, Ghislaine and Jean-Hugues Goisot, and others. Outside are teak tables and chairs on the deck, open in good weather. The guest rooms are simple yet stylish; spend the night and at breakfast taste Philippe's homemade conserves—classic strawberry, apricot, or surprising banana.

On the east side of the river at Précy-le-Moult, part of Pierre-Perthuis, is winery **Elise Villiers** (Tel: 03 86 33 27 62, elisevilliers@yahoo.fr, by appointment). Her Vézelay Le Clos Blanc, from a three-acre vineyard below the southern ramparts of Vézelay, bursts with refreshing minerals and lemon zest.

PLANCHEZ

Between the reservoirs of Setton and Pannecière in Le Morvan, Planchez is a budding gastronomic pilgrimage site. **Restaurant-Hôtel le Relais des Lacs** (Avenue François Mitterrand, Tel: 03 86 78 49 00, www.morvan-gourmand.fr or www.relais-des-lacs .com, closed Monday in fall and winter, closed end January to end February, very inexpensive to expensive), a gourmet restaurant and thirty-six-room hotel, has starched tablecloths, blue candles in silver candlestick holders, and oversized wineglasses. Owned by dynamic Parisian Philippe Morinay, in addition to hearty Morvan crapiauds and bone-in ham, you might find rack of lamb with roasted garlic and a rich potato casserole, whole roast squab, local cheeses, and fondant au chocolat. Followers of former president François Mitterrand know he ate here many times on his Morvan visits—to the sites of glory where fought la Résistance, to which he famously belonged, post-Vichy. There's a farmers market on the main square on Friday mornings.

QUARRÉ-LES-TOMBES

About eleven miles south of Avallon, surrounded by thick forests, this town—or large village—gets its name from the thick, immensely heavy stone sarcophagi in its center. About 2,000 of them once ringed the church; today perhaps a hundred stretch ominously, moss covered, in the churchyard. The tombs are 1,400 years old (Merovingian and Carolingian), and give Quarré a peculiar feel, especially in winter. The rest of the year, Quarré thrives as a resort: in spring and summer it's a sunny place. The wide main square hosts a Sunday morning market, and is lined by cafés and shops. One is an excellent (and cleverly named) bakery, chocolate, and gourmet foods emporium, **Quarré de Chocolat** (24 Place de l'Église, Tel: 03 86 32 22 21, closed Wednesday from October to March). Chocaholics drive out of their way to buy high-quality, dark-chocolate bars with dozens of herbs, candied fruits, and liqueurs. The coriander flavor is spicy, the dried-apricot bar rustically flavorful. Also made are chocolate-dipped orange or lemon peel, filled chocolates, and biscuits. House specialty Pavé Morvandiau is a cake with a biscuit base, candied orange, and crushed almonds, with Grand Marnier. In summer, a sidewalk stand out front serves waffles—thick and deeply-grooved—into which customers dribble chocolate or spoon jams. The gourmet food section and bakery next door stock artisanal jams and honeys, gingerbread, gougères, pastries, and picnic supplies.

Those who favor revival hotel-restaurants patronize **Le Saint-Georges-Hôtel du Nord** (25 Place de l'Église, Tel: 03 86 32 29 30, www.hoteldunord-morvan.com, closed Wednesday dinner, Thursday, and from early November to mid February, inexpensive to moderate), owned by the Salamolard clan. Revamped a few years ago, the varnished knotty pine paneling, Formica-top bar, black-and-white floor tiles, and heavy wooden furniture are intended to evoke the rusticity of decades past. On the sound system: 1940s crooners or jazz. The interconnecting dining rooms in shades of pink are like grandma's house. The menu features Burgundian and Morvandiaux classics, the service is friendly if halting. Don't be in a rush.

The Salamolard family's mothership is **Auberge de l'Âtre** (Les Lavaults, Tel: 03 86 32 20 79, closed Tuesday, Wednesday, February, and second half of June, moderate to very expensive). On the highway south of Quarré, this upscale operation showcases chef-owner Francis Salamolard's talents. Classic oeufs en meurette are flanked by fresh, buttery spinach. The roast squab is dabbed with local honey, the pike-perch made earthy by wild mushrooms.

Back in town, on the south end, **Le Morvan** (6 Rue des Ecoles, Tel: 03 86 32 29 29, closed Monday, Tuesday, and from late December to late February, moderate to expensive) is modern but traditional. The décor is studiously elegant, the thick wine list and ambitious *cuisine bourgeoise* follow suit (classic pâté en croûte, snails fricasséed with mushroom juices and folded into a tourte topped with creamy puréed broad beans and bacon, and pike-perch filet topped with same). The veal, flavored with dandelion liqueur and hemmed by morel mushrooms, comes in a hot pot; the filet mignon of pork cooks in its own juices with Fallot mustard. The freshly curdled goat's cheese comes drizzled with slightly salty caramel. Desserts are classic and satisfying. Among the wines are affordable, muscular Marsannay-les-Côtes Les Grasses Têtes red from Bernard Coillot & Fils, or quaffable Irancy from Thierry Richoux. There's a terrace for summer dining. The service can be slow.

To buy handsome, highly functional handmade knives, visit one of France's few remaining *ferronnerie-coutelleries*, **Philippe Soeuvre** (44 Rue de l'Etang, Tel: 03 86 32 28 91, www.forge-du -morvan.com, phone ahead).

RECLESNE

Watch for a crowded parking lot, and if you hear children and grannies laughing and chortling as they guzzle and gorge on the front terrace, where 1950s metal chairs stand under a sunbleached sign, you've probably found **Chez Daché** (Route de Lucenay l'Evêque, Tel: 03 85 82 62 63, closed Monday dinner and Tuesday, very inexpensive to inexpensive). It's the only eatery in this nowhere village six miles north of Autun. The dining room has plank floors, is prim and country-proper, with heavy old furniture; the bar area is for the constant overflow. Quantity is the thing: you'll be served two slabs per person of housemade terrine, a bowl of pickles and a giant basket of bread, or mounds of buttery, garlicky snails or frog's legs, calf's head in piquant sauce ravigote, stews or steaks, cheeses, giant bowls of antebellum chocolate mousse or crème caramel (skip the other desserts—they aren't housemade). Bells and buzzers ring as Carine Comont bustles. Chef Bernard Comont is a dying breed. Huge, he believes in More is More, and is a *saucier*—a sauce specialist. "You eat too much at Chez Daché," as devotees boast. The prices are also extremely low. Don't expect gastronomic heights, and enjoy an authentic Morvan experience.

ROUSSILLON-EN-MORVAN

In Le Morvan, halfway between Autun and Château-Chinon, pocketsized, medieval Roussillon was the birthplace of Count Girart de Roussillon and his wife Berthe, founders of Vézelay. It's also the closest village to the miniature Yosemite-style river valley Les Gorges de la Canche. Very miniature, but charming. On the main square is upscale yet old-fashioned **L'Auberge de Roussillon** (Tel: 03 85 82 75 68, www.auberge-de-roussillon.com, closed in fall and winter at dinner Sunday through Thursday, open daily for lunch, also closed mid November to mid December, from May to October open daily, inexpensive to moderate), with a handful of cozy rooms. There's a pleasant summer terrace, a brasserie section with daily specials, and a restaurant section called Le Patio, offering more elaborate, and artistically plated classics. Everything is of the region, from frog's legs on up, despite the owners' backgrounds. Run since 2004 by a friendly pair of out-of-towners—he lived in Paris for years and runs the place, she's half Dutch and half Chinese and does the cooking—this is a good spot to stop for refreshments or a meal.

SAINT-BRISSON

La Maison du Parc (Tel: 03 86 78 79 57, www.parcdumorvan.org, opening hours vary widely and seasonally) is the Morvan's park headquarters, in a farm compound, with a rose garden and arboretum, about six miles west of Saulieu. There's a well-stocked gift shop with many local gourmet items, including honey, and apple cider from Ferme des Brossiers in the Othe Valley. Next door is the fascinating **Musée de la Résistance** (Tel: 03 86 78 79 06), which recounts the story of the French Resistance in the region.

SAINT-LÉGER-SOUS-BEUVRAY

Many visitors to the battlefields of the Gallic Wars appear to despise Caesar and worship head-hunting, wife-burning Gallic chieftains Dumnorix and Vercingétorix, heroes of the nutty Native Lunatic fringe. Nuts abound in Saint Léger, chestnuts, in particular. The village hosts an annual hayseed Foire aux Marrons (Tel: 03 85 82 53 00), where you wolf chestnuts grilled, puréed, and stuffed into things, and hope the weather holds: the last weekend in October can be rainy or snowy.

Saint Léger is also home to good-value **Hôtel-Restaurant du Morvan** (Tel: 03 85 82 51 06, www.hoteldumorvan71.com, closed Monday and Tuesday in low season, and December to February,

inexpensive to moderate). From the 1880s bartop in the old-fashioned café-hotel lobby, to the old-fashioned dining room and old-fashioned but comfy guest rooms, "old-fashioned" is the operative word. Hôtel du Morvan, a time tunnel, has waxed plank floors, wooden armoires and tables, and lots of live plants in the cozy dining room. Chef Éric Mazière might look like a Roman patrician, but he's from the outskirts of Paris, a veteran of the hotel trade. His wife Laurette runs the show, serving Éric's good regional food. What you'll find nowhere else—except possibly at Le Chaudron de Bibracte atop Mont Beuvray—are authentic Gallo-Roman delights. A specialist from Bibracte helped Éric create the menu. It features plump helixes, i.e. snails, served with macerated cabbage, i.e. choucroute, meaning sauerkraut. The tender, slow-simmered stew of beef, lamb, and pork tastes surprisingly like Alsatian baekkeoffe from Strasbourg, another ancient Roman city. The farmstead goat's cheese sprinkled with minced chives has been eaten hereabouts for 2,000 years. Ditto the delicious walnut cake. The service is charming, the clients locals and tourists. The wines, luckily, are contemporary, regional and affordable.

Organic farmstead **GAEC du Rebout** (Tel: 03 85 82 54 64, phone ahead), at outlying Le Rebout, is where Denis Revel and Séverine Kovachiche make certified-organic, delicious cheeses from cow's milk and goat's milk. You can buy cheese and other organic produce at the Place Carnot covered market in Nevers, where du Rebout has a stand.

Were awards handed out for kindly enthusiasm at a B&B, the recipients would be retired farmers Paul and Janette Caré. Their tidy, attractive, affordable *chambre d'hôtes* perches atop Les Dués at **La Grande Verrière** (Tel: 03 85 82 50 32), near Saint-Léger-sous-Beuvray, ten miles from Bibracte. Beyond being adorable, and keeping rooms with pleasant views, the couple provide sumptuous breakfasts with Janette's eleven to fifteen varieties of exquisite homemade jam. The flavors change seasonally; expect to find peach or strawberry, plus elderberry blossom or elderberry fruit, and novel blends.

SAINT-LÉGER-VAUBAN

Follow abundant signage from Quarré-les-Tombes to the birthplace and house-museum (**Maison Vauban**, 4 Place Vauban, Tel: 03 86 32 26 30, www.vaubanecomusee.org, open Easter to November, hours vary) of military engineer and local hero Sébastien Le Prestre de Vauban (1633 to 1707). Have a drink or a snack here before driving onwards to the outlying hamlet of Trinquelin, home to jam-maker **La Trinquelinette** (Trinquelin, Tel: 03 86 32 20 97, closed Sunday). Bernard Berilley is celebrated for his *confitures*, compotes, and jellies, sold at gourmet shops (including Aux Bons Pâturages in Saulieu). They cost less here, but remain the Cartier of jams. The reason: the best ingredients, from the bananas, rhubarb, quince, figs, and heirloom vineyard peaches on up. He uses fifty-five percent fruit (for the jams), and no preservatives, and makes dozens of classic mono-fruit types, and unusual combinations (Poire William and greengage plum) by hand in big copper vats.

Still within Saint-Légér's municipality is monastery, spiritual retreat, and cheese factory **L'Abbaye et Ferme de la Pierre-Qui-Vire** (1 L'Huis Saint-Benoît, Tel: 03 86 33 03 73, www.abbaye-pierrequivire.asso.fr, abbey boutique open daily 10:15am to noon and 3pm to 5:15pm sharp, closed January; farm-factory open weekdays 7am to noon and 5pm to 7pm, afternoons only on weekends). Anyone familiar with Yosemite or Yellowstone will feel at home on the tendril roads curling through pine forests with granite outcroppings. The abbey is a century old; the Pierre-Qui-Vire or "spinning boulder," a triple-decker sandwich of stone raised by prehistoric inhabitants (used by Gallic Druids for ritual purposes) is older, crowned by a nineteenth-century statue of the Virgin. The abbey's farm, uphill half a mile, makes and sells eighteen organic curds, from mild cow's-milk rounds resembling and tasting like mild Soumaintrain, to flavorful chèvres and mixed-milk cheeses, fresh or aged, rolled in herbs. Visit the barns and pastures, home to 110 Swiss Brown cows and seventy-eight Alpine goats. At the abbey, the gift shop also sells herbal teas, honeys, beeswax, and books.

SAINT-PÈRE-SOUS-VÉZELAY

Forget the pilgrimage church atop the ancient Roman village of Vezeliacum. Forget the local history museum and nearby Fontaines Salées archeological site. No, soulful Saint-Père is synonymous with celebrity chef Marc Meneau and his formerly many-starred, universally hailed hotel-restaurant **L'Espérance** (Tel: 03 86 33 39 10, www.marc-meneau-esperance.com, closed Monday and Wednesday lunch, Tuesday, and mid January to mid March, astronomically expensive). Despite tribulation, the unstoppable Meneau continues to enrage or delight. Though a native son, self-taught and recognized as an original culinary genius, it would be misleading to associate his cooking with *terroir*. Highly creative, impossible to define, you either love or hate it. Any wine connoisseur should consider breaking the piggy-bank for a Meneau experience, because the maestro is a winemaker himself. Twenty years ago he spearheaded the revival of local vineyards. L'Espérance has one of the longest, deepest cellars in the business.

Across the highway is Meneau's less expensive **L'Entre Vignes** (Tel: 03 86 33 33 33, same website, closed Sunday dinner, Monday, Tuesday lunch, moderate), a classic star-chef's baby bistro, with solid, please-all food, wood and wrought iron as decorative themes, and professional service. Gourmet foods and Meneau's wines are sold in the boutique.

One outstanding organic winery is here, **Domaine de la Cabotte** (15 Rue de l'Abbé Pissier, Tel: 03 86 33 24 25, lacadette@ wanadoo.fr, by appointment). Idealistic winemaker Jean Montanet does what many others claim to do: respects the soil and *terroir*, and doesn't mask his wines' light, nuanced, only-in-northern-Burgundy flavors. You'll find Bourgogne Vézelay, Melon de Bourgogne, and Bourgogne Rouge at affordable prices.

SAINT-PÉREUSE

On the north side of highway D978 near Château-Chinon, between Tannay and Dommartin, at Coeurty, you'll spot the post-

modern factory where affable Frédéric Grobost, his wife Valérie and their staff make soft, ladyfinger meringue "sponges" (as some are wont to call them), known as Biscuits à la cuiller Grobost. The happy revival of **Biscuits Grobost** (Coeurty, Tel: 03 86 84 44 33, www.biscuits -grobost.com, open weekdays) is recent. Founded in 1901 by Eugène Grobost, who perfected the recipe, began winning medals, and made a fortune, the company passed down the generations until the 1970s, when production ceased. In 1991, great-grandson Frédéric, President François Mitterrand's personal chef, inaugurated the brash new micro-factory and began whipping up these addictive ladyfingers. Unlike others, Grobost's are tender and delicious—not merely ingredients in creamy cakes. The ingredients are high quality. Grobost packages batches for marquee restaurants (where they're sold at sky-high prices), using the client's label. From the boutique, watch through a

Plexiglas window as the sole pastry chef whips his fresh egg whites and folds them into the yellow batter with a giant wooden paddle—the real secret. Grobost makes two cookie types, each in two sizes (mini or normal): classics, or ladyfingers with chocolate chips. The other butter cookies and madeleines branded Grobost are outsourced.

SAINT-PRIX-EN-MORVAN

On the flanks of Mont Beuvray, near Bibracte, three miles northwest of Saint-Léger-sous-Beuvray, this isolated mountain village is home to insider's restaurant **Chez Franck et Francine** (Tel: 03 85 82 45 12, www.chez-franck-et-francine.fr.st, chez-franck-et-francine@wanadoo.fr, closed Sunday dinner, Monday, and January, moderate to very expensive). The basic bar-café-lobby out front is where locals hang. A spacious yet cozy dining room behind harbors comfortable chairs around widely spaced, nicely laid tables facing a fire that crackles in cool weather. Casual-hip, the restaurant is booked solid weeks in advance. Characterful Francine runs the dining room, Franck cooks the *gastronomique* and aesthetically plated food. Happily, dishes are market-based; Franck uses fresh, highest-quality local or regional ingredients, usually bought direct or at markets. You'll find foie gras and seafood, alas, but also a savory, rustic tourte Bourguignonne with a red-wine reduction sauce, roasted Charolais beef filet in a pastry shell, with wild mushrooms, and other *terroir* delights. The wine list features excellent Burgundies, the service is professional but spirited (at times jocular), the clientele savvy gourmets from miles around.

SAULIEU

On Le Morvan's eastern edge, the self-styled capital of Burgundian gastronomy, Saulieu is a pleasant small town bisected by the RN6 highway linking Paris to Lyon. Underneath the highway is a millefeuille of asphalt and stone: a Neolithic footpath, a Gallic road, the Via Agrippa consular highway, and medieval road. Tradition? Locals refer to themselves as Sédélociens, from the name the Romans gave them. Saulieu was a departure point for Paris-bound Charolais oxen. Charolais beef—from oxtails to head cheese—remains the local specialty. Beef is honored during the hayseed Fête du Charolais, a fair with a barbecue party and stands (held the third weekend of August).

Several great restaurateurs of centuries past, including Alexandre Dumaine and Bernard Loiseau, both of luxurious La Côte d'Or, set up on Saulieu's main street. Since the 1970s the autoroute has drained off much traffic, a blessing and curse. Saulieu is less noisy (though many trucks still roll through), more upscale and touristy, and less dynamic. Many townhouses stand empty. Given Saulieu's current population of 2,800, a hugely disproportionate number of fine restaurants and gourmet food shops are still found.

Don't miss the medieval Basilique Saint-Andoche, dating from the twelfth century. One of its famous capitals shows dancing pigs—or boars hunted by pagan Gauls, depending on your religion. The **Musée Pompon** (Place du Dr. Roclore, Tel: 03 80 64 19 51, closed Tuesday and holidays) abuts the church in a 1600s townhouse. Displays in and out include Roman milestones and tombstones, antique menus and crockery from the town's famed restaurants, and the sleek bronzes of mid-nineteenth-century native son François Pompon (1855–1933). Since 1948, Pompon's *Taureau* (Bull) has embellished the main highway (Rue d'Argentine), near the tourism office (Tel: 03 80 64 00 21, www.saulieu.fr) and celebrated Napoleonic Milestone (La Borne Imperiale).

Saulieu's Saturday market is held on Rue Monge; in winter it's in the covered marketplace. Among the dozens of stands is honey-maker **Jean-Louis Seguin** of nearby Saizerey-Misserey (Tel: 03 80 84 30 50, by appointment).

Places to eat and drink

Too famous to need introducing, and too expensive for most mortals is **La Côte d'Or–Relais Bernard Loiseau** (2 Rue d'Argentine, Tel: 03 80 90 53 53, www.bernard-loiseau.com, closed Wednesday lunch, Tuesday and early January to early February, astronomically expensive). It includes a super-luxury spa-hotel and gourmet boutique with about 1,000 delicacies. Loiseau committed suicide in 2003. His indefatigable widow, Dominique, flanked by longtime chef Patrick Bertron, carries on the legacy. Bertron's saddle and chops of milkfed lamb with spring vegetables is true to *terroir* yet levitates. He also makes Loiseau's Burgundian signature dishes (pike-perch braised in Pinot Noir, luscious standing rib roast seared in a frying pan, oven-roasted, then topped with an oxtail-and-red-wine reduction sauce with shallots and marrow). The cheese platter is among the country's best, the desserts are too gorgeous to eat (but you will devour them), the wine list too heavy to lift.

Loiseau was not the only local chef who worked in Alexandre Dumaine's kitchens in the 1950s and '60s. A B&W photograph on the wall of charming hotel-restaurant **La Borne Imperiale** (16 Rue d'Argentine, Tel: 03 80 64 19 76, closed Tuesday dinner and Wednesday from September through June, and January, prix fixe lunch menu inexpensive, other prix fixes and à la carte moderate to expensive) shows the restaurant's chef Jean Berteau as a beardless youth, alongside Loiseau and Dumaine. Loiseau skyrocketed in search of stars; Berteau stuck to the path of *terroir* and *cuisine bourgeoise*, taking over La Borne Imperiale in 1987 with his wife. This is Saulieu's insider address. Comfortable, with antiques, a baby grand piano, flowing curtains, and bouquets of fresh flowers, you'll be served by wife Marie-Christine. The excellent food and wine comes at a fifth the price you'd pay *chez* Loiseau. On the short, handwritten menu are jambon persillé, oeufs en meurette, earthy, luscious terrine of pig trotters, and roasted chicken livers with mild, creamy horseradish. The house ham (served with creamy mushroom sauce) comes from butcher-*charcutier* Michel Rousseau (Marie-Christine's brother, a veteran of Loiseau's kitchens). The mild but flavorful fish stew has local pike-perch (and not-so-local salmon). If you want to experience the legendary poularde façon Dumaine à la vapeur—whole Bresse poultry slowly steamed in its own juices, in a specially designed pot—Berteau will make it for you (reserve ahead). The cheeses include the region's best, the desserts are simple, seasonal, and satisfying. In summer, dine on the rear balcony. The guest rooms are comfortable and affordable; get one at the rear.

Four other excellent-value, attractive hotel-restaurants, any of which could be the top address in a lesser food town, are on the main drag. **Auberge du Relais** (8 Rue d'Argentine, Tel: 03 80 64 13 16, open daily, prix fixe menus inexpensive to moderate, à la carte moderate to expensive), run by talented young chef Serge Taverna and his wife Maïté, offers Burgundian and Morvan specialties, is decorated tastefully in rose hues, and has large dining rooms with caned chairs and a back terrace. On the southern end of town, find **La Vieille Auberge** (15 Rue Grillot, Tel: 03 80 64 13 74, open daily in summer, closed Tuesday dinner and Wednesday the rest of the year, plus the second half of January and first week of July, prix fixe menus very inexpensive to moderate, à la carte moderate). Also young and ambitious, Patrick and Catherine Auduc run this unpretentious gourmet restaurant, serving *terroir* classics in a cozy dining room (Louis Philippe chairs and many-paned, soundproofed windows).

It's rare to find a café-lunch spot as well loved by locals and visitors as Saulieu's landmark **Le Café Parisien** (4 Rue du Marché, Tel: 03 80 64 26 56, open daily nonstop 7am to 10pm from June through September; open 7am to 8pm and closed Monday lunch and dinner Tuesday through Sunday the rest of the year, meals very inexpensive). It's on the shopping street one block west of the church. Opened in 1832 and little changed since, the scuffed plank flooring, mirrors, bistro chairs, and solid tables on sewing-machine stands exude coffee, beer, wine, and gutsy food. Upstairs there's a pool hall and game room. Packed in from morning to past dinnertime are local bankers, cheesemongers, pool sharps, and hoity-toity Englishmen with reconverted farms. Blackboard daily specials—edible—cover regional ground (terrines, hams, steaks, freshwater fish, cheeses, and desserts). Most ingredients are local. This café almost disappeared. An unlikely Parisian hero stepped in: photographer Jean-Marc Tingaud. Passionate about food, wine, folklore, and photos (which hang everywhere), Tingaud hosts concerts.

Gourmet shops and food artisans

Venerable bakery, pastry and candy shop **À la Renommée** (11 Rue du Marché, Tel: 03 80 64 17 13, closed Monday) was founded by the Guillemard family around 1900. It's now run by heirs, the Duvignauds, who make the house specialties: Le Sédélocien (mini-pastries or cakes with almond paste, slivered almonds and chocolate), and Griottes du Morvan (chocolate-covered cherries).

On the opposite side, outwardly unimpressive *charcuterie* **Michel Rousseau** (42 Rue du Marché, Tel: 03 80 64 14 18, closed Sunday and Monday) is where you'll find rosette salami, jambon persillé, terrines from rabbit to duck or pork, hams, jambon en croûte, other picnic makings. Rousseau, a native son, worked for Loiseau in the 1970s, and is brother-in-law of chef Jean Berteau of La Borne Imperiale.

Backtrack to the crossroads, fifty yards north of the café, to the green-and-yellow façade of **La Fouchale Crèmerie-**

Fromagerie (4 Place de la République, Tel: 03 80 64 02 23, www .achat-cotedor.com, closed Sunday after-noon and Monday). A cow bell tinkles when you step in. Affable Marie-France and Georges Dodane's old-fashioned shop carries the region's best cheeses. You'll find chèvre from Bernard Sivignon in Génelard, raw-milk Époisses and l'Ami du Chambertin from Fromagerie des Marronniers or Gaugry, plus local wines. The Dodanes sell at Autun's covered market on Wednesday and Friday, and at Avallon's covered market on Saturday.

A hundred yards west, on the main street, another friendly, well-stocked cheese shop is **Aux Bons Pâturages** (10 Rue des Fours, Tel: 03 80 64 07 88, closed Sunday afternoon and Monday). Agnès Morizot and Marie-Jeanne Bierry have been here since 1990. Alongside Époisses, Chaource, and Nuits Saint Georges cheeses, you'll find organic *Tourtière*, a cow's-milk wheel with a moldy crust, Le Colombier de Sivry, and top specialty foods (honey from Les Ruchers du Morvan and jams from La Trinquelinette, plus Flavigny bonbons).

On the same street, find compact, modest bakery **Poulizac** (4 Rue des Fours, Tel: 03 80 64 18 92, open nonstop 6:30am to 7:30pm Monday through Saturday, closed Sunday and three weeks in July). Top-flight restaurateurs get their bread here. Try the rustic sourdough miche, or unbleached wholewheat-rye loaf with dry figs.

Fancy pastries, ice creams, and chocolates are at **Aux Délices de Morvan** (5 Rue de la Foire, Tel: 03 80 64 06 08, closed Monday), near deli Michel Rousseau. The Casssissines—candies filled with blackcurrant liqueur—plus filled chocolates, gorgeous, elaborate chocolate or fruit pastries, almond-packed Sédélociens, and crunchy rocky-road Rochers de Gouloux and Morvandiaux, are made by pastry chef Jean-Marc Joly.

Le Cellier Morvandiau (21 Rue de la Foire, Tel: 03 80 64 14 19, closed Sunday), stocks the best of Burgundy. Chummy quipster Régis Renaud will guide you.

LES SETTONS–LAC DES SETTONS

Built during the Second Empire and old enough to have transformed itself into a natural lake, Lac des Settons, a vast reservoir in Le Morvan's center, is a resort. Though unusual, the best place to eat is **Hôtel-Restaurant Les Grillons du Morvan** (Tel: 03 86 84 51 43, www.lesgrillonsdumorvan.com, info@lesgrillonsdumorvan. com, closed Wednesday, and lunch Thursday, from mid to late December, and from January 2 to March, very inexpensive to expensive). This hard-driven property is a French Baghdad Café, run by a reinvented artistic director and corporate consultant. In 2003, Claire and Fabien Gillard transformed the ramshackle place into a shabby-chic B&B–*table d'hôtes*. Eclectic retro, in mauve, cool jazz on the stereo, and an equally eclectic menu based on regional traditions, lend character to a dining experience. The terrace and backyard are pleasant; the dining room has picture windows. Salads or steaks topped with Époisses are typical fare. Avoid offerings that suggest culinary adventurism. The wild bilberry tart and tarte tatin are delicious.

LA TAGNIÈRE

At Le Morvan's southernmost tip, five miles by corkscrew from the lookout atop Mont Julien, near Uchon and Étang-sur-Arroux, south of Autun and west of Le Creusot, La Tagnière is a challenge to find. Hikers and gastronomes know its unsung, excellent-value, hotel-restaurant **À l'Auberge** (Tel: 03 85 54 57 55, aubegedelatagniere@orange.fr, closed Monday and dinner on Tuesday, and from Christmastide to late January, inexpensive to moderate). Spartan and spotless, with nine tables (and a few guest rooms), a fireplace and bar, it's run by shy Monsieur Challamel and Mademoiselle Desbois. The seasonal menu is short, the cooking authentic, the wines from co-ops at Buxy and Clessé, or André Delorme. Expect to find housemade terrine or pheasant paté with hazelnuts and thyme, baby lettuce with toasted pine nuts, perfectly cooked Charolais rumpsteak or succulent confit of rabbit slow-cooked in duck fat, trout-and-pike dumplings, and one of the creamiest potato gratins anywhere (Challamel is from the Savoy). The cheeses are local (luscious cottage cheese from Torcy or goat from Sainte-Radegonde), the desserts old-fashioned (oeufs à la neige, crème caramel, chocolate mousse, or crème brûlée with sour cherries). Everything is housemade, from scratch.

For organic duck foie gras, organic flour and beer, and comfortable B&B lodgings (and simple *table d'hôtes*), go to outlying Corfeuil and duck farm **Domaine du Petit Corfeuil** (Tel: 03 85 54 52 12 or 06 83 98 90 63, www.corfeuil.fr, phone ahead, meals for overnight guests, by reservation), run by friendly Chantal, Daniel, and Vincent Naulin. They and the waterfowl will greet you with open arms and beaks.

Near the Signal d'Uchon panoramic point, find **Auberge la Crois de Messire Jean** (Tel: 03 85 54 42 06, closed Tuesday dinner, Wednesday, and Christmastide, very inexpensive), a rustic eatery. Enjoy the view from the terrace, buy a take-out picnic, or overnight in a hostel environment. Uchon proper is home to a Romanesque church, and France's largest Orthodox monastic community (Ukrainian, Russian, and Greek, Tel: 03 85 54 47 75, phone ahead).

TANNAY

On the upper Yonne, ten miles south of Clamecy on highway D985, Tannay is so unfindable you wonder why perfidious Cardinal Richelieu demolished its walls in 1630. Was the monarch displeased with Tannay's wine? Wine? Indeed. The resurgent Coteaux de Tannay, killed by the end of Yonne river traffic (Tannay wines floated to Paris with Morvan timber) and phylloxera, reborn in the 1990s, this micro-growing area of 115 acres on Le Morvan's western edge, is home to welcoming **Les Caves Tannay-siennes** (11 Rue d'Enfer, Tel: 03 86 29 31 59, www.caves-tannay.com, open daily without appointment May to October, closed Monday the rest of the year, also open by appointment). A co-op with eleven partners who've invested millions in the venture, the winery is in a landmark 1568 building, with medieval cellars.

Cyril Ponnelle transforms Chardonnay, Melon, Gamay, and Pinot Noir into about 120,000 bottles of highly quaffable, silver and bronze medal-winning wines. (The other Cyril—Cyril Raty—the co-op's loquacious communications officer, has managed to underwrite a theme restaurant, Les Coteaux de Tannay (www.restotannay.com), in Paris's seventh arrondissement. The grapes grow in grassy (not organic) vineyards, are hand-picked and selected. The oak barrels are three to five years old; the co-op's delicate wines aren't over-oaked. The Chardonnay is refreshing yet plump; the Melon has light Muscat flavors. The fruity Pinot Noir might be from Alsace.

Tannay has a pleasant hotel-restaurant tucked in the center of the village: **Le Relais Fleuri** (2 Rue de Bèze, Tel: 03 86 29 84 57, le-relaisfleuri@wanadoo.fr, closed Sunday dinner, Monday, Christmastide to March, and a week in early September, inexpensive to expensive). Lace on the windows, polished planks, comfortable caned chairs, and a patio for summer dining, lend charm. Chef Blondeau is a veteran. He took over in 2004, and does *cuisine bourgeoise*, serving chicken-liver salads, housemade terrine with hazelnuts, calf's head with gribiche sauce, steaks, roasts, cheeses, rich desserts, and a good citrus terrine. Wines include the co-op's bottlings.

Visit Tannay on a Sunday in late November, during the Foire de Sainte-Catherine (the village's patron saint), when the main square fills with stands. Phone the winery or restaurant and get the exact date.

VÉZELAY

Ancient Vezeliacum (buried under Saint-Père-sous-Vézelay), on the Via Agrippa consular highway, gave the perched medieval

Vézelay its name. The basilica of Mary Magdalene, a UNESCO World Heritage Site, draws an estimated 1 million visitors per year. Vézelay, nicknamed "The Eternal Hill," a reference to Rome and Catholicism, claims, since the eleventh century, to have Mary Magdalene's relics in its crypt. The basilica is still a pilgrimage site and starting point on the Way of Saint James pilgrim's route. The village sheltered 10,000 daily, incredible given the current population of 500. A revival is underway, though most who flock here enjoy its earthly pleasures. A dozen cafés, snack bars, hotels, and restaurants beckon from a space the size of several football fields. If you stray into one of the traps awaiting, you might find yourself elbow-to-elbow with the busloads.

Not much risk of that at **Le Saint-Etienne** (39 Rue Saint-Etienne, Tel: 03 86 33 27 34, www.le-saint-etienne.fr, closed Wednesday, Thursday, and from mid January to late February, moderate to very expensive), the fief of veteran chef Gilles Lafontaine and his wife Catherine. For decades, Gilles headed a team of forty sous-chefs at Paris's Le George V. The Morvan native took over Le Saint-Etienne in 1998. White linen tablecloths reach to the gleaming floor; chandeliers twinkle; a fire crackles; thick timbers and tasteful objets d'art are reflected in antique mirrors. Squint and you might be in the old Le George V. Gilles buys high-quality, fresh ingredients locally. If you stroll by before dawn, you'll see him at work, preparing everything from scratch. House seasonal specialties range from summery salads with smoked fish and fresh edible flowers, to winter fare (lièvre à la royale simmered in its own blood), or venison grand veneur with Burgundy truffles. The Charolais filet, served year-round, is sliced into small mignonettes and flambéed with cognac. If you reserve ahead (and for the whole table), Gilles will make what might be the best boeuf bourguignon, coq au vin, or other classic dish, you'll ever eat. The higher the price, the nicer the nice. Ditto the wines. There's a sidewalk terrace. Expect to dine with the local gentry and free-spending travelers.

Less expensive but also good when fresh ingredients are obtainable, is long-established, retro-neo-bistro **Le Bougainville** (26 Rue Saint-Etienne, Tel: 03 86 33 27 57, closed Tuesday and Wednesday, and Monday from October to March; seasonal closing mid November to mid February, inexpensive to moderate). Philippe and Sylvie Guillemaud offer daily blackboard specials (onion soup, beef à la mode with carrots) and hearty regional food (oeufs en meurette, snails, pot roast). The cheese platter is outstanding, the wine list strong on Yonne bottlings. The sidewalk terrace is pleasant.

Hôtel de la Poste et du Lion d'Or (Place du Champ de Foire, Tel: 03 86 33 21 23, www.laposte-liondor.com, restaurant closed Monday and Tuesday in spring; restaurant and hotel closed early January to end February, moderate to expensive) is reliable. On the square fronting Porte du Barle, this traditional hotel-restaurant is a favorite among well-heeled pilgrims. The décor and food match: a pious bourgeois family's dining room (thick curtains and carpets, Louis XV-style chairs, wall sconces, a wooden effigy of Saint James). The food, much improved of late, is well made. The menu changes every two months, with regional specialties, from garlicky snails to slow-cooked pork jowl. It includes conservatively creative dishes, and variations on the theme of scallops (the symbol of Saint James). The cheese platter is excellent, the desserts classic, the wine list includes fine local bottlings. There's an outdoor terrace; the comfortable guest rooms offer views over Eternal hillsides.

With similar regional, upscale food (snails in a crisp pastry shell with mushrooms, foie gras, scallops a go-go), a spacious terrace, also facing the city gate, three small, cozy dining rooms of the timbers-and-tiles variety, and the best coffee in town (Illy), is **Hôtel-Restaurant Le Cheval Blanc** (Place du Champ de Foire, Tel: 03 86 33 22 12, restaurant closed Wednesday and Thursday; restaurant and hotel closed late January to late February, inexpensive to expensive). This is a fine option if what you really want is a snack and an espresso.

For decent coffee and homey desserts, try two rustic-spiritual-bobo places: **Hôtel La Maison des Glycines** and **Caballus Café**, both on the main street, a hundred yards from the basilica, facing the Centre Sainte-Madeleine. Each has a cobbled courtyard shaded by wisteria.

Excellent gourmet foods and remarkable wines are sold by a trio of shops on the main street, all owned and operated by the Blanco family. Step into **Le Saint Vincent** (28 Rue Saint Etienne, Tel: 03 86 33 27 79, www.bourgogne-vin.com, vezelay@bourgogne-vin .com), **Au Tastevin** (Tel: 0t3 86 33 22 08) or **Bourgogne-Vin** (Tel: 03 86 33 35 63, all open 9am to 7:30pm daily from Easter to mid November), and ask for Roger or Jocelyne Blanco. They started out in 1976 with one tiny outlet and have grown into Central Burgundy's top winesellers. Among the hundreds on offer the Blancos will find you the right bottling at the right price. See Top Burgundian Winesellers' Favorites, page 56, for the Blancos' picks.

CHAPTER 3

....

EASTERN BURGUNDY

Département: Côte d'Or.

Population: 510,000.

Population density: 58 inhabitants/sq. km.

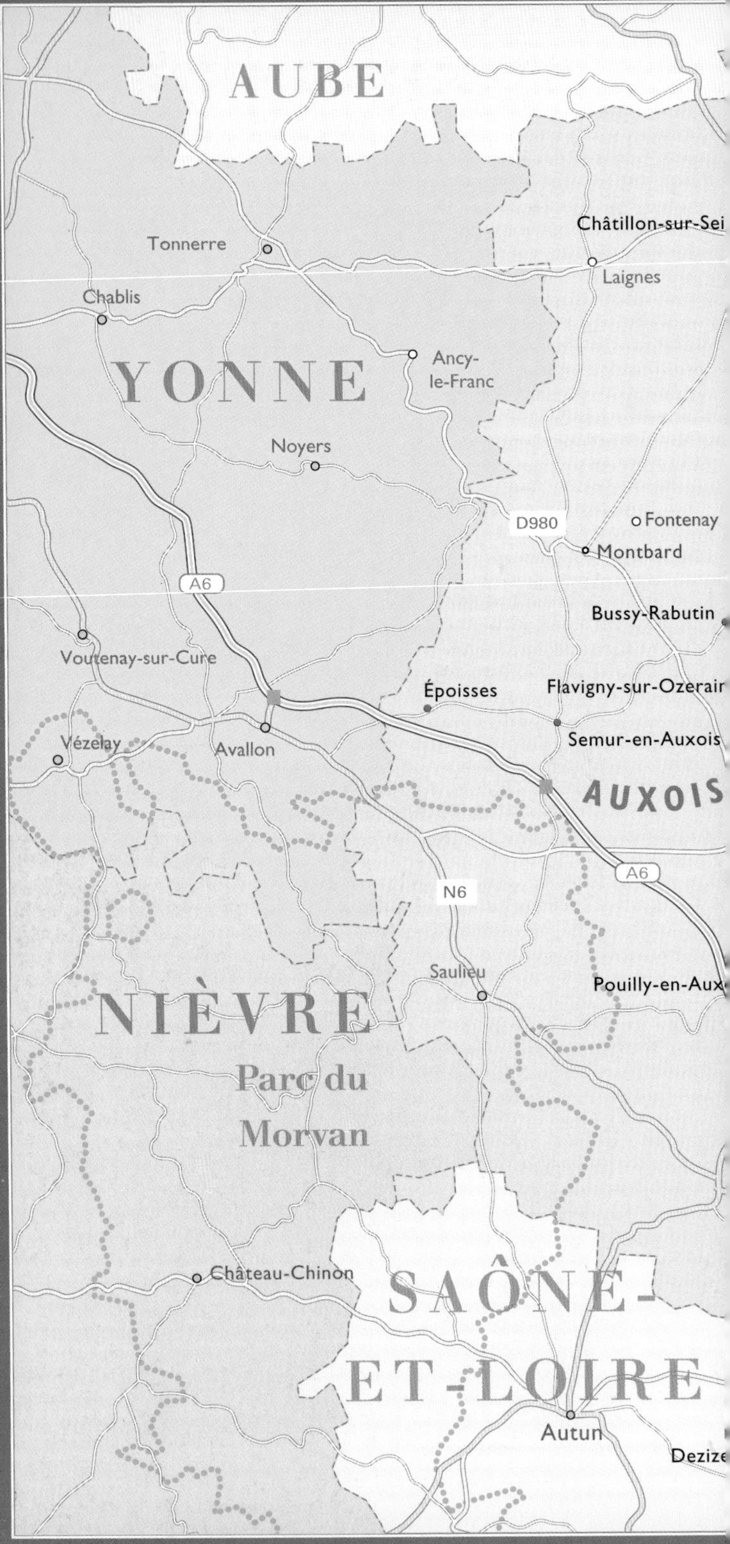

AUBE

Châtillon-sur-Sei

Tonnerre

Laignes

Chablis

YONNE

Ancy-
le-Franc

Noyers

D980

o Fontenay

Montbard

Bussy-Rabutin

A6

Voutenay-sur-Cure

Époisses

Flavigny-sur-Ozerair

Vézelay

Avallon

Semur-en-Auxois

AUXOIS

A6

N6

Saulieu

Pouilly-en-Aux

NIÈVRE

Parc du

Morvan

Château-Chinon

SAÔNE-

ET-LOIRE

Autun

Dezize

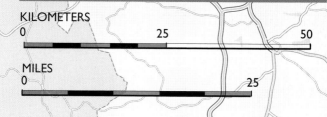

AUXOIS,
CHÂTILLON-SUR-SEINE,
VALLÉE DE L'OUCHE

*Includes: Châteauneuf-en-Auxois, Châtillon-sur-Seine,
Époisses, Flavigny-sur-Ozerain, Lusigny-sur-Ouche,
Pouilly-en-Auxois, Semur-en-Auxois*

STRETCHING FROM CHAMPAGNE SOUTH TO THE SCENIC OUCHE RIVER VALLEY ON THE OUTSKIRTS of Dijon, the northernmost and central-northern sections of the immense Côte d'Or are remarkably different from the stony vineyards of the Côtes south of Dijon. Rivers, marshes, forests, fields, and pastureland are typical; the Seine River rises near Chanceaux, flowing north to Châtillon-sur-Seine. Époisses cheese comes from the village of the same name. The only characteristic the upper and lower Côte d'Or share is winegrowing, in the north, limited to the Châtillonnais. In style, character, and quality, the Châtillonnais resembles the Tonnerrois in Northern Burgundy's Yonne.

Work-a-day Montbard, birthplace of eighteenth-century naturalist Georges-Louis Leclerc, Comte de Buffon, is also a TGV station; high-speed trains to Paris take one hour. Lovers of history and monuments will not want to miss the medieval abbey at Fontenay, a UNESCO World Heritage Site as attractive and moving as better-known Vézelay; the excavations at Alésia, where Julius Caesar's army defeated Vercingétorix and his Gallic tribes; and the Château of Bussy-Rabutin, among the best preserved in France. Semur-en-Auxois and Flavigny-sur-Ozerain are handsome medieval fortified towns poised over river valleys; the first has wonderful chocolates, the second, celebrated aniseed candies (and curious Coteaux de l'Auxois wines). Running through the scenic Ouche River Valley, alongside the river, the Canal de Bourgogne links Dijon to Tonnerre and Joigny.

CHÂTEAUNEUF-EN-AUXOIS

A handful of perched fortresses in Burgundy vie for the title of Book-of-Hours Gold Medal Winner. They include Châteauneuf-en-Auxois. This particular crow's nest is populated by self-styled artists, artisans, and mercantile cuckoos, perched above the A6 autoroute, halfway between the Vallée de l'Ouche and Pouilly-en-Auxois. It's worth the tilting, curving detour for the views and atmosphere (out of season). When capturing stray tourists becomes the main source of income for locals, the quality of the dining experience is less than brilliant. You can get good please-all food at the village's "gastronomic" hotel-restaurant, **Hostellerie du Château** (Tel: 03 80 49 22 00, www.hostellerie -chateauneuf.com, moderate to expensive, closed Monday and Tuesday from September through June, and December, January, February). The guest rooms provide oohs-and-ahs, as does the glassed-in dining room with Louis Philippe–style chairs and yellow tablecloths. The pocketsized outdoor terrace has teak chairs—but plastic tables, and no view.

For a snack, the grill across the street is acceptable, and you can also eat a filling meal without anxiety at **L'Auberge du Marronnier** (Place du Marché, Tel: 03 80 49 21 91, inexpensive to moderate, open daily in summer, for weekday lunch and weekend dinner from September to mid November and from February through June, closed from mid November through January), amid the requisite collection of ye olde peasant's tools nailed to the timbers.

If in Châteauneuf on the last weekend in July, 2010 or 2012 (on even-numbered years), you'll see the biannual Marché Médiéval. Locals and savvy hawkers from miles around dress like Robin Hood and display edibles of a kind possibly sold, eaten, or dreamed of in the Bad Old Days. At the BBQ on Place du Marché, sides of beef, pork, and lamb are roasted, and bread is baked in a mobile wood-burning oven. Highlights at the château of Châteauneuf include a fireplace, frescoes partly visible, and the view.

CHÂTILLON-SUR-SEINE

Sizeable—7,000 inhabitants—and watered by the nascent Seine and vigorous Douix River, which rises on the edge of town, at the foot of a cliff, leafy Châtillon is a Burgundo-Champagnois border town rich in virtual history. The medieval fortress is in ruins; most of the town was rebuilt after heavy damage in both World Wars, though the Saint-Vorles Romanesque church survived. Antique charm isn't a strong suit. However, the setting is attractive, and much is being done to reclaim the city and its monuments. The new home for the **Musée du Pays Châtillon-nais**, reopened in 2009, is the restored Notre-Dame Abbey (Tel: 03 80 91 51 76, www.pays-chatillonnais.fr). Archeology, history, and wine enthusiasts will want to see the Vase de Vix, the largest ancient wine crater—a ritual drinking or display vessel—yet found. It holds 300 gallons, weighs 450 pounds and stands 5' 4" tall, is stunning, and was brought to the area by merchants from Magna Graecia, probably circa 500 BC. At the time, a Gallic queen reigned, though no trace of her pre-Roman city survives. The crater would be proof, were any needed, of the region's long association with wine. Should you be present on the third Saturday of March, you'll see the Fête du Crémant, a boozy sparkling wine festival with ancient roots, revived in the late 1970s (same telephone number and website as above).

The Crémant de Bourgogne can be good hereabouts (the reds and still whites are often thin). Sip some downtown at co-op **Les Vignerons de Haute Bourgogne** (26 Rue Maréchal-de-Lattre-de-Tassigny, closed Sunday and Monday). Buy picnic supplies, especially terrines of duck, rabbit, and pork, and bone-in baked or boiled ham, across the street at **Charcuterie Barder** (33 Rue Maréchal-de-Lattre-de-Tassigny, Tel: 03 80 91 04 47, closed Sunday and Monday). The best pastries, chocolates, coffee, tea, and housemade ice creams are at **Pâtisserie Serge Barbier** (27 Rue Maréchal-Leclerc, Tel: 03 80 91 13 22, closed Monday). Also good are the light lunches and snacks (fresh quiches, terrines, and salads).

To go the whole *terroir* hog (or beef, chicken, and squab), head to traditional **Hôtel de la Côte d'Or** (2 Charles Ronot, Tel: 03 80 91 13 29, remillet.gerard@club-internet.fr, closed Monday, Tuesday, and January to March, very inexpensive to expensive), in a 1737 coaching inn. Gérard Remillet does a good job with the Charolais and morel mushrooms, and simply roasted or simmered Bresse poultry; his desserts are classic and copious. The wine list is strong on northern Burgundian and local bottlings.

ÉPOISSES

This is a happy tale of revival. Lovers of Époisses wishing to see the village, in hopes, perhaps, of purchasing the authentic item and watching ye olde cheese-maker, must swallow a bitter pill. Though your nose may twitch with delight, you cannot see the *fromage* fashioned at the famous, dauntingly sterile Fromagerie Berthaut (Place du Champ de Foire, Tel: 03 80 96 44 44, www .fromagerie-berthaut.com, closed holidays and Sundays, except in July and August). No hay or dung, and no visitors. However, you may buy *époisses d'Époisses*, as it's called chez Berthaut, and rounds of milder Soumaintrain, plus gourmet delicacies—Fallot mustard, Mulot & Petitjean gingerbread, honeys from the Morvan or Rouvray, Quarré de Chocolat jams, vinegars, wines—at the compact **Berthaut** boutique on the homely main square. Follow the crowds: they're not heading to landmark **Château d'Époisses** where the epistolary queen Madame de Sévigné lived (Tel: 03 80 96 40 56, hours vary widely). As bona fide cheese bores know, it was the Berthaut family who reinvented Époisses, the cheese (usually with a lower-case *é*) and the village (upper case), half empty by 1956. That's when the dairy dynasty dusted off local monks' sixteenth-century recipe, and made modern Époisses, an old lush, at fifty percent fat. (The bone of capitalization can't be picked here.) Berthaut's Époisses is made from pasteurized, not raw, milk, but is very good, nonetheless. Buy a round, and several raw-milk rivals (Gaugry, Ferme des Marronniers), and do a tasting, preferably with the windows open.

FLAVIGNY-SUR-OZERAIN

Imagine Flavinius, the wandering Roman who plucked aniseed while in Syria and then rode on the leather skirt-tails of Julius Caesar, glimpsing the site of his (future) namesake Flavigny, cupped by the meandering Ozerain River, and two other flickering streams, a magical site thirty-five miles northwest of Divio (now Dijon). No wonder Flavinius decided to build a villa, presumably with a stock of aniseeds in the cellar. That was during the Gallic Wars. "Flavinius" morphed to "Flavien" and "Flavigny" in Gallic, Frankish, and Burgund mouths, and the Roman town became the stronghold of pious Burgund chieftain Widerard, who presumably also liked aniseed, and probably had a sweet tooth. Widerard's abbey appeared in the early 700s AD; at some point the monks discovered how to coat aniseed with something sweet. By the Renaissance, that something was sugar, and, by 1591, the famous aniseed candies of the abbey of Flavigny were born. Whether entirely accurate or not, a similar tale is spun by enterprising Catherine Troubat, proprietor of the town's last remaining aniseed candy factory, **L'Anis de l'Abbaye de Flavigny** (Tel: 03 80 96 20 88, www.anisdeflavigny.com, boutique open daily from April to November; visits to the factory and abbey weekdays 9am to 11am only, closed weekdays, holidays, the first three weeks in August, and Christmastide). Troubat and her loyal staff make traditional aniseed-flavored and other sweet "bonbons." The aniseeds are from Spain, Turkey, and Syria and are tumbled—like headache pills—in copper basins, slowly picking up a sugary coating. The tumblers turn for fifteen days. The candies, also perfumed with fourteen different flavors, from violet or jasmine to orange flower water, are sold in attractive little tins and make delightful gifts. A visit to the shop and abbey is also delightful.

Though tourism has worked its magic, strolling through Flavigny is still appealing: medieval houses shoulder along sloping streets, there are ramparts, views, and a remarkable Romanesque church. In the crypt of the candy factory-abbey, the martyrized remains of Sainte-Reine, she of the nearby village Alise-Sainte-Reine, once reposed.

In Flavigny in spring, summer, or fall, get a hearty meal at **La Grange** (Place de l'Église, Tel: 03 80 96 20 62, open March to late November weekends and holidays, daily except Monday July

to mid September, very inexpensive). Farmstead ingredients are cooked by local farm ladies and milkmaidens: omelettes, salads, cold cuts, roasted poultry in thick cream, beef or pork stews, rabbit in mustard sauce, sweet or savory crêpes. The menfolk don't do the cooking, but might pour you some local wine.

Otherwise, if you give the Atlantic fish a miss, you can get a perfectly decent *terroir* meal at timbers-and-pink **Relais de Flavigny** (Place des Anciennes Halles, Tel: 03 80 96 27 77, www .le-relais.fr, open daily in summer, closed Monday dinner and Tuesday from November to Easter, very inexpensive to inexpensive), run by affable Natacha and Philippe Guillier.

Unlikely though it seems, Coteaux de l'Auxois wine is grown hereabouts, and is more than drinkable. Head out of the village toward Alésia downhill on Rue de l'Abbaye, following signs to Pont-Laizan and **Vignoble de Flavigny-Alésia** (Tel: 03 80 96 25 63, vignoble-de-flavigny@wanadoo.fr, www.vignoble-flavigny .com, open daily 10am to 6/7pm, phone for detailed directions if you get lost), in a hulking winery building. Courageous, affable winegrower Ida Nel makes many wines of all colors, including a very honorable Aligoté she calls La Vivacité.

LUSIGNY-SUR-OUCHE

In the Ouche Valley, at the junction of highways D17 and D970, at the fountainhead of the Ouche River, **L'Auberge des Sources** (Tel: 03 80 20 10 52, lunch only, daily except Saturday, inexpensive to moderate) is a premodern country hostelry, the delight of savvy travelers. Family-run, in constant operation since at least 1903, the building is centuries old, with thick timbers, thicker walls, and heavy furnishings. The short menu features simple classics, from egg to apple tart. Across the way, in the park at the river's springs, the auberge runs an outdoor *guinguette*—refreshments stand—under soaring old trees.

POUILLY-EN-AUXOIS

Akin in atmosphere and weathered looks to nearby Arnay-le-Duc, this sprawling farm town has many claims to fame, and one good reason to visit it: outwardly unimpressive, chalk-white **Hôtel-Restaurant de la Poste** (Place de la Libération, Tel: 03 80 90 86 44, open daily in July and August, closed Sunday dinner, Monday, Tuesday lunch the rest of the year, inexpensive to moderate). On Pouilly's graceless main square, it's among the best gourmet values around. In 2000 young Antony Bonnardot, survivor of triple-starred Alain Senderens and Lameloise, took over from his journeyman father (and grandfather) at this 200-year-old, family-run inn. Having noticed how certain masters of haute and their itty-bitty portions fail to win a local following, Bonnardot has not thrown out the boeuf bourguignon with the bathwater, wisely offering a *terroir* menu. The result: this unlikely venue is packed yearround by locals (and out-of-towners). The cavernous dining room is comfortable; if you enjoy sunlight, reserve on the glassed-in terrace. Never mind the naïf canvas (Burgundian natives toiling in the vineyards). Stick to the frog's legs, oeufs en meurette, braised or oven-roasted pike-perch and Charolais steaks, and you're sure to eat very well. To fly to Asia, Africa, or California, order the creative food.

A fine supplier of picnic foods is on the main street: **Boucherie-Charcuterie de l'Auxois** (Avenue du Générale de Gaulle, Tel: 03 80 90 71 54). The rabbit terrine and jambon persillé are outstanding.

As of July 2008, Pouilly has a weekly open market— Le Marché—a revival. It's held from 4pm to 8pm on Fridays downtown. A Christmas market is held on December weekends, around Le Colombier, a landmark dovecote which houses the tourism office (Tel: 03 80 90 74 24, www.pouilly-auxois.com); many stands sell gourmet items.

A final reason to exit at Pouilly: near the traffic circle flanking autoroute A6 (Créancey) the postmodern, government-subsidized **Maison de Pays** (Le Seuil, Tel: 03 80 90 75 86, www.maison-auxois.com, closed Sunday). A showcase for crafts, gourmet food and wine are also sold.

SEMUR-EN-AUXOIS

Fortified, medieval, and with a natural, cliff-edged moat provided by the Armançon River, Semur is handsome yet soulful. The imposing duncecap towers—seen in the postcards—have wide cracks, caused, it's said, by heavy trucks (a highway wraps the fortifications). The trucks also rumble over the many-arched Pont Joly, a pretty bridge. The views from the ramparts and bridge are lovely nonetheless. Fans of tilts and other costumed spectacles should visit in May or September (Office de Tourisme: 2 Place Gaveau, Tel: 03 80 97 05 96, www.ville-semur-en-auxois.fr).

It's hard to get lost. Head for the main square, Place Notre Dame, fronting the ungainly, over-restored Gothic cathedral. You can't miss **Charcuterie Notre Dame** (10 Place Notre Dame, Tel: 03 80 97 06 17, closed Sunday and holiday afternoons and Monday, and late August to mid September). Traditional and many times awarded for its jambon persillé, boned ham, garlic salami and rabbit terrine, the shop also makes many other terrines, pâtés, quiches, tourtes and take-out dishes (from snails or blood sausage to duck à l'orange).

Across the square is wine boutique **Oenothèque** (20 Place Notre Dame, Tel: 03 80 97 30 38, www.oenotheque-semur.com, closed Sunday afternoon and Monday). Of the 1,000 wines sold, the choice of Burgundies isn't vast—about 150—but you'll find many good buys and top wineries. Accessories (including Riedel tasting glasses) are also sold, plus a selection of gourmet foods.

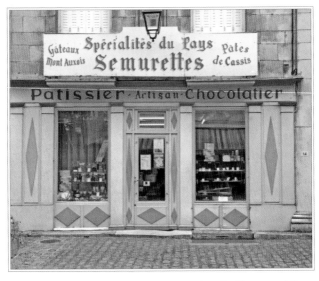

One hundred yards up pedestrianized Rue Buffon toward Porte Sauvigny find adorable chocolate and pastry shop **Pâtisserie-Chocolaterie Coeur** (14 Rue Buffon, Tel: 03 80 97 09 40, closed Monday). Compact and attractive, in business since the 1800s, the décor is original. Bruno Coeur took over in 1993. A master chocolatier, Coeur worked in Dijon and Miami (he speaks fluent English), and will proudly tell you that www.wine.com in Oakland, California, sells his Semurettes. The recipe for these truffle-like chocolates (without butter) is from the early 1900s. Coeur also fashions Le Mont Auxois, a paving stone of chocolate cake, chock-a-block with almonds. The other specialty is Bouchons au Marc de Bourgogne—chocolate corks filled with liqueur, a fine gift, if you can resist drinking them. Coeur's classic pastries, and excellent ice creams, are luscious; in summer he sets up tables on the car-free street.

Just outside Porte Sauvigny is **Alexandre** (1 Rue de la Liberté, Tel: 03 80 97 08 94, closed Sunday afternoon and Monday). Namesake chocolatier Alexandre and wife took over from longtime owner Alain Pellé, who made this shop famous. The couple craft chunks of Granite Rose de L'Auxois (chocolate, almonds, and orange), which look like Auxois pink granite, and Joyaux de Bourgogne (marzipan with blackcurrant liqueur or Marc de Bourgogne), plus two dozen classic filled chocolates, ice creams, and other treats. Alexandre also sells Cartron liqueurs.

Down the dog's-leg street on the slope from Place Notre Dame to the cracked tower overlooking the bridge, find **Le Saint-Vernier** (13 rue Févret, Tel: 03 80 97 32 96, open daily, very inexpensive to moderate). A wine bar—restaurant with bistro décor, this is where local twenty- and thirty-somethings flock to strike poses, while older regulars watch, amused. Lunch is best, unless you're spending the night in town. Don't expect culinary fireworks. The food is hearty and traditional, the chalkboard menu changing regularly. Order a glass of Chablis or Irancy to go with your calf's head or ribsteak sauced with Époisses.

Cookie lovers can visit the factory of **Biscuiterie du Mistral** (Route de Dijon, Tel: 03 80 89 66 66, www.biscuits-mistral.com or www.biscuits.fr, closed Sunday), on the highway to Dijon. Based in Saint-Andiol-en-Provence, Mistral has baked in Semur for over thirty years. Taste free of charge a dozen types of quality cookie, some in handsome tins, and buy at factory prices, should you need a gross during your travels.

DIJON

....

THE ROMAN SETTLEMENT OF DIVIO LIES BENEATH TODAY'S DIJON AND EXPLAINS THE CITY'S NAME. It became the capital of the Dukes of Burgundy, and is still the region's capital and biggest city. There are 153,000 inhabitants downtown, about 240,000 counting the suburbs. They spread far, embracing Chênove and Marsannay, the Ouche River Valley, and Val de Saône, and are framed by autoroutes and train lines. The TGV to Paris takes ninety minutes; many Dijonais commute.

Luckily, Dijon's contemporary attractions and historical treasures are within a radius of half a mile from the Ducal Palace and pedestrianized, semi-circular Place de la Libération. Though five times as big as rival Beaune, Dijon's heart is about the same size.

Several factors provide charm, life, and authenticity not found elsewhere. Dijon's university has 30,000 students. Faculties are scattered. Cafés, bars, restaurants, hotels, and ungentrified buildings signal hormonal youths and budding young minds. Second, as the administrative seat, Dijon harbors fleets of well-heeled *fonctionnaires*. It fills with Burgundians come to battle the bureaucracy. Machinery abounds: mustard factories, manufacturing, factory farming, high tech, transportation, and tourism. They make modern Divio a lively, real place and not merely a bobo playground.

Dijon is also very handsome. Toss a coin and watch it land on a church or townhouse, the latter stone-built or half-timbered, the timbers, probably, painted like those of a gingerbread house. This is the cradle of mustard, but it's also the great urban bakery of *pain d'épices*. The architecture is a mix of late medieval, Renaissance, and seventeenth- to nineteenth-century styles. While the suburbs are banal, within the ring of central boulevards you'll find few eyesores. Chain stores are spreading their contagion, yet most pedestrian streets are still pleasant, rather than mall-like.

The main crosstown thoroughfare and shopping street linking Place Darcy to the Ducal Palace is Rue de la Liberté. The so-called antiques dealers' quarter (Quartier des Antiquaires) is east of Notre-Dame on rues Chaudronnerie, Jean-Jacques Rousseau, and Verrerie. Dijon's tourism office is on Place Darcy (Tel: 08 92 70 05 58, pay-per-minute, www.dijon-tourism.com, www.dijon .fr, open daily); more convenient, a smaller office is at 11 Rue des Forges, near the Ducal Palace. Pick up free maps at the station, tourist offices, museums, city hall, and many restaurants and hotels. If you get lost, raise your eyes to the towering, medieval Tour Philippe le Bon and you'll find your way back to the bull's-eye: the Ducal Palace.

A miniature and unscrubbed Louvre, **Le Musée des Beaux-Arts/Palais des Etats de Bourgogne** (Tel: 03 80 74 52 70, www .musees-bourgogne.org, www.ville-dijon.fr, closed Tuesday), in the Ducal Palace, has one of France's largest and eclectic collections of artworks from antiquity to the present. Don't miss the tomb of Philippe le Hardi. If it's open, scale the **Tour Philippe le Bon** (Tel: 03 80 74 51 51), accessed via city hall, for a panorama of rooftops (open daily Easter to the third Sunday in November, open Wednesday afternoons and weekends the rest of the year). Overlooked, the **Musée Archéologique** (5 Rue du Dr. Maret, Tel: 03 80 48 83 70, same website, closed Tuesday), in the medieval Saint Bénigne Abbey, houses pre-Roman treasures and, in the subterranean former scriptorium, ex votos and treasures excavated at Les Sources de la Seine (including a Gallo-Roman bronze of river goddess Sequana, hauntingly displayed).

Since November 2008, Dijon boasts France's first à la carte cooking school—*table d'hôtes*. Walk-in clients take hands-on courses from professional chefs, lasting thirty minutes to four hours, eat what they've cooked, or take it home. It's called **L'Atelier des Chefs** (18 Rue Chaudron, Tel: 03 80 31 72 75 or 06 16 57 06 88, www.atelierdeschefs.com, info@atelierdeschefs.com, meals very inexpensive). You'll find the school in contemporary, ground-floor premises near gingerbread-makers La Rose de Vergy. If you pre-plan your cooking course, you can choose your favorite classic Burgundian or French recipes and eat while learning.

Les Halles (rues Odebert, Bannelier, Quentin), a few hundred yards northwest of the Ducal Palace, is open Tuesday, Thursday, Friday, and Saturday mornings from 5:30am to noon/12:30pm; Friday and Saturday are days of bustle. This 1883 glass-, iron-, and brick-built marvel is similar to what speculators destroyed in Paris in the 1960s. It's encircled by family-run fruit and vegetable stands. Among the many excellent, permanent stalls inside, don't miss Triperie Dijonnaise (on the southern end), run by smiling Jean-François Moreau, maker of award-winning jambon persillé; outstanding cheesemonger **Pascal Benner–Crèmerie Porcheret** (whose sumptuous shop and cheese-aging cellar are a hundred yards away, and a must-see, at 18 Rue Bannelier, cremerie. porcheret@wanadoo.fr, shop closed Sunday and Monday), selling the best of Burgundy; and organic bakery Cheval Gris (in the center aisle). The street market (clothing and sundries) is open Tuesday, Friday, and Saturday mornings, facing Les Halles and on Rue François Rude.

Places to eat and drink

Hundreds of restaurants in and around Dijon offer the gamut of regional, French, and international food. Burgundian traditions remain, but the city is not immune to nationwide trends. Dijon is a real city, like Paris, and not a bobo playground like Beaune. You'll find plenty of down-to-earth, affordable food.

Affable Jean-Pierre Billoux owns two restaurants downtown. Packed by regulars, **Le Bistrot des Halles** (10 Rue Bannelier, Tel: 03 80 49 94 15, billoux@club-internet.fr, closed Sunday, dinner Thursday, very inexpensive to moderate) faces the north side of the covered market, source of chef François Temmermann's fresh ingredients, and many customers. The décor matches the food: bentwood chairs, red banquettes, mirrors, old prints, brass sconces. Daily chalkboard menus feature hearty terrines, soups, and stews. The lunch prix fixe is so delicious— slow-roasted lamb with potato gratin, blanquette de veau—that you might never try the perennial housemade jambon persillé with veal trotters and mustard mousse, old-fashioned pâté en croûte, caramelized pork shanks, or desserts (crème brûlée with gingerbread, spiced orange marmalade in a compote). That would be a pity. Wines: Marsannay, Côte de Nuits, and Pernand-Vergelesses, quaffable and affordable, by the glass, carafe, or bottle. The service is remarkably friendly and professional. The bistro is so good that many prefer it to elegant, excellent,

Michelin-starred **Le Pré aux Clercs** (13 Place de la Libération, Tel: 03 80 38 05 05, www.jeanpierrebilloux.com, contact@jean-pierrebilloux.com, closed Sunday dinner, Monday, two weeks in February and one week in August, expensive to astronomically expensive), Billoux's other restaurant. It faces the Ducal Palace. The cooking, done primarily by Billoux's son Alexis, takes *terroir*—Charolais, Burgundy truffles, pike perch, Dijon mustard, Bresse poultry—and raises it into airy plated artworks, more attractive, it must be said, than the contemporary art on the walls. The choice of Burgundies is vast.

Dijon's second Michelin-Musketeer is **Stéphane Derbord** (10 Place Wilson, Tel: 03 80 67 74 64, www.restaurantstephane derbord.fr, closed Sunday, lunch Monday and Tuesday, one week in February, and two weeks in early August, inexpensive to astronomically expensive). His restaurant with a mere dozen tables, presided over by wife Isabelle, is on a busy traffic circle edging central Dijon. The décor—blond wood, upholstered armchairs, Asian touches and live bamboo in the patio—makes for comfortable, sunny dining. Derbord transforms seasonal Burgundian ingredients: snails done three ways, including in a frothy *nage* with cardamom essence; hearty calf's trotter in phyllo dough; succulent pike-perch wrapped in bacon; local venison in an earthy shepherd's pie; or pheasant tourte with Burgundy truffles. The desserts are exquisite and complicated (caramelized pear with acacia honey and pannacotta, light cream and sorbet). The wine list features 800 different bottlings, from affordable organic Goisot Côtes d'Auxerre to Domaine de la Romanée Conti at well over 4,000 euros. The service is polished, the clientele business-oriented at lunch, romantic at dinner. The inexpensive weekday lunch is remarkable.

To mix metaphors, the third Michelin-Musketeer is rebel-without-a-cause William Frachot. His **Hostellerie du Chapeau Rouge** (5 Rue Michelet, Tel: 03 80 50 88 88, www.chapeau-rouge .fr, open daily, closed first two weeks of January, expensive to astronomically expensive), also a designer hotel, serves outspokenly anti-*terroir* cuisine, excellent in its fusion genre, in an Asian-Californian-style dining room.

Frachot's garrulous, mustachioed father, Dominik, runs hotel—restaurant—wine bar **Restaurant et Caveau de la Porte Guillaume** (Hôtel du Nord, Place Darcy, Tel: 03 80 50 80 50, www .hotel-nord.fr, inexpensive to moderate, open daily, closed Christmastide), facing the city's triumphal arch. In the family since 1907, this is where you explore classic Burgundy *terroir*—from eggs to snails, pike-perch with Aligoté and coq au vin to boeuf bourguignon—plus gutsy lamb brains with lemon-butter

and capers, or tripe stewed in rosé from Marsannay. Frachot serves 44,000 garlicky snails per year, 1.2 tons of jambon persillé, and 40,000 oeufs en meurette. Each is described on the nine foreign-language menus. Unsurprisingly, Frachot considers himself an ambassador of regional cooking. Among the desserts, the ginger-bread ice cream with Marc de Bourgogne stands out. Everything is housemade (except the jambon persillé) by veteran Hervé Panart; the ingredients are fresh. While the cooking won't win Michelin stars, you'll certainly enjoy dinner, the laden cheese trolley, smiling, professional service and pleasant, wood-paneled dining room, complete with grandfather clock. The wines include good bottlings from Faiveley, Jadot, Chanson, La Chablisienne, and by-the-glass selections. The vaulted, bright Caveau wine bar downstairs serves the restaurant's food, plus wine-tasting menus (from three to five glasses) with platters of cold cuts and cheeses. Indulge: an elevator will whisk you to your comfortable room above.

Upscale and contemporary, with reluctant nods to *terroir*, the cooking at **Les Oenophiles** (Hôtel Philippe le Bon, 18 Rue Sainte-Anne, Tel: 03 80 30 73 52, www.hotelphilippelebon.com, closed Sunday, inexpensive to expensive) thrills some; the wine list thrills many. The restaurant is on the ground floor of several Gothic buildings knocked together, on a side-street south of Place de la Libération. On site is a wine museum. The summer patio is pleasant; the neo-medieval, high-design dining room is bright, even in winter. Chef Stéphane Cattane did the marquee circuit; his cooking bursts with daring surf-'n'-turf combinations, matched to wines by the glass. Stick to the prix fixe menus with classics, order a bottle from Faiveley or Amiot-Servelle, and you'll be safe. The guest rooms are classy.

Similar yet wholly different, in a rib-vaulted, thirteenth-century cellar, is cushy **La Dame d'Aquitaine** (23 Place Bossuet, Tel: 03 80 30 45 65, closed Sunday and lunch Monday, inexpensive to very expensive). Aquitaine, the region, has little to do with the menu. Order the lightened, nicely presented Burgundian classics and you'll eat well. One drawback: the architecture is so striking, you and the tourists distanced from each other at lavishly draped tables, risk being distracted from your meal.

For traditional food in a simple, neighborhood setting, head to **Restaurant L'Escargot** (43 Rue Jean-Jacques Rousseau, Tel: 03 80 73 33 85, www.lescargot-dijon.com, closed Sunday, very inexpensive to inexpensive), in the antiques dealers' quarter, near gourmet shop Gautier. A paradise of snails and well-prepared, unfussy regional dishes, it's run by chummy young Carmen and Gilles Guinot.

Students and bobos in search of casual-hip surroundings favor grill-restaurant **Le Sauvage** (64 Rue Monge, Tel: 03 80 41 17 33, open daily, very inexpensive to moderate). It faces l'Academie de Dijon, near Place Émile Zola, in a rustic 1400s inn. The bistro décor with colorful touches, timbers and fireplaces (one sporting a rotisserie), lend charm. In summer, the cobbled courtyard fills with tables. Order oeufs en meurette, jambon persillé from *charcutier* Gérald Martenot, calf's head or frog's legs, plus grilled steaks and poultry. The cheeses are from neighboring cheesemonger Crèmerie La Grapillotte. Never mind the preening staff.

Dijon's other center-city rotisserie is **Le Grill Laure** (8 Place Saint Benigne, Tel: 03 80 41 86 76, open daily, very inexpensive to inexpensive), fronting the church near the archeological museum. Namesake Laurette Demougin not only roasts lamb, poultry, and beef of excellent quality, she also serves *terroir* dishes, housemade desserts, and remarkable wines from Bouchard Père et Fils and Alain Gras (of Saint Romain).

La Causerie des Mondes (16 Rue Vauban, Tel: 03 80 49 96 59, la.causerie.des.mondes@wanadoo.fr, open nonstop 10am to 7pm, closed Sunday, Monday, and the last half of August, meals very inexpensive). Without question, this cosmically pleasing establishment brews (and sells) Dijon's best artisanally roasted, perfectly extracted coffee (fifteen monovarietals); to-die-for, unadulterated hot chocolates (five variations); and dozens of outstanding teas and herbal infusions. Snack on housemade pastries and fruit tarts, warming soups, and simple, fresh daily luncheon dishes with a Mediterranean bent. World music plays as you settle into the cozy, narrow rooms, with old wooden tables, African tribal art, antique lutes, and burlap wallpaper. You might feel like chatting: the shop's name means "chat-room of the world(s)," first through third. Jean-François Mazuer—a compact Brad Pitt lookalike—is no star-gazer. A reinvented medical professional, he buys top-quality ingredients direct. Mazuer does the roasting and cooking, with state-of-the-art equipment, and chats, and chats. In summer, there's a terrace on the pedestrian-only road. Don't miss it.

Comptoir des Colonies (12 Place François Rude, Tel: 03 80 30 28 22, open nonstop 8am to 8:30pm, closed Sunday). A hip café (with its own roasting facility nearby), tea salon (with 140 Mariage Frères teas), coffee-and-tea retail boutique, and all-around brassy hangout, on the main pedestrian-only square 200 yards south of Les Halles, this is where locals gauge the mood, sip hot cocoa, or listen to jazz and live piano music (a baby grand sits by the cash register). Bustling, especially on market days, the terrace tables out front are prized.

Maison Millière (10 Rue de la Chouette, Tel: 03 80 30 99 99, closed Sunday and Monday). In a labyrinthine 1483 townhouse flanking landmark Hôtel de Vogüé, behind Notre-Dame, this café-restaurant-gift shop with timbers, tiles, and bentwood chairs serves about thirty different teas, fine hot chocolate, and excellent Illy coffee (downstairs). In the tastefully decorated, cozy upstairs dining room, you'll eat perfectly good classic fare.

La Part des Anges (5 Rue Vauban, Tel: 03 80 49 89 56, open from 5:30pm to 11:30pm only, closed Sunday and Monday, meals very inexpensive). A hundred yards from Place de la Libération, on a pedestrianized street, this likeable wine bar with vintage photos has a studenty feel, serves simple, market-based daily dishes and snacks, and wines from small, independent winemakers. The lack of pretension is refreshing, the summertime terrace pleasant.

Au Vin des Rues (26 Rue Odebert, Tel: 03 80 30 77 13, open 10:30am to 3pm and 6pm to midnight, closed Sunday, Monday, and in January, meals inexpensive to moderate). Within hailing distance of Les Halles, this hip, recently opened wine bar is Dijon's most ambitious, stocking 350 different bottlings, many sold by the glass (inexpensive but excellent Mâcon-La Roche Vineuse by Olivier Merlin, Patrick Javillier's Meursault Clos du Cromin, or Robert Arnoux's Vosne-Romanée les Hautes-Maizières, vintage DRC at nearly 5,000 euros a bottle). The food: tapas, or Beaune-style *gastronomique* bistro food whipped up by chef

Gilles Magnien, a follower of anti-*terroir* kingpin Jean-Michel Lorrain. The blond wood-and-chalkboards décor speaks volumes about the clientele. (A similarly hip wine bar—restaurant, with a less impressive list, decent food, and nonstop, daily opening hours, also inexpensive to moderate, is **Le Quentin** at 6 Rue Quentin, Tel: 03 80 30 15 05, on the opposite side of Les Halles).

Gourmet shops and food artisans

Pascal Benner—Crèmerie Porcheret (see page 181 for details). Dijon's biggest, best-stocked cheese shop, with many gourmet foods, including organic jams and other products from Ferme de la Guye.

Boutique Maille (32 Rue de la Liberté, Tel: 03 80 30 41 02, www.maille.com, open nonstop 9am to 7pm, closed Sunday). On Dijon's main drag, this famous shop from 1845, now owned by a multinational corporation, showcases the nearly thirty mustards of Maille. Above all a feast for the eyes, Maille also sells vinagers, condiments, and oils. The mustard is made from imported seed; there's nothing artisanal involved.

Carbillet (58 Rue des Forges and 84 Rue de la Préfecture, Tel: 03 80 30 38 82 and 03 80 73 43 13, closed Sunday and Monday). Among Dijon's longest-established pastry and chocolate shops, of Carbillet's two boutiques, the original, near the prefecture, is less afflicted by attitude. The glitzy, designer outlet near the Ducal Palace is run by beautiful-but-difficult ladies in black. Of the dozens of delights, the Fleur de Guerande (milk chocolate mousse, caramel syrup, and salted butter) and Montaigne (butter biscuit mounded with buttery, caramelized pears or apples, almond pastry cream and whipped cream) stand out. The filled chocolates are fresh and flawlessly fattening.

Le Chalet Comtois (28 Rue Musette, Tel: 03 80 30 48 61, closed Sunday, and Monday morning). Near Les Halles, this aged, excellent cheese shop specializes in Comté from the Jura east of Dijon, but also stocks many of the best Burgundian cheeses, from Époisses to Mâconnais AOC, Cîteaux to Amis de Chambertin. Run by friendly Patrick Rouaud, father of the celebrated pastry chef of Dix Carnot in Beaune, the shop carries a dozen or more artisanal jams and honeys.

Daniel Chenu (14 Rue Guillaume Tell, Tel: 03 80 41 56 29, closed Sunday, Monday, and August). Caterer-*charcutier*-butcher Daniel Chenu is probably central Dijon's best, and a fine source for picnic supplies, from award-winning jambon persillé or baked bone-in ham to quiches and salads. The shop is outlying, north of Place Darcy, near the luxurious Sofitel La Cloche hotel.

Crèmerie La Grapillotte (26 Rue Monge, Tel: 03 80 30 36 91, closed Sunday afternoon and Monday). A neighborhood cheese shop between restaurant Le Sauvage and Mulot & Petitjean, owned by helpful Rachel Nicolas, La Grapillotte sells exquisite, raw-milk Époisses from Ferme des Marronniers in Origny sur Seine, Gaugry's Ami de Chambertin, and Mâconnais AOC from Ferme des Coteaux, plus delicious artisanal jams from **Au Paradis des Saveurs** (Charmoy, Tel: 06 10 32 77 35, phone ahead).

Le Creuset (14 Rue Musette, Tel: 03 80 30 69 41, www .lecreuset-bourgogne.fr, lecreuset21@free.fr, closed Sunday afternoon and mornings on Monday and Wednesday). Though small and recent, this regional foods boutique 150 yards from Les Halles, run by friendly, tongue-twisting Myriam Schlagdenhauffen, is probably Dijon's best for ethically produced, authentic, artisanal goods. It ships worldwide and has an active internet site. You'll find antique mustard pots—some from the eighteenth-century—and new oddities (handmade ceramic jam funnels). Among the treats are Burgundy truffles and truffled terrines and mustards from Thierry Bezeux of **L'Or des Valois** (97 Rue Paquier d'Aupre, Tel: 03 80 73 46 20, www.truffesdebourgogne .fr, phone ahead); biodynamic Pinot Noir, unusual Melon white wines, and liqueurs, from idealistic Guy Bussière of **Domaine du Val de Saône** (Bonnencontre-Cîteaux, Tel: 03 80 36 36 62, by appointment); mustard with figs and honey-sweet, moist gingerbread from beekeeper–mustard maker Hélène Noluveau of **La Dame de la Marlière** (Saint-Vincent-en-Bresse, Tel: 03 85 76 55 66, http://damedelamarliere.free.fr, phone ahead); equally excellent gingerbread (fifty percent honey) from **Les Ruchers Debroye** (Losne, Tel: 03 80 29 17 62 or 06 07 59 47 05, phone ahead); and exceptional foie gras from Philippe Labonde of **Ferme Rivault** (Autun, Tel: 03 85 52 43 52, phone ahead).

La Cuisinerie (6 Rue Charrue, Tel: 03 80 30 18 07, www .lacuisinerie.fr, closed Sunday, and Monday morning). Dijon's trendy, spotlit kitchen tools and accessories boutique, in the center of town, La Cuisinerie stocks oven dishes for baking snails plus the spear-like forks and clamps you'll need to encourage les escargots out of their shells.

Etablissement Maillard (35 Place Bossuet, Tel: 03 80 30 00 70, closed Sunday, and Monday morning). Affable Odile Mantei-Maillard is the third generation to run this touchstone cooking tools and pastry-maker's supply depot, in the family since 1909, kitty corner to the deconsecrated Saint-Jean church (now a theater). On shelves are hundreds of molds for cakes and pastries—from hearts to Christmas trees—in tin, aluminum, stainless steel, or silicon, plus cooking pots and tools from Staub and de Boyer, and bags of nuts or dry fruits bought by bakers and chefs.

Patrick Fremont (23 Rue Verrerie, Tel: 03 80 50 19 80, closed Monday). In the antique dealers' quarter facing wine shop Aux Grands Crus, this handsome bakery in a landmark building bakes excellent specialty breads, some with sour dough, others studded with chunks of chestnut, or figs, raisins, or pumpkin. The butter cookies and pastries—usually three dozen of them—are remarkable.

Gautier (77 Rue Jean-Jacques Rousseau, Tel: 03 80 67 17 19, closed Sunday afternoon, and Monday). In the antiques dealers' quarter, this long-established, upscale fruit, vegetable, and gourmet foods emporium with an attractive green shopfront and tempting displays, bursts with thousands of regional, artisanally produced items, from snails to vinegar, honey to cheese and oil, plus house-branded duck or quail pâtés, wines, Champagne, and caviar.

La Gerbe d'Or (12 Rue François Rude, Tel: 03 80 30 72 04, closed Sunday and Monday). A fine, family-owned, classic bakery on the main street between Les Halles and Rue des Forges, what you'll find made here and nowhere else are giant-sized sablé butter cookies—an inch or more thick—chock-a-block with hazelnuts, figs, raisins, pistachios, pine nuts, and such like. The gougères are also delicious, crafted with good Comté cheese.

André Grillot Articles de Cave (4 Place François Rude, Tel: 03 80 30 18 97, closed Sunday, and Monday morning). Facing Comptoir des Colonies and Rue des Forges, this shop stuffed with corks and corkscrews, wineglasses and cellar accessories, was founded in 1871 and has been run by the Grillot family since 1931. You'll find *rats de cave* candlestick holders and *coupes de Bourgogne* drinking cups for newlyweds, pewter mustard pots, cheese cages and much else.

Fabrice Gillotte–Au Parain Généreux (21 Rue du Bourg, Tel: 03 80 30 38 88, fabrice.gillotte@wanadoo.fr, www.chocolat-gillotte.com, closed Sunday, Morning morning, and end July to mid August). Writ large across this chic, spotlit chocolate boutique are the initials M.O.F., signifying that Gillotte won the prestigious "best of" prize among French chocolate makers. That was in 1991, when Gillotte was twenty-six. Since then he's won just about every gourmet prize in France, and his creations have become increasingly complex and ethereal—edible jewels displayed as such (with an irreverent, high-tech twist or two). The Terroirs de Bourgogne series are filled chocolates with scientifically studied stratification: seventy-percent cocoa dark chocolate shell, fresh raspberry ganache, raspberry jelly, and more raspberry ganache. Other flavors include blackcurrant, blackberry, and heirloom vineyard peach. There are too many filled chocolates to describe, plus excellent gingerbread, macarons, and chocolate bars. The shop is half a block from Dijon's main crosstown thoroughfare.

Mulot & Petitjean (13 Place Bossuet, Tel: 03 80 30 07 10, www.mulotpetitjean.fr, closed Sunday, and Monday morning). Gingerbread aficionados who enjoy spreading butter on their lightly sweet, firm, somewhat dry pain d'épices, which is flavored with aniseed, or like to use it as an ingredient in cooking, maintain that family-run Mulot & Petitjean makes the best of its type. They

may well be right. Founded in 1796, M&P is currently owned by affable, enthusiastic Catherine Petitjean-Dugourd. She has expanded manyfold and made M&P a nationwide success. The gingerbread is baked at a semi-industrial facility near Dijon's train station, and sold in select gourmet shops throughout France. Even if the gingerbread weren't as great as it's made out to be, the original gingerbread shop—with turn-of-the-nineteenth-century décor—in a gingerbread, half-timbered building in the center of town, would be a must. On offer

are all M&P products, from individually wrapped miniature Petits Mulots (tender gingerbread bites), to giant loaves of the classic item, nonnettes, and dozens of excellent Burgundian gourmet foods, from Flavigny aniseed candies, to mustards, wine (excellent Réserve de la Chèvre Noir Monopole from Albert Ponnelle in Beaune), and Cassis and fruit liqueurs (from Briottet and Cartron). Note: Mulot & Petitjean also has boutiques at 1 Place Notre-Dame and 16 Rue de la Liberté (plus one on Beaune's main square). It owns both giant **Bourgogne Street** (61 Rue de la Liberté, formerly Auger, open daily) and cozy, handsome **A. Michelin** (18 Rue Musette, specializes in sugar-coated Jacqueline candies and chocolates); these shops also stock gingerbread (with orange-perfumed variations on the M&P theme), and many gourmet items.

Robert Vannier (4 Rue François Rude, Tel: 03 80 30 27 17, closed Sunday and Monday). Pastries—over forty types daily— are the main draw at this old-fashioned, artisanal bakery, opened in 1987 and still run by Robert Vannier. Don't miss the chocolate-

meringue finger cookies, glazed chocolate cherries, or crispy almond-hazelnut Craqueline candies. The gougères are gigantic, the savory tarts and quiches a meal in themselves. Vannier has another shop a few blocks away at 12 Rue de la Liberté.

La Rose de Vergy (1 Rue de la Chouette, Tel: 03 80 61 42 22, contact@rosedevergy.com, www.rosedevergy.com, open nonstop 9:30am to 7pm, closed Sunday and Monday). In a landmark half-timbered building a hundred yards southeast of the apse of Notre-Dame, this quiet, tastefully decorated tea salon is home to Dijon's leading artisanal bakers—friendly Annette and Marc Planchard—of gingerbread and nonnettes. They're made downstairs, using honey as the sole sweetener (forty-five percent by volume). The coffee and tea (from Maloka in Beaune) are very good, and you'll also find delicious artisanal cookies, jams, liqueurs from Jean-Baptiste Joannet, mustards, spices, honeys, and more.

Wine shops

Au Vieux Millésime (82 Rue Monge, Tel: 03 80 41 28 79, www .auvieuxmillesime.com, closed Sunday, and Monday morning). Less conveniently located—about a hundred yards south of grill-restaurant Le Sauvage—but also excellent and independent, this wine emporium run by Ludovic Flexas and Christophe Voisin stocks about 700 different wines, many old, impossible-to-find vintages, and also prides itself on promoting good-value wines at around ten euros a bottle. If you've failed to find Anne-Claude Leflaive's outstanding biodynamic wines, or that vintage Clos des Lambrays (or DRC) you've always dreamed of, you might just get lucky here.

Aux Grands Crus (22 Rue Verrerie, Tel: 03 80 31 68 71, www .auxgrandscrus.com, closed Sunday and Monday). Across from bakery Patrick Fremont, this pintsized, independent corner shop—with a spacious fifteenth-century cellar—run by serious wine master Philippe Perrin, stocks dozens of fine Burgundies, including, as the name suggests, top-flight Grand Cru vintages, and rare wines. By arrangement, and for a fee, Perrin will hold wine tastings and teach neophytes the art. Not for bargain hunters.

La Carte des Vins (1 Rue Musette, Tel: 03 80 30 45 01, www .lacartedesvins.com, dijon@lacartedesvins.com, open nonstop 10am to 8pm, closed Sunday). Jean-Luc Roblin, chef de cave, and Adrien Tirelli run this handsome boutique, part of a high-end French mini-chain, on Dijon's main pedestrianized street, near the covered market. Among the 450 or so French wines stocked you'll find about 130 Burgundies, each from an excellent wine-grower, many of them organic, all at the least practicing *agriculture raisonnée*. But respect for the soil isn't the only criteria: the wines sold here are outstandingly good. You'll find everything from Alain Michelet's Nuit-Saint-Georges to Étienne Sauzet's Puligny-Montrachet, plus Pernand Vergelesses from Rapet Père et Fils, and curiosity-value Vins de Table from Flavigny-sur-Ozerain, plus scores of other outstanding, difficult-to-find bottlings. Roblin and Tirelli are friendly and an invaluable resource. See Top Burgundian Winesellers' Favorites, page 58, for their picks.

NUITS SAINT GEORGES and CÔTE-DE-NUITS, HAUTES-CÔTES-DE-NUITS, UPPER VAL DE SAÔNE

....

Includes: Arcenant, Auvillars-sur-Saône, Brochon, Chambolle-Musigny, Cîteaux, Concoeur, Couchey, Échevronne, Fixin, Flagey-Echezeaux, Gevrey-Chambertin, Gilly-lès-Cîteaux, Marsannay, Morey-Saint-Denis, Nuits Saint Georges, Premeaux-Prissey, Saint-Nicolas-lès-Cîteaux, Villars-Fontaine, Vosne-Romanée, Vougeot

A THOUSAND YEARS AGO, WHEN WINEMAKING TOOK OFF IN BURGUNDY, THE LOCALS DID NOT DIVIDE their lands with the express purpose of confusing visitors. However, the result of millennial division and sub-division, particularly after the French Revolution, is today's daunting nomenclature covering wines, vineyards, and districts, many of uneven contour and each a different size, like the pieces of a jigsaw puzzle. Within the Côte-d'Or *département*, the Côte de Nuits sub-region begins in the southern suburbs of Dijon, at Marsannay-la-Côte, and runs south to Aloxe-Corton and

Ladoix, which are in the northern outskirts of Beaune. Côte de Nuits is famed above all for its red wines, though many villages also produce outstanding whites. The village names are often hyphenated and include a vineyard name: Chambolle-Musigny, Gevrey-Chambertin, Morey-Saint-Denis, Vosne-Romanée, and others. They're world renowned, usually for good reason. The district is named for Nuits Saint Georges, the largest but not necessarily the most attractive town between Dijon and Beaune.

The Val de Saône extends from the bottomlands east of the main north-south RN 74 highway (on some maps marked D974) and A6 autoroute, to the banks of the slow-flowing Saône River, and beyond, east to the Jura. Tucked into these lowlands you'll find the Cîteaux Abbey.

Above the Côte de Nuits, behind Nuits Saint Georges, begin the Hautes-Côtes-de-Nuits, nearly always hyphenated. This is Burgundy's blackcurrant heartland, home to some of France's best distillers; the wines of this mountainous area are improving, in part thanks to global warming.

ARCENANT

This appealing village in the Hautes-Côtes is on the Raccordon, a creek; it has a landmark church, and prehistoric grottoes. Few drive here to visit them: Arcenant is the capital of Cassis. With so many vineyards around—plus forests and pasturelands—it takes courage to focus on blackcurrants and other fruit, and transform them into fruit-based liqueurs and eaux-de-vie. Though small, Arcenant boasts two rival distillers from the same family. To keep the peace, most connoisseurs agree they're equals with Cassis, and approach them alphabetically. **Gilles Joannet** (Rue Basse, Tel: 03 80 61 22 80, www.gillesjoannet.com, by appointment only, closed the second half of August) started a quarter century ago, and excels at fruit liqueurs, particularly heirloom vineyard peach liqueur. Reserve ahead to visit and taste (and designate a driver). Gilles also masters apricots, wild plums, melons, tomatoes, and beets, and has distinguished himself by being the first to make fresh milk liqueur. To call the result unusual is an understatement. **Jean-Baptiste Joannet** (Rue Amyntas Renevey, Tel: 03 80 61 12 23, liqueurs.joannetjb@wanadoo.fr, open weekdays without appointment) is now in the hands of (the late) Jean-Baptiste's daughter, Viviane Joannet. This branch started earlier, in 1978, makes the same or similar products from similar ingredients, but appear to have the edge when it comes to raspberries. In truth, both Joannets are outstanding; you'll be happy with the products of either.

Certified-organic winery **Domaine Aurélien Verdet** (Rue de la Combe, Naudron, Tel: 03 80 61 08 10, by appointment) is in outlying Naudron. The estate's best wines are true to type Aligoté, and Hautes-Côtes-de-Nuits red and white.

AUVILLARS-SUR-SAÔNE

L'Auberge de l'Abbaye (Tel: 03 80 26 97 37, auberge-abbaye@ wanadoo.fr, http://pagesperso-orange.fr/auberge-abbaye/, open daily for lunch, for dinner Thursday through Saturday, closed ten days in February and the last week in August, always reserve ahead; inexpensive to moderate) is a roadside restaurant on highway D996, near the junction with highway D201, south of Cîteaux Abbey. A shade tree stands out front, there's a bar in the entrance, and the dining room, with timbers and stone walls, is decorated like a Parisian neo-bistro. From the rear terrace for summer dining you won't see or hear passing traffic. Young, ambitious Jean-François Vachey and his wife Chrystel serve at most thirty guests per seating—they don't have staff. No groups are accepted. Insiders have cottoned on; reserve ahead to get a table. Don't be rushed. You'll eat updated classics from Burgundy, Jura, and Val de Saône, plus lightened French classics (terrines with fresh nuts and compotes, stuffed, roasted rabbit, deep-dish fruit tarts). The wine list is short, with a few good bottlings.

BROCHON

One compelling reason to stop on the busy main highway between Gevrey-Chambertin and Fixin is **Fromagerie Gaugry** (10 RN74, Tel: 03 80 34 00 00, www.gaugryfromager.com, closed Sunday and holidays). Founded in 1946 but wholly remodeled recently and turned into a glassed-in showcase, with tours and tastings (wine by request), this family-run cheese factory makes some of the best raw-milk Époisses, Soumaintrain, Ami du Chambertin, and Plaisir au Chablis anywhere, period. Also sold are other cheeses from further afield, and high-quality regional specialities. Gaugry's founder Raymond Gaugry invented Ami du Chambertin in 1950 at a time when Époisses was practically extinct. Both cheeses are gently brushed or "washed" with Marc de Bourgogne.

CHAMBOLLE-MUSIGNY

In 1999 Éric and Martine Claudel took over **Le Chambolle-Musigny** (28 Rue Basse, Tel: 03 80 62 86 26, www.restaurant-lechambolle.com, closed Wednesday and Thursday; from December to mid April closed Sunday at dinner; also closed the first half of July, moderate to expensive). This old village restaurant is a gourmet destination, with devoted local clients, including winemakers. Martine runs the restaurant, Éric cooks, updating, lightening, and reinventing regional food. You'll find delicious oeufs en meurette but also scrambled eggs with local Burgundy truffles, housemade duck foie gras terrine studded with sour cherries, snails baked in a parsley-filled savory tart, kidneys in mustard sauce, coq au vin, boeuf bourguignon, pike-perch sautéed and napped with (unnecessary but delicious) Époisses sauce, a wildly rich, thick, firm pure-chocolate tart, and luscious spoon sweets and fruit tarts. Everything is made in-house. The service is professional, but leisurely. The wine list boasts bottlings from the best (including Comte de Vogüé). Reserve ahead.

La Maison Vigneronne (1 Rue Traversière, Tel: 03 80 62 80 37, www.caveaudesmusignys.com, closed Monday, very inexpensive to moderate). In what might be the area's most physically charming village, affable chef Matthieu Mazoyera turns out traditional food, from pig's trotters or snails to beef oxtails, coq au vin and more, plus scatter-shot dishes for the tourist trade. Alas, the Flamingo-pink chairs, orange roller blinds and naïf mural do not stimulate the appetite. Downstairs, in the **Caveau des Musigny** (Tel: 03 80 62 84 01), you'll fine a handsome, vaulted cellar where the wines of 110 Côte de Nuits and Côte de Beaune wineries may be tasted and purchased, accompanied by a tasty, simple snack (reservation only, inexpensive). A good fallback in case Le Chambolle-Musigny is closed or fully booked.

If you're an overnight guest at hotel-winery **Château André Ziltener** (Rue de la Fontaine, Tel: 03 80 62 41 62, www.chateau -ziltener.com, info@chateau-ziltener.com, meals expensive, rooms extremely expensive), a luxurious boutique property, reserve ahead and ask your hosts to cater a Burgundian *table d'hôtes* meal. The wine list will include the winery's own labels, and bottlings stored in the cellars for other fine winemakers. Anyone can enjoy the vaulted cellar wine bar, where you can taste, accompanying your wines with simple, regional foods.

CÎTEAUX

The isolated **Monastère de Cîteaux** (Tel: 03 80 61 35 34, boutique closed Sunday morning and Monday), in the Val de Saône, is famous for its cow's-milk cheese. It belongs to the Benedictine Order. From Nuits Saint Georges drive fifteen miles east on highway D8. You'll see Montbeliard brown-and-white cows, a parking lot full of tour buses, and a landscaped pay-to-enter complex,

❖ OTHER WINERIES ❖
IN CHAMBOLLE-MUSIGNY

Domaine Amiot Servelle (34 Rue Basse, Tel: 03 80 62 80 39, www.amiot-servelle.com, domaine@ amiot-servelle.com). Note: this excellent winery is in the process of getting organic certification. *Best wines:* Chambolle-Musigny 1er Crus Les Charmes and Les Amoureuses, Chambolle-Musigny Village, Bourgogne AOC red.

Domaine Remy Boursot (7 Rue de la Fontaine, Tel: 03 80 62 80 82, www.remyboursot.com, open daily without appointment, closed Sunday afternoon). *Best wine:* Chambolle-Musigny Les Chatelots.

Domaine Digioia-Royer (Rue du Carré, Tel: 03 80 61 49 58, micheldigioia@wanadoo.fr, by appointment). *Best wine:* Chambolle-Musigny Les Fremières Vieilles Vignes.

Domaine Gilbert et Christine Felettig (Rue du Tilleul, Tel: 03 80 62 85 09, gaecfelettig@wanadoo. fr, open without appointment, closed Sunday). *Best wines:* Chambolle-Musigny 1er Crus Les Fuées.

....

as much a didactic museum as a place of worship. Few of the medieval buildings survived the French Revolution. Benedictine monks do not merely contemplate God; they work. Of the several dozen brothers resident, those able to do heavy physical work keep busy. Many are over eighty years old. The factory is closed to visitors; the boutique stocks the delicious, mild, fifty-percent fat Cîteaux cheese, each round weighing 700 to 800 grams. Also sold is Trappe de la Coudre, a smaller, similar cheese from the Mayenne in northwestern France. Spartan, as befits a monastery, the boutique nonetheless stocks many delicacies, including the abbey's own acacia honey, beeswax, gingerbread, biscuits, herbal liqueurs, Rocamandines (crisp cookies), jams, candied fruit, and more, all fashioned by the hands of churchmen and women.

CONCOEUR

You'll enjoy the drive on highways D109 and D25 through the scenic Hautes-Côtes, parcelled into berry and fruit orchards. Roll down your windows and sniff. When the scent of macerating fruit hits, you've arrived. **Fruirouge** (Tel: 03 80 62 36 25, www.fruirouge.fr, closed mornings on Tuesday and Wednesday) is among the area's makers of liqueurs from "red fruit"—raspberries, strawberries, redcurrant, cherries—but also blackcurrant, heirloom peaches, and others. Founded in the mid 1990s by Sylvain and Isabelle Olivier, Fruirouge now competes with top artisanal *liqueuristes* Joannet or Cartron. Unlike them, the Oliviers use their liqueurs to create innovative foods, from the sublime (blackcurrant-flavored butter and naturally sweet fruit jellies and jams) to the ridiculous (ketchup with Cassis). Take a tour and tasting (very inexpensive), and learn about blackcurrant and the monks of Cluny. This is the non–Las Vegas response to the glitzy Cassissium below, in Nuits Saint Georges.

COUCHEY

Between Marsannay and Fixin, Couchey is home to winery **François Brugère** (7 Rue Jean-Jaurès, Tel: 03 80 52 13 05, www.francoisbrugere.net, phone ahead), also a comfortable *chambres d'hôtes*. François Brugère is a traditionalist, making about 35,000 bottles a year of good-value, underrated red and white Marsannay. The winery is wrapped by the northernmost vineyards of the Côte de Nuits. For overnight guests, memorable breakfasts, with homemade everything, are served by Brugère and his wife Anne.

Also in Couchey, very good and accessible is **Daniel Fournier** (1 Rue Raymond Poincaré, Tel: 03 80 52 18 38, open daily without appointment). His best wine: Fixin AOC red.

Not usually open to the public, **Européenne de Condiments– Moutarderie Téméraire** (7 Rue Jean Moulin, Tel: 03 80 51 52 20, by appointment only) is just east of RN74, edging the ZA des Champy industrial park. This revival mustard factory has refloated a brand created in 1816; it now makes fifty different mustards.

ÉCHEVRONNE

In the Hautes-Côtes' blackcurrant country, behind Pernand-Vergelesses, off highway D18, find **Domaine Lucien Jacob** (Tel: 03 80 21 52 15, lucien-jacob@wanadoo.fr, open weekdays, on Saturday by appointment only, closed Sunday). Chantal Forey-Jacob and Jean-Michel Jacob continue the family tradition of transforming blackcurrants into Cassis. They also make excellent blackberry and raspberry liqueurs. You'll be warmly welcomed in the small boutique.

FIXIN

Between Couchey and Gevrey-Chambertin, Fixin (pronounced *Fissahn*) is the site of a sprawling park dedicated to Napoléon Bonaparte, and produces fine AOC Fixin and Côte-de-Nuits-Villages red wines. Of its two restaurants, one is in transition, with a new owner and chef since 2008: **Au Clos Napoléon** (4 Rue Perrière, Tel: 03 80 52 45 63, www.clos-napoleon.com, closed Sunday dinner and Monday, very inexpensive to moderate). After decades of honest, *terroir* cooking, with beef bourguignon, served in simple surroundings, the new team has redecorated, adding a summer terrace amid the vines, and is offering regional special-ties and the inevitable *gastronomique* hodgepodge—gambas with pesto, help! The wine list is long—for a reason: the wine store and tasting room next door are owned by the restaurant, **Caveau l'Imperial** (8 Rue Perrière, Tel: 03 80 52 45 63, caveaulimperial@ orange.fr, open daily). Stocked are around fifty Burgundies (many local, from independents), at a reasonable mark-up.

Many locals favor **Chez Jeannette** (7 Rue Noisot, Tel: 03 80 52 45 49, chezjeanneatte@orange.fr, closed dinner Sunday and Christmastide, inexpensive to very expensive). A simple, old-fashioned hotel-restaurant, known for its generous servings and prix fixe menus, here, too, the seafood with sauces and squab with exotic spices are gaining ground. Luckily, you can still get

❧ WINERIES IN FIXIN ❧
OPEN TO THE PUBLIC

Domaine Vincent et Denis Berthaut/Caveau Napoléon (9 and 18 Rue Noisot, Tel: 03 80 52 45 48, open daily without appointment, closed January). Note: this is a winery and shop. *Best wines:* Fixin 1er Cru Les Arvelets, Fixin AOC (both red).

Domaine Clos Saint Louis (4 Rue des Rosiers, Tel: 03 80 52 45 51, clos.st.louis@wanadoo.fr, open daily except Sunday without appointment, 9am to 7pm). *Best wine:* Fixin 1er Cru Hervelets (red).

Manoir de la Perrière • Joliet Père et Fils (Tel: 03 80 52 47 85, open daily without appointment). Note: Bénigne Joliet of the celebrated family of winemakers, here since 1853, is the oenologist, flanked by Philippe Charlopin of the equally famous family. *Best wines:* Fixin 1er Cru Clos de la Perrière Monopole (red), Fixin AOC Perrière (white).

Domaine Pierre Gelin (2 Rue du Chapitre, Tel: 03 80 52 45 24, gelin.pierre@wanadoo.fr, open daily except Sunday without appointment). *Best wine:* Fixin 1er Clos Napoléon.

....

Burgundian classics, choose from the cheese trolley, and enjoy housemade desserts (Cassis-flavored almond tuiles, caramelized pears and apples). The wine list is good; winegrowers are regulars.

FLAGEY-ECHEZEAUX

Joined at the hip to Vougeot, two miles north, this village may have a difficult name, but it's worth driving to for a *terroir* lunch or more elaborate *cuisine bourgeoise* at family-run **Chez Simon** (12 Place de l'Église, 03 80 62 88 10, famille.simon7@wanadoo. fr, closed dinner Sunday, Wednesday, ten days in early August, and Christmastide, moderate to very expensive). Winemakers come for the traditional décor and fresh, high-quality, seasonal ingredients, prepared by François Simon. Skip the scallop "carpaccio" and other nonsensical offerings. The fine wine list includes liqueurs from Cartron. The weekday lunch prix fixe is good value, and inexpensive.

GEVREY-CHAMBERTIN

Fabulous wines are the main reason to visit this celebrated village, whose hyphen points to the great Grand Cru vineyard, Chambertin, owned by winemaker Bertin (Champ de Bertin, shortened to Chambertin). The village's administrative area comprises nine Grand Crus and twenty-six 1er Crus, plus village and regional appellations. The village's handsome château is open to the public (**Château de Gevrey**, Tel: 03 80 34 36 77, open Friday through Sunday, or by appointment), of interest for its spiral staircase, thick walls, and history (the wine is fine).

Another reason is **Chez Guy & Family** (3 Place de la Mairie, Tel: 03 80 58 51 51, www.hotel-bourgogne.com, open daily, closed holidays, very inexpensive to expensive). Run by ambitious young chefs Eric Cherval and Yves Rebsamen, survivors of starred-restaurants, this is a surprisingly unpretentious, affordable restaurant. Though chic and packed with bobos, it has become a favorite among winemakers. The terrace at the village's crossroads is pleasant in good weather. The interior is more attractive: blond wood, contemporary art, wooden beams, and when cold, a crackling fire. Cherval and Rebsamen are confident enough to avoid over-sophisticated, vertical haute, and keep most dishes simple. Following the seasons, they update and lighten classics (with occasional flights of fancy). You'll find fricasséed snails with parsley butter and a judicious dose of garlic, Burgundy truffles sliced onto rustic toasts, housemade jambon persillé, beef cheeks in a winey bouguignon sauce, and other hearty dishes that somehow levitate. Wild game is available in season (venison with cranberry sauce and puréed Jerusalem artichokes); Atlantic fish or oysters lurk among the fussy *cuisine d'auteur* fish dishes. The desserts embrace fresh truffles, Italian pannacotta, roasted pineapple with raspberry sorbet, gingerbread ice cream, and creamy blackcurrant financiers. The wine list includes affordable bottles and Gevrey's top Crus, often impossible to find elsewhere.

La Rotisserie du Chambertin and **Le Bonbistrot** (Rue du Chambertin, Tel: 03 80 34 33 20, www.rotisserie-bonbistrot.com, closed Sunday dinner, Monday, Tuesday lunch, three weeks in February, and the first half of August, moderate to very expensive). On the village's south end, in a gated courtyard, this classic "two-fer" offers a pricey, ultra-traditional restaurant out front (regional and pan-French *cuisine bourgeoise* in style and comfort, with a mile-long wine list and prices to match); in back is **Le Bonbistrot**, a cozy bistro with good-value, though not cheap, regional food. There's a tin-topped bar, bentwood chairs, cheek-by-jowl wooden tables with check tablecloths and butcher paper, and a summer terrace. The menu ranges from "winegrower's salad" (with poached eggs en meurette) to duck pâté, garlicky snails, chicken fricassée with a winey coq-au-vin sauce, pike-perch quenelles, beef bourguignon, and rich desserts. The wine list is shorter, the service more casual. Either is a good choice.

On the main road to Beaune, a new *table d'hôtes* with regional food and wine tastings is **La Table de Pierre Bourée** (40 Route de Beaune, Tel: 03 80 34 13 97, www.pierre-bouree-fils.com, latabledepierrebouree@orange.fr, open 11am to 4pm Monday to Saturday, closed Sunday and from the third weekend in November to the third weekend in March, moderate, by reservation only). The wines come from the family's winery, **Pierre Bourée Fils** (same address, Tel: 03 80 34 30 25, by appointment when La Table is closed), with vineyards at Beaune, Gevrey-Chambertin, and Puligny-Montrachet. Affable Jean-Christophe Vallet is your host. A red napkin awaits atop your wooden table, wineglasses at the ready. The formula: a progression from gougères to jambon persillé, boeuf bourguignon to local cheeses, and a sobering cup of coffee. Menu options regard the number of wines served to accompany your fare: five (two whites, three reds; moderate), seven (three whites, four reds; expensive), or nine (three whites, six reds including a 1er and Grand Cru, very expensive). The

❧ OTHER WINERIES ❧
IN GEVREY-CHAMBERTIN OPEN TO
THE PUBLIC BY APPOINTMENT

Unless otherwise specified, these wineries' best wine is AOC Gevrey-Chambertin.

Camus Père et Fils (21 Rue du Marechal-de-Lattre-de-Tassigny, Tel: 03 80 34 30 64).

Dupont-Tisserandot (2 Place des Marronniers, Tel: 03 80 34 10 50, open weekdays without appointment; weekends by appointment only). *Best wine:* Gevrey-Chambertin Lavaux Saint-Jacques 1er Cru.

Mortet Thierry (16 Place des Marronniers, Tel: 03 80 51 85 07).

Gérard Quivy (7 Rue Gaston Roupnel, Tel: 03 80 34 31 02, open daily except Friday, by appointment only). *Best wine:* Gevrey-Chambertin Les Corbeaux 1er Cru.

Jane et Sylvain Raphanaud (9 Rue du Chêne, Tel: 03 80 34 16 83). Note: in the process of organic certification. *Best wines:* Bourgogne AOC red, Gevrey-Chambertin, Gevrey-Chambertin 1er Cru.

Domaine Henri Richard · Patrick Maroillier (75 Route de Beaune, Tel: 03 80 34 35 81). Note: certified organic since 2000. *Best wines:* Marsannay, Charmes Chambertin Grand Cru.

Rossignol-Trapet (4 Rue de la Petite-Issue, Tel: 03 80 51 87 26, www.rossignol-trapet.com). Note: in the process of organic certification. Wines typically sell out. *Best wines:* Gevrey-Chambertin 1er Crus aux Combottes and Les Corbeaux, Chapelle-Chambertin Grand Cru, Latricières-Chambertin Grand Cru, Chambertin, Morey Saint Denis.

Domaine Tortochot (12 Rue de l'Église, Tel: 03 80 34 30 68, www.tortochot.com). Note: remarkable Mazy-Chambertin Grand Cru, more affordable Gevrey-Chambertin Village Les Corvées.

wines include pleasant Bourgogne AOC white and red, Marsannay white, a meaty Gevrey-Chambertin 1er Cru Les Cazetiers, Beaune 1er Cru Les Epenottes, and Charmes Chambertin Grand Cru. Make sure to visit the eighteenth-century cellars.

Trapet Père & Fils (53 Route de Beaune, Tel: 03 80 34 30 40, www.domaine-trapet.com). Note: certified organic. *Best wines:* Gevrey-Chambertin, Chapelle-Chambertin, Latricières-Chambertin, Marsannay, Chambertin.

GILLY-LÈS-CÎTEAUX

Two reasons to drive east of the old north-south highway are **Fromagerie Delin** (Tel: 03 80 62 87 20, www.fromagerie-delin .com, open daily), makers of cow's milk Le Régal de Bourgogne cheeses (with everything imaginable on or in them, from herbs to raisins, pepper to mustard seed, truffle oil to cranberries), plus award-winning l'Eclat de Nuits (seasoned and aged with Aligoté), and classic Brillat-Savarin and L'Amour de Nuits. The drawback: they're from pasteurized milk.

Nearby is ultra-luxurious **Château de Gilly** (Tel: 03 80 62 89 98, www.chateau-gilly.com, inexpensive to astronomically expensive), with fancy pan-French food in baronial surroundings; surprisingly, the **Côté Terroirs** bistro, also on the property, serves a good, inexpensive *terroir* prix fixe lunch (closed Sunday).

MARSANNAY

Like Chablis, Marsannay is Burgundy's second self-styled "Golden Gateway"—La Porte d'Or. It has a suburban feel, just south of Dijon and Chenôve (site of the historic Pressoirs and Cuverie des Ducs wine presses and winery, Tel: 03 80 51 55 00, open daily afternoons only in summer, or by advance arrangement).

For the antithesis of *terroir*, but an amazing wine list: **Restaurant Les Gourmets** (8 Rue Puits de Têt, Tel: 03 80 52 16 32, www.les-gourmets.com, closed Monday and Tuesday, inexpensive to extremely expensive).

You can't miss **Château de Marsannay** (Tel: 03 80 51 71 11, www.chateau-marsannay.com, open daily March to November, closed Sunday the rest of the year). Like Château de Meursault, this winery is owned by the Boisseaux family, which also owns Kriter of Beaune, mega-makers of sparkling wines (and still wines, some excellent). The formula here and in Meursault is similar: guided visits, tastings, buffet lunches of regional food, and retail sales in a well-stocked boutique. Whereas whites are king in Meursault, reds are the specialty here. The best are Chambertin

Grand Cru Rouge and Ruchottes-Chambertin Grand Cru Rouge; the Clos-de-Vougeot holds great promise.

For subtle, underrated, low-priced Marsannay red wines redolent of violets, try **Domaine Bart** (23 Rue Moreau, Tel: 03 80 51 49 76, domaine.bart@wanadoo.fr, by appointment), a small, independent, hospitable winery. The best wine is from Les Grandes Vignes vineyard. Bart's Fixin 1er Cru Hervelets, also red, is exceptional, and the fruity Marsannay Les Favières white is uplifting.

For advice from a pair of seasoned winesellers: **La Cave Jacques François** (4 Route de Beaune, Tel: 03 80 52 06 02, www.cave-jacquesfrancois.com, closed Sunday). Hundreds of Burgundies and other bottlings fill this vast, big-box emporium run by Celine Pansiot, of the winegrowing family of Corgoloin.

MOREY-SAINT-DENIS

Many of the best wineries here sell out and are not accessible. That's what makes **Caveau des Vignerons** (Place de l'Église, Tel: 03 80 51 86 79, caveau-des-vignerons@wanadoo.fr, open daily) of interest. Most local winegrowers' bottlings—between 160 and 180—are available to taste and buy, from Village AOC to Grand Crus Clos des Lambrays and Clos de Tart. The mark-up is reasonable.

The third or fourth weekend of March, Morey hosts an annual regional foods festival in the municipal Salle des Fêtes (everything from cookies, candies, and cheese to great wines; phone the Caveau for info, since it's often difficult to raise anyone at town hall).

❧ WINERIES ❧
IN OR AROUND MOREY-SAINT-DENIS
OPEN TO THE PUBLIC

Domaine Pierre Amiot et Fils (27 Grande Rue, Tel: 03 80 34 34 28, domaine.amiot-pierre@wanadoo.fr, by appointment). *Best wine:* Clos-Saint-Denis Grand Cru.

Domaine Arlaud (41 Rue d'Epernay, Tel: 03 80 34 32 65, by appointment only). *Best wine:* Clos-Saint-Denis and Clos-de-la-Roche Grand Crus.

Domaine Castagnier (20 Rue des Jardins, Tel: 03 80 34 31 62, by appointment only). *Best wine:* Clos-Saint-Denis Grand Cru.

Domaine Robert Gibourg (RN74, Tel: 03 80 34 38 32, rgibourg@club-internet.fr, by appointment). Note: Gibourg's Corton vineyards are over sixty years old. *Best wines:* Corton Grand Cru Renardes and Ladoix Les Toppes Coiffées (both red).

Domaine des Lambrays (31 Rue Basse, Tel: 03 80 51 84 33, clos.lambrays@wanadoo.fr, open daily without appointment). Note: this prestigious winery owns almost the entire Clos des Lambrays vineyard, and produces between 20,000 and 25,000 bottles per year. Their best and only wine is Clos des Lambrays and it is extremely expensive.

Domaine Jean-Paul Magnien (5 Ruelle de l'Église, Tel: 03 80 51 83 10, www.domainemagnien.com, open daily except Sunday without appointment). *Best wine:* Clos-Saint-Denis Grand Cru.

Domaine Louis Remy (1 Place du Monument, Tel: 03 80 34 32 59, domaine.louis.remy@wanadoo.fr, by appointment). *Best wine:* Clos-de-la-Roche Grand Cru.

Domaine Taupenot-Merme (33 Route des Grands Crus, Tel: 03 80 34 35 24, domaine.taupenot-merme@wanadoo.fr, by appointment). Note: this seventh-generation winery has adopted organic grape growing. *Best wines:* Morey-Saint-Denis 1er Cru La Riotte.

. . . .

NUITS SAINT GEORGES

Improved of late by traffic limitations, Nuits Saint Georges is no longer the homely sister to Beaune, with a neglected Hôspices and dusty shops. It's a lively, authentic winemaking town. For better or worse, it's also a major stop on the Burgundy Wine Route and mass tourism circuit. The main square is well proportioned, overlooked by a Baroque belfry whose carillon plays on the hour. The tables of interchangeable eateries spread across it. Other archetypal *pièges à touristes* dot surrounding streets. Skip them. The best updated regional food is served on the busy RN74 artery on the south end of town, in the cellar restaurant **L'Alambic** (Rue du Générale de Gaulle, Tel: 03 80 61 35 00, www.lalambic.com, closed Sunday dinner and Monday lunch, inexpensive to expensive). If you enjoyed the costumes and knights-of-the-round-table atmosphere at Clos Vougeot, you'll love L'Alambic, named for the century-old copper still in the dining room. *Terroir* is the strongest suit, from the oeufs en meurette and jambon persillé, to the stews of veal, sweetbreads, and Charolais. Chef Christophe Dumay sometimes strays onto uncertain ground. Don't follow. The desserts are rich, the wine list 500 bottles long, the service professional. Cartron liqueurs are served.

Another serious upscale restaurant, on the main pedestrian street, is trendy **La Cabotte** (24 Grande Rue, Tel: 03 80 61 20 77, lacabotte@wanadoo.fr, closed Saturday and Monday at lunch, Sunday all day, and the first week in January, moderate to expensive). Brash Thomas Protot, trained by multiple-star chefs, regularly reinvents his *cuisine d'auteur*, which ranges from the sublime to the nonsensical. Traditionalists beware.

Excellent pastries, outstanding chocolates and twenty-five delicious seasonal flavors of ice cream are the specialty of long-established **Olivier Bourau** (28 Grande Rue, Tel: 03 80 61 04 44, closed Sunday afternoon, Monday, and two weeks end of August), in the center of town. The shop is compact, with a few tables squeezed in. In summer, sit under a parasol on Place Monge and enjoy good coffee or tea, and sublime sweets.

The best picnic supplies in town, including outstanding chicken liver terrine forestière with wild mushrooms, and other earthy, regional specialties, come from outwardly unimpressive **Charcuterie Vié** (7 Rue Paul Cabet, Tel: 03 80 61 05 18, closed Sunday, Monday afternoon, and August), on the narrow road running uphill toward the church.

❧ WINERIES ❧
IN OR AROUND NUITS SAINT GEORGES OPEN TO THE PUBLIC

Unless otherwise specified, these wineries' best wine is Nuits Saint Georges.

Barbier et Fils and **Dufouleur Père & Fils** (17 Rue Thurot, Tel: 03 80 61 10 65, open daily 9am to 7pm without appointment). Note: Barbier, a twenty-five-acre estate, is now owned by major winemakers Antonin Rodet and Dufouleur Père et Fils. The wines are polished, the winery open to visitors. *Best wines:* Gevrey-Chambertin Les Murots, Nuits Saint Georges Belle Croix (Sous les Pruliers).

Jean-Pierre Bony (5 Rue de Vosne, Tel: 03 80 61 16 02, fabiennebony@wanadoo.fr, open weekdays without appointment, closed weekends).

Philippe Gavignet (36 Rue Docteur Louis Legrand, Tel: 03 80 61 09 41, www.domaine-gavignet.fr, open weekdays without appointment, weekends by appointment). *Best wines:* Nuits Saint Georges 1er Cru Les Bousselots, and Les Argillas (village).

Alain Michelot (6 Rue Camille Rodier, Tel: 03 80 61 14 46, by appointment only). Note: this is a fine independent winery. Good-value wines, warm welcome to serious wine lovers. *Best wine:* Nuits Saint Georges 1er Cru Les Cailles.

Domaine T. Liger Belair (32 Rue Thurot, Tel: 03 80 61 51 16, www.domaine-liger-belair.com, by appointment only). Note: this winery is in the process of organic certification.

Domaine Prieuré-Roch (22 Rue du Général de Gaulle, Tel: 03 80 62 00 00, by appointment). Note: certified organic.

Henri et Gilles Remoriquet (25 Rue de Charmois, Tel: 03 80 61 24 84, domaine.remoriquet@wanadoo. fr, open daily without appointment).

Thomas-Moillard (Chemin Rural 59, Tel: 03 80 62 42 22, nuicave@wanadoo.fr, open daily 10am to 6pm, closed January or February).

....

Distillers

....

Nuits Saint Georges and nearby villages are known for their distilleries. Among top traditional makers of Cassis, Vieille Prune, Poire Williams, Marc de Bourgogne, and dozens of eaux-de-vie and fruit-, herb-, or nut-based liqueurs is **Joseph Cartron** (25 Rue du Docteur Louis Legrand, Tel: 03 80 62 00 90, www .cartron.fr, open daily, telephone ahead of time if possible). The distillery is about 150 yards east of highway D974. Medium-sized, Cartron uses both old oak vats and stainless steel, centuries-old techniques and cutting-edge technology, to produce about 1.5 million bottles per year. The company was founded in 1882 by Joseph Cartron and is run by fourth-generation Xavier Cartron. Mild-mannered yet passionate, Cartron was born here and will hand over one day to his daughter Judith. Cartron does not advertise or solicit visits, selling direct to wine or gourmet food boutiques and restaurants. However, if you're a serious liqueur-lover, and phone ahead to request a tasting and visit, Xavier will happily show you the facility, and atmospheric, vaulted cellars. If you know to ask, he'll also take you into the loft of the oldest building, purposely un-insulated, so that temperatures inside top 100°F in summer and below zero in winter, with marked differences in the course of each day. This is where straw- or wicker-wrapped demijohns repose, filled with decades-old Poire Williams. It's the "thermal shock" that gives this pear eau de vie its complexity. Don't miss the classic Double Crème de Cassis, or wild raspberry liqueur. If you enjoy exotic flavors, try the watermelon, vanilla, kiwi, banana, or pineapple. A wonderful experience.

If blackcurrants were grown in Disneyland you might not be surprised to see the postmodern **Le Cassissium** (Avenue du Jura, Impasse des Frères Montgolfier, Tel: 03 80 62 49 70, www .cassissium.com, open daily from April 1 to November 19, closed Sunday and Monday the rest of the year). In Burgundy, where tourism used to be quiet and high end, Le Cassissium shocks. On the east side of the train station, accessible via an overpass, by car or, more likely, tour bus, this is the corporate showcase of award-winning, mega blackcurrant distiller Pagès-Védrenne. A **Boutique Védrenne** (Rue Fagon, Tel: 03 80 61 15 55, www .vedrenne.fr, closed Sunday and Monday) is in the center of town, with others in Beaune and Dijon. You'll learn more than you ever wanted to know about these berries, how to recognize a good one and pick it, how to taste Cassis, mix it into white wine to make a

Kir, and more. There's a multimedia show, a step-by-step on how Cassis is made, a tasting bar and boutique with regional products (Anis de Flavigny, Fallot mustards, Rose de Vergy and other gingerbreads, jams, babas au rhum, even olive oil). In case you missed a beat, try turning your headphone dial. Scripts are in six languages. *In unserer Boutique finden Sie Souvenirs . . .*

If you're still standing, nearby, on the same road, find the even glitzier **Imaginarium, la Magie des Bulles**, www.imaginarium -bourgogne.com, the same formula applied to Louis Bouillot's sparkling wine—part of the Jean-Claude Boisset wine empire.

PREMEAUX-PRISSEY

One of this prestigious area's most prestigious winegrowing villages, Premeaux-Prissey is home to **Domaine de la Vougeraie** (Rue de l'Église, Tel: 03 80 62 48 25, www.domainedelavougeraie .com, by appointment and only for serious buyers). Certified organic, this winery is the peacock-feather in the cap of multifarious winemaker-merchant Jean-Claude Boisset. Note: it's difficult to find Domaine de la Vougeraie wines in stock, and casual visits are discouraged. *Best wines:* Gevrey-Chambertin 1er Cru Bel-Air, Charmes-Chambertin Les Mazoyères Grand Cru, Gevrey-Chambertin Village La Justice.

The same caveat applies to **Domaine des Perdrix** (Rue des Écoles, Tel: 03 85 98 06 62, www.domainedesperdrix.com, contact@domainedesperdrix.com, by appointment only and only for serious buyers). Owned by the Devillard family, based in Mercurey, this estate consistently wins awards for its Nuits Saint Georges villages and Nuits Saint Georges 1er Cru Aux Perdrix.

Château de Premeaux (Rue de la Courtavaux, Tel: 03 80 62 30 64, chateau.depremeaux@wanadoo.fr, by appointment only) is more approachable. The estate's best wines, made by Alain Pelletier, are true to type Aligoté, and Hautes-Côtes-de-Nuits red and white.

SAINT-NICOLAS-LÈS-CÎTEAUX

Rusticity rhymes with authenticity: local farmers, hunters, and winemakers drive to this hamlet to eat hearty meals at **Café-Restaurant Le Vieux Relais** (Tel: 03 80 62 12 29, open for lunch daily, for dinner on Wednesday night by reservation only, very inexpensive). A stag's head trophy adorns the wall of the dining room. Count the points: there are fourteen. From the pleasant outdoor terrace you'll view the local church. Lunch is a *repas* *ouvrier*—blue-collar special—consisting of all-you-can-eat cold cuts, hams and shaved carrots or creamy mayo salad, a daily special (blanquette de veau, beef bourguignon, roast chicken), cheese, dessert, a quarter liter of wine, and coffee. On Wednesday evening, reserve ahead and enjoy wild game (in season), or Burgundian classics. This is the only café for miles around, a place to stop for coffee, beverages, and the facilities.

VILLARS-FONTAINE

Mountainous at 1,300 feet, the local vineyards declined from cooling trends, from the fifteenth century until recently, when winemakers noticed grapes thriving again. They're producing better than decent wines now, ironically, thanks to global warming. Don't ask the tourism office or the well scrubbed where to eat; ask a winemaker, distiller, or farmer. They'll steer you to cheap-and-cheery **Auberge du Côteau** (Route de Côte-de-Nuits, Tel: 03 80 61 10 50, closed Monday, Tuesday, and from December 23 to January 23, very inexpensive to moderate), three miles west of Nuits Saint Georges, edging the Hautes-Côtes. It has an outdoor terrace and a cozy dining room where you'll enjoy grilled steaks, stews, and affordable bottles of local wine.

In the same neighborhood is **Domaine Patrick Hudelot** (Route de Segrois, www.domaine-patrick-hudelot.com, open daily, phone ahead before showing up), a forty-five-acre estate. Formerly a subsistence farm, in the family since 1960, Patrick took over in 1982, improved the quality, and adopted organic methods. The grapes are hand-picked and selected. Expect red fruit in the reds, and minerals, flint, and toasted almonds in the Chardonnay whites (he also makes typical Aligoté). These wines spend up to fourteen months on oak, a portion of it new, most of it not.

Haute-Côtes pioneer Bernard Hudelot, a professor of oenology at Dijon University, has a grander estate, including a luxurious B&B, and specializes in old vintages (from 1987 forward), at handsome, peaked-roof **Château de Villars-Fontaine** (Tel: 03 80 62 31 94, www.chateaudevillarsfontaine.fr, tastings and retail sales from Monday to Saturday without appointment, on Sundays and holidays by appointment only). This Hudelot makes wines to keep—his hobby horse. Some are oaked eighteen months. The best is an Hautes-Côtes-de-Nuits Blanc Le Rouard, which might be mistaken for a fatso from lower slopes, were it not for the lemon zest typical of high-altitude wines.

VOSNE-ROMANÉE

Anyone who has tilted at Domaine de la Romanée Conti knows the difficulty involved in approaching some Vosne-Romanée wineries. Take heart: accessible and enthusiastic, and available on her estate, the award-winning winemaker Anne Gros of Domaine Anne Gros runs a contemporary-design B&B, **Maison d'Hôtes La Colombière** (11 Rue des Communes, Tel: 03 80 61 07 95, www .maison-lacolombiere.com, domaine.annegros@orange.fr, by reservation only). She quietly reserves bottles to sell to overnighters. The scion of a winemaking clan, in 1995 she took over the seventeen-acre property from her father François. Her holdings are scattered (and include new vineyards in Provence). Anne enjoys sharing her expertise, especially with her B&B guests, for whom she also arranges vineyard visits and guided tastings (expensive). However, she routinely runs out of stock. Gros's best include Clos-de-Vougeot Rouge Le Grand Mauperthui, Vosne-Romanée Richebourg Grand Cru Rouge, Vosne-Romanée Villages Les Barreaux, and an affordable (unfindable) Bourgogne Rouge.

At **Domaine Armelle et Bertrand Rion** (8 RN74, Tel: 03 80 61 05 31, www.domainerion.fr, armelle@domainerion.fr, by appointment) you might scent truffles in late fall and winter. That's not overripe wine: affable Armelle and Bertrand are also truffle-growers. By reservation (and for a fee), they'll take you truffle-hunting, and teach you about Burgundy's earthy, nutty, sweet *tuber uncinatum*. They're also highly respected vintners: the winery dates to 1880. The simple, affordable red Bourgogne AOC is remarkably good; the Vosne-Romanée 1er Cru Les Chaumes and Clos-de-Vougeot Grand Cru Vieilles Vignes are excellent.

Eating in Vosne-Romanée means **La Toute Petite Auberge** (RN74, Tel: 03 80 61 02 03, closed Tuesday dinner and Wednesday, and two weeks in February, very inexpensive to very expensive). Recently remodeled, this roadside eatery is bigger and classier than it looks, with picture windows and a garden out back. The chef, Franck Boyer, is increasingly slipping from solid *terroir* into the realm of creative cuisine. Stick to the classics and you'll be fine. The wine list is long. In summer, reserve a table on the terrace.

VOUGEOT

With the exception of Vosne-Romanée, no other Burgundian winegrowing name is better known. In truth, it's Clos-de-Vougeot, the 125-acre vineyard and château, that are the stars: the

✦ OTHER WINERIES ✦
IN VOSNE-ROMANÉE

Domaine Bruno Clavelier (6 RN74, Tel: 03 80
61 10 81, by appointment). Note: this winery is
certified organic. *Best wines:* Vosne-Romanée Village
and 1er Cru, Corton Grand Cru.

Domaine Lalou Bize-Leroy (15 Rue de la Fontaine,
Tel: 03 80 21 21 10, by appointment only, better if
made by someone intimate with Bize-Leroy). Note:
Bize-Leroy was long affiliated with Domaine de
la Romanée-Conti, which her family owned. She
now runs her own winegrowing and *négociant*
business. The winery is certified organic and uses
biodynamic techniques. Bize-Leroy makes many
wines, many of them exceptional (most astronomically expensive). They routinely sell out, from the
Aligoté and Bourgogne AOC red and white on up;
the domaine is not easily accessible. *Best wines:*
Nuits Saint Georges, Chambolle-Musigny Les
Fremières, Romanée Saint Vivant, Richebourg.

Domaine Cécile Tremblay (1 Rue de la Fontaine,
Tel: 03 80 21 46 75, domainetremblay@yahoo.fr, by
appointment). Note: this winery is getting organic
certification.

....

unremarkable village is strung along the main highway, and has 200 inhabitants. **Château du Clos de Vougeot** (Tel: 03 80 62 86 09, www.tastevin-bourgogne.com, open daily for visits, closed Christmas Eve, Christmas and New Year's Eve) is too celebrated to need introducing. The Renaissance château atop medieval foundations has been headquarters of the Chevaliers du Tastevin since 1944. You've seen the square towers, gabled roof and yawning twelfth-century cellars (and antique wine presses) in every postcard or tour brochure extolling Burgundy's must-sees. It's difficult to avoid being gimlet-eyed. Yet the château is authentic, handsome, and set among some of the most prized vineyards anywhere. The Chevaliers du Tastevin (the "s" is silent) may be excused for wearing four-cornered hats, gold and scarlet robes, and carrying silver tasting cups. Beyond the marketing and PR value at their origins (they banded together in 1934 to promote flagging sales of Burgundy), they are bona fide professionals. Their job is to rate the region's wines twice yearly; only a third of bottlings submitted get the stamp of approval. Scores of winegrowers—currently seventy—own tiny parcels in the Clos-de-Vougeot vineyard, all of it Grand Cru; the quality of their wines depends on their skill, but is generally very high. Note: the château does not sell wines or do tastings.

Don't overlook the village's more affordable but often excellent 1er Cru (four of them) and Villages AOCs. Though a red-wine area, the white wines can be remarkable (particularly Vougeot 1er Cru Clos Blanc).

Domaine Bertagna (Rue du Vieux Château, Tel: 03 80 62 86 04, www.domainebertagna.com, open daily without appointment except Sunday and January). No longer up-and-coming, Bertagna has arrived, yet remains friendly and accessible. The bottlings are still good value. *Best wines:* Nuits Saint Georges 1er Cru Les Murgers (red) and Vougeot 1er Cru Les Cras (white).

Surprisingly, **Domaine du Château de la Tour** (Clos de Vougeot, Tel: 03 80 62 86 13, open daily except Tuesday without appointment, closed from December to March), a nineteenth-century château, is open to visitors. You might not be able to buy the wine of your dreams, either because it has sold out, or is breathtakingly expensive—typically over $100 for a fresh bottle—but you can nose the air and admire the cellars. The best: Clos-de-Vougeot Grand Cru.

BEAUNE and CÔTE-DE-BEAUNE, HAUTES-CÔTES-DE-BEAUNE

Includes: Aloxe-Corton, Auxey-Duresses, Beaune,
Bouze-lès-Beaune, Change, Chassagne-Montrachet,
Chorey-lès-Beaune, Corgoloin, Corpeau, Dezize-les-Maranges,
Ladoix-Serrigny, Meursault, Monthelie,
Nantoux, Nolay, Pommard, Puligny-Montrachet, Saint-Aubin,
Saint-Romain, Saint-Sernin-du-Plain, Santenay,
Savigny-lès-Beaune, Volnay

HANDSOME, PROSPEROUS AND PROUD, BEAUNE IS THE WORLD-RENOWNED WINE CAPITAL OF Burgundy, a major tourism destination with a high concentration of food- and wine-related properties. It has ancient Gallic and Roman roots—the Roman name was Belenos—but what you sense more than anything as you amble amid its scores of button-bright boutiques, luxury hotels, wine shops, wine bars, restaurants, museums, and landmark townhouses, are the concentric rings of medieval streets, alleys, and ramparts. Remarkable churches and monuments crop up at every turn of the twisting, sometimes cobbled road. At night, with spotlighting, few towns could be more spectacular. Beaune is also the liveliest small city in the region. With 22,000 year-round inhabitants, the population doubles or triples much of the year thanks to out-of-towners. The crowding, and the smugness of some locals, can impart an artificial, Disneyland feel, not helped by the sleek "Visiotrain," which conveys tired visitors from place to place, sounding its merry horn.

Detractors—there are many—speak of "Beaunification" when pointing to plastified, big-money tourism, or the Bourgeois Bohemianism behind the term bobo. Luckily, authenticity lurks below Beaune's glitzy surface. It was the medieval capital of Burgundy (which eventually drew together into a powerful duchy) before Dijon became supreme in the 1300s. Though smaller nowadays than other, less glamorous cities in the region, it has remained the heartland for winegrowing. Beaune itself is a base for many fine wineries.

The surrounding Côte de Beaune and Hautes-Côtes-de-Beaune reach from Aloxe-Corton north of town south to Santenay, and from the Bresse Bourguignonne in the east to Le Morvan. With the Côte de Nuits, this is Burgundy's prime vineyard area.

ALOXE-CORTON

Four miles north of Beaune and with highly sought-after wine-growing parcels, Aloxe-Corton is celebrated for Corton-Charlemagne Grand Cru whites, and Bressands, Vergennes, Renardes, Clos du Roy, Les Languettes and other Grand Cru reds—the only red Grand Cru of the Côte de Beaune. Another curiosity: no other Burgundy AOC has more Grand Cru acreage. Vineyards are tiny, however, typically between half an acre and three acres, the yields low, the prices high, and therefore the ability of winegrowers to share with casual visitors limited. That is one reason to enjoy a luncheon at **Domaine Comte Senard** (Les Meix, Tel: 03 80 26 41 65, www.domainesenard.com, table@domainesenard.com, open from March to December, closed Sunday and Monday, moderate to expensive, by reservation only). Hearty, traditional food accompanies wine tastings. Don't expect culinary fireworks. The family's history is glorious. They are Chevaliers du Tastevin, among them a Grand Master. Current scion Philippe Senard's excellent Corton Grand Cru Blanc is grown on the estate's one-acre Clos dex Meix, producing about 1,300 bottles—far too little to satisfy thirsty clients. Comte Senard also makes a fine Bressandes Rouge and other, more accessible Villages and 1er Crus: Beaune, Chorey-lès-Beaune, Corton, Pernand-Vergelesses, and Savigny-lès-Beaune. The *table d'hôtes* and tastings are in an attractive, pink building from the 1800s set among the vines. Tastings and guided tours of the estate and twelfth-century cellars are by reservation. (Note: the winery's offices are in Beaune: 7 Rempart Saint Jean, Tel: 03 80 24 21 65).

Maison Pierre André–Château de Corton André (Rue des Corton, Tel: 03 80 26 44 25, www.pierre-andre.com, open daily, closed Christmas and New Year's Day). In the village proper, with a glistening tile roof, you can't miss this château, one of the few wineries open without an appointment. The Liogier d'Ardhuy family still owns some vineyards here, but the company's *négociant* and other activities were ceded to the Ballande group. There are summertime classical concerts on the property. Top wines: Corton-Charlemagne Grand Cru, Aloxe-Corton Les Paulands 1er Cru, Nuits Saint Georges Cru Communale, Pommard 1er Cru Rouge Les Arvelets, Savigny-lès-Beaune Clos des Guettottes Rouge.

Follow signs to **Domaine Maurice Chapuis** (3 Rue Boulmeau, Tel: 03 80 26 40 99, www.domainechapuis.com, open mornings only, preferably by appointment). Family-run for the last 160 years, the current head of the clan is Maurice, flanked by wife Anne-Marie; they took over in 1995, and have made the property more accessible. With twenty-seven acres, the estate turns out various AOC wines; the best are Chorey-lès-Beaunes and Corton-Charlemagnes. Chapuis is also a *négociant*.

Domaine Didier Meuneveaux (9 Jardin des Brunettes, Tel: 03 80 26 42 33, by appointment), fair-sized, independent, and highly regarded, makes fine wines from nine AOCs. The best: brawny red Aloxe-Corton 1er Cru, Corton Grand Cru Rouge Bressandes, Grand Cru Chaumes, and Perrières. Not for casual visitors or bargain hunters.

AUXEY-DURESSES

On the lower Côte de Beaune, Auxey-Duresses is not a culinary desert. At the main crossroads, **La Crémaillère** (Route de Beaune, Tel: 03 80 21 64 48, closed Tuesday and Wednesday, inexpensive to moderate) is a typical auberge. Authentic if unexciting, it does the right things, from the hearty, housemade terrines to the boeuf bourguignon, with accommodating service, and a local clientele. On one side is the café, on the other the spartan dining room; the terrace is open in good weather. The restaurant belongs to the many-branched family of Domaine Michel Prunier & Fille, a fine winery, across the way. This doesn't mean other winemakers are not on the *carte des vins*. Bottlings from most of the best are available.

✢ WINERIES ✢
IN AUXEY-DURESSES

These wineries' best wine is AOC Auxey-Duresses.

Domaine Château de Melin (Melin, Tel: 03 80 21 21 19, www.chateaudemelin.com), also a dreamy, luxury B&B.

Domaine de Mac Mahon Véronique (Rue du Dessous, Tel: 03 80 24 63 14)

Domaine Labry André et Bernard (Melin, Tel: 03 80 21 21 60)

Domaine Lafouge Jean et Gilles (Rue du Dessous, Tel: 03 80 21 68 17)

Domaine Piguet-Chouet Max et Anne-Marye (Route de Beaune, Tel: 03 80 21 25 78)

Domaine Prunier Jean Pierre and Laurent (Rue Traversière, Tel: 03 80 21 27 51)

Domaine Prunier Michel et Fille (Route de Beaune, Tel: 03 80 21 21 05)

Domaine Prunier-Damy Philippe (Rue du Pont Boillot, Tel: 03 80 21 60 38)

Domaine Vecten Pascal et Clotilde (Chemin sous la velle, Tel: 03 80 21 67 99)

....

BEAUNE

Of the estimated 150 restaurants in and around town, scores of hotels, B&Bs, cafés, and wine bars, some are excellent, a few are outstanding. This is not an exhaustive list. Eating places, and gourmet food and wine shops, stand shoulder-to-shoulder throughout the city center and are thickest on the main square, Place Carnot. They encircle the Hôtel-Dieu, also known as **Hôspices de Beaune** (Tel: 03 80 24 45 00, open daily year-round). This is where the annual November gala charity wine auction takes place; the benefits go to running the hospice, which is no longer a general hospital but rather a museum, geriatric hospital and retirement home. Magnificent is not too strong to describe the art collection, or the former hospital dormitory (Grand' Salle) and the courtyard inside the half-timbered Renaissance complex, topped by colorful Burgundian tiles.

At the Hôspices and other attractions, much of the year you will wait in line, and be entertained by street-corner minstrels. Worth the musical interlude is Beaune's **Musée du Vin/Burgundy Wine Museum** (Rue du Paradis, Tel: 03 80 22 08 19, closed Tuesday from December to March), if for no other reason than to see the architecture, and where the Dukes of Burgundy lived. An attentive visitor will learn much about wine, and see many, many displays of antique bottles, glasses, tools, pitchers and carafes, plates and so forth, plus several pieces of remarkable, wine-related religious art (the Virgin Mary with grapes, for instance).

It's hard to know whether to consider some of Beaune's huge wine shops museums, theme-parks of oenology, or retail sales operations. Dozens of them means you can get lost searching for the right landmark cellar in which to open your wallet. (For smaller winesellers, some independent, see Wine shops and wineries). Of the various only-in-Beaune, medieval extravaganzas, several are owned by or associated with giant **Caves Patriarche Père & Fis** (5–7 Rue du Collège, Tel: 03 80 24 54 78, open daily). This winery claims to have millions of bottles in its three-mile long cellars; a visitor must wonder who does the inventory, and how often. Should you actually hike through this labyrinth, or explore parts of cellars open to the general public, you will be thirsty at journey's end. A dozen Burgundy wines await you in the subterranean medieval tasting room.

Probably the most rewarding medieval cellar, though still extravagantly touristy, is **Caves des Cordeliers** (6 Rue de l'Hôtel-

Dieu, Tel: 03 80 25 08 21, closed Wednesday and Thursday, Christmas, and three weeks in January). It's in the thirteenth-century convent of the same name, facing the Hôspices, down the road from (but still within the proprietorial orbit of) Patriarche. The methodology is similar. Here, if you buy an etched wineglass, you may taste five wines free of charge. If that kind of incentive appeals to you, read on, because another, comparable cellar awaits. Attached to the Cave des Cordeliers, and eerily familiar, also affiliated with Patriarche, is **Marché aux Vins** (2 Rue Nicolas Rolin, Tel: 03 80 25 08 20, www.marcheauxvins.com, open daily). This emporium is in the same underground maze of church cellars and chapels, in parts not covered by the properties described above. Here you experience a guided tasting of fifteen Burgundy Crus, and admire an encyclopedic collection of Hôspices wines from decades past.

Not in the bull's-eye but rather on the wide boulevard outside the ramparts, **Maison Bouchard Ainé et Fils** (4 Boulevard Maréchal Foch, Hôtel du Conseiller du Roy, Tel: 03 80 24 06 66) is another major winery offering an entry-level, low-priced wine discovery tour and tastings, in a handsome townhouse whose cellars, alas, are merely from the 1700s. The distinguishing factor here lies in methodology; "initiations" take you by the palate through the five senses (smell, hearing, touch, taste, sight). Irreverent pupils might realize that when it comes to wine, it's the sixth sense that counts. Naturally, a retail boutique awaits you (and may be patronized tour or not). Note: do not confuse Bouchard Ainé et Fils with the other Bouchards in Burgundy, including Beaune's top-flight Bouchard Père et Fis, only open by appointment to wine professionals, or by special arrangement.

Maison Champy (5 Rue du Grenier à Sel, Tel: 03 80 25 09 99, www.champy.com, closed August and Christmastide through New Year's) is Burgundy's oldest house of *négociants*, founded in 1720, owned in recent decades by ambitious Pierre Meurgey, whose fortunes have improved since oenologist Dimitri Bazas began improving quality and taking the business upmarket and global. Some of the grapes, from forty-three acres scattered from Chablis south to the Côte Chalonnaise, are grown organically (without pesticides and herbicides). Though visitor-friendly, Champy isn't a tourist trap. The retail shop is open weekdays without appointment (weekends by appointment); you may also tour and taste. By arrangement, a wine-tasting lunch is now available, by reservation. Of Champy's wines, the biggest are its Chablis Grand Cru

Les Preuses (3,000 bottles annually, and sometimes superior to the Chablis Grand Cru Grenouilles, which Champy also makes); the Charmes-Chambertin Grand Cru Rouge and Gevrey-Chambertin Villages Vieilles Vignes, and Chambolle-Musigny Villages Rouge Les Bussières are outstanding. For thinner wallets, try affordable Bourgogne Blanc (less New World in style than Bourgogne Blanc Signature).

In Beaune, you can taste at wine shops, wineries, wine "museums," restaurants, and wine bars. The most professional way to learn to judge and appreciate wines by color, scent, and flavor is to take a course at **L'École des Vins de Bourgogne** (6 Rue du 16éme Chasseurs, Tel: 03 80 26 35 10, www.ecoledesvins -bourgogne.com, ecoledesvins@bivb.com). This well-equipped school with individual tasting booths for students is operated by the Bureau Inter-Professionnel des Vins de Bourgogne (BIVB), an industry association funded by winegrowers. On offer: twenty-two courses from two-hour to five-day wine-tasting, oenology, and wine master classes for professionals and enthusiasts. Customized courses are also available. The school organizes visits to wineries and vineyards.

Beaune's small Wednesday and big Saturday morning covered market and street market are on Place de la Halle fronting the Hôspices. The faux-medieval hall houses sellers of perishables, from fish and cheese to wine. Nearby streets can become chaotic on Saturdays in high season. Seek out beekeeper and honey-maker Julien Borlot of Aiserey; organic greengrocers Alain and Ghislaine Péchoux-Loubet; and bakery Le Pétrin Ribeiron from Dijon, whose specialty is a long, narrow, flat loaf with a thick crust.

Places to eat and drink

L'Auberge Bourguignonne (4 Place de la Madeleine, Tel: 03 80 22 23 53, www.auberge-bourguignonne.fr, closed last week in November to mid December, Christmastide, and Mondays except holiday Mondays, inexpensive to moderate). In southeast Beaune's Faubourg Madeleine neighborhood, this traditional, reliable Burgundian hotel-restaurant is a Beaune touchstone. Chef Jean-Pierre Autun uses fine *terroir* ingredients, respecting time-tested techniques. The setting is classic: two stone buildings joined together, with many-paned windows, a pleasant terrace and a comfortable dining room of the timbers-and-tiles variety. Expect to find perennials, from jambon persillé and oeufs en meurette, to snails in an earthy stew or in puff pastry, steaks, long-stewed beef, sweetbreads, grilled, roasted or stewed poultry and lamb, a cheese platter, fruit tarts and spoon sweets, a long wine list with affordable and big bottlings, and professional service. The clientele includes a fair proportion of out-of-towners, and bona fide Beaune bourgeois, rarely Bohemian.

Le Bénaton (25 Rue du Faubourg-Bretonnière, Tel: 03 80 22 00 26, www.lebenaton.com, closed Wednesday and Thursday from December through March, closed Wednesday and Thursday lunch and Saturday dinner the rest of the year, one week in July and one week in December, moderate to very expensive). A few shopfronts from the ramparts at Faubourg Bretonnière, this prototypical Michelin-starred restaurant is where Bruno Monnoir takes Burgundy truffles, Fallot mustard, snails, Bresse squab, calf's head and piquant gribiche sauce, salted codfish or, who knows why, giant prawns, and transforms them into novel, unexpected, impossible-to-classify, beautifully plated dishes. The rich chocolate cake bursts with blackcurrant sauce. The décor matches: old and new, with the inevitable Asiatic touch. The service is friendly and polished, the clientele regulars or well-heeled tourists. The wine list accents local bottlings, some with four-digit prices. Not *terroir* in the usual sense. The lunch prix fixe menu is good value.

Le Caveau des Arches (10 Boulevard Perpreuil, Tel: 03 80 22 10 37, closed Sunday, Monday, from late July to late August, and Chistmastide to mid January, inexpensive to expensive). Favored by locals keen to please professional out-of-towners, and upscale tourists, this good, reliable, and attractive restaurant occupies vaulted, brightly lit, white-painted cellars from the 1400s, edging the boulevard at Porte Saint-Jean. There are plank floors, modern bentwood chairs, and faux-candlestick lights atop each table. Dishes run the gamut of Burgundian and French classics, and are lighter and more professionally cooked, plated, and served than at many Beaune restaurants.

La Ciboulette (69 Rue de Lorraine, Tel: 03 80 24 70 72, closed Monday, Tuesday, three weeks in February and from early to late August, inexpensive to moderate). The name means "chive," and describes the color theme. Summery, with rattan chairs, it's in the otherwise challenging Porte Saint-Nicolas area, near the northern ramparts. Reserve several days ahead; La Ciboulette is often booked solid. The updated regional food by chef Laurent Mâle is made with local ingredients from good suppliers. He also does Atlantic or Mediterranean fish (seabass with fennel, for instance). The wine list is strong on Côte de Beaunes.

Le Comptoir des Tontons (22 Rue du Faubourg Madeleine, Tel: 03 80 24 19 64, closed Sunday, Monday, Christmas Eve to mid January, and the first seventeen days in August, very inexpensive to moderate). On the busy radial artery east of Porte Saint-Jean, this pintsized restaurant has a comic-book theme and décor, affable owner Richard Grocat's passion. Luckily, it doesn't carry over to the cooking. Wife Pépita, from southern climes, has mastered Burgundian cuisine, often with a piquant twist. On her weekly, affordable prix fixe menus, discover tiny tastes, including biscuit à l'Ami du Chambertin, snails in a herb boullion, Charolais boeuf bourguignon with puréed vegetables, winter-wheat mini tart topped with bleu de Bresse (from Ferme la Gauloise), and pear sorbet with blackcurrant syrup and gingerbread. The main menu items can be delicious (roasted veal shoulder with citrus-sage) or not (goat's-milk cheese mousse with anchovy). Most ingredients are organic, ditto many of the excellent wines. Organic specialty foods are also sold. This is probably Beaune's most idealistic venture. Expect to dine with right-thinking locals, organic winemakers, and stray tourists.

Le Conty (5 Rue Ziem, Tel: 03 80 22 63 94, closed Sunday, Monday, and from mid February to mid March, very inexpensive to expensive). In the bull's-eye and besieged by tourists, this restaurant with an animated outdoor terrace, semi-subterranean dining room, and a slightly less chaotic upper floor, is owned by Isabelle and Laurent Parra. There's a zinc-topped bar with a grapevine motif, and rustic-snazzy décor. Le Conty is a good fallback. You'll eat good Burgundian classics and updated variations on predictable themes, plus creative or Italianate dishes. The wine list includes 500 different bottlings, reasonably priced, some sold by the glass.

Le Jardin des Remparts (10 Rue de l'Hôtel-Dieu, Tel: 03 80 24 79 41, www.le-jardin-des-remparts.com, closed Sunday, Monday, and early December to mid January, moderate to very expensive). Beaune's luxury gourmet restaurant, in a 1930s townhouse with a garden and terrace facing the city walls, offers refined, complicated food that is loosely *terroir*-rooted. Michelin-starred Roland Chanliaud and wife Emmanuelle cater to out-of-towners and a business clientele. The son of a Burgundian butcher, Chanliaud's upbringing has clearly influenced his meat-based dishes. He still cooks pork jowls, but makes them with gingerbread and fennel, flavored with tea. The seabass also gets a dose of gingerbread. The cheese trolley is excellent, the

desserts elaborate. The wine list has about 450 bottlings, including the region's best. The lunch prix fixe is a bargain.

Loiseau des Vignes (31 Rue Malfoux, Tel: 03 80 22 12 06, www.bernard-loiseau.com, closed Sunday and Monday, moderate to extremely expensive). In the Hôtel du Cep, Beaune's luxury hotel, near the Hôspices, this chic Bernard Loiseau-spinoff is run by Loiseau's widow Dominique. His photo hangs from one wall; anyone who knew him might feel gooseflesh. The décor evokes a château—neo-bistro with Asiatic touches, if such can exist. There are backlit bottles on shelves, designer tableware, red-upholstered black-frame chairs and matching, glistening, red laquered walls. The studiously casual atmosphere and service are in keeping with other Loiseau properties. The menu includes Loiseau favorites, from the luscious pâté en croûte façon Alexandre Dumaine, to the oeufs en meurette and pike-perch quenelles. A few originals are available (seabass filet with shellfish and buttery fresh spinach).

The desserts (dark chocolate and candied orange peel, Grand Marnier soufflé) are rich and satisfying. The seasonal luncheon prix fixes are low-priced; the draw for most clients is the by-the-glass selection of up to seventy wines. They range from affordable Bouzeron or fabulous Montagny 1er Cru from Stéphane Aladame to giants costing over $50 per glass. Keep your eye on the right-hand column.

Ma Cuisine (Passage Sainte Hélène, Tel: 03 80 22 30 22, macuisine@wanadoo.fr, closed Saturday, Sunday, Wednesday, and August, inexpensive to expensive). Pierre Escoffier runs the small, simply decorated, cluttered but cozy dining room of this insider's restaurant, known for its 650-bottle wine list (primarily Burgundies). Fabienne, née Parra, is chef. Her childhood at luxurious Ermitage de Corton, run by her parents, shows. She takes fresh, seasonal ingredients sourced at markets or from local growers, and makes rustically delicious food, as solid as the wooden tables and chairs. The menu changes constantly; expect to find fresh salad with plump chicken livers, slabs of succulent pure-pork pâté; poultry in the style of coq au vin; whole squab or half a gamehen roasted in its own juices; beef or pork stews; fresh goat's-milk or cow's-milk cheese with cream, salt and pepper, or chives; Époisses aged with Marc de Bourgogne. For dessert: seasonal tarts—fig, apple, lemon—and spoon sweets (cream pot with hazelnut praline). Wind up with Illy espresso. Wines range from by-the-glass simplicity to the biggest, rarest, and best. To buy a bottle, follow Pierre: he retails next door at **Cave Sainte-Hélène**. Ma Cuisine is often closed (or fully booked). Don't give up. Reserve ahead. This is one of Beaune's best.

P'tit Paradis (25 Rue Paradis Tel: 03 80 24 91 00, closed Sunday, Monday, and two weeks each in March, August, and December, inexpensive to moderate). Compact and stylish, on Rue Paradis, facing the wine museum, P'tit Paradis in its way is paradisiacal. You can dine on a street-side terrace (no sidewalks, no traffic, either). The dining room is bright, with cream-colored walls, niches, timbers, and spiraling wrought iron wall sconces. A two-woman show, the ten tables inside and six out are served by waitress-manager Aurelie Desserprit. Talented young Vanessa Laudat (latterly at La Bouzerotte, in Bouze-lès-Beaune) makes the food from scratch. Inventive, generously served seasonal dishes, most rooted in *terroir*, include slabs of rabbit terrine with tarragon-flavored Fallot mustard; flavorful, tender, long-cooked pork jowl with cumin; thick Charolais steak with Époisses flanked by creamy potato gratin. Desserts: nougat glacé with red fruit; frothy grape nage with mild spices; Toblerone chocolate mousse with housemade hazelnut gianduja ice cream. On the list, a hundred bottlings, from Maison Alex Gambal, Bouchard Père et Fils, Matrot, Alain Gras, and Rapet. Liqueurs are from Cartron. This is among Beaune's best, most affordable, and least pretentious restaurants. Reserve ahead.

La Table du Vieux Vigneron (6 Rue du Faubourg Madeleine, Tel: 03 80 24 07 78, www.aubergeduvieuxvigneron.com, closed Sunday, Monday, early January, ten days in February, and two weeks in August, very inexpensive to moderate). On the busy axial road leading east from Porte Saint-Jean, this rustic-retro wine bistro is run by winemaking family Jean-Charles Fagot (of Corpeau). Reserve ahead; the auberge is often thronged. Set perilously close in the narrow dining room, the tables are painted black and topped with brown butcher paper. Wine barrel lids with stenciled names adorn walls, with wine racks overhead. Blackboard items range from solid to silly. *Escarboeuf* merges long-cooked beef jowl with snails, and is eminently forgettable. The jambon persillé with mustard seed comes from Eddy Raillard, a sure bet, served with good bread and pickles. The sautéed chicken gizzard salad is delicious, there's good fresh crayfish-tail gratin, and the grilled ribsteak is memorable. Desserts are straightforward (ice creams aren't housemade). The white wines (and the perfectly drinkable reds) are from the owners' estate. Also available though often changing: glasses, carafes, or bottles from Vougeot 1er Cru La Vougeraie to Pommard Épenots from Violot-Guillemard. The jocular, chummy waiters linger with regulars, slowing service; if you're in a rush, go elsewhere.

WINE BARS **Le Bistrot Bourguignon** (8 Rue Monge, Tel: 03 80 22 23 24, www.lebistrotbourguignon.com, closed Sunday and Monday year-round, plus Tuesday and Wednesday evening in low season, food inexpensive). An easy address in the pedestrianized area between Place Monge and the Hôspices, a few shopfronts from Eddy Raillard, this darkish wine bar (with a shaded street-side terrace) features jazz on the sound system and live jazz on (some) Saturday nights in the back room. Beaune's first wine bar, among Burgundy's pioneers, founded in 1985, its owner is aging boomer Jean-Jacques Hegner. He initiated the Beaune Jazz Festival. The Paris-bistro, fell-off-a-truck décor draws an anti-bobo crowd of local regulars and laid-back outsiders. The food is good and affordable. Stick to simplicity—hams, cold cuts, cheeses, snails with garlicky butter and parsley, and traditional daily specials. Among remarkable bottlings: Hubert Lamy of Saint-Aubin, Vincent Dauvissat of Chablis, and Vincent Girardin of Meursault. Up-and-coming wineries include the outstanding Bret Brothers.

Caves Madeleine (8 Rue du Faubourg Madeleine, Tel: 03 80 22 93 30, closed Sunday, Thursday, and Friday lunch, inexpensive to moderate). Two shopfronts away from La Table du Vieux Vigneron and Le Comptoir des Tontons, this wine bar—restaurant has bare-bones décor: one long wooden table and benches, a handful of smaller tables, farm tools, coconut-fiber flooring, and bottles of fine wine in cubby holes. The choice isn't huge, and embraces all of France and Europe. This is one Beaune hangout where local wine gurus, winemakers, and wine lovers enjoy meeting. You'll share your table with them, and eat good, unfussy *terroir* food cooked by second-generation chef Lolo.

Les Mille et Une Vignes (61 Rue de Lorraine, Tel: 03 80 22 03 02, in summer open 11:30am to midnight Tuesday through

Saturday, closed Sunday and Monday; the rest of the year, also closed Wednesday, food inexpensive). Near La Ciboulette and Porte Saint-Nicolas, this funky wine bar stocks about 1,001 different wines. It's known for its dusty *vieux millésimes*, typically given to loved ones to mark anniversaries or birthdays, wars, revolutions, coups d'état, illegal invasions, and rigged elections. The oldest might be the 1795 Terrantez Madeira. Also collecting dust are an 1848 Château de Bourdieu Armagnac, and 1934 Châteauneuf du Pape Clos des Papes. The 2004 Givry Clos de la Brûlée from Domaine Masse is highly drinkable. Voluble Marine and Didier Sévestre are in charge, and the food they serve is simple: terrines, sausages, cold cuts, hams and cheeses, salads. Local boozers and amused tourists crowd the noisy tables, knocking back glasses or bottles new and old.

Via Mokis (1 Rue Eugène Spüller, Tel: 03 80 26 80 80, www.viamokis.com, open daily, lunch menu inexpensive, other menus moderate to expensive). The name merges something Ancient Roman or astronomical, and the Japanese for "hot cooking stones," or so it's claimed by the surprisingly earnest, studiously fashionable young staff. Beaune's trendy, high-design wine bar, feel-good spa, and pricey boutique hotel, could be anywhere, and seems made for nouveau hayseeds and bobos seeking a loft-style home away from home. Beyond the curiosity value, it's worth a peek. Fifty bottles plugged into air-tight necks dispense the perfect dose of La Fontenotte from Marc Colin et Fils (Saint Aubin), Aloxe-Corton from Domaine Latour, Gevrey-Chambertins by Dupont-Tisserandot, Bernard Moreau's Chassagne-Montrachet, Beaune du Château from Bouchard Père & Fils, and scores of others—at the press of a button. If you crave Frenchified *pasta alla carbonara au siphon* blended and run through a seltzer bottle, consider eating here. The menu changes weekly. Playing with edible arabesques on slate slabs is the brainchild of David Zuddas (of Dijon.) Also offered is transmogrified *terroir* (pike-perch in Pinot Noir, calf's head sliced "snackée" style, whatever that means in French or English). The food is a foil. Expect to find 300 bottlings. They start low and soar. You'll either laugh or weep.

Gourmet shops and food artisans

Alain Hess (7 Place Carnot, Tel: 03 80 24 73 61, alain.hess@wanadoo.fr, closed Sunday afternoon). Hess is one of Burgundy's top cheese-makers and mongers. His shop showcases about one hundred types daily: Aisy Cendré, Petit Vougeot, Chaource,

Charolais, Pourly, Soumaintrain, AOC Mâconnais (they arrive on Wednesday morning), Grand Vatel and, of special note, domed Delice de Pommard, which Hess invented. A temple of gastronomic luxury, Hess stocks many specialty foods, from raw ham and bread to wine, vinegar, artisanal pasta, excellent jams from Cadole aux Douceurs, and oils from Leblanc in Iguerande.

Les Arômes de la Chancellerie Torrefaction Cafés François (18 rue Poterne, Tel: 03 80 24 79 58, closed Sunday, Monday, and in August) has been run since 1984 by François-Xavier Rudloff. Coffee is his passion. He opens early to beat the heat and roasts small batches of excellent Arabica—twenty varieties—the mildest of which is medium-roast Moka Sidamo Bouana, with Kenya and Costa Rica beans. Excellent monovarietals include New Guinea, Marogogype, Guatemala, and Jamaican Blue Mountain. This is among the best roasting houses in Burgundy. For tea lovers: 150 varieties. Artisanal chocolate bars are also sold. The shop is behind Place Carnot via Passage Sainte Hélène. Follow your nose.

L'Athenaeum de la vigne et du vin (5 Rue de l'Hôtel-Dieu, Tel: 03 80 25 08 30, www.athenaeumfr.com, open daily 10am to 7pm, closed Christmas and New Year's Day). Facing the Hôspices, this vast bookstore created in 1989 by André Boisseaux, at the time president of Maison Patriarche (next door), stocks volumes on wine, regional gastronomy, history, entertaining, and more. It's also a wine-accessory boutique and wine shop with hundreds of bottlings to taste and buy. Upstairs are wine-theme toys, stuffed-animal toys, books and CDs for children.

Aux 3 Épis (31 Rue d'Alsace, Tel: 03 80 22 09 35, closed Sunday and Monday, ten days in February, and a week in October). East of Petite Place Carnot, on the corner of Rampart Saint-Jean, this neighborhood bakery uses a sourdough sponge to make excellent breads, possibly the best in town. Of the thirty types baked daily, don't miss the cornbread or multi-grain loaves. The gougères, croissants, and apple turnovers are excellent.

Bouché (1 Place Monge, Tel: 03 80 22 10 35, closed Monday), founded in 1925, is in the same family. In 1970s style, the upstairs tea salon is done in flamingo pink. Happily, there's a tiny outdoor terrace. Bouché makes dozens of chocolates and pastries, and rich ice creams. House classics include Tarte Vigneronne (shortbread sablé topped with sabayon and pears cooked in red wine) and Concorde (meringue and chocolate mousse). Original chocolates with a *terroir* twist are piquant Sévénés, with Aligoté and Fallot mustard.

Boutique Védrenne (28 Rue Carnot, Tel: 03 80 22 16 30, www
.vedrenne.fr, closed Sunday and Monday). In case you missed
the Cassissium, or Védrenne's other boutiques in Dijon, this is
Burgundy's biggest and brashest Crème de Cassis (and much
else) distiller, founded in 1923. The spotlit, luxurious shop on
the corner of Place Carnot is a good source for high-quality (and
expensive) gourmet foods.

Le Comptoir Viticole (11 Rue Samuel-Legay, Tel: 03 80 22 15
73, closed Sunday). Off Beaune's main square, this is accessory
Mecca for wine lovers, founded in the 1930s. Jacqueline Passe-
mard stocks corks and pipettes, wine racks, corkscrews, bottling
machines, aprons, dishcloths, crystal cleaners, vinegar-makers,
carafes and about a hundred different wineglasses, plus *rats de
cave* candlestick holders. Among easy-to-pack objects are enameled metal plaques with wine or grape varieties, for the cubby
holes in your cellar.

Dix Carnot (10 Place Carnot, Tel: 03 80 24 62 06, open daily
nonstop 8am to 7pm). The nonstop opening hours alone make this
trendy chocolate and pastry shop on the main square a tempting
choice. The complexity, beauty, and deliciousness of pastry chef
Fabien Rouaud's edible artworks is breathtaking. If such is your
cup of tea (enjoy one here), don't miss Dix Carnot. The macarons,
and the neo-crème-brûlée-cum-chocolate-biscuit called Adélaïde
(itself a mouthful), are outstanding.

Eddy Raillard (4 Rue Monge, Tel: 03 80 22 23 04,
raillardeddy@wanadoo.fr, closed Sunday afternoon from December to May and Monday year-round, July, and the last week in
November). At age thirteen Eddy Raillard started making the

hams, rosette salami with Marc de Bourgogne, jambon persillé, savory tarts, and other specialties that have won him gold medals and recognition as Beaune's top *charcutier*. In 2003 he and his wife took over this landmark 1800s butcher shop-deli and have been mobbed ever since. Buy picnic supplies here. Raillard also sells Fallot mustard.

Jean Ourvois (8 Rue Carnot, Tel: 03 80 22 35 40, www .jeanourvois.com, open daily March through December, closed Monday in January and February). Traditionalist, dessert-loving Beaunois either prefer Bouché or Ourvois. The two are a hundred yards apart. Ourvois's old-fashioned main outlet serves good coffee, tea, pastries, chocolates, ice creams, savory snacks, and salads, and has tables on pedestrianized Rue Carnot. Its fancy, postmodern chocolate boutique across the street sells lemon- or orange-custard tartelettes, dark-chocolate tarts, chocolate-coated tuile cookies, chocolate truffles, chocolate-dipped candied orange peel and suchlike, all excellent.

Moutarderie Fallot (31 Rue du Faubourg-Bretonnière, Tel: 03 80 22 10 02, www.fallot.com, by appointment only through the Office de Tourisme de Beaune, Tel: 03 80 26 21 30, www .ot-beaune.fr, contacts@ot-beaune.fr). Burgundy's only medium-sized, family-run mustard mill, and the only one using Burgundian mustard seed, Fallot is housed in a mustard-yellow building on a courtyard in the outskirts, south of the ramparts and Boulevard Bretonnière. Marc Désarménien, grandson of Edmond Fallot, has transformed the 1840s factory, now open to individuals and small groups. Through plate glass windows you look into the sterile, modern production facility and watch mustard being milled, only to disappear into state-of-the-art vats and presses and mixers. It reappears in the packaging area as it plops at the rate of 4,000 jars per hour into the distinctive mustard bottles Fallot uses. This is an interesting, eye-stinging experience—there's lots of vinegar and salt in the air. More enlightening and pleasant is the history lesson next door, followed by a visit to the reconstructed, no-longer-functioning, 1800s Fallot millworks. To cap things, taste mustard in the museum-boutique, and nibble bites of jambon persillé and savory snacks daubed with many Fallot mustards. Fallot produces old-fashioned mustard with mustard seeds, white wine mustard, tarragon-, cassis-, gingerbread-, honey-and-balsamic-, and green peppercorn—flavored mustards. All are sold on site, and are remarkably good. Once you've tried them, you'll be hard-pressed to eat industrial mustard.

Mulot et Petitjean (1 Place Carnot, corner Rue Carnot, Tel: 03 80 22 06 18, open daily in summer, closed Sunday and Monday the rest of the year) is synonymous with gingerbread. In its luxurious Beaune boutique, this historic, Dijon-based *pain d'épices* maker sells variations on the theme, plus a vast assortment of gourmet delights, from chocolates to cookies, filled nonnettes to candies, Cassis and Fallot mustard.

Palais des Gourmets (14 Place Carnot, Tel: 03 80 22 13 39, closed Tuesdays from October to April). Another pillar of Beaune's chocolate-and-pastry establishment, preferred by some to Jean Ourvois, Bouché, and Dix Carnot, this upscale shop has a terrace on the main square, and offers pastries by chef Jacky Tavenet, including patented toasted-hazelnut-and-chocolate "snails," liqueur-filled Roulés au Cointreau and meringue-and-blackcurrant Nuages de Bourgogne, plus classic chocolates, mini tarts, dozens of types of butter cookies, nearly a dozen ice creams, and other sweet or savory treats (from crêpes to sandwiches). The coffee and tea are very good.

Wine shops and wineries

Denis Perret (40 Rue Carnot, corner Place Carnot, Tel: 03 80 26 22 35 47, www.denisperret.fr, closed Sunday afternoon Easter to late November, all day Sunday the rest of the year). Compact and upscale, facing equally luxurious Mulot et Petitjean, it's the oenological equivalent, stocking vintages from hundreds of top Burgundy wineries. The polite, professional staff are among Beaune's best with old and rare wines, kept below the boutique in a cellar. Talk over your important purchases before buying.

Upstairs, the more affordable wines are divided by growing area, whites on one side, reds on the other. You'll also find corkscrews, decanters, wineglasses, and other accessories.

Domaine Philippe Dufouleur—Les Jardins de Loïs (8 Boulevard Bretonnière, Tel: 03 80 22 04 62, www.jardinsdelois .com, tastings by appointment, B&B for overnight guests). Affable Philippe Dufouleur and his grape-grower wife Anne-Marie run Beaune's first winery-luxury B&B. It's hidden on the outer edge of the ring-road encircling the town's ramparts. There's a leafy garden; a winery on the ground floor; and a rambling cellar full of the oak casks—a third of them new—in which the Dufouleurs age their 1er Cru and other reds, and small quantities of white (fifteen percent of production). It's here you'll taste up to seven wines, guided by Philippe, who looks like Jean Gabin playing l'Inspecteur Maigret. The pride of the 12.5-acre estate are reds Le Clos du Roi, Le Clos des Perrières, Les Cent Vignes, and Le Clos du Dessus des Marconnets, plus white or red 1er Cru Champs-Pimonts. Philippe's reds macerate for three weeks in wooden tanks, repose unracked for up to eighteen months on their lees in oak, and are then racked and filtered once before bottling. Round, balanced, and medium-bodied, the best will grow for years. Total production is 35,000 bottles. No pesticides are used, the grapes are hand-harvested. The Dufouleurs also sell wines from other estates. The B&B's four guest rooms (one of them a suite) sit above the winery, have capacious wooden armoirs, fuddy-duddy but comfortable armchairs, tile floors, tree-trunk timbers, and bathrooms with showers large enough for a horse and rider. There's a Turkish steam bath down the hall. Running the B&B, and giving advice on wines, restaurants, museums, vineyard tours, and wine-tasting courses, is affable Dutchman Wim Nugteren.

La Grande Boutique du Vin (Avenue du Général de Gaulle, Tel: 03 80 24 08 09, www.vinscph.com, closed Sunday). This bare-bones wine emporium, in the outskirts, is a favorite of locals. It sells Champagne (150 bottlings), and wines from outside Burgundy. Among the 1,000 wines on wooden shelves are the region's best, plus little-known discoveries. The prices are competitive. There's also a selection of gourmet foods.

Maison Albert Ponnelle (38 Faubourg Saint-Nicolas, Clos Saint Nicolas, Tel: 03 80 22 00 05, open daily without appointment, closed August). This family-run *négociant* makes about 200,000 bottles yearly from grapes bought widely. Visit the fourteenth-century cellars. The red Réserve de la Chèvre Noir Monopole is organic (not certified), the vineyard ploughed by horse. Also remarkable: Gevrey-Chambertin Villages, Nuits Saint Georges Villages Les Crêts, and Beaune 1er Cru Bressandes (reds); Saint-Aubin Cuvée Catherine Bastide and Pouilly Fuissé Vieilles Vignes (whites).

Maison Alex Gambal (14 Boulevard Jules Ferry, Tel: 03 80 22 75 81, www.alexgambal.com, info@alexgambal.com, by appointment). Distinguished Bostonian Alex Gambal has done the unthinkable: breach the fortifications of Beaune's wine establishment. He began in 1997, and, now flanked by oenologist Fabrice Laronze, crops up among Beaune's most promising. He's certainly among the more versatile, making fine whites and reds from grapes picked up and down the côtes. Gambal's bottlings

are balanced; don't shun the "lesser" ones, some to be preferred
to the big Crus. His best: Fixin Blanc, Clos de Vougeot, Meursault
Villages Blanc Clos du Cromin, Puligny Montrachet Villages.

La Vinothèque (4 Rue Pasumot, Tel: 03 80 22 86 35, www
.bourgogne-vinotheque.com, open daily, nonstop), between Place
Carnot and Place de la Halle, Beaune's oldest independent,
family-owned wine shop is run by second-generation Jérôme Filliatre. The entry-level bottles are on the ground-floor. Downstairs,
the cellar hides *vieux millésimes* and finer wines for which La
Vinothèque is known. They range from Domaine de la Romanée
Conti down. This is Beaune's only wine shop open daily. Filliatre,
who's cordial, helpful, and not condescending, delivers to hotels
and ships worldwide. He also stocks the finest liqueurs and accessories. See Top Burgundian Winesellers' Favorites, page 59, for
Filliatre's picks.

BOUZE-LÈS-BEAUNE

Eight miles east of Beaune, Bouze has an unfortunate name
(Bouze means dung). Happily, one of the area's best-value restaurants is on the main highway: **La Bouzerotte** (Tel: 03 80
26 01 37, closed Monday and Tuesday, three weeks in January,
early September, and Christmastide, inexpensive to moderate).
There's a tiered garden with umbrellas, tables and chairs, and a
sunny dining room with contemporary touches and old wooden
armoirs painted white, a fireplace in one corner. Millésime, the
dog, greets guests and watches as they enjoy carefully updated,
nicely presented, seasonal meals based on Burgundian tradition
(pâté en croûte, snails, duck breast stuffed with pork and topped
with creamy mushroom sauce, boeuf bourguignon, soufflé with
ham) and creative, sometimes less successful, dishes. Robert
Olivier was a pastry chef and did the marquee circuit; his wife
Christine Fevre worked at Hostellerie de Levernois when it had
multiple stars. Their professionalism is matched only by their
lack of pretension. Everything is housemade except the jambon persillé, ham, and bacon (from award-winning Moron in
Pommard). The excellent cheeses are from Gaugry. Desserts:
dark-chocolate mini-tart with chocolate ice cream and raspberry
coulis. The Café Monika coffee is good; the short wine list includes
affordable carafes and half bottles (plus Marc Colin's excellent
Saint Aubin, Morey Saint Denis from Ponsot, and Domaine de
la Romanée-Conti Echezeaux at nearly a thousand euros). If you
can't finish your bottle, Christine will give you *un sac à vin*—a
doggy bottle-bag. The lunch prix fixe is a steal.

CHASSAGNE-MONTRACHET

Halfway up the golden slopes that grow golden wines, Chassa-gne-Montrachet's tidy stone houses emanate prosperity. Some of the 412 acres of vineyards here, notably Grand Crus Bâtard-Montrachet, Bienvenues-Bâtard-Montrachet, Chevaliers-Montrachet, and Criots-Bâtard-Montrachet, produce white wines whose excellence—and price tags—make the head spin. Less well-known is that nearly as much (350 acres) of fine red-wine vineyards also fall within the municipal area, which abuts Santenay, Puligny-Montrachet, and Saint-Aubin. The RN74 highway runs at the base of the village's lesser AOC vineyards, and another busy highway, RN6, links nearby Chagny to Nolay and Autun. Most premium wineries here are not open to the public, not even by appointment.

Foodwise, other than one grocery-bakery, there isn't much in the village, exception made for startling **Le Chassagne** (4 Impasse des Chevenottes, Tel: 03 80 21 94 94, closed for dinner Sunday and Wednesday, all day Tuesday, mid December to mid January, and the first half of August, moderate prix fixe weekday lunch only, à la carte expensive to astronomically expensive). Imagine the cushy dining room of a well-off French family, with a penguin-suited Japanese butler, maids and nannys scraping to classical music, and hushed voices, many foreign. Then glance at the contemporary art, bring on the food, and watch guests swoon—from shock or delight. The seasonal menu changes year to year, whisking together guacamole with giant prawns and an exotic African galangal-root-flavored vinaigrette, grilled scallops with pistachio oil and a Granny Smith emulsion, a crème-brûlée of foie gras with green apple-and-tarragon sorbet, or day-boat sole with kumquats, and lobster with laquered veal shortribs and squid-ink-sauced spaghetti. Were they not delicious, they would be ludicrous. Happily, the veal rib-roast and sweetbreads with kidneys and fricasséed wild mushrooms, or Saône pike-perch, also with Morvan crèpes, and winey Vin Jaune, or braised thigh of suckling wild boar with chestnut purée, evoke Burgundy's *terroir*. The wine list features 400 bottlings, many unfindable, most running into the hundreds of euros. A few are available by the glass, but aren't always stellar. Chef Stéphane Léger is openly seeking Michelin stars. The set-up is clearly intended to *épater le bourgeois*, and you might feel like screaming as the waiter or sommelier rushes over and pours, or swoops on your wayward napkin. But the cooking is extraordinarily fine. You're unlikely to forget your meal.

Just below the village, amid vineyards, is winery-luxury B&B—*table d'hôtes* **Château de Chassagne-Montrachet** (5 Rue du Château, Tel: 03 80 21 98 57, www.michelpicard.com, open year-round for visits and tastings Monday to Saturday 9am to 6pm, lunch March to November by reservation only, moderate to expensive, wine included). To distinguish it from next door, also in parts of the older château, with claims to the same name, locals call this neoclassical mansion "Chez Michel Picard." The owner is a dynamo winemaker, mayor of Chagny, and a remarkable success. Picard started young as a merchant with a three-wheeled delivery truck, and currently owns 325 acres of vineyards, including prime Grand Cru and 1er Cru parcels, plus others in Châteauneuf-du-Pape AOC, Condrieu and the Loire Valley. He bought into the Côte Chalonnaise, and snapped up this château in 1997. A decade and countless millions later, the restoration is complete, from the maze of cellars up. They're in part eleventh-century (the property was demolished during the French Revolution, divided and rebuilt) and included on the tour, which you take before tasting half a dozen or a dozen wines. The tasting room is high-tech; each taster gets a private spitoon. Manager Marie-Florence Grimm reminds you that "chalk in the soil makes wines manly, while limestone makes them feminine." A bit of both and you get androgynous wines—virile whites and delicate reds. Oak abounds here. Of the 790 barrels, about 200 are new, with a five-year cycle; wines spend up to fifteen months in them, from new to older. The barrels come from four different makers using wood from different regions to impart complexity. Among the best bottlings, from the top down: Corton Grand Cru Clos des Fiètres (red), Clos de Vougeot (red), Puligny-Montrachet Village (white), Chassagne-Montrachet Village en Pimont (white), Chassagne-Montrachet Village Les Chaumées (red), and unpretentious, quaffable Bourgogne Blanc and Bourgogne Rouge (from grapes grown at the Domaine Voarick estate in the Côte Chalonnaise). Lunch is devised to accompany tastings: gougères, raw ham, pâté en croûte, and terrine de campagne, followed by Bresse chicken with wild rice. Cheeses: Époisses and Cîteaux. Dessert: fruit sorbet and finger cakes. The coffee is Illy, served with squares of Valrhona Caraïbes chocolate. Overnight guests choose among five vast, wildly luxurious bedrooms and suites, several with the kind of sunken bathtubs a family could sink into.

Next door in part of the original fortress is family-run **Domaine du Château de Chassagne-Montrachet Bader-Mimeur** (1 Rue du Château, Tel: 03 80 21 30 22, www.bader-mimeur.com, by appointment). The Bader-Mimeur family has owned the vineyards wrapping the château since 1919. From them and other grapes (from farther-flung vineyards) it produces Chassagne-Montrachet Villages whites (the Vieilles Vignes is very good) and reds, Saint-Aubin 1er Cru en Remilly (white), Pommard 1er Cru Les Grands Epenots, and Volnay 1er Cru Santenots (both red), plus other Villages or Régionales AOC wines. The affable scions divide their time between here and Paris (they are professionals). Though not organic, the vineyards are grassy. The grapes are hand-picked and transported in cases to prevent damage. Wines are barrel-aged for up to a year (a quarter of barrels are new).

Domaine Lamy-Pillot (31 Route de Santenay, Tel: 03 80 21 30 02, www.lamypillot.fr, contact@lamypillot.fr, by appointment only). Winemakers René and Thérèse Lamy (aided by daughters Florence and Karine, and sons-in-law Sébastien Caillat and Daniel Cadot) run this family estate. René has a remarkable corkscrew collection, which he will show if requested. Their Chassagne-Montrachet Pot Bois is a classic white with memorable complexity. The other four 1er Crus are remarkable (Les Caillerets, a white, is exceptional).

Other wineries in Chassagne-Montrachet open to the public include **Bachelet-Ramonet Père & Fils** (11 Rue du Parterre, Tel: 03 80 21 32 49, www.bachelet-ramonet.com, open weekdays without appointment, Saturday by appointment only, closed Sunday and first half of August). *Best wine:* Chassagne-Montrachet Villages (white). Also open to the public is **Vincent et François Jouard** (2 Place de l'Église, Tel: 03 80 21 30 25, by appointment). *Best wines:* Chassagne-Montrachet 1er Cru La Maltroie Vieilles Vignes, Chassagne-Montrachet Villages Vieilles Vignes Blanc.

CHOREY-LÈS-BEAUNE

This drive-through village on the outskirts of Beaune has many fine wineries. A few are open to the public, including **Domaine Maillard Père et Fils** (2 Rue Joseph Bard, Tel: 03 80 22 10 67). Run by father-and-son team Alain and Pascal Maillard. *Best wines:* Aloxe Corton Rouge, Beaune Rouge, Chorey-lès-Beaune Blanc, and Savigny-lès-Beaune Rouge. The exceptional wines made at **Tollot-Beaut & Fils** (Rue Alexandre Tollot, Tel: 03 80 22 16 54) include Chorey-lès-Beaune Rouge Pièce du Chapitre and Savigny-lès-Beaune 1er Cru Rouge Champ-Chevrey, but they sell out years in advance and are not available at the estate.

CORGOLOIN

If you're hankering to visit a vine-clad aristocratic manor surrounded by a monopole vineyard, and taste the wines as you
might in the Napa Valley, detour to unsung Corgoloin and
Domaine d'Ardhuy (Tel: 03 80 62 98 73, www.ardhuy.com, by
appointment only, closed Sunday). Owners the Liogier d'Ardhuy
clan long owned the bricks-and-mortar at Château Corton-André
and Reine Pédauque in Beaune. They still have vines, but this
property, Clos des Langres, is the d'Ardhuy family's real fief
and monopoly. It produces muscular Côte-de-Nuits Villages
Rouge Clos des Langres, even bigger Corton Grand Cru Rouge
Hautes Mourottes and Corton-Charlemagne Grand Cru Blanc,
and affordable, excellent Savigny-lès-Beaune 1er Cru Rouge
Aux Clous. D'Ardhuy vineyards total 103 acres, from Gevrey-
Chambertin to Puligny-Montrachet, in twenty-two AOCs (with
an additional seventy-five acres in the Rhone Valley, labeled
Domaine de la Cabotte). Guided tours, tastings, and meals, can
be reserved with advance notice.

CORPEAU

East of highway RN74 on the southern Côte de Beaune, Corpeau is home to Jean-Charles Fagot and family, who own and
operate the casual, rustic-retro **L'Auberge du Vieux Vigneron**
(Route de Beaune, Tel: 03 80 21 39 00, closed Monday and Tuesday, inexpensive to moderate). At affordable prices, you taste the
winery's quaffable wines, and those from other estates. The food
is straightforward, sometimes updated Burgundian, served in the
wine-theme eatery. This is the original branch of Beaune restaurant La Table du Vieux Vigneron.

LADOIX-SERRIGNY

In outlying Buisson, where Ladoix-Serrigny and Aloxe-Corton
overlap along the highway, find country auberge **La Buissonière**
(RN74, Tel: 03 80 26 43 58, closed Tuesday dinner and Wednesday,
always reserve ahead for dinner, moderate). Claude Chevalier,
president of Burgundy's winegrowers association, took over in
2006 and has turned this roadside eatery into an insider's address
for winegrowers and professionals. The décor is contemporary in
the glassed-in dining room; there's a veranda and a cellar dining
room. You'll find perennials and updated regional classics. The
wine list is well-chosen, with dozens of bottlings from affordable
little-knowns on up—and up.

Also on the highway, with a back terrace, and a spartan but sunny dining room, **Les Terrasses de Corton** (RN74, Tel: 03 80 26 42 37, days closed vary widely according to the season; closed mid January to mid March and Christmastide, plus several nights and at least one day at lunch, always phone ahead, inexpensive to moderate), with bewildering business hours, is small, family-run and serves traditional cooking updated to suit tourists. A handful of guest rooms await upstairs, should you indulge and crack your piggy-bank on the wines.

A mile from the highway, on the road to Corgoloin, find more rustic **Auberge de la Miotte** (4 Rue de la Miotte, Tel: 03 80 26 40 75, closed Sunday, Monday, and Tuesday, first half of August and Christmastide; also closed Thursday out of season, inexpensive to moderate). The wooden tables, stone floor, and proximity of woodlands where hunters tramp, bespeak the auberge's origins as a hunting lodge of yore. Customers include crusty hunters, wine-makers, farmers, and merchants who enjoy giving city-slicker friends a wood-scented thrill. No surprises from the kitchen, just good, solid, seasonal fare. The wine list offers both good deals and pricey bottlings.

Wineries in Ladoix-Serrigny open to the public: **Domaine Edmond Cornu et Fils** (Le Meix Gobillon, 6 Rue du Bief, Tel: 03 80 26 40 79, by appointment only). Long-established, with vines over fifty years old. *Best wines:* Aloxe-Corton Vieille Vigne, Corton Grande Cru Les Carrières, Ladoix Vieille Vigne. **Domaine Robert et Raymond Jacob** (Buisson, Tel: 03 80 26 40 42, by appointment only). Aloxe-Corton 1er Cru, Corton-Charlemagne Grand Cru, Ladoix Blanc and Rouge. **Domaine Jean-René Nudant** (11 Route de Dijon, Tel: 03 80 26 40 48, no appointment needed weekdays, by appointment only Saturday, closed Sunday and August). *Best wines:* Aloxe-Corton Clos de la Boulotte Monopole, Corton Grand Cru Bressandes, Ladoix and Nuits Saint Georges villages.

MEURSAULT

Friday mornings are best for visiting Meursault; that's when the market animates Place de l'Hôtel de Ville, the main square. There's nothing much to see: on one flank of the trianglar square stands town hall, with remnants of a medieval tower. The barn-like Saint-Nicolas church kitty corner is capacious and grace-less, with a skyscraper belltower, designed to evoke the wealth of the winemaking gentry. The bakery facing the church, run by **Hélène and Jacky Sancenot** (11 Place de l'Hôtel de Ville, Tel: 03 80 21 21 08, closed Wednesday), is the town's best, with fabulous breads and good pastries; the other food shops in town are interchangeable.

The tourism office (Place de l'Hôtel de Ville, Tel: 03 80 21 25 90, www.ot-meursault.fr, closed Sunday in summer, weekends the rest of the year) flanks the bakery. You will want to buy tickets through it to attend De Bach à Bacchus, Meursault's July music-and-wine extravaganza, in the church, the Château de Cîteaux, and Château de Meursault.

Whether "Meursault" derives from "rat" and "leap"—*muris saltus*—in Latin, or from *murus altus* ("high wall") is immaterial. The high stone walls around Meursault's handkerchief-sized vineyards, and the town's history from pre-Roman to Roman encampment, militates for *murus*. No, insist experts: "Rat's Leap" is what Burgundians call the geological separation between the town's 155 acres of Chardonnay from its neighbors'.

Some of the fattest, most expensive whites in the world come from Meursault. Pseudo-sophisticates chanting "Anything But Chardonnay" are laughed merrily out of town. Bone white in color, and strung out between sloping vineyards and the valley, Meursault is larger than most nearby villages. It boasts a bewildering number of wineries: signs at crossroads point every which way. Meursault retains authenticity, though it's feeling increasingly like Beaune, with an influx of city slickers and foreigners. A wine-therapy and beauty spa, **Vignes et Bien-Être** (14 Place de l'Hôtel de Ville, Tel: 03 80 21 19 91, by appointment only, closed Sunday), opened recently. A bobo restaurant scene is growing, and slick, corporate wineries are snapping up properties.

Updated regional and creative cuisine are served at trendy **Le Bouchon** (1 Place de l'Hôtel de Ville, Tel: 03 80 21 29 56, closed Sunday dinner and Monday, inexpensive to moderate), run by chef Laurent Chandelier. It has a contemporary, neo-bistro atmosphere, blond-wood décor, a shaded terrace, professional service, and an affordable *terroir* menu with lightened food (the coq au vin and pike-perch with a flavorful Pinot Noir sauce with shallots, and authentic calf's head with piquant sauce gribiche, are excellent).

Across from it, with a sidewalk terrace, comfortable dining room, and shady courtyard, is more traditional **Les Arts** (4 Place de l'Hôtel de Ville, Tel: 03 80 21 20 28, closed Thursday and from mid December to end January, inexpensive to moderate). Franck Laroche makes classics (snails, jambon persillé, beef bourguignon, gutsy shepherd's pie with tripe sausage). Desserts include

seasonal fruit tarts; the wine list features Meursault whites and many unsung local reds, at reasonable prices.

Facing both is traditional, good-value, rustic **Hôtel du Centre** (4 Rue de Lattre-de-Tassigny, Tel: 03 80 21 20 75, inexpensive to moderate, closed Sunday and Monday), where veterans Xavier and Martine Foret, and their cheerful daughter Aurélie, serve mountains of garlicky snails, quantities of good beef bourgui gnon (made with beef shanks, and cooked for three hours), and solid, predictable specialties.

Beyond the church, nearer to the château, is **Le Chevreuil** (Place de l'Hôtel de Ville, Tel: 03 80 21 23 25, www.lechevreuil. fr, closed Tuesday and Wednesday at lunch year-round, February, and Sunday and Tuesday dinner the rest of the year, inexpensive to very expensive). Evelyne and Jean Gouges are moving upscale, with a self-consciously modernized version of regional haute. The décor captures a countryman's vision of luxury. Happily, they've kept the old house specialty on the menu, a rich, meaty terrine served hot "in the style of La Mère Daugier."

Space limitations keep most tour buses and their famished loads out of downtown, so they head east toward the train tracks, to sprawling **Relais de la Diligence** (23 Rue de la Gare, Tel: 03 80 21 21 32, www.relaisdeladiligence.com, closed Wednesday in summer, also closed Tuesday dinner the rest of the year, and mid December to mid January, inexpensive to moderate), a fallback. This coaching inn has been remodeled, with rustic-bourgeois décor, and is a favorite among Japanese and Russian tourists. It posts photographs of the food, signed Gérard Lejeune. Please-all dishes, plus some daring inventions, flank traditional, safe choices. The most compelling thing about this restaurant is the elevated outdoor terrace overlooking a tiny vineyard.

Wine shop and wineries

Cave des Vieilles Vignes (13 Place de l'Hôtel de Ville, Tel: 03 80 21 29 07, www.cavedesvieillesvignes.com, open daily year-round) is an option if you don't have time (or don't want) to visit Meursault's wineries. Multilingual Fabien Cipriano will guide you through 500 different bottlings from Côte d'Or and the Côte Chalonnaise. The prices are fair, often the same as those offered by the wineries. (The shop's second outlet is in Santenay.)

Imposing **Château de Meursault** (Rue du Moulin Foulot, Tel: 03 80 26 22 75, www.meursault.com, open daily, closed late December to the second week in January) is owned by sparkling

wine maker Kriter of Beaune, a.k.a. André and son Jacques Boisseaux. Boisseaux senior also created Aethenaeum bookstore and
the Patriarche group. It comes as no surprise that Château de
Meursault is the top tourist attraction, with 20,000 paying visitors annually. They see 2,000 barrels in the vaulted cellars, and
700,000 to 800,000 bottles on display. Tours wind up with a guided
tasting (seven wines), at the end of which you're presented with
an engraved glass. By reservation only are Etapes Gourmandes
(buffet lunches with tastings), and Balades Oenophiles (sit-down
meals, and wider-ranging wine tastings). Vertical theme tastings feature Meursault 1er Cru Blanc; horizontal tastings cover
the château's red wines. Wines are from various growing areas:
Aloxe-Corton, Puligny-Montrachet, Meursault. Best: Beaune
1er Cru Rouge Cent-Vignes, Beaune Villages Rouge, Pommard
Village Rouge Les Petits Noizons, Puligny-Montrachet 1er Cru
Blanc Champ Canet.

MONTHELIE

There's one good reason to detour to Monthelie: **Domaine
de Suremain-Château de Monthelie** (Tel: 03 80 21 23 32,
desuremain@wanadoo.fr, by appointment). The excellent wines
are bio-dynamic. Eric and wife Dominique Suremain took over
the family château, behind Volnay and Auxey-Duresses, and,
starting in 1978, converted the vineyards. Their pricey Monthé-
lies (1er Cru Sur la Velle), and accessible Rully reds and whites,
are highly regarded. Eager to share his expertise, Eric's brother
Arnaud (and wife Lydia) will walk you through bio-dynamic
vineyards at Agneux, in Rully, with a tasting of ten wines and a
simple *table d'hôtes* meal.

NANTOUX

Nantoux is in truffle-hills behind Pommard in the lovely Hautes-
Côtes. Once you've arrived at isolated **Domaine de la Combotte**
(Tel: 03 80 26 02 66, www.lacombotte.com, info@lacombotte
.com, by reservation only), on the edge of vineyards and woodlands, you'll find a warm welcome, fine food and wine, comfortable lodgings, and thick-tailed Ruffe and Clochette, Golden
Retrievers, with *truffes* tipping their snouts. (In French, a dog's
nose is called a *truffle*). From November to mid January, they lead
friendly Denis François and his guests on a merry truffle-chase,
through oak, hornbeam, black pine, and hazelnut. Denis and
his wife Nathalie run this modern, well-designed B&B known
for truffle-hunting adventures and truffle meals, old-fashioned

✦ OTHER WINERIES ✦
IN MEURSAULT OPEN TO THE PUBLIC
BY APPOINTMENT

Hours vary widely; few if any wineries are open
from noon to 2pm or on Sunday (special opening
hours are noted). Make an appointment (unless
otherwise noted), and plan to buy a bottle or two
after a tasting.

Château de Cîteaux (20 Rue de Cîteaux, Tel: 03 80
21 20 32).

Château Genot Boulanger (25 Rue de Cîteaux, Tel:
03 80 21 49 20). *Best wines:* Meursault Village Blanc
Les Levrons, Meursault 1er Cru Blanc La Garenne.

Alain Coche Bizouard (5 Rue de Mazeray, Tel:
03 80 21 28 41). *Best wines:* Aligoté, Meursault,
Meursault Goutte d'Or.

Bernard Delagrange (10 Rue du 11 Novembre, Tel: 03 80 21 22 72, open without appointment daily, 10am to 7pm).

Gauffroy G.A.E.C. (2 Rue de la Liberté, Tel: 03 80 21 26 87, open daily without appointment 8am to 8pm).

Marc Gauffroy (4 Rue du Pied de la Fôret, Tel: 03 80 21 21 09, www.meursault-gauffroy.com, open Monday through Saturday mornings without appointment, Sunday by appointment only).

Jerome Gerbeault-Les Caves du Vieux Pressoir (RN74, Tel: 03 80 21 28 91, open without appointment, closed Sunday).

Patrick Javillier-Cave St. Nicolas (Place de l'Europe, Tel: 03 80 21 27 87, open Monday, Friday, and Saturday, and Sunday morning, closed November to March).

Jean Javillier et Fils (6 Rue Charles Giraud, Tel: 03 80 21 24 61, by appointment). Note: certified organic.

Domaine Pierre Morey (9 Rue Comte Jules Lafon, Tel: 03 80 21 21 03, morey-blanc@wanadoo.fr, by appointment). Note: certified organic.

Bernard Millot (27 Rue de Mazeray, Tel: 03 80 21 20 91, www.domaine-millot.com, open daily by appointment).

Jean Monnier et Fils (7 Place de l'Hôtel de Ville, Tel: 03 80 21 20 82, www.domaine-jeanmonnier. com, open Wednesday through Monday 10am to 6pm without appointment, closed Tuesday).

Maison Ropiteau Frères (13 Rue du 11 Novembre, Tel: 03 80 21 24 73, www.caves-ropiteau.com, open daily 10am to 7pm without appointment, closed mid November to January).

....

breakfasts, and wines made by Denis's brother and relatives at excellent-value, sixth-generation **Domaine François Charles & Fils**, Tel: 03 80 26 01 20, phone ahead for a visit and tasting, truffle meals expensive). Ruffe, Clochette, and Denis work seamlessly, unearthing *tuber uncinatum* without damaging the forest.

Denis starts preparing meals a week ahead by nesting fresh truffles with eggs, cream, and butter (to flavor them). He makes truffle-topped toasts, omelettes, oeufs en meurette, truffle risotto, truffled mashed potatoes with cream, truffled cheeses, and more. Fats bring out the essence of *uncinatum*; the combination is irresistible when accompanied by red wine. The family winery makes sixteen bottlings, many award-winners, from rough-and-ready Aligoté to Meursault or 1er Cru reds from Volnay (Les Fremiets) and Beaune (Les Boucherottes and Les Epenottes). Grapes are hand-harvested and -selected; most wines spend eighteen months on oak (a quarter of it new). The best-value sleeper: Bourgogne Haute-Côtes-de-Beaune Vieilles Vignes red, which is complex, powerful, yet fresh and balanced. Reserve six months ahead for a truffle meal. Denis hosts half a dozen adventures per year. They feature guided wine-tastings, and truffle dinners, served in the B&B's dining room, where you sit at a wooden table, a fire roaring, Ruffe and Clochette at your feet.

Another fine winery, near the old train station, is **Domaine Christine et Didier Montchovet** (Rue de la Gare, Tel: 03 80 26 03 13, www.montchovet.fr, domaine@montchovet.fr, by appointment). Montchovet was the first in the Côte d'Or to get organic and biodynamic certification. The pioneering parcel is AOC Côtes de Beaune 1er Cru Aux Coucherais, less than an acre, producing 1,500 bottles in a good year. With about twenty-five acres now, all biodynamic, Montchovet is medium-sized; its wines routinely sell out. *Best wines:* Côtes de Beaune 1er Cru red, Hautes-Côtes de Beaune red, Pommard red.

NOLAY

On busy RN6 from Chagny to Autun, in hills footing the Hautes-Côtes, medieval Nolay has seen better days, but is revitalizing. The covered marketplace, back from the highway, is handsome. A lively market takes place on Monday morning (and there's a food fair at Eastertide and on August 15th). Antiques shops, self-styled *artisans d'art*, and boutiques offering items of questionable utility, abound. Happily, there's also a bakery and tea salon on the highway, and signs of life in restaurant **Le Bourgonde** (35 Rue de la République, Tel: 03 80 21 71 25, closed dinner on Sunday and Tuesday, and Wednesday, inexpensive to expensive), also on

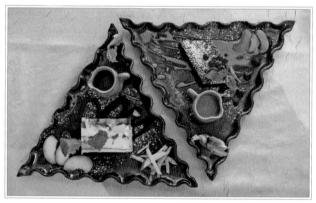

the main road, in a reconverted variety store. Knickknacks still fill glass cases. Endearing, this revival venture has a glassed-in patio, and a dining room with polished plank floors, comfortable chairs, and big tables. The plates are oversized, the food falling between neo-Baroque and Jackson Pollock. Jean-Noël Aprikian often succeeds with his updates. The oeufs en meurette are farmstead eggs and classic; the rolled chicken breasts are doused with tasty Époisses sauce. Delicious breast of veal is braised with baby

❧ WINERIES ❧
IN OR NEAR NOLAY
OPEN TO THE PUBLIC

Nolay's wines are often pleasant, rarely memorable. They're Hautes-Côtes-de-Beaune, Côtes-du-Couchois or Bourgogne AOC, in red, white, and rosé. The reds are far superior. Business hours vary widely; few if any wineries are open from noon to 2pm or on Sunday. With family-run properties, make an appointment ahead of time, and plan to buy a bottle or two after a tasting.

Domaine François Bergeret (15 Rue Franche, Tel: 03 80 21 88 72, bergeret.francois@cegetel.net, by appointment). *Best wine:* Hautes-Côtes-de-Beaune red.

Domaine Sylvain & François Changarnier (14 Route de Cirey, Tel: 03 80 21 70 92, syl.changarnier@wanadoo.fr, preferably by appointment). *Best wine:* Hautes-Côtes-de-Beaune red.

Domaine de La Confrerie · Christopher Pauchard (37 Rue Perraudin, Cirey, Tel: 03 80 21 89 23, www.domaine-pauchard.fr, by appointment only). *Best wines:* Aligoté, Santenay.

Domaine Nicolas Père et Fils (38 Route de Cirey, Tel: 03 80 21 82 92, nicolas-alain2@wanadoo.fr, Monday to Saturday without appointment, Sunday by appointment only). *Best wine:* Hautes-Côtes-de-Beaune red.

Domaine Gilles Gaudet (3 Rue de la Fontaine, Saint-Sernin-du-Plain, Tel: 03 85 49 62 12). *Best wine:* Côtes-du-Couchois red.

. . . .

vegetables; the luscious soft chocolate dessert, fruit mousses, and peaches cooked in local rosé are winners. The wine list features quality wines at fair prices (Maranges 1er Cru from Claude Nouveau, Vougeot 1er Cru Les Petits Vougeut from Roux Père et Fils, local Couchois reds from Gilles Gaudet, Aloxe Corton red from Domaine Maillard in Chorey-lès-Beaune).

POMMARD

Charming, tucked into hills south of Beaune, and with a large church and unusually unprepossessing fountain showing a sculpted artichoke, Pommard has long been renowned for its reds. Thomas Jefferson famously patronized **Domaine Parent** (3 Rue la Métairie, Tel: 03 80 22 15 08, by appointment only). Parent's great, great, great grandchildren Anne and Christine have recently turned around the business and again make excellent Beaune 1er Cru Rouge les Epenottes, Corton Grand Cru Rouge Les Renardes, Ladoix 1er Cru Rouge La Corvée, Pommard 1er Cru Rouge Les Chaponnières, Pommard 1er Cru Rouge Les Chanlins, and Pommard 1er Cru Rouge Les Epenots.

There are nearly thirty 1er Cru and dozens of Village appellations here, and many wineries, the best difficult or impossible to visit. One place to buy gourmet items is **Cave de Pommard** (3 Route de Beaune, Tel: 03 80 24 62 42, www.cavedepommard.com, open daily 10am to 7pm), an easy address on the main highway, representing Domaine de la Crea and Clos de la Perrière. The wines come from a dozen AOCs; it's the honey, mustard, potted pâtés and other foods that should retain your attention.

Pommard boasts an outstanding butcher-deli, unfortunately named **Moron** (Tel: 03 80 22 02 61, closed Sunday afternoon and Monday). Moron is on the narrow roads between the highway and artichoke fountain. Moron routinely wins medals for jambon persillé, and makes excellent terrines and salami.

Restaurants in or near the village are okay; none is outstanding. On the highway at the crossroads, find **Hôtel du Pont** (Rue Marey-Monge, Tel: 03 80 22 03 41, open daily, very inexpensive to moderate), where locals, truck drivers and tourists nurse wine, beer, or coffee. The terrace out front, and bigger one on the side, or rustic café-dining area, are fine for a snack or rustic lunch (snails, coq au vin, tripe sausage with mustard sauce).

At wineries in Pommard, hours vary widely; few if any wineries are open from noon to 2pm or on Sunday. With family-run properties, make an appointment, and plan to buy a bottle or two after a tasting: **Maison Michel Arcelain** (Rue Mareau, Tel: 03 80

22 13 50). **Château de Pommard** (15 Rue Marey Monge, Tel: 03 80 22 12 59). **Coste-Caumartin** (2 Rue du Parc, BP19, Tel: 03 80 22 45 04). **Jean-Luc Joillot** (6 Rue Marey Monge, Tel: 03 80 24 20 26). **Lejeune (**1 Place de l'Église, La Confrèrie, Tel: 03 80 22 90 88). **Michel Rebourgeon** (7 Place de l'Europe, Tel: 03 80 22 22 83).**Virely-Rougeot** (Place de l'Europe, Tel: 03 80 24 96 70).

PULIGNY-MONTRACHET

The name feels round and fat in the mouth; the wines and restaurants are a match. A good bakery is on the main square: **Boulangerie-Pâtisserie Joël Guenot** (12 Place du Monument, Tel: 03 80 21 38 29, closed Sunday afternoon and Monday). You'll find homey pastries and delicious bread (served at La Table d'Olivier Leflaive).

Le Montrachet (1 Place des Marronniers, Tel: 03 80 21 30 06, www.le-montrachet.com, open daily, moderate to astronomically expensive) dates to 1824. Its perfect stone façade, white shutters, mansard roof, and geraniums cannot prepare you for the creative, contemporary cooking of Thierry Berger. Traditionalists should seek elsewhere. Snails are unrecognizable as crispy mouth-fuls. The Bresse poultry, cooked in two ways is remarkable, the cheeses excellent, the desserts elaborate. The wine list includes an extravagant 1,050 bottlings, many hard to find and costing hundreds or thousands of euros. With the 1.8-million euro 2008 remodel, there is now a wine bar—blond wood, scarlet stools— where you can sip and snack without going bankrupt. There's also a wine shop in the cellar, with dozens of top bottlings, reserved for overnight guests. The lunch prix fixe is fine value.

On the main square find **La Table d'Olivier Leflaive/Domaine Olivier Leflaive Frères** (Place du Monument, Tel: 03 80 21 37 65, www.olivier-leflaive.com, closed Sunday and from late December to mid February, lunch only, restaurant inexpensive without wine tasting, expensive to very expensive with tasting, reserve ahead). Leflaive pioneered the *table d'hôtes*–winery concept, now mined by many. Suave, silver-haired Olivier and his brother Patrick are the seventeenth generation at this 400-year-old estate. In 1995, the premises were tastefully reconverted as a lunch-only *table d'hôtes* with wine tastings. Now, in bigger, swanker premises, the business is also a luxury hotel, with a summer patio. The winery is on the edge of town; the public is welcome to visit, touring from 11:30am to lunch. Affable Patrick will show and tell you everything, in great detail, from the care of vines to harvest and transport of grapes (hand-picked and placed in color-coded

plastic buckets to avoid crushing the contents). Leflaive buys seventy percent of grapes, from sixty-five different AOCs. Modern
and traditional winemaking methods range from temperature-
controlled environments and equipment to slow-aging. Presses
and bottling lines are slow, operating at low pressures. Exported
wines are shipped, not air freighted. Cork stoppers are used—
Leflaive isn't a screwtop convert, believing in micro-oxidation.
Slow-everything is the hobby horse. White wines are the forte.
They ferment and age in medium-toasted new oak for up to eighteen months, some aging afterwards in older barrels. Leflaive is
big by Burgundy standards, making 800,000 bottles annually, of
which 130,000 are red. Some Leflaive giants total as few as 900
bottles (certain Montrachets). In the cavernous yet elegant dining

room at the *table d'hôtes*, seated at an oak table, you may judge for yourself. Olivier's charming, efficient daughter Julie is aided by astonishingly talkative sommelier-waiters, who sometimes linger to discourse. Three formulas are available: eat without wine (inexpensive but pointless); select-taste ten wines (expensive); Grande Dégustation of fourteen wines, including three 1er Cru whites and one 1er Cru red (very expensive). Grapes arrive from as far away as Chablis (pleasant Les Deux Rives) and Rully (underrated 1er Cru Vauvry). The best are big Pommard 1er Cru Charmots, Chassagne-Montrachet 1er Cru La Grande Montagne, Meursault 1er Cru Charmes, and Puligny-Montrachet 1er Cru Champ Gain. The higher the price, the nicer the nice. Among the winery's best (not included in tastings) is Chablis 1er Cru

❧ PULIGNY-MONTRACHET WINERIES ❧ OPEN WITHOUT APPOINTMENT

Business hours vary; none of these wineries is open from noon to 2pm.

Chartron-Dupard (13 Grande Rue, Tel: 03 80 21 99 19, www.jeanchartron.com, open daily without appointment, closed mid November and April). *Best wines:* Jean Chartron's Chassagne-Montrachet Les Benoites red and white.

Domaine Guillemard-Clerc (19 Rue Drouhin, Tel: 03 80 21 34 22, www.guillemard-clerc.com, closed Sunday afternoon). *Best wine:* Bienvenues-Bâtard-Montrachet (astronomically expensive and reserved years ahead—only about 600 bottles of it are made).

Domaine Veuve Henri Moroni (1 Rue de l'Abreuvoir, Tel: 03 80 21 30 48, www.vins-moroni .com, open daily without appointment). *Best wine:* Puligny-Montrachet.

. . . .

Fourchaume. The food isn't the object of the exercise. Good, a meal typically includes gougères, jambon persillé, housemade terrine, range-raised chicken stewed in Leflaive's own Chardonnay, regional cheeses, liqueurs, and a cup of Illy espresso with squares of Valrhona chocolate. Lunch chez Olivier Leflaive is enjoyable and instructive. Just remember the house motto: slow.

SAINT-AUBIN

Long overlooked, this AOC situated at the eastern border of the Hautes-Côtes west of Chassagne-Montrachet has taken off. With 350 acres of vineyard, about six in ten planted with Chardonnay, the rest is Pinot Noir. There are a few 1er Crus. Nearby Gamay is included in the AOC, not simply because it has excellent *terroir*, but also to avoid confusion with the name (the Gamay variety is not grown here).

If you visit one winery in Saint-Aubin, try to make it **Hubert Lamy** (20 Rue des Lavières, Tel: 03 80 21 32 55, domainehubert lamy@wanadoo.fr, by appointment only). Young Olivier Lamy took over in 1996 and has turned this family-run estate into a superstar. He often runs out, so don't be surprised if you're unable to arrange a visit. His wines are light on the oak and respectful of *terroir*. Outstanding: 1er Cru Blanc Les Murgers des Dents de Chien. Other excellent wines, all 1er Cru whites: Clos de la Chatenière, Derrière Chez Edouard, Les Frionnes. The Saint-Aubin Village Le Paradis red is also remarkable.

Outstanding, respectful of *terroir*, and of the natural freshness of Saint-Aubin whites is Domaine **Marc Colin et Fils** (Gamay, Tel: 03 80 21 30 43, by appointment only). Marc is gradually handing over to his children. The winery often sells out, and the

❧ OTHER FINE WINERIES ❧
IN SAINT-AUBIN AND GAMAY

These wineries are open by appointment only.

Domaine Gilles Bouton (24 Rue de la Fontenotte, Gamay, Tel: 03 80 21 32 63, by appointment only, closed two weeks in August and Christmastide). *Best wines:* 1er Cru Blanc en Remilly, 1er Cru Blanc Les Champlots.

EARL Derain (46 Rue des Perrières, Tel: 03 80 21 35 49, dc.derain@wanadoo.fr, by appointment only). Note: this winery is certified organic. *Best wines:* Saint Aubin 1er Cru, Mercurey (red), Pommard.

Domaine Larue (32 Rue de la Chatenière, Tel: 03 80 21 30 74, dom.larue@wanadoo.fr, by appointment only). *Best wines:* 1er Cru Blanc en Remilly, 1er Cru Blanc Les Murgers des Dents de Chien.

Domaine Bernard Prudhon (15 Rue du Jeu de Quilles, Tel: 03 80 21 35 66, by appointment only). *Best wines:* 1er Cru Rouge Les Castets, 1er Cru Blanc Les Combes.

Domaine Henri Prudhon et Fils (32 Rue des Perrières, Tel: 03 80 21 36 70, henri-prudhon@ wanadoo.fr, by appointment only). *Best wine:* 1er Cru Blanc en Remilly.

Domaine Roux Père et Fils (8 Rue de Ban, Tel: 03 80 21 32 92, roux.pere.et.fils@wanadoo.fr, by appointment only). *Best wine:* 1er Cru Blanc Les Murgers des Dents de Chien.

Domaine Gérard Thomas et Filles (6 Rue des Perrières, Tel: 03 80 21 32 57, by appointment only). *Best wine:* 1er Cru Blanc Les Murgers des Dents de Chien.

....

only way to taste these wines is from a shop or in a restaurant. *Best wines*, all 1er Cru whites: en Créot, en Remilly, La Chatenière.

SAINT-ROMAIN

Compelling reasons make a detour to this ancient, hillside village obligatory. The scenery is gorgeous: limestone cliffs, rugged hills sculpted by vineyards, and tiers of stone-built houses on streets with see-forever views. Archeological digs at the base of the cliffs have revealed fourteen layers of occupation—five more than at Troy—from 5000 BC to 1600 AD.

Two celebrated barrel-makers operate here (François Frères and Claude Gillet, both for professionals only). On a swelling of the road between lower (*bas*) and upper (*haut*) Saint-Romain, flanking the town hall, **Les Roches** (Place de la Mairie, Tel: 03 80 21 21 63, www.les-roches.fr, closed Monday and Tuesday, inexpensive to moderate) is the village's only hotel-restaurant. Spacious, sparkling, and echoing, the rustic-bourgeois dining room is directed by Séverine Crotet. Her husband, second-generation chef Guillaume Crotet, stays behind the scenes, not a bad thing, since he appears entirely aware of his pedigree. Crotet updates and lightens classics, from "grandmother's terrine" to snails with potatoes and creamy herb sauce on up. One specialty, *tatin d'oreille de cochon à la sauge*—an upside-down tatin tart of pig's ears perfumed with sage sauce—sounds unappetizing but is delicious, despite the crunchy cartilage. Among daily specials you might find a delicious shepherd's pie. The desserts are classics. The wine list includes nearly everyone in the AOC. There's a terrace open in summer. In case you need a nest, the rooms are comfortable, clean, and simply decorated.

Jovial and overwhelmed by his success, winegrower **Alain Gras** (Saint Roman le Haut, Tel: 03 80 21 27 83, by appointment), aided by his vintage father, young wife, and children, makes some of the finest wines in this AOC, plus outstanding whites and reds from others. Many holdings are tiny: only 3,000 bottles each of Auxey-Duresses and Meursault (whites). Gras will gladly welcome you and let you taste his excellent Saint-Romains. *Best wines:* Auxey-Duresses Blanc les Crais, Saint-Romain Rouge, Saint-Romain Blanc, Auxey-Duresses Rouge Vieilles Vignes, Meursault.

Another outstanding winery, in expansion to meet growing demand, is **Domaine Christophe Buisson** (Rue de la Tartebouille, Tel: 03 80 21 63 92, domainechristophebuisson@wanadoo.fr, by appointment). A one-man show created in the mid 1990s, Buisson continued to sell out, one reason Christophe began buying

grapes from other growers, and has taken over his father-in-law's vineyard in Nuits Saint Georges. *Best wines:* Saint-Romain Blanc, Auxey-Duresses Rouge.

Other fine wineries in Saint-Romain include **Domaine Henri et Gilles Buisson** (Impasse du Clou, Tel: 03 80 21 27 91, www .domaine-buisson.com, open Monday to Saturday without appointment, closed Sunday). *Best wines:* Auxey-Duresses Blanc Les Ecusseaux, Monthelie Rouge, Saint-Romain Blancs Les Perrières, and Sous la Velle. **Domaine Patrick Germain Père et Fils** (Rue de la Pierre Ronde, Tel: 03 80 21 60 15, www.domaine -germain.com, by appointment). *Best wines:* Saint-Romain Blanc, Saint-Romain Rouge Sous Le Château. **Domaine Pierre Taupenot** (Rue du Chevrotin, Tel: 03 80 21 24 37, by appointment only, closed Sunday afternoon). *Best wine:* Saint-Romain Blanc.

SANTENAY

Santenay is the southernmost village on the Côte de Beaune, separated from the Côte Chalonnaise by the Dheune River Valley and Canal du Centre, and overlooked by majestic Mont de Sène. It was once nicknamed the "Nice of the Côte d'Or," a moniker supposedly coined by the celebrated mayor of Dijon, Canon Kir, better known for inventing the aperitif. There is a casino as in Nice, and a spa resort of the nineteenth-century variety, which gives the town a landlocked, Second Empire feel. The water has high saline and lithium content; this may explain the sense of well-being, and the distinctive character of the wines, or maybe it's just because Santenay is likeable.

Santenay encompasses the unsung Maranges AOC, between Santenay, Nolay, and points south. Like Maranges, Santenay was

Château de la Crée (11 Rue Gaudin, Tel: 03 80 20 63 36, la.cree@orange.fr, by appointment). *Best wine:* Santenay Beauregard 1er Cru Blanc, Santenay Le Clos Faubard 1er Cru Rouge.

Domaine Hervé de Lavoreille (10 Rue de la Crée, Santenay le Haut, Tel: 03 80 20 61 57, delavoreille.herve@wanadoo.fr, by appointment). *Best wines:* Santenay Clos des Gravières 1er Cru Blanc, Santenay Clos du Haut Village Rouge.

Maison Prosper Maufoux (1 Place du Jet d'Eau, Tel: 03 80 20 60 40, www.prospermaufouxwines.com, open daily March to November without appointment, by appointment the rest of the year). *Best wine:* Santenay Rouge.

Domaine Mestre Père et Fils (12 Place du Jet d'Eau, Tel: 03 80 20 60 11, gilbert.mestre@wanadoo.fr, open daily without appointment). *Best wine:* Santenay Beaurepaire 1er Cru Blanc.

Domaine Lucien Muzard et Fils (11bis Rue de la Cour Verreuil, Tel: 03 80 20 61 85, Lucien-Muzard-et-Fils@wanadoo.fr, by appointment). *Best wines:* Maranges Rouge, Santenay Clos des Mouches 1er Cru Rouge, Santenay Clos Faubard 1er Cru Rouge, Santenay Vieilles Vignes Champs Claude Rouge.

Domaine Olivier Père et Fils (5 Rue Gaudin, Tel: 03 80 20 61 35, domaineolivier@orange.fr, by appointment). *Best wines:* Santenay Le Bievaux Perle de Grêle Blanc, Santenay Les Charmes Rouge.

Domaine Prieur-Brunet (Rue de Narosse, Tel: 03 80 20 60 56, www.prieur-santenay.com, by appointment only). *Best wines:* Santenay Maladière 1er Cru Rouge La Fleur de Maladière Cuvée Claude.

Domaine Sorine et Fils (4 Rue Petit, Tel: 06 86 98 04 77, christiansorine@club-internet.fr, by appointment only). *Best wines:* Santenay Maladière 1er Cru Blanc, Santenay Beaurepaire 1er Cru Rouge.

Domaine Claude Nouveau (Marchezeuil, Change, Tel: 03 85 91 13 34, by appointment). *Best wine:* Maranges 1er La Fussière Rouge.

Domaine Jean François Bouthenet (4 Rue du Four, Mercey, Cheilly-les-Maranges, Tel: 03 85 91 14 29, by appointment). As the name of the flagship wine suggests, it spends a long time on new oak. *Best wine:* Maranges sur Le Chêne Blanc.

Domaine Marc Bouthenet (10–11 Rue St-Louis, Mercey, Cheilly-les-Maranges, Tel: 03 85 91 16 51, open Monday to Saturday without appointment, Sunday by appointment only, closed the second half of August). *Best wine:* Maranges 1er La Fussière Rouge.

Domaine Fernand Chevrot et Fils (19 Route de Couches, Cheilly-les-Maranges, Tel: 03 85 91 10 55, www.chevrot.fr, open daily without appointment, closed Sunday afternoon). This friendly, family-run winery is in the process of switching to organic methods. *Best wines:* Maranges Blanc, Maranges sur Le Chêne Rouge.

Domaine France Dessauge (Place de l'Église, Cheilly-les-Maranges, Tel: 03 85 91 13 73, dessauge@free.fr, by appointment). *Best wines:* Maranges sur Le Chêne Rouge.

Domaine Maurice Charleux et Fils (1 Petite Rue, Dezize-les-Maranges, Tel: 03 85 91 15 15, by appointment). *Best wines:* Maranges 1er Cru Clos Roussots Rouge, Maranges 1er Cru Clos des Rois Rouge, Maranges 1er La Fussière Rouge, Maranges Vieilles Vignes Rouge.

Domaine Bernard Regnaudot (Route de Nolay, Dezize-les-Maranges, Tel: 03 85 91 14 90, by appointment). *Best wines:* Maranges 1er Cru Clos des Rois Rouge, Maranges 1er Cru Clos des Loyères Rouge.

one of the least prestigious AOCs of the Côte d'Or. Both are experiencing a gastro-oenological boom; quality has improved manyfold.

On the main square, recently landscaped, though still occupied in large part by a parking lot, is old-fashioned, family-run **Hôtel-Restaurant L'Ouillette** (16 Place du Jet d'Eau, Tel: 03 80 20 62 34, closed Tuesday and Wednesday, open daily in July and August, very inexpensive to expensive). The archetype of family-run bourgeois restaurants, it's the kind of place merchants and winemakers take clients or families for Sunday lunch. Well-spaced tables, upholstered armchairs, waxed, heavy wooden armoirs and buffets, lend authority to the *cuisine bourgeoise*. Updated classics arrive on outsized plates. Chef Éric Oudin—wife Martine runs the dining room—is a pro. The snails come tucked into puff pastry with a delicate, creamy nettle-tip sauce. The juicy pan-fried Charolais rib-eye steak is garnished with the right dose of earthy morel mushrooms; the exquisite roasted breast of guinea fowl is flanked by lemon confit. You can also get classic jambon persillé, coq au vin, and beef bourguignon, all well made, and often available on the prix fixes. The cheese platter is remarkable. The desserts are light, often featuring seasonal fruit. The service and wine list are in keeping. In summer, dine on the terrace facing the square's fountain. The lunch prix fixe is extremely good value. Reserve ahead.

Next door, and preferred by certain French food critics and many migratory bobos, **Le Terroir** (19 Place du Jet d'Eau, Tel: 03 80 20 63 47, closed Sunday dinner and Thursday, and Wednesday dinner from November to March, inexpensive to expensive) is a good fallback. The décor is more Provence than Burgundy. Fabrice Germain makes classics—oeufs en meurette, jambon persillé, coq au vin—plus delicious fricasséed snails, a crispy Époisses-filled puff pastry, and other authentic or updated regional classics. Seasonal desserts include, in summer, vanilla-raspberry Vacherin (the semi-frozen dessert, not the cheese). The wine list features local winegrowers; the service is friendly and professional, and there's a terrace here, too.

As in Meursault, at the main branch of this wine emporium, **Cave des Vieilles Vignes** (22 Place du Jet d'Eau, Tel: 03 80 20 69 33, www.cavedesvieillesvignes.com, open daily year-round) is a good idea if you don't have the time or desire to tour wineries. Like brother Fabien, Aurélien Cipriano guides you through 500 or so different Côte d'Or and Côte Chalonnaise bottlings. The oldest vintages are from 1959. The prices are often the same as at the wineries.

If you visit only one winery in Santaney, make it Yvette and Jean-François Chapelle of **Domaine Chapelle** (Le Haut Village,

Tel: 03 80 20 60 09, www.domainechapelle.com, open weekdays without appointment, weekends by appointment only). In the same family since 1893, Jean-François took over in 1991 and revolutionized things. The vineyards are organic. The Santenay Rouge Clos des Cornières—10,000 bottles per year—is remarkable. The AOC Bourgogne Rouge is also a winner—and a bargain. Bigger, expensive bottlings are excellent but difficult to come by, especially the Corton Rouge Grand Cru (1,300 bottles), and Gevery-Chambertin (1,800 bottles). The winery makes around 120,000 bottles per year; it all disappears.

An easy address is unmistakable **Château de Santenay** (1 Rue du Château, Tel: 03 80 20 61 87, www.chateau-de-santenay.com, open 10am to 6pm from April to November without appointment, by appointment—hours vary widely—the rest of the year). Remodeled for Burgundy's first Duke, Philip the Bold, in the late 1300s, this pocketsized pile with a glistening tile roof goes back to the ninth century, though it's been tidied and replastered many times since. The estate covers nearly 250 acres, from Clos-de-Vougeot and Aloxe-Corton to Mercurey. The Santenay 1er Cru Rouge holds pride of place. Taste, buy wines, and visit the property.

SAVIGNY-LÈS-BEAUNE

Joined at the hip to Beaune, Savigny has excellent wineries, a medieval museum-winery in a castle, Château de Savigny (see Volnay and Le Cellier Volnaysien for details), and a serviceable traditional restaurant, **La Cuverie** (5 Rue Chanoine-Donin, Tel: 03 80 21 50 03, closed Tuesday, Wednesday, and late December to late January, inexpensive to moderate). A winery centuries ago, the décor—stucco-pointed stone walls, timbers, knickknacks and antique coffee pots—is in keeping with the classic, nicely presented Burgundian cooking. Expect everything from snails and jambon persillé on up, served to tourists and a few locals.

Domaine Henri de Villamont (Rue du Docteur Guyot, Tel: 03 80 21 52 13, www.hdv.fr, open daily 10am to 6pm). Owned by Swiss corporation Schenk, this winery makes a wide variety of wines, some outstanding, and owns twenty-five acres dotted around Savigny and Chambolle-Musigny; it also buys grapes. Visit the vineyards and winery, and do a tasting in the cellars. *Best wines:* Auxey-Duresses Blanc Les Hautés, Chambolle-Musigny 1er Cru Rouge Les Châtelots, Nuits Saint Georges Villages Rouge, Savigny-lès-Beaune 1er Cru Rouge Clos des Guettes, Savigny-lès-Beaune Villages Rouge, and Saint-Véran Blanc Les Plantés.

VOLNAY

Strikingly similar in appearance to Pommard, Chassagne-Montrachet, and a score of other winegrowing villages, Volnay has too many excellent wineries to count, most impossible to visit without investing time and treasure.

On the lower edge of Volnay's vineyards, roadside **Auberge des Vignes** (RN74, Tel: 03 80 22 24 48, www.aubergedesvignes .fr, closed Monday and for dinner on Sunday and Wednesday, inexpensive to expensive), looks like a tourist eatery. Not so. Unless you know it's there, you won't be able to pull over in time before its façade appears in your rearview mirror. The blight of the Route Nationale is compensated by a cozy dining room of the timbers-tools-vintage photos-and-fireplace variety. The glassed-in terrace and, in good weather, the tables outside, fronting Volnay's vineyards, are a treat. It's tempting to pluck grapes; you'll have plenty, as wine, in your glass. The list is longer than you'd expect, with by-the-glass wines from Vincent Naudet (of Marchiseuil) and François Mikulski (of Meursault). Everything—from the cheese sticks on up—is housemade. Every Burgundian specialty is here, prepared with a light touch, plus seasonal dishes. In fall: earthy pheasant pâté, roast duck, boned squab or wild boar slow-cooked in its own juices, lièvre à la royale with a winey red-wine-and-blood reduction sauce. There's also fresh pike-perch with coriander. One outstanding dessert: rich chocolate-and-raspberry bar with lightly salted caramel-butter and crispy hazelnut praline. This is a friendly, family-run restaurant with relaxed but efficient service. Expect to dine with winemakers and merchants.

A different experience awaits on the main square at ivy-hung **Le Cellier Volnaysien** (2 Place de l'Église, Tel: 03 80 21 61 04, www.le-cellier-volnaysien.com, lunch only Thursday to Tuesday, dinner Saturday only, closed Wednesday, very inexpensive to moderate; wine-tasting room open daily 9am to 4pm). Nathalie Gente-Pont transformed the family manor into a restaurant and wine-tasting bar. She's accustomed to crowds of voracious Europeans, who arrive by the busload and fill her subterranean dining room—La Cave—while winelovers and quieter customers choose the garden, wine tasting room, or a table in the upper room, confusingly called Le Cellier. You'll find studiously rustic décor throughout, in an authentically antique setting. The food: regional from egg (oeufs en meurette), via coq au vin or boeuf bourguignon, to apple (tart). Nathalie's father, Michel Pont, owns Château de Savigny in Savigny-lès-Beaune, a museum and winery, whose 1er Cru and other wines Nathalie serves. (Pont's passion is vintage motorcycles, racing cars, tractors, airplane models, and fighter jets, which dot the grounds). Also sold here for take out, at low prices, are hard-to-find vintages from many estates.

CHAPTER 4

SOUTHERN BURGUNDY

Département: Saône et Loire.

Population: 546,000.

Population density: 64 inhabitants/sq. km.

SOUTHERN BURGUNDY

KILOMETERS
0   25   50

MILES
0   Château-Chinon   25

Autun

AUTUNOIS

Chas
Couche
St.-Léger-sur-D

Le Creusot   St.-

Torcy

D994   D980

Marcilly-lè
Monta

Blanzy

Chenôves—L

Collonges-en-Charollais

SAÔNE-ET-   Mont-St.-Vincent
                   St.-Gengoux-

Bourbon-Lancy   Perrecy-les-Forges

LOIRE   Cray

Génelard

Chevagny-sur-Guye

St.-Vincent-Bragny   N70   St.-Martin-de-Salencey   Sa
                                                                     sur

Digoin   St.-Bonnet-de-Joux

Paray-le-Monial

ALLIER   Charolles   Suin   C

                                             N79

Nochize
Poisson   CHAROLLAIS

                 Amanzé   Gibles   Montmelard

Oyé   Lavaux   Matour

                            Châtenay
St.-Christophe-en-Brionnais   La Clayette

St.-Laurent-en-Brionnais   MÂ

St.-Julien-de-Jonzy   Châteauneuf
Iguerande   Mailly   Chauffailles
Outre-Loire

RH

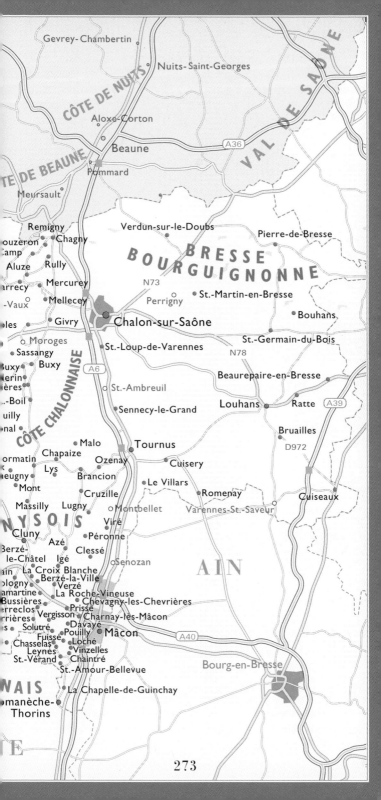

Gevrey-Chambertin

Nuits-Saint-Georges

CÔTE DE NUITS

Aloxe-Corton

VAL DE SAÔNE

A36

Beaune

CÔTE DE BEAUNE

Pommard

Meursault

Remigny

Verdun-sur-le-Doubs

Pierre-de-Bresse

ouzeron
Camp

Chagny

BRESSE

Aluze

Rully

BOURGUIGNONNE

arrecy

Mercurey

N73

St.-Martin-en-Bresse

-Vaux

Mellecey

Perrigny

les

Givry

Chalon-sur-Saône

Bouhans

Moroges

St.-Germain-du-Bois

Sassangy

St.-Loup-de-Varennes

Buxy
erin
ères

Buxy

A6

N78

Beaurepaire-en-Bresse

-Boil

St.-Ambreuil

uilly

Louhans

Ratte

A39

nal

Sennecy-le-Grand

CÔTE CHALONNAISE

Bruailles

Malo

Tournus

D972

ormatin

Chapaize

Ozenay

Cuisery

eugny

Lys

Brancion

Le Villars

Romenay

Cuiseaux

Mont

Cruzille

Massilly

Lugny

Montbellet

Varennes-St.-Saveur

NYSOIS

Viré

AIN

Cluny

Péronne

Berzé-
le-Châtel

Azé

Clessé

ain

Igé

Senozan

ologny

La Croix Blanche

amartine

Berzé-la-Ville

Bussières

Verzé

La Roche-Vineuse

rreclos
rières

Vergisson

Chevagny-les-Chevrières

s

Solutré

Prissé

Charnay-lès-Mâcon

Chasselas

Davayé

Fuissé

Pouilly

Mâcon

Leynes

Loché

St.-Vérand

Vinzelles

Chaintré

A40

St.-Amour-Bellevue

Bourg-en-Bresse

NAIS

La Chapelle-de-Guinchay

manèche-
Thorins

E

CHALON-SUR-SAÔNE
and CÔTE CHALONNAISE

Includes: Aluze, Blanzy, Bouzeron, Brancion Buxy, Chagny, Chalon-sur-Saône, Charrecey, Chassey-le-Camp, Chenôves—Les Filletières, Le Creusot, Genouilly, Givry, Jambles, Malo, Marcilly-lès-Buxy, Mellecey, Mercurey, Montagny-lès-Buxy, Mont-Saint-Vincent, Moroges, Ozenay, Remigny, Rully, Saint Boil, Saint-Gengoux-le-National, Saint-Léger-sur-Dheune, Saint-Vallerin, Sassangy, Sennecey-le-Grand, Tournus, Le Villars.

THE CÔTE CHALONNAISE BEGINS SOUTH OF THE DHEUNE RIVER AND CANAL DU CENTRE. CHAGNY and Remigny, in bottomlands, and hilltop Bouzeron (where excellent Aligoté is made), are on its border. This is a geographical, topographical, and administrative divide: the Côte d'Or *département* lies north, the Saône et Loire south. The soil is markedly different, the wines are softer and less inclined to last, though there are exceptions, particularly in AOCs Givry, Mercurey, and Rully. The scenery is greener, gentler, and, many would argue, extremely appealing.

This sub-region's largest city (Burgundy's second city) is Chalon-sur-Saône, fifteen miles south of Chagny. A solid place of half-timbered buildings, Chalon gives its name to the Côte

Chalonnaise. An important historic city, its pedigree is ancient Roman. Many authentic restaurants, neighborhood food and wine shops, a major river port, two museums, and an urban edge, have preserved it from mass tourism. One of Burgundy's liveliest markets is held twice weekly.

The Côte stretches south to fortified hilltop Brancion. Tournus, an attractive riverside center of ancient origin, is east of Brancion. The area's western hinterlands reach the Dheune River, which runs northeast to southwest, past formerly coal-rich Le Creusot and Montceau-les-Mines. Halfway between Chalon and the Autun is Couches. The unsung Couchois winegrowing district spreads across pretty hills; some Couchois wines are made by winegrowers in Hautes-Côtes-de-Beaune villages.

ALUZE

Medieval in appearance, handsome hilltop Aluze sits atop one of the region's oldest settlements. Excavations are underway. The Via Agrippa ran nearby, after traversing Mercurey, due west three miles. The site's beauty, isolation, fine reputation for winegrowing, and relative lack of contamination, are what induced Alain and Isabelle Hasard to move their winery here from Saint-Sernin-du-Plain. Their new winery is **Alain et Isabelle Hasard–Domaine les Champs de l'Abbaye** (Tel: 06 09 57 77 52, by appointment only). The Hasards went organic in 1999, and their Bourgogne Côtes du Couchois Le Clos and Les Rompeys (both red), Bourgogne AOC red, Bourgogne Aligoté, and even the humble Passetoutgrain, are outstanding. They're also hard to buy: the winery sells out. Restaurant Le Petit Blanc in nearby Charrecey serves them.

BLANZY

Joined to Montceau-les-Mines, Blanzy is also a former mining town, with a museum of mining, and low-cost housing projects. It's home to **Le Plessis** (33 Route de Mâcon, Tel: 03 85 57 46 08, www.restaurant-le-plessis.com, closed Sunday dinner, Saturday lunch, and Monday, inexpensive to expensive), on terraces overlooking a lake. Le Plessis is the town's best, an excellent place to enjoy a classy bourgeois-*terroir* meal while waiting for your train: the Montchanin TGV station is only minutes away.

BOUZERON

On a hillside overlooking the northern Côte Chalonnaise, Bouzeron is celebrated for its Aligoté, here known simply as "Bouzeron," and drunk straight. At its best, it has a pleasant citrus quality and abundant acidity. Some of the finest Bouzeron is made not in the village but elsewhere, by prestige wineries Bouchard Père et Fils of Beaune, and Faiveley of Nuits Saint Georges, as well as Marinot-Verdun (in Saint-Sernin-du-Plain) or Domaine Belleville—Marc Dumont, in Rully.

Bouzeron now draws gourmets, since chef Olivier Philippeau remodeled a bedraggled property with the requisite contemporary flair, turning it into a self-styled *restaurant gastronomique*: **Le Cavochon** (2 Rue de la Mairie, Tel: 03 85 87 33 92, closed Monday dinner, Tuesday, and Wednesday lunch, inexpensive to moderate). Think black metal tables and chairs with white seat cushions, red runners on top, tiles and polished planks. Spotlights pick out the timbers, local winemakers, and migratory bobos. Dine in summer on the back terrace. The food is updated Burgundian: snail salad with crayfish and garlicky cream sauce, frog's leg soup with flat-leaf parsley and hot chili pepper, classic pike-perch in a red wine sauce, fricasséed veal kidneys with mustard seed. The desserts, seasonal, are light, the wine list rich in local Aligoté, smoother whites, and lovely reds from Rully, Givry, Maranges, and Santenay.

Ambitious winemakers Anne-Sophie and Daniel Chanzy of **Domaine Chanzy** (1 Rue de la Fontaine, Tel: 03 85 87 23 69, daniel@chanzy.com, www.chanzy.com, open weekdays without appointment, weekends by appointment only, closed two weeks in August) have nearly ninety acres in various AOCs. Chanzy is bigger than many, and recent. The Bouzeron AOC (Aligoté) is true to type. Oak shows up in many bottlings, but the Rully L'Hermitage white respects *terroir* nonetheless; the red is also good. Better than either is modest Bourgogne AOC Clos de la Fortune white, redolent of peachy, overripe fruit. Chanzy also makes oaky Mercurey AOC Les Carabys in red and white.

Next door is **Domaine Aubert et Pamela de Villaine** (2 Rue de la Fontaine, Tel: 03 85 91 20 50, www.de-villaine.com, open weekdays by appointment only), early converts to pesticide-free winemaking. The De Villaine's nephew Pierre de Benoïst now makes the wines, most of them organic, including one of the best Bouzerons around, and very good Bourgogne Côte Chalonnaise red and white.

BRANCION AND MARTAILLY-LÈS-BRANCION

Perched over bluffs and vineyards on the southernmost Côte Chalonnaise, Brancion is the picture-book, hilltop fortified village, a lovely place to stroll. Visit the Romanesque church, with its crusader's tombstone and magnificent views. You're better off limiting your caloric intake to a snack and coffee at the only place in the village. Footing Brancion, within the commune of Martailly-lès-Brancion, at the crossroads of highway D14, an organic food market, Marché Biologique (Tel: 03 85 51 11 41), is held under antique linden trees on the first and third Sunday morning of the month. Expect to find organic cheeses, fresh fruit and vegetables, honeys and gingerbread, and organic wines. Facing the marketplace is another café-eatery where you can safely tank up on coffee before heading elsewhere to eat.

BUXY

On the wine route half an hour from Chalon-sur-Saône, Buxy is hardly touristed. Once surrounded by ramparts, the main drag follows the former moat, a sycamore-lined oval. This medieval sleeper has charm, pleasant cafés, good food and wine, and a fine restaurant. Buy picnic supplies (terrines, jambon persillé) at **Charcuterie Guy Berny** (3 Place Halle, Tel: 03 85 92 01 28, closed Monday). Buxy's weekly market on Thursday mornings counts among its fruit, vegetable, and chèvre cheese stands the soft-spoken Gilles Valentin-Smith, a beekeeper from Montagny-lès-Buxy, who makes excellent honeys (try light-colored *miel de fleurs des chaumes*, from scrubby limestone tablelands). He also makes artisanal mustard with hydromel-flavored vinegar. Christophe Thibault and Valérie Pamart of Ferme de la Cré grow organic vegetables, and make excellent organic jams and conserves. Chocolate-maker Caroline Curt of Caro d'Choc in Saint Ambreuil (Tel: 03 85 44 22 05), south of Sennecey le Grand, sells her fine, handmade filled chocolates, candied orange peel dipped in chocolate, and chocolate bars.

The restaurant's gourmet food boutique, **L'Épicurien des Vignes** (19 Grande Rue, Tel: 03 85 92 14 12, closed Sunday and Monday afternoon, and Tuesday) sells excellent take-out foods (ready-to-eat garlicky snails, casseroles of frog's legs, house-smoked salmon), desserts (crème brûlée, chocolate and raspberry tarts), and gourmet foods (honey, jam, cookies, liqueurs).

Practically next door is fine bakery and chocolate shop **J. I. Bailly** (Grande Rue, Tel: 03 85 92 13 87, closed Monday). Of the pastries, chocolates, and candies don't miss crisp cookies called Gallettes Bourguignonnes (with blackcurrant, orange, or lemon). Bailly also sells artisanal nougat with candied fruits, pistachios, and other nuts.

For an outstanding home-cooked Burgundian meal featuring garden-grown produce and local ingredients of the highest quality, reserve a comfortable room at **Chambre d'Hôtes—Table d'Hôtes Davenay** (Davenay, Tel: 03 85 92 04 79, dav_christine@hotmail.com, http://davenay.chez-alice.fr, meals inexpensive, reserve ahead). The challenge is finding it: follow signs from central Buxy. The house is modern, on a steep hillside a quarter-mile southwest, amid grapevines. Garrulous, plucky hostess Christine Davanture makes gougères from scratch, serving them with classic Kir to guests, most of whom are astonished by the view from the terrace (where you dine in summer). Next: exquisite jambon persillé, which she makes from pork shoulder slow-cooked in a double-boiler. The perfect boeuf bourguignon follows; meltingly tender and flavorful, it has marinated with herbs and Pinot Noir for up to forty-eight hours. Christine cooks it, on and off, over a period of a day, for about three hours, at low heat. Garden-grown vegetables and salad accompany the meal. Homemade dessert (pears poached in Pinot Noir with cinnamon and sugar, or sliced oranges flambéed with Marc de Bourgogne) wraps things up. Christine learned from her mother and grandmother, and proudly upholds Burgundian traditions, which few restaurateurs respect. The wine? Montagny 1er Cru white, and local reds, from the co-op. Thierry, her husband, supplies the co-op with his grapes, grown below in the grassy vineyards. They're not organic, but almost. Request the bedroom on the east side, with the view: when clear, you'll see to the Mont Blanc.

The area's best wineries are in Montagny-lès-Buxy. But don't overlook **Cave des Vignerons de Buxy** (2 Route de Chalon, Tel: 03 85 92 04 30, www.cave-buxy.fr, open daily except Sunday without appointment), a.k.a. La Buxinoise, founded in 1931, now in a modern, user-friendly facility edging town. It produces 6.4 million bottles, some surprisingly good, many good-value, especially the "limited series" selections for individual estates. *Best wines*: Montagny Premier Cru Montcuchot (white) and Domaine Laborbe-Juillot Givry 1er Cru Clos Marceaux Monopole (red).

CHAGNY

Bordering the Côte d'Or, and crossed by the Canal du Centre, Chagny is a hard-driven town that once thrived off river transportation and steel. It's in the process of refitting for tourism (canal cruises and wine). There's a good Sunday morning market that fills the center of town.

One of the region's most famous, luxurious restaurants edges the main square: **Lameloise** (36 Place d'Armes, Tel: 03 85 87 65 65, www.lameloise.fr, closed lunch on Tuesday and Thursday, Wednesday, and from December 23 to end January, astronomically, impossibly expensive). The food at Jacques Lameloise's perennial three-star temple is sublime, fashioned from the finest ingredients, with many an updated Burgundian classic—snails with parsley cream and grilled fingerling potatoes, frog's legs done in half a dozen ways, Charolais filet with red-wine butter sauce and a mini tarte-tatin of shallots, to name a few. The sumptuous desserts include a parade of chocolate confections. The trolley offers possibly the best selection of Burgundian cheeses in the region. The wine list is too heavy to lift, with hundreds of bottles costing hundreds or thousands of euros. Service? Impeccable, rarely starchy. The sole drawback—beyond the slightly ceremonious atmosphere—is the price.

Country-style, in a historic salt cellar with vaults and a giant fireplace, is **Le Grenier à Sel** (4 Rue Marc Boillet, Tel: 03 85 87 09 10, open daily, inexpensive to moderate). Follow signs to the Casino Géant supermarket on the outskirts and you'll find it. The rotisserie chicken, beef, and lamb are deliciously simple, the desserts generously served (classic tarte tatin), the atmosphere relaxed. You'll discover reasonably priced wines to send down your meal with a smile.

The butcher shops, *charcuteries*, and bakeries in town are many, and equally good. If you're in the market for regional gourmet items, however, head to **Marie l'Or de Bourgogne** (39 Rue Ferté, Tel: 03 85 87 21 77, closed Sunday and Monday, in summer open Sunday morning), on the main square. You'll find everything from mustard and gingerbread to jams, terrines, wines, and wine accessories.

CHALON-SUR-SAÔNE

Call it Chalon—no one in Burgundy but bureaucrats or visiting Parisians says Chalon-sur-Saône. With 50,000 inhabitants, Chalon is the second largest city in Burgundy, after Dijon. It's a real place, the ancient Cavillonum (or Cabilonnum) of the Romans, who unloaded their wines and other weapons here during the conquest of Gaul; an important market city of the Middle Ages; the cradle of Burgundian heavy industry in the 1800s, with shipbuilding and steel; the French headquarters, recently defunct, of Kodak; and now a bustling blend of suburban big-box emporiums and historic businesses, all of them rattling along, transitioning toward high-tech and tourism. The monuments of antiquity are gone, except for remnants of Roman towers and walls, but the half-timbered houses, and stone cathedral of later centuries, abide. Many landmarks have been restored, and the center city is off limits to cars, at least some of the time. Chalon has atmosphere, and edge. Like Mâcon and Dijon, low-cost housing projects dot the scruffy outskirts, unemployment is high, and there's an at times rowdy party crowd on the streets. Not that Chalon is dangerous: by any standard it isn't. But this is certainly not a bobo playground like Beaune.

The Tourist Office, on the riverside, near the Pont Saint Laurent, hands out free, detailed maps and is a good source of information on cultural events: 4 Place du Port-Villiers, Tel: 03 85 48 37 97, www.chalon-sur-saone.net.

There are scores of fine restaurants in and around Chalon, and many appealing cafés with outdoor terraces. With few exceptions, the best are near the cathedral, or on Île Saint Laurent, midstream in the Saône, along the island's axis, Rue de Strasbourg, restaurant alley.

Note that almost all food-related businesses are closed Sunday afternoon and Monday; those not closed on Monday are closed on Wednesday.

Cultural nourishment is available from two museums. As the cradle of heavy industry and photography—pioneering heliographer Nicéphore Niepce was born nearby and lived in Chalon—it seems natural to find the **Musée Nicéphore Niepce** (28 Quai des Messageries, Tel: 03 85 48 41 98, www.chalonsursaone.fr, closed Monday and Tuesday from October to June, open daily the rest of the year) on the riverside drive. Anyone remotely interested in the origins of photography must visit. Chalon's second trove is across from city hall, the ideal provincial museum, in a landmark, neoclassical building, easy to visit and stuffed with fascinating treasures of local history: **Musée Denon** (Place de l'Hôtel de Ville/3 Rue Boichot, Tel: 03 85 94 74 41, closed Tuesday and holidays). Head downstairs to the Gallo-Roman rooms, where objects, sculptures, and tombstones are displayed. Many finds, such as amphorae from Chalon, the bed of the Saône, and villages or farms throughout Southern Burgundy, evoke Caesar and his WMD—weapons of mass drunkenness. The wicker grape-picker's basket from 2,000 years ago is identical to those still occasionally seen in Burgundian vineyards. Ditto farm and vineyard tools.

The markets of Chalon are held nearly every day somewhere in town. Tuesday: Les Aubépins (outlying), Rue Porte-de-Lyon,

Place Saint-Laurent; Wednesday: Place de l'Hôtel de Ville, Place du Marché aux Prés Saint Jean; Thursday: Cité du Stade (outlying); Friday and Sunday: Rue aux Fèvres and Place de la Cathédrale, aka Place Saint-Vincent, plus Rue Porte-de-Lyon, and Place du Général de Gaulle/Place de Beaune; Saturday: Avenue Boucicaut, Rue Porte-de-Lyon.

The most exciting markets are on Friday and Sunday on Rue aux Fèvres and Place Saint-Vincent, but Wednesdays are also fun. Among the stalls on Place Saint-Vincent, seek out La Chév'rit for goat's-milk cheeses incorporating herbs, nuts, pepper, and fruit. Market gardener Monsieur Maudeit of GAEC des Riottis sells herbs, fruit, and vegetables. At tiny Rue Porte-de-Lyon's market, fourth-generation farmers the Tareaux sell homegrown fruit and vegetables, and always share smiles.

Places to eat and drink

120 Cent Vins bar à vins (3 Rue du Blé, Tel: 03 85 93 29 91, familleclaing@orange.fr, closed Monday, Wednesday until 6pm, Friday after 6pm, Sunday afternoon, inexpensive to expensive). The name plays on words—*cent vins* (100 wines) sounds like *cent vingt* (120), or the other way around. Whether there are 100 or 120 wines on the blackboard when you visit, they're excellent. Sommelier Gregory Clain, in partnership with Pascal Laville of Cellier Saint Vincent, picks favorite, up-and-coming or established wineries and showcases them, serving ham, olives, and warm snacks such as garlicky snails. The décor is contemporary. Perch at a tall table out front, sit at a wooden table, or lounge in the back on upholstered armchairs.

L'Air du Temps (7 Rue de Strasbourg, Tel: 03 85 93 39 01, closed Sunday and Monday, inexpensive to moderate). The food at this contemporary bistro follows the seasons and the often felicitous inspiration of chef Cyril Bouchet, who worked under three-star Joël Robuchon, with many a nod to regional classics, from pike-perch to Charolais. The ingredients are high quality and fresh, the service is friendly and efficient, and the wine list is strong on Burgundian bottlings at reasonable prices.

Au Grain de Café (19 Avenue du Châtelet, Tel: 03 85 48 49 33, closed Sunday and Monday, inexpensive). Though billed as a coffee roaster, this neighborhood café with tables on the main pedestrianized road actually buys from Le Moulin à Café, the roaster facing the cathedral. You'll find twenty-two types of coffee—monovarietals or blends—and sixty-six different teas, served and

sold. For espresso or cappuccino in the Italian style, make sure to ask for it *serré*. The proprietors are generous with water.

Le Bistrot (31 Rue de Strasbourg, Tel: 03 85 93 22 01, closed weekends, inexpensive to moderate). This likeable revival eatery with old posters, enameled plaques, and woodwork, serves revival food with Burgundian and bistro classics reinterpreted by Patrick Mézière, whose affable wife runs the dining room. The food is not as traditional as at Le Bourgogne or Chez Jules, but the ingredients are excellent; Mézière grows his produce, and the seasonal menus are good value. Like most others on restaurant alley, Le Bistrot has a terrace out front. The wine list is better than most.

Le Bourgogne (28 Rue de Strasbourg, Tel: 03 85 93 39 10, www.restau-lebourgogne-chalon.fr, closed Saturday lunch, Sunday dinner, and Monday, inexpensive to expensive). On "restaurant alley," this comfortable, authentically bourgeois establishment is a minor temple—a side chapel, perhaps—of classic Burgundian food. The building goes back to the 1400s; the long, narrow, thickly carpeted dining room is from the 1600s, according to the affable lady of the house. The vaulted cellar—for groups—is older than either. The décor, service, and food match: chintz on faux Louis XIII chairs, fresh flowers, timbers, wall sconces and antique armoirs, outsized plates atop well-spaced tables, and quality cutlery that feels weighty when wielded on the perfect rabbit terrine, Charolais steak, or coq au vin. Also served are French classics—scallops with mild spices, the inevitable duck with caramelized peaches—but the regional register is more satisfying. If you're wondering why the beef bourguignon or soufflé of local pike with a piquant crayfish sauce are so exquisite, the reason lies in Jean-Luc Civade's decades in the kitchens of l'Hôtel de Paris, in Moulins, a multiple-starred property during his tenure. The premodern desserts—pêche Melba, poires Belle Hélène—sound tempting but sweets don't seem to be Civade's forte. The cheeses, instead, are delicious, the wine list—with many half bottles—includes Meursault 1er Cru Les Génevrières from Bouchard Père et Fils, excellent, underrated Givry 1er Cru from Clos Salomon, and 1973 Château de Pommard. In summer, dine outside.

Café Charbon (14 Place de l'Hôtel de Ville, Tel: 03 85 94 06 11, closed Sunday and Monday, inexpensive). The café's distinctive blue detailing and blue chairs face city hall. The owners are Swiss, evident from the cozy décor (turn-of-the-century tiles, banquettes), to the cleanliness and efficiency. The Lavazza coffee is perfectly made, the desserts particularly delicious. Café Charbon serves jambon persillé and ham from Charcuterie Jussiaux. Lunch platters have silly names (Chalonuus, Classicus), but the cheeses, soups, toasts, salads, and daily specials are remarkably good. Many wines are available by the glass. In nice weather, enjoy the terrace and market.

Chez Jules (11 Rue de Strasbourg, Tel: 03 85 48 08 34, closed Saturday lunch and Sunday, two weeks in February, and three weeks in August, inexpensive to moderate). On restaurant alley, bisecting Chalon's island, this long-established, pleasantly decorated, hip, young bistro is a local favorite. The prices are low, the décor a mix of authentically old and faux-antique. The menus change seasonally; always served are regional or French classics (Saône pike-perch, Charolais steak and Bresse poultry, roast lamb with garlic cloves). Desserts are luscious (fruit tarts, rich chocolate constructions). You'll find good-value regional wines. In warm weather, the dining room opens French windows onto a long streetside terrace.

Le Petit Comptoir d'à Côté (32 Avenue Jean-Jaurès, Tel: 03 85 90 80 52, closed Saturday lunch and Sunday, very inexpensive to moderate). The baby bistro of l'Hôtel Saint-Georges, whose main restaurant is next door—*à côté*—this is the best spot near the train station for lunch or casual dinner. The décor is contemporary-retro, brass-and-wood, bistro-wine bar; the daily blackboards specials, not always Burgundian, follow the seasons, and are fresh and well-prepared (salads, cold cuts, classic entrées, veal meatballs in ragout, skewers of lamb with a red-wine or creamy Béarnaise sauce, luscious seasonal desserts). Wines are reasonably priced and good.

La Rôtisserie Saint Vincent (9 Rue du Blé, Tel: 03 85 48 83 52, closed Sunday and Monday, and the first three weeks in August, very inexpensive to inexpensive). This spartan but lively retro-hangout on a narrow street twenty yards from the cathedral square, has big windows, which let in plenty of light. Diners watch the rotisseries turn; on them are quality meats and poultry, skin browning and juices trickling, the air scented. Though there are the requisite timbers to recall centuries gone by, this isn't an authentic dive haunted by crusty Chalonnais. White collar regulars and tourists wolf the straightforward grilled food, spicy tripe sausage, and salads, some elaborate. The desserts range from antebellum profiteroles to fresh fruit tarts, and while the wine list is short, it features good local bottlings, some by the glass.

Le Verre Galant (Place Saint Vincent, Tel: 03 85 93 09 87, closed Sunday and Monday from May to September, also Tuesday to Friday night the rest of the year, inexpensive to moderate). This retro-style café facing the cathedral is the best perch during Friday and Sunday market days. Philippe and Martine Petit are pros; you'll find plenty of decent and some very good wine, hearty daily dishes and snacks.

Gourmet shops and food artisans

Allex (11 Place de l'Hôtel de Ville, Tel: 03 85 48 04 52, closed Sunday, Monday, one week in February, and August). Chalon's luxury chocolate shop, facing the Musée Denon, Allex was founded by master chocolatier Michel Allex, a local potentate (he was also Chalon's mayor). He died in early 2008, but his widow carries on, flanked by the longtime chocolatiers Allex trained. They make the base-chocolate from scratch, buying the beans and toasting them in-house. The marble-clad, spotlit interior, with its dozens of exquisite filled chocolates, bars, confections, and pastries, displayed like jewelry, is a culinary landmark.

L'Amboisie—Artisan Pâtissier-Chocolatier (6 Avenue Jean-Jaurès, Tel: 03 85 48 09 88, closed Sunday, Tuesday afternoon, and Wednesday). Neo-Baroque and colorfully decorated, this pastry and chocolate shop-cum-tea salon is on the dreary street to the train station, near the elevated highway. Among the irresistible confections: Trio Chocolate (white, milk, and dark chocolate mousse and chocolate sponge cake); Mona Lisa (almond biscuit with creamy candied hazelnut and chocolate ganache with honey and nougat), guaranteed to put an enigmatic smile on your face; and dashing Le Monte-Cristo (chocolate biscuit, raspberry mousse, dark chocolate mousse, and raspberry jam). You'll also find housemade ice creams, classic and exotic chocolates, macarons, jellied fruit candies, and savory snacks served at lunchtime. The hot chocolate and coffee are very good.

Aux Délices (12 Place de Beaune, Tel: 03 85 48 04 32, closed Monday). At the north end of Grande Rue, this old-fashioned, high-quality pastry, chocolate, candy, and ice cream shop owned by the Hurel family has tables indoors, and is a good place to enjoy a pick-me-up and good coffee or tea.

Boulangerie du Théâtre (48 Rue aux Fèvres, Tel: 03 85 93 46 99, www.boulangerieduthéatre.com, closed Sunday afternoon and Wednesday). The bread is baked three times daily to insure perfect freshness; the bakery looks unpromising—a sandwich shop—but

actually has good snacks and is also loved for its *pâté à choux* pastries (cream puffs resembling profiteroles sans ice cream).

Bugaud Traiteur (8 Place de Beaune, Tel: 03 85 48 04 24, www.bugaudtraiteur.com, closed Sunday afternoon and Monday). Topping Grande Rue, Bugaud is Chalon's trendy deli and gourmet boutique, selling everything from seafood salad or "osso bucco of monkfish" with lemon and orange zests, to Parma or Spanish hams, cheese from everywhere imaginable, and many regional specialties.

Charcuterie Jussiaux (7 Rue Gloriette, Tel: 03 85 48 30 15, closed Sunday afternoon and Monday). Michel Rageot and wife Colette run this excellent *charcuterie*, between city hall and the highway. They make delicious hams, salads, jambon persillé, and Cornets de Lucullus—miniature horns of plenty with foie gras mousse or other delights. The Rageots have been at it for forty years, but haven't lost an iota of their passion. Everything is housemade.

Charcuterie Noirot (2 Rue Gloriette, Tel: 03 85 48 05 90, closed Sunday afternoon and Wednesday). This handsome corner deli 200 yards west of town hall has been in the same family since 1970, is only fifty feet from equally excellent Charcuterie Jussieux, and also handmakes dozens of delicacies, from boned and stuffed quail, to suckling pig with morel mushrooms, pheasant terrine or puff pastries with frog's legs, meats, salads, coq au vin, and more, ready to become your picnic.

Coutellerie Jacques Micheron (32 Rue Pasteur, Tel: 03 85 48 22 49, closed Sunday and Monday). This old hardware-style store is a must for lovers of knives—of every shape, size, and cost.

La Ferme Saint Hubert (47 Rue aux Fèvres, Tel: 03 85 48 12 88, closed Sunday afternoon, and a month in summer, usually from late July to end August). Chalon's longest-established cheese shop is about a hundred yards from the cathedral. You'll find just about every type of cheese made in Burgundy (and many others), all of high quality.

Jean-Luc Genet (40 Rue du Général Leclerc, Tel: 03 85 48 10 53, closed Tuesday and Wednesday). The specialty of this friendly, family-owned bakery, pastry, and chocolate shop is chocolate-dipped tuiles—cookies resembling mini-terracotta roofing tiles.

Gallet (8 Rue Saint Vincent, Tel: 03 85 48 39 15, closed Sunday afternoon and Monday, and two weeks mid August). Chalon's fanciest *charcuterie* and catering operation, half a block west of the cathedral square, is the fief of Meilleur Ouvrier de France (M.O.F.) Patrice Gallet; his hams, jambon persillé, salami, terrines of pork, veal, and quail are among the most beautiful in Burgundy. Gallet is famous for his Saint-Vincent, a deliriously complicated savory construction of ingredients wrapped in a pastry crust and oven baked.

Légendes Gourmandes (Place Saint Vincent, Tel: 03 85 48 05 64, closed Sunday afternoon and Monday). On the cathedral square, across from the coffee roaster, this gourmet food emporium stocks jams, honeys, candies, chocolates, and bizarrely, artisanal French pasta, flavored with everything from aniseed to curry, chocolate, or tomatoes and beets.

La Meulière (21 Rue du Général Leclerc, Tel: 03 85 42 90 90, closed Sunday and Monday). Twenty-one types of certified-organic bread (from baguettes to black bread), crunchy organic cookies, classic pastries made with organic butter, and classical music: all tucked into the tempting display cases of this modest little bakery on the main north-south road, near Place du Général de Gaulle.

Le Moulin à Café (1 Place Saint Vincent, Tel: 03 85 48 91 44, closed Sunday afternoon and Monday). The Plissonniers took over this corner coffee roasting and tea shop in 2006. (It was formerly Le Grain d'Or.) You can't miss it, facing the cathedral, in a half-timbered landmark. The scent is irresistible. Choose among twenty monovarietals and blends, or four dozen teas. The Plissonniers supply the putative competition, Au Grain de Café, a few hundred yards west (which they themselves ran for many years). Coffee grinders and accessories are also sold.

Pâtisseries Vincent Tourret (17 Rue Pasteur, Tel: 03 85 48 05 10, closed Sunday afternoon in summer and Monday year-round). Tourret took over from his father in 1998, and continues to make the specialties of this favorite neighborhood pastry and chocolate shop, which has a few tables and serves good coffee and tea. Le Saint Pierre, invented in 1964, is a meringue cake with candied hazelnut cream. The ice creams are remarkably good, made with cream, eggs, and fresh, top-quality ingredients. Vincent toasts and crushes the hazelnuts that go into that flavor (the only semi-processed paste he buys is for pistachio). Of Chalon's many *pâtisseries*, this is among the least hyped and best.

La Volaillerie Saint-Vincent (10 Rue aux Fèvres, Tel: 03 85 48 04 01, closed Sunday and Wednesday afternoon, and Monday). An historic poultry shop, this is *the* place to buy Bresse chicken, wild game (in season), and many ready-to-cook poultry dishes, plus canned snails, tinned foie gras, and duck or chicken gizzards long cooked and preserved in their own fat.

Marc Wettling (45 Rue aux Fèvres, Tel: 03 85 93 57 86, closed Sunday afternoon and Wednesday morning, and from late July to early September). The maestro uses Valrhona chocolate as his base, and transforms it into classics, from filled chocolates to bars. The house specialty are Kyriettes, luscious ganaches with Crème de Bourgogne liqueur. He also makes chocolate sculptures and complicated delicacies you'll hesitate to eat, because of their beauty.

Wine shops

Cellier Saint Vincent (14 Place Saint Vincent, Tel: 03 85 48 78 25, www.bourgognepassion.fr, closed Sunday afternoon and Monday). Dapper Pascal Laville's mustache twitches when asked for guidance through the maze of Burgundy wines. He's among the region's top winesellers. His spotlit shop on the corner of the cathedral square may appear small, but is cleverly designed. Bottles lie on custom-built, sliding racks. Underneath the 500-year-old building, his premium wine cellars extend across the street to the basement of 120 Cent Vins bar à vins, in which Laville is a partner. Laville stocks affordable, above-ground Mâconnais whites to subterranean giants from the Côte d'Or, worth 1,000 euros or more. See Top Burgundian Winesellers' Favorites, page 59, for Laville's picks. Laville also sells micro-brewery beers.

Maison des Vins de la Côte Chalonnaise (Promenade Sainte-Marie, Tel: 03 85 41 66 66, www.maison-des-vins.com, tastings and retail sales daily 9am to 7pm except Sundays and holidays). At this government-sponsored wine shop and restaurant, taste and buy dozens of Saône et Loire wines at estate prices (wine accessories are also sold). The management has bona fide expertise; however, perhaps jaded by droves of tourists, some viewing a visit as entertainment with free drinks, the staff can at times be less than gracious. From Bouzeron, Givry, Mercurey, Montagny, Rully, plus AOCs Bourgogne Côte Chalonnaise, Passetoutgrains, and Crémant, you'll find estates Domaine Chanzy, Michel-Andreotti, Jean-Paul Berthenet, Domaine des Moirots, Château de Chamirey, Château de Cary Potet, Goubard & Fils, Lumpp, de Suremain, Guillot, and others—a one-stop tour of Southern Burgundy. The upstairs restaurant is a fine idea; ideas are hard to eat.

CHARRECEY

Halfway between Mercurey and Saint-Léger-sur-Dheune, off highway D978 at a crossroads near Aluze, find **Auberge Le Petit Blanc** (Le Pont Pilley, Tel: 03 85 45 15 43, lepetitblanc@orange. fr, closed Sunday dinner, Monday, and Thursday from October to June, also Sunday lunch the rest of the year, Eastertide, the second half of August, and from Christmas through New Year's, inexpensive to moderate). This family-run auberge is favored by winemakers and is a cult hangout, drawing devotees from Sydney to San Francisco. Though authentic, it looks and feels retro-revival (there's a hand-cranked telephone, 1950s television set, and red-and-white check tablecloths). Luckily, Florent Prost and his family haven't been ruined by success, and refuse

to go bobo or change the tried-and-true formula. The menus, on blackboards, might include classic housemade terrine, oeufs en meurette, fricasséed chicken, oysters and chicken livers in mushroom sauce, fricasséed snails, calf's head with gribiche sauce, beef bourgignon, coq au vin, or wild boar stew (in season). Cheeses, and old-fashioned desserts (profiteroles with housemade chocolate sauce, seasonal fruit tarts, mousses) wind up a copious meal. The wine list is longer and deeper than you'd expect—one reason Le Petit Blanc is a hit. Among bottlings are excellent local wines (Rully, Givry, Bouzeron, and Mercurey), many of them—Alain and Isabelle Hasard, for instance— impossible to buy from the winery. The outdoor terrace has comfortable teak furniture. Reserve ahead.

CHASSEY-LE-CAMP

The "camp" in this hillside hamlet in a valley deep in the Côte Chalonnaise, near Aluze, is an ancient Roman encampment. Neolithic man was here first; you may visit the virtual neolithic site, and gaze upon stones, imagining the rest. Edging Chassey find classy, panoramic hotel-restaurant **Auberge du Camp Romain** (Tel: 03 85 87 09 91, www.auberge-du-camp-romain.com, open daily, very inexpensive to expensive). What cave men or Caesar would make of the geranium-hedged terrace with see-forever views, or the stone-paved dining room with columns, heavy curtains, cushy upholstered chairs, and handsomely set tables, is a fine question. The delicious grilled meat and poultry would delight anyone. On the menu is about every Burgundian specialty, from jambon persillé to frog's legs, snails to Charolais steaks with or without Époisses or mustard sauce, pike-perch or trout (from local fish farms), beef bourguignon and coq au vin. The cheeses include fresh goat with cream; the desserts range from gingerbread or pears poached in red wine, to nougat glacé, fruit tarts and antebellum Ile Flottante. The service is professional, the wine list strong on local, reasonably priced bottlings.

CHENÔVES–LES FILLETIÈRES

Don't confuse this Chenôves with the celebrated Chenôves near Dijon. Here, on the main D981 highway, in the hamlet of Filletières north of Saint Boil, you'll find award-winning **La Chèvrerie des Filletières** (Tel: 03 85 44 02 92, closed Sunday afternoons in January). This tidy little farm and cheese factory is celebrated for its Tour du Charollais—a towering lump of goat's curd—Saint Biquet (about half the size), and Cabrilou (even smaller), plus classic Boutons de culottes, Briquettes (flat and long), fresh cheeses, and pungent, powerful Fromage fort. You can visit the barn and pet the goats if you so desire.

LE CREUSOT

Le Creusot is a former mining, heavy industrial and armaments town, an untouristed, real place with character. Nowadays it has a green belt, with a park and lake; the old glass factory, **Château de la Verrerie** (Tel: 03 85 55 02 46, www.creusot.net), houses **Le Musée de l'Homme et de l'Industrie**, about the city's industrial past. It's also the HQ of Greater Creusot-Montceau, and the tourism office, and well worth visiting for the eighteenth-century architecture—duncecap towers and vast salons—the views, and the displays.

Le Creusot's outdoor market is held on Saturday morning. In the former slaughterhouse, on the southeastern outskirts, beyond the steam-driven, ore-crushing Marteau-Pilon, a towering iron hammer, the area's great landmark, find the hip, popular **Le Restaurant** (Rue des Abattoirs, Tel: 03 85 56 32 33, closed weekends, very inexpensive to moderate). The décor is modern, and though it's chilling to think of the building's former use, the reconversion is laudable and successful. The prix fixe menus are affordable, seasonal, and play variations on regional themes. Many dishes use organic, locally grown produce, meat, and fish. There's a long wine list featuring regional bottlings, many available by the glass. In good weather, eat outside on the terrace overlooking the lake.

Food purveyors include pastry and chocolate shop **Aux Buchettes du Morvan-Godillot** (27 Rue du Maréchal Leclerc, Tel: 03 85 55 10 75, closed Sunday afternoon, and Monday), on the main, curving boulevard from the château to Esplanade François Mitterrand. The shop's namesake Buchettes are chocolates resembling miniature logs.

GIVRY

Atmospheric Givry is the showcase of Chalonnais architect Émiland Gauthey, who designed the Canal du Centre, city halls in Tournus and Givry, churches in and around Givry and the Vaux Valley, and countless other solid pieces of infrastructure. Givry's unusual eighteenth-century gates are also his, ditto the matching main square, in whose middle rises a rotonda, La Halle Ronde de Givry (Tel: 03 85 44 43 36), which used to be a grain market. The helicoidal staircase is remarkable. This is Givry's tourism information center, where the annual wine market— Le Marché aux Vins—is held in early April. The weekly outdoor market is held Thursday morning on the parking lot on the highway, Place d'Armes.

On Place d'Armes you'll also find **Auberge & Bar à Bières de la Billebaude** (#4, Tel: 03 85 44 34 25, closed Sunday and Monday, very inexpensive to inexpensive), a beery youth hangout, with a terrace, near Gauthey's church. The prices are extremely low; among the unlikely, oft-changing dishes you'll find a few safe, edible items. Don't expect gourmet food.

Givry has a tapas bar; several café-restaurants (the nicest terrace is at **Le Givry**, 2 Place de la Halle, Tel: 03 85 44 39 86, open daily), a classic bakery–pastry and chocolate shop (**Fèvre**, 48 Rue de la République, Tel: 03 85 44 34 04, closed Tuesday), a fancy chocolate boutique (**Dessolins**, 18 Rue de l'Hôtel de Ville, Tel: 03 85 44 31 44, closed Monday), and several good *charcuteries* and grocery stores, which come in handy for picnics.

However, the main attraction is the wine. If you're not interested in hitting the wineries, you can find about twenty local producers (and others from further afield) at glitzy new shop **Le Cellier Henri IV** (6 Rue de la République, Tel: 03 85 44 36 81, www.cellierhenri4.com, open nonstop 10am to 6:30pm, closed Wednesday).

Givry is remarkably good value; the best is red. Relatively little white is made, though that is changing. Among top producers are Ludovic du Gardin de Séveirac and his partner Fabrice Perrotto of **Clos Salomon** (16 Rue du Clos Salomon, Tel: 03 85 44 32 24, open daily except Sunday without appointment for sales, tastings by appointment only). The winery is on Givry's southern edge, on the road to Poncey. A single-vineyard estate, Clos Salomon has been in the family for over 300 years. Though outwardly modest, the cellars go back to the 1300s. The estate's vineyard totals 17.5 acres; no chemical treatments or herbicides are used, and grass grows between the rows. The best and only red is Givry 1er Cru Clos Salomon Monopole, a balanced, powerful, meaty wine. It's made to last, and needs five years to come into its own. The estate also makes outstanding white Givry 1er Cru La Grande Berge; judging by the color, nose, and complexity, it might come from Meursault.

Also outstanding and down the same road is **Domaine Ragot** (4 Rue de l'École, Poncey, Tel: 03 85 44 35 67, www.domaine-ragot .com, open Monday to Saturday without appointment, closed Sundays and holidays), a sixth-generation, family-run winery with 22.5 acres, eighty percent of which grows Pinot Noir. Their best wines are Givry 1er Cru La Grande Berge and Givry AOC Vieilles Vignes reds.

Domaine Joblot (4 Rue Pasteur, Tel: 03 85 44 30 77, by appointment). Jean-Marc and Vincent Joblot are among the area's most reliable winegrowers. They have a handful of prime 1er Cru parcels. *Best wines:* Givry 1er Cru Clos de la Servoisine (red and white), Givry 1er Crus Clos des Bois-Cheveau and Clos du Cellier aux Moines (both red).

Domaine Armelle et Gérard Mouton (6 Rue de l'Orcene, Tel: 03 85 44 37 99, open Monday to Saturday by appointment, closed Sunday) is another fine family-run winery, known for its simple Givry Champ Pourot white and Givry 1er Crus, including Clos Jus (red).

JAMBLES

The landscape is particularly scenic around Jambles, which falls within the Givry AOC. On the southern edge of the village find award-winning, family-run **Domaine Michel Sarrazin et Fils** (Charnailles, Tel: 03 85 44 30 57, sarrazin2@wanadoo.fr, open daily without appointment, closed Sunday afternoon). Though the estate's facilities look modern, they've been in the same family since 1671. The reds are big and meaty, and are meant to be drunk with substantial fare. *Best wines:* Givry 1er Cru Les Grands Prétants and Givry AOC Champs Lalot (both red).

Another fine winery with excellent, affordable, classic Givry is **Domaine René Bourgeon** (2 Rue du Chapître, Tel: 03 85 44 35 85, by appointment).

MALO

To experience a rustic working farm, and eat wholesome, home-grown food, try **Ferme-Auberge de Malo** (Malo, Champlieu,

Étrigny, Tel: 03 85 92 21 47, www.aubergemalo.com, open for lunch and dinner, preferably by reservation, from Easter to November, inexpensive). It's a few miles west of Brancion, off highway D159. The chickens scrabble around, animals braying, moo-ing, clucking, and so forth, as you await your meal. You can also buy fruits, vegetables, pork terrines, and housemade delicacies. Owners Pascal Goujon and family may look vaguely like French Hell's Angels, but they seem to know how to farm and cook: they've been at it since 1988. Each May, June, July, August, and September, so-called Marchés Paysans are held here on Saturdays, mid-month, during which other local farmers sell their goods. Check the website or phone ahead for dates and details.

MARCILLY-LÈS-BUXY

Outstanding organic honey and derivatives are the specialty of far-flung **L'Abeille de Guye–Biobourgogne D & D Savoye Apiculteurs** (Tel: 03 85 96 10 68, 06 88 50 10 29, labeilledeguye@yahoo.fr, open weekday afternoons only, closed weekends and holidays). Bearded and wearing a chef's uniform, honeymaker Monsieur Savoye makes half a dozen delicious honeys in a good year. He does everything by hand, without treatments. Ask ahead for a tour. If he has time, Savoye will take you to the hives. Don't miss the chestnut honey and *miel de sapins*, and the housemade, pure-honey gingerbread, which is outstanding.

MELLECEY

A mile north of Germolles and its château, by an information kiosk and old wine press, in what resembles a tract home at the traffic circle on highways D981 and D978, find **Le Guide de Marloux** (Tel: 03 85 45 28 46, www.leguidedemarloux.com, closed Sunday and Thursday dinner, and Monday, very inexpensive to moderate). Also known as Chez Jean and Corinne Lagareiro, this simple restaurant serves locals and tourists. The yawning dining room with wooden tables, white tiled floors, and barn-style timbers isn't exactly cozy in winter. But there's a nice terrace (with umbrellas from an industrial ice cream maker). Stick to the Menu Classique (oeufs en meurette, tripe-sausage terrine with mustard, a classic main dish, good local cheeses, and dessert). Desserts are good: Duchess of Burgundy is gingerbread with candied-hazelnut nougatine, white chocolate, and blackcurrant, a nod to the great Lady of Germolles. The wine list features good-value bottlings from Givry and Rully.

Do many Burgundian culinary icons (and artworks) actually come from the Low Countries? Maybe. It's widely acknowledged that in the late 1300s, Duchess Marguerite de Flandre, wife of Duke Philippe le Hardi, brought to her weekend residence at Germolles the gingerbread of her native Flanders. Apparently, she also had farm animals herded along with her. Charolais, it's claimed, is none other than a cross of indigenous Burgundians with the Duchess's heifers and bulls. Is boeuf bourguignon really Dutch *stamppot* stew with wine? Blackcurrants, and Dijon mustard, too, may have come in the grand lady's trousseau. At least Pinot Noir and Chardonnay are safe.

Gastronomy aside, the hodgepodge Château de Germolles has charm, and is a must for anyone interested in the progression of medieval architecture, from a barn on the ancient Roman road, to twelfth-century fort, to fourteenth- and fifteenth-century Gothic château. (Tel: 03 85 45 10 55, open daily in high season, closed Monday in low season, and from mid November to May.)

MERCUREY

Little visited, Mercurey lies eight miles west of Chalon. Named for the (undiscovered) temple to Mercury that (presumably) once stood here, Mercurey is known for its powerful, under-valued reds, and the traditional, cozy, luxurious Michelin-starred hotel-restaurant **Hôtellerie du Val d'Or** (40 Grande Rue, Tel: 03 85 45 13 70, www.le-valdor.com, closed Monday, lunch Tuesday, mid December to mid January, and one week in February, moderate to astronomically expensive). This is one of the few Michelin-starred properties in Burgundy with real food—lightened, beautifully presented, and served with ceremony—in pleasantly fuddy-duddy surroundings (and the lunch prix fixe is a deal). Chef Pascal Charreyras is famed for his house-smoked eel, torpedo fish and eel terrine with wild mushrooms, Saône pike-perch, tender Bresse chicken cooked and served in its own juices, excellent cheeses, Marc de Bourgogne soufflé-glacé, and long wine list. Among affordable bottlings is gold-medal-winning Mercurey Village white from Château de Chamirey, which is muscular yet balanced and delicate (a quarter of it spends sixteen months in new oak casks).

Speaking of which, gentleman winemaker Bertrand Devillard, his son Amaury, and daughter-in-law Aurore are the faces behind picture-book **Domaine du Château de Chamirey** (Tel: 03 85 45 21 61, www.domaines-devillard.com, by appointment), Mercurey's prestige property, south of the main highway. The

Devillards are quietly passionate, and while they aren't shy about using new oak, their wines capture the meat and muscle of Chardonnay without much flab. They also own a brace of prestige properties, among them outstanding Domaine des Perdrix (in Premeaux-Prissey) and La Ferté (in Givry). *Best wines:* Mercurey 1er Cru Les Ruelles, Mercurey Village, Givry 1er Cru Clos de la Servoisine (all red), Mercurey La Mission Monopole 1er Cru, Mercurey Village (both white).

Excellent **Domaine Émile Juillot** (4 Rue de Mercurey, Tel: 03 85 45 13 87, e.juillot.theulot@wanadoo.fr, open weekdays without appointment, weekends by appointment only) is more accessible. Run since 1986 by Nathalie and Jean-Claude Theulot, this estate routinely wins awards for its round, fruity reds. *Best wines:* Mercurey Vieilles Vignes, Mercurey 1er Cru Les Combins (both red).

Much bigger is winegrower-*négociant* **Maison Antonin Rodet** (Grande Rue, Tel: 03 85 98 12 12, www.rodet.com, by appointment). Rodet produces Château de Rully, Château de Mercey, recently bought Dufouleur Père et Fils and Clos de Thorey, and distributes Château de Chamirey wines, and others.

On the highway west of town, watch for **Restaurant Le Charme** (Route d'Autun, Tel: 03 85 45 28 49, www.restaurant-lecharme.com, closed Tuesday and Wednesday, inexpensive to moderate). Small, upscale, with chandeliers and faux Louis XIII furniture, run by a husband-and-wife team, and serving updated *cuisine bourgeoise*, Le Charme is a favorite of locals when they can't quite manage Val d'Or, and want something a little more refined than Le Petit Blanc in Charrecey. Chef Fabien Benoît worked at three-star Lameloise in Chagny, and it shows. Stick to the simplest dishes.

MONTAGNY-LÈS-BUXY

Perched on a mountainside above Buxy, Montagny has see-forever views. A handful of winegrowers here are outstanding. **Jean-Paul Berthenet** (Tel: 03 85 92 17 06, domaine.berthenet@free.fr, by appointment) is in an old village house on the corner of the main road, near the cypress hedge as you enter the village. Formerly a member of Buxy's co-op, Berthenet went independent in the early 2000s. His reputation and fortunes have soared. *Best wines*: Montagny 1er Crus Tête de Cuvée, Vieilles Vignes, Les Saint-Morilles.

Budding organic superstar **Stéphane Aladame** (Rue du Lavoir, Tel: 3 85 92 06 01, stephane.aladame@wanadoo.fr, by appointment) is higher up on the same road. Aged eighteen, he threw himself into the vat, and now, in his mid 30s, is hailed for his derring-do (sinking several hundred bottles of his best wine into the sea for a year, at seventy feet, to test the effects of pressure, oxygen-saline transference, and constant low temperature). Most of his landlocked wines sell out; don't be surprised if he has nothing for you to taste. *Best wines*: Montagny 1er Crus Les Burnins, Les Coères, Le Vieux Château.

Domaine Feuillat-Juillot (Tel: 03 85 92 03 71, domainefeuillatjuillot@wanadoo.fr, open daily without appointment, closed the second half of August). This recent, easy-to-visit winery on the back road to Saint-Vallerin is run by Françoise Feuillat-Juillot and has its oak-adoring adepts—many foreign. Luckily, only ten percent of the barrels are new, and several of the best wines are spared oaking, notably the Montagny 1er Crus Les Crêts, and Cuvée Les Grappes d'Or, which have a subtle, clean, fresh quality. Bigger, fruitier, fatter, oaky Les Coères unsurprisingly wins plaudits.

MONT-SAINT-VINCENT

With clear-day views reaching to Switzerland or the Beaujolais, this hilltop village ten miles south of Montceau-les-Mines is a favorite excursion. Despite the giant broadcasting tower, it has charm—narrow, winding streets, a hulking tenth-century church. If you're starving, there's a tavern on the square in the middle of the medieval tangle. Better food is a half mile downhill at Les Perrons, on the road to Montceau, at **Le Relais des Perrons** (Les Perrons, Tel: 03 85 79 80 87, closed Tuesday dinner and Wednesday, inexpensive to moderate). The décor: stuccoed stone walls, timbers, tiles, comfortable wooden furniture, plus a terrace for fine-weather dining. The menu: classics, plus fancy *gastronomique* flambéeing of Cognac-sauced beef, and beggar's-purses for tasty snails. Desserts include unusual goùre, a kind of waffle, with wine-reduction syrup and a scoop of vanilla ice cream. Stick to the local wines. Regulars, and, in season, hunters and hikers, don't seem to mind the lack of a view.

OZENAY

Between Tournus and Chapaize on highway D14, Ozenay is a charming village with a Romanesque church and pocketsized château fronted by old lindens. Roadside restaurant **Le Relais d'Ozenay** (Tel: 03 85 32 17 93, open daily in summer, closed Wednesday the rest of the year, very inexpensive to moderate), remodeled and redecorated in a rustic-contemporary style, has timbers, colorful runners across the tables, terraces, and a front barroom where locals hang (and hearty workers' lunches are served). Like many such, it has *gastronomique* pretensions. Run by a pair of eager youths who worked in Switzerland before returning to native climes, the presentation and service are polished. On the seasonal menus are updated classics, plus inventions for traveling Swiss, Lyonnais, and Parisians, many with vacation homes nearby. Stick to snails, pike-perch, Charolais beef with or without winey sauce, Bresse poultry in cream or with wine, and long-simmered lamb. The desserts are light and seasonal, the wine list adequate.

REMIGNY

On the Canal du Centre, between Santenay and Chagny, Remigny is home to canalside **Restaurant L'Escale** (Route de Chassey-le-Camp, Tel: 03 85 87 29 13, closed Sunday dinner, Wednesday, and Thursday lunch, inexpensive to moderate). A local favorite patronized by winegrowers, the canal-cruise set, and stray tourists looking for the neolithic site at Chassey-le-Camp, this traditional restaurant with a glassed-in terrace and tables on the canal is run by affable Florence and Fabrice Dubois. The menu features well-made classics generously served. Affordably priced, the wines are local.

RULLY

Rully has too many wineries to count or visit in a lifetime. Crémant is one specialty; if you enjoy this sparkling wine you'll want to visit **Louis Picamelot** (12 Place de la Croix Blanche, Tel: 03 85 87 13 60, louispicamelot@wanadoo.fr, open weekdays without appointment, by appointment on Saturday, closed Sunday), an old winery run by Philippe Chautard, grandson of the founder. Chautard makes outstanding Crémant rosé (primarily Pinot Noir, with about a fifth Gamay), and, additionally, a good blanc de blancs (Chardonnay and Aligoté).

Perched over the area's walled vineyards, 800-year-old **Château de Rully** (Tel: 03 85 87 20 89, www.chateau-rully-bourgogne .com, hours vary widely and seasonally) has been in the de Ternay family since the 1200s. Countess Brigitte de Ternay has her wines made by Antonin Rodet of Mercurey. The estate's Rully 1er Crus Les Molesmes and single-vineyard La Bressande Monopole are good and may be tasted and purchased here. Make sure to tour the property, starting with the turreted, walled courtyards, and the kitchen the size of a barn, with an oak table from the 1500s, and tools from centuries past.

More of a challenge to find is **La Cave Bio'te d'Agneux** (4 Impasse d'Agneux, Rully, Tel: 03 85 87 37 31, cavebiote@aol .com, open Monday to Saturday without appointment, Sunday by appointment only, *table d'hôtes* lunch by reservation only, inexpensive). The de Suremain family of Château de Monthelie, in the southern Côte de Beaune, is also established in Rully, with estates and houses amid the vineyards. In handsome Agneux, due west a quarter mile, on the narrow road to prehistoric grottoes, Arnaud de Suremain and wife Lydia offer wine tastings, vineyard visits, and a wine-and-cheese *table d'hôtes* lunch for groups (of six or more). The de Suremains were organic and biodynamic pioneers, certified in 1996. Arnaud will scoop up his soil, lead you to a nearby "traditional" vineyard, fill his other hand, and raise them to your nose. Close your eyes and smell the samples. One is pleasant, natural, and smells of life; the other smells dead, tainted by chemicals. Now guess which is which. You might be converted on the spot. At table, you'll be served estate wines, crusty bread and delicious cold cuts, jambon persillé, excellent cheeses from Fromagerie Gaugry (in Brochant), chocolate mousse, and coffee.

On Rully's triangular square, **Hôtel-Restaurant Le Vendengerot** (Place Sainte-Marie, Tel: 03 85 87 20 09, www .vendangerot.com, closed Tuesday, Wednesday, and from February to mid March, very inexpensive to expensive) was run for decades by Marie-Laurence and Armand Lollini, who made Le Vendengerot a touchstone, with honest, well-prepared, delicious *cuisine bourgeoise*, and many *terroir* specialties, sourced locally. In March 2009 they retired, but Lollini's sous chef, Florian Cauzeret, has taken over the kitchen, and, for the time being, is still preparing the same earthy cassolette d'escargots with mushrooms, roasted pike-perch, coq au vin, Charolais beef, and tender roast lamb, as before. Florent Martin, the new owner, has been running the place since mid 2008, and, with luck, the transition will continue seamlessly. The terrace faces a splashing fountain, while the dining room is done up with eclectic flair, the waiters dressed like penguins. The cheese trolley is exceptional, the desserts light and luscious, the wine list honest and local.

SAINT BOIL

The name is enough to keep most English-speakers out. Saint Boil is bisected by the main highway, amid a sea of grapevines; put on your turn signal, and, in the middle of the village, find outwardly unprepossessing **Le Cheval Blanc** (Tel: 03 85 44 03 16, www.auberge-cheval-blanc.net, open for dinner only, closed Wednesday, and mid February to end March, prix fixe menu only: moderate to expensive). This auberge has a tastefully decorated dining room—old prints, ceramic roosters, fine china on well-spaced tables—and a pleasant back garden with a few tables under trumpet vines. The menu, handwritten, is short, and features well-crafted, traditional food from good sources. Everything is housemade. A tiny gougère and minuscule boudin noir will stir your appetite, followed, perhaps, by local ham and melon, and tournedos of Charolais with a confit of shallots, wild mushrooms, and potato cakes. The persillade of garlicky snails is tasty; ditto the terrines and foie gras, and freshwater fish when available. Don't miss the cheeses from Chèvrerie des Filletières. In summer, for dessert, you'll eat blackcurrant sorbet or a light fruit tart. The wine list has affordable, good, local bottlings (Gérard Mouton, Jean-Claude Brou, Domaine Andreotti, Stéphane Aladame). The only sour note is sung by the lady of the house, Martine Cantin, a very rough diamond. Chef Jany Cantin stays out of harm's way. The auberge has comfortable guest rooms across the highway in a late-1800s house, with views from the quiet, east side, and serves memorable breakfasts.

Saint Boil hides its treasures. Ask and discover that third-generation beekeeper and honey-maker **Hervé Balland** operates out of an unmarked tract home on the north side of Rue Blondin (Tel: 03 85 44 05 56 or 09 62 05 39 38, lesruchersballand@orange.fr, by appointment). It branches east off the highway, near the square. With over a century of experience in his family (his great-grandfather started out in 1895), Balland is a trove of anecdote, from bee-breeding on up. Like most of his colleagues, he worries about the future of bees—and man—because of pesticides and novel crops—hybrids and, possibly, GMOs—which poison or disorient bees, causing high mortality. The die-off was ten percent a few decades ago; it's fifty percent or higher now. Rapeseed and sunflower—lucrative subsidy crops—pose clear dangers. That's why Balland moves his bees to safety. Of his many honeys, the acacia and prairie-flower stand out. Balland's dark, earthy miel de sapin is a treat. A "great harvest" occurs only every nine years (with a decent one between). The taste is astonishingly similar to pure, untreated maple syrup. Don't miss it.

SAINT-GENGOUX-LE-NATIONAL

Unsung Saint-Gengoux lies at the southern edge of the Côte Chalonnaise. Below sloping forests, pastures, and vineyards, a tangle of narrow alleys reveals Gothic arches and Romanesque columns jutting from the walls of tumbledown houses. The pencil-tipped main church tower rises over this appealing jumble which, like Buxy, is on the cusp of gentrification. The Rue Cesarée and Rue Jouvance hint at a pedigree: Saint-Gengoux was an Imperial-era town on the Roman road from Tournus. It grew during Merovingian times, and became a pilgrimage stopover. Jouvence was the Merovingian name. The name flipped back and forth from Saint-Gengoux-le-Royal to Jouvence to Saint-Gengoux-le-Royal.

More compelling is the name Gengoux (See Avallon, page 130). The tourist office is to be found on the sycamore-lined main street, La Promenade (Tel: 03 85 92 52 05).

A lively open market is held on Tuesday mornings, and on the mornings of the first and third Thursday of each month, plus Saturdays at certain times of year (phone the tourist office for specifics). Among many stands are producers of organic vegetables, eggs, wines, and flour **Damien Gressard** (Moulin de Foulot, Tel: 03 85 92 60 52, phone ahead). Ask to visit his cousin's flour mill (near the former train station) and see organic flour milled. Also here with good farmstead goat's cheeses are **Ferme des Chavennes** (Burzy, Tel; 03 85 96 29 13, open weekday mornings or by appointment) and, on the first and third Tuesday of the month only, certified-organic **Fromagerie Fermière de la Petite Guye** (Chevagny-sur-Guye, Tel: 03 85 24 50 45, open daily, mornings only).

Saint-Gengoux-le-National offers servicable cafés on main street, two bakeries and a good butcher-*charcuterie*, a glitzy boutique selling tableware, and a remarkable, premodern chocolate and pastry shop, **Jean-Pierre Demortière** (Rue Commerce, Tel: 03 85 92 60 86, closed Monday), in the medieval heart of town. Demortière faces a turret sprouting from a wall; on display are unlikely chocolates made to resemble French cheeses; filled chocolates with spices and liqueurs; ganaches; chocolate bars; housemade nougat; and irresistible chocolate or lemon custard tarts or classic millefeuilles with strawberry or chocolate.

Saint-Gengoux is home to a branch of the area's co-op winery, **Cave des Vignerons de Buxy** (Tel: 03 85 92 61 75, www.cave-buxy.fr, closed Sunday year-round and Monday from September through June; see Buxy entry for details), where you can taste wines to your liver's content. It's on the western edge of town, near the big-box garden shop.

Recently remodeled by an ambitious, friendly chef, Monsieur Dejou, **Restaurant de la Gare** (Route de la Gare, Tel: 03 85 94 18 50, hotelrestaurantdejou@wanadoo.fr, open daily, very inexpensive to moderate), faces the old train station and Voie Verte linear park. It's the best place to eat in town. Savvy workers, farmers, and winegrowers crowd in at lunch for the low-priced, tasty, fill-you-to-burst menu—quiche, salad, sautéed duck drumsticks and ratatouille, plus cheese, fruit tart, wine, and coffee. It changes daily, and is served in the bar area or the bedraggled, enclosed terrace. The dining room—in contemporary style, aspiring to chic—is for bigger prix fixe menus or à la carte meals. It's often empty at lunch, and filled at dinner by foreign tourists, winemakers, and white-collars. The food: updated, stylized, elaborately plated, and professionally executed dishes from the regional and pan-French repertoire.

For a home-cooked meal at a friendly, comfortable, pleasant B&B, seek out **Chambre d'hôtes–Table d'hôtes Marie-Claude and Jean-Luc Reumaux** (7 Rue de la Tuilerie, Tel: 03 85 92 55 76, www.tilleuls71.com, meals very inexpensive, for overnight guests only). Distinguished retiree Jean-Luc Reumaux spent his boyhood summers in this turn-of-the-nineteenth-century house. His love for the place is contagious. He and wife Marie-Claude are reinvented innkeepers. Everything is authentic, original, and sturdy, from the tile or polished plank floors, to the oak staircase, fireplaces with stone surrounds and pedestal sinks. Marie-Claude's cooking is simple but real: lentil-and-quail-egg salad, roast pork, and homemade apple pie, washed down with local wine. The homemade raspberry jam and pure-butter croissants are memorable.

SAINT-LÉGER-SUR-DHEUNE

Bisected by the Canal du Centre, this village has picnic supplies, restaurants and hotels, plus a maker of fine artisanal jams. The traditional restaurants are perfectly okay, but you'll probably have a more enjoyable time at **Au P'tit Kir** (16 Rue du Pont, Tel: 03 85 45 46 80, closed Sunday and Monday, inexpensive to moderate), flanking the bridge on highway D978. This trendy canalside wine bar is run by a bilingual, transplanted Englishwoman. You eat outdoors, on the canal, or in an airy dining room with big windows and tables unencumbered by cloths or mustard jars. The foreign river-cruise set flocks here, and locals too. Blackboard daily specials range from salads to hearty sausage meat in a pastry shell, andouillette with mustard, steaks, stews, and seasonal fruit salads or tarts. The wines are local, and many are good value. Don't expect culinary fireworks.

Across the street is **Boulangerie Pâtisserie Gilles Poirier** (7 Rue du Pont, Tel: 03 85 45 36 94, closed Monday). The specialty: Le Saint-Léger, a vanilla-flavored mousse pastry.

A few hundred yards west on the highway, in a former tile works, is jam factory **Péché Sucré** (3 Route de Couches, Tel: 03

85 45 36 44, www.peche-sucre.fr, closed Monday, and mornings on Tuesday, Wednesday, and Sunday; in December open daily nonstop 10am to 7pm). Master jam-makers Laurence and Xavier Augagneur reconverted the landmark building and make dozens of excellent jams, jellies, conserves, fruit pastes, and gingerbread, in a state-of-the-art kitchen. Of the thirty-seven jams half are classics (plum, apricot, strawberry), the rest are unexpected (apricot-almond, kiwi-strawberry-mint, apple-caramel-Calvados, orange-rhubarb-banana). They also make spreadable nut, caramel, and chocolate "butters." In the gourmet boutique they stock Fallot mustard, savory jellies made from wine, local wines, and liqueurs, absinthe, and their own crispy butter biscuits flavored

with everything from orange to strawberry, pistachio or walnut. Don't miss it.

SASSANGY

In the scenic back-country west of Buxy, seek out **Château de Sassangy-Domaine Jean et Geno Musso** (Tel: 03 85 96 18 61, musso.jean@wanadoo.fr, by appointment), in a landmark with landscaped grounds. Idealistic Jean and Geno Musso own three estates, totaling eighty-five acres. This is where all the wines are made and aged. The family has been in the business for centuries, but was among the first to go organic, in 1979. The wines are clean, refreshing, and remarkably balanced. They routinely win medals at important competitions in Burgundy and beyond. Of the six made, the best are Bourgogne Pinot Noir, Bourgogne Côte Chalonnaise, Bourgogne Hautes-Côtes-de-Beaune, and Santenay, all red.

SENNECEY-LE-GRAND

A town of 3,000 strung along the old highway eleven miles south of Chalon, Sennecey isn't anywhere you'd rush to unless you're looking for chic, recently Michelin-starred **L'Amaryllis** (78 Avenue du 4 Septembre, Tel: 03 85 44 86 34, closed Sunday dinner, Monday lunch, and Wednesday, very inexpensive to very expensive). Cédric Burtin did time with starred gurus of haute, predictably remodeled in contemporary-globalized style, and tossed out the *terroir*. Of course, the exquisite food is plated Cartier. The wine list features organic Montagny 1er Cru Les Burnins, Les Coères, and Le Vieux Château from Stéphane Aladame.

TOURNUS

Tournus, a town of 6,000 with a particularly ancient pedigree, was founded by the Gauls on the banks of the Saône before Julius Caesar showed up and spoiled things. Under the Romans, it became a thriving port, used, like Mâcon and Chalon-sur-Saône, in the Gallic Wars. Wine was the WMD of the day: soldiers and amphorae came upriver, slaves—traded for wine—went downriver to Rome. The outlines of Roman Tournus are visible, but the many historic vestiges are mostly medieval, starting with the 1,000-year-old Saint Philibert Abbey. It feels like a fortress, with a cavernous narthex, columns the diameter of giant redwood trees, and a labyrinthine crypt.

The abbey, and recently restored history museum, dedicated to eighteenth-century court painter and native son Jean-Baptiste

Greuze (**Hôtel Dieu–Musée Greuze**, 21 Rue de l'Hôpital, Tel: 03 85 51 23 50), would alone make a trip here worthwhile. Further enticements are the half-timbered houses, sycamore-lined riverbanks, charming atmosphere, and excellent food and wine. If not Beaune, Tournus is the Saulieu of Southern Burgundy. Its prosperity, and the modern shopping malls hemming it, are attributable to the A6 autoroute and RN6 highway, which blight the town's eastern edge.

For most of the twentieth century, **Restaurant Greuze** (1 Rue A. Thibaudet, Tel: 03 85 51 13 52, www.restaurant-greuze.fr, closed mid November to early December, moderate to extremely expensive), fief of traditionalist two-star chef Jean Ducloux, was the town's claim to fame. Ducloux was the heir of legendary Alexandre Dumaine, and retired only in 2003, handing over to Laurent Couturier, who redecorated in the usual classico-contemporary luxury style, and five years later tossed in his toque. In April 2008, Yohann Chapuis, a Lameloise veteran, arrived. Perhaps with Couturier in mind, Chapuis has toned down the globalized and emphasized the *terroir*. A sop to longtime regulars, he's kept exquisite classics on the menu, including pâté en croûte, which Ducloux inherited from Dumaine. Other heirlooms are pike-perch dumplings and crayfish tails *à la nage*—in a frothy emulsion—or ribsteak nonparée with marrow cooked down in Pinot Noir (with Chapuis's unnecessary Parmigiano-Reggiano tossed in), and Grand Marnier soufflé served hot. Also expect to find saddle of rabbit, roasted duck breast with gingerbread, and other earthy dishes. Cheeses are the best, desserts are elaborate and beautiful. The service is Teflon, the wine list novel length. The prix fixe lunch Marché menu is a deal (moderate).

Tournus boasts other renowned *grandes tables*. One is comfortable **Le Rempart** (Avenue Gambetta, Tel: 03 85 51 10 56, www.lerempart.com, open daily, moderate to very expensive), in the hotel of the same name, with a cushy dining room and a nice patio; also on the property is the more casual, good-value **Le Bistrot** (inexpensive to moderate). The town's other gastronomic pilgrimage site is **Aux Terrasses** (18 Avenue du 23 Janvier, Tel: 03 85 51 01 74, www.aux-terrasses.com, closed Sunday dinner, Monday, and Tuesday lunch, January, and ten days in June, moderate to extremely expensive). Family run and in an unlikely spot, facing the ATAC supermarket on the southern edge of town, this is where second-generation chef Jean-Michel Carrette and wife Henriette welcome guests in two dining rooms, or on the summer terrace. The eager youngsters' world view was formed in the luxury establishments of France, notably Troisgros, hence the décor. The food is also contemporary, artistic, and most has little to do with Burgundy. However, the quality is high, the flavors undisguised, and some *terroir* shines through. Snails come in a large "ravioli" but are earthy and luscious; the duck terrine in a pastry crust is served warm; the pike-perch braised in wine is wrapped in Morvan ham; the squab is roasted with whole cloves of garlic. Inevitably, the seasonal desserts are vertical and architecturally impressive, with raspberries, chocolate, caramel, and spices teetering or cascading. The excellent cheeses come from Crèmerie de Tournus. Also happily, there's little of the stuffy self importance of other Michelin-starred places. The service is friendly; the wine list features local, affordable wines, some by the glass.

Down the scale but serving authentic, traditional, *terroir* food in a rustic-cozy dining room is **Le Bourgogne** (Rue Alexis Bessard or Rue du Dr. Privey, Tel: 03 85 51 12 23, closed Tuesday and Wednesday, inexpensive), 200 yards south of the abbey. Christophe Canet worked for Ducloux at Greuze, and is a specialist in *charcuterie*—jambon persillé, hams, head cheese. He also excels at variety meats, pig's trotters, hamhocks, beef bourguignon, coq au vin, and Lyonnais cooking. His wife Maryline is your efficient hostess. All the classics are here, from frog's legs and snails on up, plus a few Spanish-leaning dodos that seem out of place. This isn't your average tourist trap: locals love it. Don't miss the clubby backroom café, where regulars perch on caned chairs and shoot the breeze. The décor hasn't changed for a century.

The best bakery in town is upscale **Jean-Marc Krzeminski** (4 Place de l'Hôtel de Ville, Tel: 03 85 51 02 13, closed Sunday and Monday, two weeks in August and two weeks in November), near city hall. You can't miss the truck-wheel-sized loaves of sourdough bread, sold by weight, which keeps three days or more. The classic pastries and tarts are delicious.

You might not be in the market for fruits and vegetables, but you'll still want to visit outstanding greengrocery **Le Verger de l'Abbaye** (4 Place du Champ-de-Mars, Tel: 03 85 51 03 61, closed Sunday afternoon and Monday, two weeks in February and the first week of November), near the municipal parking lot flanking the highway. The gastronomical advice from owner Daniel Prely is invaluable. You find the finest local produce plus fine gourmet items, from Hervé Balland's honeys, to artisanal oils from Leblanc, or wines from local growers such as organic Guillot-Broux.

Half a dozen pleasant, interchangeable, inexpensive cafés await on the riverbanks (and serve perfectly edible daily specials).

Bar Le Charleston (12 Rue Jean-Jaurès, Tel: 03 85 51 20 95, closed Sunday) has the best coffee, from Le Moulin à Café in Chalon-sur-Saône. The owner collects ceramic, plush, or plastic frogs. Her pink glass seltzer bottles are from the days of yore.

On the north-south shopping street sloping toward the abbey, find one of the region's top cheesemongers: **Crèmerie de Tournus-Y et E Giroud** (63 Rue du Dr. Privey, Tel: 03 85 51 70 66, closed Sunday afternoon and Monday, and three weeks in January). Blackboards and decorated window displays attract passersby. Every imaginable Burgundy cheese is here, from local goats to raw-milk Époisses and L'Ami du Chambertin from Gaugry, Plaisir au Chablis to Cîteaux, and Mâconnais AOC from La Racotière in Génelard. Also sold are jams, canned snails, honey, and wines.

Next door is **Charcuterie Saveurs et Terroir** (61 Rue du Dr. Privey, Tel: 03 85 51 05 01, closed Sunday afternoon and Monday), fief of Stéphane Gambin, who makes excellent hams, terrines, and jambon persillé. Outstanding chocolatier **Gilles Lathuilière** (55 Rue du Dr. Privey, Tel: 03 85 51 06 61, closed Sunday afternoon, Monday, two weeks in February, and from end August to early September) is a few shopfronts north. Strapping Gilles's elegant wife Sonia runs the shop. The beam holding up the front hints at centuries past, everything else is ultra modern. Gilles crafts the pastries and chocolates, sometimes too beautiful to devour. The specialty is Le Tournusien (almonds, vanilla-flavored butter, and hazelnut nougatine). Among chocolates, Greuze Emotion (a candied hazelnut praline coated with chocolate) and Les Délices de Tournus (Cointreau-flavored nuggets) are outstanding. Chocolate sculptures, a dozen types of butter cookie, and just as many ice

creams, make this little shop a must. Also sold are the jams of Cadole des Douceurs.

Across the street is highly professional **Les Caves Saint-Valérien** (58 Rue du Dr. Privey, Tel: 03 85 51 78 74, closed Sunday from September to February, open daily the rest of the year), where affable Jean-Paul Bayet stocks about 1,000 different wines from top independents. You'll find otherwise-unfindable bottlings from Chablis, Nuits Saint Georges, Meursault, and Beaune, plus outstanding, unsung locals.

Facing the abbey is a shop with postcards and trinkets, but also fine organic wine from Guillot in Cruzille, honey from Les Ruchers du Morvan, and jams from Ferme de la Guye, among other delectables: **Siècles et Arts** (3 Gabriel Jeanton, Tel: 03 95 51 11 13, closed Monday afternoon in winter).

LE VILLARS

Two miles south of Tournus on the Saône, Le Villars is a food-lover's Mecca thanks to rustic **L'Auberge des Gourmets** (Place de l'Église, Tel: 03 85 32 58 80, www.aubergedesgourmets.fr, contact@aubergedesgourmets.fr, closed Sunday and Tuesday dinner, Wednesday lunch, holidays, Christmastide, several weeks in January, and one week in June, inexpensive to expensive). Forget the timbers, caned chairs, and red tablecloths. This isn't your average auberge. Daniel Rogié was chef at Le Rempart in Tournus when it had a Michelin star. His pedigree explains the professional cooking, presentation, service, and rave reviews from regulars, glossy magazines, and guidebooks. It also explains why, if you don't reserve ahead, you won't get a table, day or night. Market-based seasonal cooking is the specialty.

BRESSE BOURGUIGNONNE

·······································

Includes: Beaurepaire-en-Bresse, Bouhans, Bruailles,
Cuiseaux, Cuisery, Louhans, Pierre-de-Bresse,
Ratte, Romenay, Saint-Germain-du-Bois,
Saint-Martin-en-Bresse, Verdun sur le Doubs

A MERE 70,000 INHABITANTS ARE SPRINKLED OVER THE VAST SAÔNE RIVER VALLEY. MÂCON and Beaune mark this rural, sparsely populated sub-region's western edge. The Jura rises to the east. By and large, the area has been spared the attentions of tourists. Burgundy's least adulterated district, its many farms specialize in AOC Bresse and Louhanais poultry. One of France's biggest, authentic farmers markets is held Monday in surprisingly appealing Louhans.

Bresse Bourguignonne is also the heartland of la pocheuse, hearty mixed freshwater fish stew from the Saône and smaller rivers, streams, and lakes that draw anglers. A historical and administrative anomaly, Bresse Bourguignonne occupies the northern and western sections of the larger Bresse, not in Burgundy (it's capital is Bourg-en-Bresse). The scenery isn't spectacular, but lush and attractive. Older buildings are low, with half-timbering, wattle, and river rocks. Locals eat big; specialties are rich and creamy. Few chefs attempt nouvelle or global. Wines are not produced; those consumed come equally from Burgundy and the Jura.

BEAUREPAIRE-EN-BRESSE

A few miles from the Jura, on highway RN78, Beaurepaire may be short on charm, but the updated, well-prepared and affordable *terroir* meals at **Auberge de la Croix Blanche** (Tel: 03 85 74 13 22, closed Sunday dinner and Monday from September through June), prepared by chef Émilie Jacquard, are a good reason to stop. There's a shaded terrace out front, where you can enjoy refreshments, and a tidy dining room.

BOUHANS

Three miles north of Saint-Germain-du-Bois, near highways D13 and D996, this isolated hamlet hosts an annual jamboree, La foire de la Balme, held since 1645 (the last weekend in August). Expect dozens of food, wine, clothing, and other stands, seniors with accordions, vacationing French families, and a loud, garish funfair.

Another, better reason to visit (perhaps after Louhans and Saint-Germain-du-Bois), is **Ferme-Auberge La Bonardière** (Tel: 03 85 72 00 08, by reservation only, very inexpensive to inexpensive). From April 1st to mid November lunch or dine weekends (and Friday nights), and in July and August daily, at this farm, which isn't in Bouhans proper, but several miles away, near highway D13. Follow the Ferme-Auberge signs. They tend to disappear among corn stalks and other crops. Semi-retired Bresse poultry farmer Jean-Paul Bonardière, wife Marie-Thérèse, and son Nicolas, raise thousands of birds. They wing around, building up the muscles that make Bresse poultry so good, or fatten up in the barn. The auberge is a nicely restored, spartan, freestanding building with half-timbering, heavy wooden furniture, and caned chairs. You'll savor homemade terrines and salads, and poultry simply roasted or slow-simmered in heavy cream with button mushrooms, cheese, and fruit tarts. Expect the company of retirees on the farm circuit, and local families. Lunch is more practical than dinner; even in daylight, finding the farm is challenging.

BRUAILLES

Luxurious, boutique B&Bs are few hereabouts, especially those serving traditional food. A lively Parisian former advertising executive owns **La Ferme de Marie Eugenie** (225 Allée des Chardenoux, Chardenoux, Tel: 03 85 74 81 84, www.lafermede marieeugenie.fr, closed at Christmastide, meals moderate). It boasts half-timbered buildings from the 1700s, leafy grounds, and tastefully decorated rooms with four-poster beds. Marie Eugenie Dupuy, aided by reserved husband Dominique, serves housemade chicken liver terrine, guinea fowl with peaches, Bresse chicken roasted or with cream and morel mushrooms, long-cooked shoulder of lamb, beef bourguignon, plus chocolat fondant and classic desserts. The cheeses are excellent; the fine red and white wines are from François Mikulski of Meursault, or Labet (in the Jura). The turn off to the B&B is five miles southeast of Louhans on D972 and is easy to miss.

CUISEAUX

Bordering the Jura, astride highway D996, this once-important frontier post has medieval and Renaissance houses, and remnants of ramparts. The castle built by the Princes of Orange, rebuilt in 1477, 1602, and 1886, now houses the Bresse Bourguignonne's Ecomusée (see Pierre-de-Bresse), here called **Le Vigneron et**

sa Vigne. It's also home to a landmark oil mill, **l'Huilerie Jail-let**. Watery and flat, without a vine in sight, this may seem an unusual venue for a museum of winemaking and rural life. Until phylloxera, Cuiseaux was a major winegrowing town. Enjoy good bottlings from Burgundy and the Jura, and good, *terroir* food, at two old-fashioned establishments owned by the Vuillot family since 1886. The mothership is **Hôtel-Restaurant Vuillot** (36 Rue Vuillard, Tel: 03 85 72 71 79, hotel.vuillot@wanadoo.fr, very inexpensive to moderate, closed Sunday dinner and Monday from September through June), with a stone façade, swimming pool, and spacious, cozy dining room. The other, **Hôtel de Bourgogne** (1 Rue Vuillard, Tel: 03 85 72 71 79, hotel.vuillot@wanadoo.fr, very inexpensive to moderate, closed Sunday dinner and Monday from September through June), is down the street, has bright blue shutters and a yellow façade, and is also cozy and comfortable. Take your pick. At either you'll savor succulent, premodern snails, terrines, salads, stews and steaks, torpedo fish cooked in the style of pike-perch in a red-wine reduction sauce, peppery tripe sausage in white Jura wine, local cheeses, classic desserts, and wines from both sides of the border. The service is friendly and professional—they've had 125 years of practice.

CUISERY

In the 1990s "rural desertification" and the malls of the Saône Valley, emptied this town ten miles east of Tournus. Most businesses went belly up. So council members and the regional government reinvented Cuisery as the **Village du Livre** (Tel: 03 85 40 16 08, www.cuisery-livre.com), Burgundy's capital of used books, some valuable, most not, plus antiques, objets d'art, porcelain souvenir thimbles, and the collectibles you'd find at flea markets. Empty shops were rented for symbolic sums to booksellers. The strategy worked. Cuisery, reborn, has about 1,600 inhabitants. You can find everything from leather-bound volumes on medieval cuisine, or first-editions by Jules Verne, at the dozens of bookshops on central Grande Rue. Visit on the first Sunday of each month, when the streets fill with stands. Don't miss the church: the dunce-capped turret sprouting from the belfry, and flying gargoyles, would've delighted Disney.

Dine (and spend the night in a comfortable motel-style room on a quiet, leafy courtyard) at upscale **Hostellerie Bressane** (56 Route de Tournus, Tel: 03 85 32 30 66, www.hostellerie-bressane .fr, hostellerie.bressane@wanadoo.fr, closed Wednesday, Thursday, and January, inexpensive to expensive). Jean-Francis Beaufays—a

Maître Cuisinier de France—and elegant wife Nathalie bought this century-old inn when Cuisery bottomed. They upgraded in a flowery, summery style, created a shady garden terrace, and now do brisk business with locals and gourmets. Beaufays worked at marquee properties and knows his craft. But he opted for lightened regional *cuisine bourgeoise*, buying his ingredients from local farmers: chickens from Guillot-Cobrea, fish from Frédéric Jasser, honey from Monsieur Michon, and so on. The nettle tops and mild garlic in the fresh frog's leg soufflé are gathered in Beaufays's herb garden, with sage, thyme, fennel, and sorrel. The smoked torpedo fish is succulent, the Louhans squab a classic (rich red-wine reduction sauce, and sautéed force-meat). Beaufays's sublime, perfect Bresse chicken *à la crème* is slow-cooked at low heat four hours in court-bouillon, then finished with cream, mushrooms, carrots, and fresh peas. The perambulator–cheese cart groans with excellent curds from Fromagerie Giroud in Tournus. Desserts: lavish, teetering, triple-chocolate delights, or superb tuiles made with gingerbread and fresh sorbet with Marc de Bourgogne. The wine list is thick, with reasonable and huge, expensive, Burgundy and Jura bottlings. For breakfast, you'll savor exceptional housemade jams. The plates and glasses may be outsized, the décor pinkish, and the friendly service somewhat stylized, but the food is remarkable, the atmosphere pleasant.

On the main square find bakery **Philippe Gamarre** (Tel: 03 85 40 16 22, closed Monday), celebrated for its housemade ice creams, chocolates, and Gallettes de Gaudes (made with toasted corn flour). Around the corner is **Cave à Vin Navoiseau** (Rue Neuve, Tel: 03 85 40 04 27 and 06 80 84 08 90, closed Sunday and Thursday), the town's only wine shop, with a good choice of regional bottlings, from bag-in-box up.

LOUHANS

If you visit only one market in Burgundy, make it Louhans. It ranks among the top three in France. Held since the 1200s, from dawn to 1pm Mondays, the biggest gatherings, dubbed Foires, are each first and third Monday of the month. A three-day Christmastide extravaganza, Les Trois Glorieuses, with a poultry theme, caps the year. Stands mushroom all over this surprisingly charming, little-known farm town of 6,000 inhabitants. Bresse poultry is also known as Louhannais. (Strangely, given the dearth of cattle, the other specialty is calf's head.) You'll find eggs, live chicks, mature birds, the feeds and treatments for them, cages, poultry-farmers' tools, and chicken-theme knickknacks. Live ducks, geese, rabbits,

goats, porkers, sheep, and other livestock are ranged amid items normally found at other markets, from fruits and vegetables, to wines and cheeses (Burgundian and Jura), terrines, salamis, pâtés, candy, chocolates, herbs, plants, and seeds. Refreshment stands sell grilled tripe sausage, chicken wings, and waffles. Farmers buy boots, bibs, hats, saddles, and whips, plus pots and pans, troughs and tanks. Of the many cheese sellers, Nathalie and Raymond Schneider (from La Chapelle-Naude), near the traffic circle, are remarkable for chèvres rolled in black pepper or herbs. The south-side of Place B. Thibert, near the tracks, is for professionals only. Arrive early: tens of thousands attend, the atmosphere is festive, and traffic snarls. Louhans, livelier than Charolles, is also a site of gastronomical excellence, according to the Conseil National des Arts Culinaires.

Louhan's trademark Corniottes are triangular shortbread pastries turned up at the corners and topped by a tiny, sweet puff pastry.

The medieval center's main artery is Grande Rue, 450 yards long, with 157 arcades—more than anywhere else in France (the thick oak pillars date to the 1500s). Grande Rue runs east-west; instead of indicating cardinal directions, locals tell you to go toward le Comté—the Jura, meaning east—or la Bourgogne—west.

Important: on holiday Mondays the market is held in the afternoon; nearly all Louhans businesses are closed on Tuesday.

Places to eat and drink

Skip the upscale hotel-restaurants on the northwestern and eastern edges of town. Louhan's best food is served near Place Saint Jean, at modest, traditional **Hostellerie du Cheval Rouge** (5 Rue d'Alsace, Tel: 03 85 75 21 42, closed Monday, inexpensive to moderate). A red horse, after herds of white ones. Cheval Rouge offers Burgundian dishes, from gougères, snails, and jambon persillé up, and wonderful Bresse-Louhans chicken simply roasted, in rich cream, or in piquant wine sauce, and calf's head. The cooking is solid, the décor classic, the service professional. The main drawback is, Cheval Rouge is closed on market days. Say the owners, it's too chaotic, and many market-goers spoil their appetites on street foods.

Consequently, the best place on market days is **L'Arlequin** (5 Place de la Libération, Tel: 03 85 75 00 25, closed Tuesday, dinner on Sunday and Monday, and the second half of September, inexpensive to moderate). The sidewalk terrace faces a parking lot, and the interior might easily be that of a harlequin-theme pizzeria. However, the calf's head is authentic and gutsy. The Bresse chicken with cream or winey vin jaune is moist and delicious. Don't expect fireworks, but good, simple food with decent wines at reasonable prices.

A fallback, farther out, where the D12 leads south to Montpont-en-Bresse, **Le Saint-Claude** (Chemin des Toupes, Tel: 03 85 75 47 64, closed Saturday lunch, Sunday dinner, Wednesday, and ten days in February, inexpensive to moderate) has a shady terrace and comfortable dining room, and serves updated regional cooking. Like other understaffed restaurants, the service mimics *les escargots.*

A foursome of hangouts, very inexpensive to inexpensive, serve daily specials, lunch, coffee, and snacks. **La Halte Bressane** (21 Place de l'Eglise, Tel: 03 85 74 93 50, closed Tuesday dinner and Wednesday), is on the church square. Nearby **Le Mère Jouvenceaux** (26 Rue Lucien Guillemaut, Tel: 03 85 74 00 51, closed Tuesday and weekday dinner) faces the market, and is more ambitious (good Bresse chicken cooked in cream, and local trout napped with *vin jaune sauce*). Ditto **Chez Alex** (19 Rue Lucien Guillemaut, Tel: 03 85 74 11 75, closed weekends and three weeks in January or February), on the same street, with animated outdoor tables. **L'Hutau** (9 Rue Bordes, Tel: 03 85 75 35 94, closed Wednesday, dinner Thursday, and several weeks in winter, usually late December), near the local tax office, also has tables on the sidewalk, traditional food, friendly service, and a raucous atmosphere.

Cafés locals favor are **Café Saint Jean** (on Place Saint Jean, facing the tourism office), **Café Saint Martin** (under the arcades at 74 Grande Rue), and **Bar de l'Hôtel de Ville** (facing town hall at 10 Place du Générale de Gaulle).

Gourmet shops and food artisans

Good coffee (from Café Monika), and delicious pastries and chocolates, are at old-fashioned **Aux Fiançailles** (12 Grande Rue, Tel: 03 85 75 12 24, closed Tuesday), run by third-generation Christian Bouvier and gracious wife Noëlle. Bouvier makes the least sugary Corniottes in town. Locals gobble them morning, noon, and night. Another specialty is tarte au fromage blanc—lightly sweet cheesecake. The friendly service helps you overlook the 1960s faux wood paneling and tables.

A few doors west, toward la Bourgogne, is **Liberge** (Grande Rue, Tel: 03 85 75 44 68, closed Tuesday), an upscale cheese shop.

Marie-Paule and Patrick Liberge are master cheesemongers, who age cheeses in their cellars. The best of Burgundy and the Jura (including flavorful two-year-old Comté), are here. Made in-house, Cancoillotte is a fresh cheese crushed and mixed with milk, butter, and garlic; Fromage Fort Bressan, potent aged, crushed cow's-milk cheese with milk, salt, pepper, and cream, is warmed, crushed, and cooled for five days. Also sold are bottled confit of Bresse chicken, jams, and honeys.

A few shopfronts toward le Comté, top butcher shop–deli **Gallet Frères** (22 Grande Rue, Tel: 03 85 75 13 71, closed Tuesday), is run by brothers Claude and Gilles Gallet. They excel with AOC Bresse chicken—they're authorized sellers—and everything derived from beef and pork. The tête roulée is head cheese with tongue, and is rolled and sliced to create a jellyroll. The pâté in a pastry crust and jambon persillé are remarkable.

N. Cadot (68 Grande Rue, Tel: 03 85 75 19 54, closed Tuesday) is another excellent pastry and chocolate shop under the arcades. The Corniottes are slightly sweeter and more fragrant here. Granite counters and spotlights give Cadot a jewelry store feel; the cakes, chocolates, candies, sweets, and enameled Bresse ceramics sold here are attractively displayed.

Also under the arcades, recently established gourmet foods, tea shop, and coffee roaster **Torrefaction T'es ou Café** (89 Grande

Rue, Tel: 03 85 75 44 20, closed Sunday and Tuesday, open nonstop 9am to 7pm) may have a silly name, and décor to lure bobos, but the Arabica house blends and monovarietals are excellent, there are dozens of teas, and the cookies, chocolates, and candies are handsomely packaged and tempting. Perch and taste the wares.

WINE SHOP **La Cave des Cordeliers** (59 Grande Rue, Tel: 03 85 75 36 69, cbuatois@club-internet.fr, closed Sunday afternoon January to December, and Tuesday) looks like a fashion boutique. Owners Christine and Eric Buatois are interested in more than aesthetics. They're among the region's most qualified wine experts. They opened in 2000. On site is a tasting salon and shady rear terrace. *Terroir* is the Buatois forte; they also seek wines with a good price-to-quality ratio. So, while they stock Domaine de la Romanée Conti and astronomically expensive bottlings, they also promote up-and-coming winemakers who hand-harvest, use little or no pesticide, and do not overwhelm their wines with excess oak, fruit, or alcohol. Among the 300 Burgundies are bottlings from Stéphane Aladame of Montagny, Nicolas Maillet of Verzé, and Alain and Isabelle Hasard of Aluze, all organic and excellent. You'll also find thirty Jura wines, including *vins jaune*, *vins de paille*, and Arbois. See Top Burgundian Winesellers' Favorites, page 60, for their picks.

PIERRE-DE-BRESSE

Even if rural life, local history, forestry, and farming don't thrill you, consider driving out of your way to the junction of D73 and D203 and **Château de Pierre-de-Bresse**, housing **Ecomusée de la Bresse Bourguignonne** (Tel: 03 85 76 27 16, www.ecomusee -de-la-bresse.com, open daily mid May to end September 10am to 7pm, afternoons only the rest of the year). Built atop feudal foundations, the château has pepper-pot towers, mansards, box-wood, and parterres. This is the mothership of many "ecological museums," each dedicated to a facet of Bresse Bourguignonne. Here, learn more than you need know about flora, fauna, and the natives; afterwards, settle down under sculpted plasterwork for coffee, tea, pastries, ice creams, or savory snacks in a parquet-floored, circular salon. The museum boutique sells wooden crafts and gourmet foods. On the last weekend of June, the château hosts an organic jamboree, La Gaudriole; taste and buy organic foods, and learn about organic farming and energy conservation.

The Château of Pierre-de-Bresse is the headquarters of several museums of rural life. Don't miss its sisters in Verdun sur le Doubs

(**Maison du Blé et du Pain**, bread and wheat), Saint-Martin-en-Bresse/Perrigny (**Maison de la Forêt et du Bois**, forests and wood), Saint-Germain-du-Bois (**L'Agriculture Bressane**, farming), Louhans (**L'Atelier d'un Journal**, printing presses), Cuiseaux (**Le Vigneron et sa Vigne**, winemaking), Rancy (**Chaisiers et Pailleuses**, chair-making and caning), Sagy (**Les Moulins**, seven flour and other mills), and Varennes-Saint-Sauveur (**La Tuilerie**, tile factory). Information is available from the château, and www .ecomusee-de-la-bresse.com.

For a down-home meal, Monsieur and Madame Petitjean at **Hôtel de la Poste** (9 Place Comte André d'Estampes, Tel: 03 85 76 24 47, closed dinner Sunday, inexpensive to moderate) will serve you classics from Burgundy, the Bresse, and Jura, including delicious chicken roasted or cooked with cream.

RATTE

The potato of a name shouldn't put you off this hamlet on RN78 four miles east of Louhans. In two quiet courtyards find the terraces and tables of **Le Chaudron** (Tel: 03 85 75 57 81, www .lechaudron.fr, closed Tuesday and Wednesday, inexpensive to moderate). Eager Alessandra Pagès and Sophie Pouthier, graduates of hotel-and-restaurant school, offer lightened regional food from highest-quality ingredients, plated on tasteful china, and served with shy good manners. There are two large, spartan dining rooms with country décor. They fill with locals, often glad to have delicious, locally baked bread to nibble as they wait. And wait. With many tables, Le Chaudron is understaffed, the service can be frustratingly slow, especially at lunch on market days in Louhans. A pity: the food is remarkable, seasonal, and sourced responsibly. Expect snails (in summer, perfumed with absinthe and bedded on fresh chopped tomatoes), freshwater fish grilled, baked, or poached, and elaborate vegetarian dishes. They, and the fruit-based desserts, are the strongest suit. The Bresse chicken (from Monsieur Thibert) is excellent quality, but needs to cook longer at lower temperature. The cheeses are outstanding, from Liberge in Louhans. Wines include many fine Burgundies. Not for anyone in a hurry.

ROMENAY

Six miles south of Cuisery on highway D975, this medieval fortified village has charm—but not many inhabitants or businesses. If you haven't seen enough rural life, a building behind harbors the **Musée du Terroir** (Tel: 03 85 40 36 27, opening hours devised to thwart even determined visitors). Ditto **Musée de la Volaille de Bresse** (same info), behind the *terroir* museum, where you learn about blue-clawed Bresse poultry. Enjoy a meal with regional specialties at ivy-clad **Hôtel du Lion d'Or** (Tel: 03 85 40 30 78, closed Tuesday dinner and Wednesday, inexpensive to moderate) flanking the Gothic-arched gatehouse leading to Romenay's narrow alleys. There's a veranda, and a cozy dining room, and the service, food—crayfish, Bresse chicken, Charolais—and wine, served by the Chevauchet family, are good.

If the Lion d'Or is closed, on the main highway, chicken out at **La Maison du Poulet de Bresse** (Tel: 03 85 40 33 48, closed Monday dinner and Tuesday, inexpensive to moderate). The name is a giveaway. Spit-roasted, pan-fried, with cream and mushrooms, and so forth. The desserts are particularly luscious.

SAINT-GERMAIN-DU-BOIS

Ten miles north of Louhans on D13, this sleepy village has two inexpensive-to-moderate hotel-restaurants with *terroir* food. **Hostellerie Bressane** (Tel: 03 85 72 04 69, www.giot -hostelleriebressane.fr, closed the first week in September, ten days in February, Sunday dinner September through June, and Monday) is the more ambitious. Run by pros Christelle and Didier Giot, it's in a 300-year-old coaching inn with turn-of-the-century murals and rustic, copper-pot décor, fine service, and a long wine list. **Le Saint-Germain** (32 Place du Marché, Tel: 03 85 72 02 47, www.le-saint-germain.com, closed Wednesday), fief of Françoise and Pierre Bruchon, on the main square, is simpler, with an indoor-outdoor terrace.

In the so-called **Maison Collinet** is L'Agriculture Bressane (www.ecomusee-de-la-bresse.com), the local Ecomusée, this one dedicated to farming, poultry, corn, and wheat, plus farm machinery (tractors were once manufactured nearby).

SAINT-MARTIN-EN-BRESSE

Two things make a detour down highway D35, east of Chalon-sur-Saône, worthwhile. In Perrigny, part of Saint-Martin, there's an Ecomusée, **Maison de la Forêt et du Bois**, in a reconverted school, with a reconstructed carpenter's workshop and displays on forestry and charcoal-making. Second, and more enticing, is multi-generational, centuries-old **Au Puits Enchanté** (1 Place René Cassin, Tel: 03 85 47 71 96, www.aupuitsenchante.com, closed Sunday dinner and Tuesday, three weeks in January, one week mid March, ten days end September to early October, and Monday dinner from

March to October, inexpensive to moderate). You'll recognize the yellow façade and steeply pitched roof. In cool weather a big fireplace roars. The cozy dining rooms have heavy wooden furniture and comfortable chairs. The cooking is traditional, but lightened. Snails are wrapped in pasta and cooked in garlicky bouillon with parsley essence. Bresse chicken is fricasséed with morel mushrooms; thick Charolais steak has red wine reduction sauce. Owners Jacky Chateau and family are pros. The wine list is thick.

VERDUN SUR LE DOUBS

At the confluence of the Saône and Doubs, soulful Verdun is a medieval stronghold whose heyday has passed. River traffic and timber-floating made it wealthy. The autoroute drained the last traffic off highway D970 from Beaune. Verdun is nice and quiet. Sports fishermen wet lines—pike-perch and torpedo fish abound— riverboat owners and visitors explore the Verdun branch of the ecology museum (dedicated to the growing of wheat, milling of flour, and making of bread, Maison du Blé et du Pain, see Pierre-de-Bresse). One of Burgundy's longest-established flour mills still operates; its silos are on the east side of the Saône.

Flanking the mill, surrounded by landscaped grounds, find **Hostellerie Bourguignonne** (2 Avenue Président Borgeot, Tel: 03 85 91 51 45, www.hostelleriebourguignonne.com, closed Tuesday, lunch Wednesday, three weeks in February, and Sunday dinner in winter, moderate to very expensive). This excellent-value gourmet restaurant is one of two remaining in Verdun, famed cradle of pocheuse fish stew. (The pocheuse festival is held on the main square, end August). In 1997, bearded, bouncy Didier Denis and his elegant wife took over this century-old, half-timbered inn and have made pocheuse their specialty. He prepares the authentic, garlicky, palate-bucking, flambéed version (with eel, torpedo fish, carp, pike-perch, and Aligoté) plus lighter, creamier, easier-to-eat stew many guests prefer. Denis' cooking courses (spring and fall on Monday, Thursday, and Friday) usually include hands-on pocheuse-making. A veteran of Le Nôtre and Michel Rostand in Paris, Denis will also teach you to craft house specialties. Leaving aside the small spring rolls and samosas, lobster salads, and foie gras, eat wild crayfish from Lac Leman in a frothy nage with star anise, pike-perch roasted on its skin, with torpedo fish fritters, or perfect Bresse chicken stuffed with morel mushrooms with *vin jaune*–reduction sauce. There's boned quail with sweetbreads, foie gras and spices, pan-fried Charolais filet with thyme (from the herb garden), and squab cooked in three ways. The cheeses are excellent; the pre-, actual, and post- desserts are wildly good if neo-Baroque (runny Guayaquil chocolate "dome" with fresh mint sorbet; giant macarons with strawberries, cream and ice cream with aniseed candy from the Abbey of Flavigny). The wine list is among the region's best: from reasonable Montagny 1er Cru, via Maranges 1er Cru La Fussière (Domaine M. Bouthenet), or Domaine Jacqueson's remarkable, organic Rully 1er Cru, to outstanding Echezeaux from Domaine Devillard, or even more extravagant Bouchard Père & Fils La Romanée (plus rare Domaine de la Romanée Conti). You can buy wines to take with you, at significant discounts. There's a terrace with comfortable teak tables and chairs, and a handsome dining room with timbers, thick carpets, heavy old furniture, copper pots, and wine racks. The service is professional, the guest rooms tastefully done with antiques and classic contemporary furniture. Business people and high-end tourists are clients. Ask in advance and Denis can arrange visits to the landmark flour mill next door.

MÂCON and MÂCONNAIS

....

Includes: Bussières, Chaintré, La Chapelle de Guinchay,
Charnay-lès-Mâcon, Chasselas, Chevagny-les-Chevrières, Clessé,
La Croix Blanche, Cruzille en Mâconnais, Davayé, Fuissé,
Leynes, Loché, Lugny, Mâcon, Péronne, Pierreclos, Pouilly,
Prissé, La Roche Vineuse, Romanèche Thorins,
Saint-Amour-Bellevue, Saint-Vérand, Sologny, Solutré,
Vergisson, Verzé, Vinzelles, Viré

A BUSY CITY OF 35,000, MÂCON FILLS THE SOUTH-
EAST CORNER OF BURGUNDY. IT'S BOUNDED ON
the east by the Saône, traversed by the many arched,
eleventh-century Pont Saint-Laurent (also remodeled and
restored many times). Of ancient Roman origin, Mâcon's first
name was Matisco. Like Chalon-sur-Saône upstream forty
miles, Julius Caesar used the river port here during his conquest
of Gaul. Mâcon is still a crossroads, now on the A6 and A40
autoroutes, and RN79 expressway. There are two train stations,
one downtown, another for TGVs only, at Mâcon-Loché five
miles west.

The Mâconnais relies on winegrowing, trans-European trucking, and provincial administration. Most tourists stick to vineyards and villages, giving Mâcon a miss. A pity. Sturdy rather than handsome, soulful and hard-working, Mâcon only recently cleaned up its historic center and is trying to lure customers off the wine route.

The Mâconnais extends from the Beaujolais north to Tournus; the north is referred to as the Haut Mâconnais. It reaches west to mountains hemming Cluny. Though the Saône Valley doesn't win beauty contests, wine country is scenic, a mix of vineyards, forests, and pasturelands. Some of Burgundy's best chèvre—AOC Mâconnais—is made here.

The monks of Cluny Abbey perfected the vintner's art and were particularly active in this area. Their former summer residence borders the Clunysois and Mâconnais, at Berzé-la-Ville; they maintained wineries in many villages. Red wines, nearly all made from Gamay, are often challenging to appreciate. Chardonnay, the village, in the Haut Mâconnais, is called by some "the cradle of Chardonnay."

Whether the Romans or Gauls brought winemaking to the region, after the Clunysian monks' toil, the Mâconnais became the fief of mediocre co-ops. That's why its reputation suffers to this day. After a century of mediocrity, the co-ops are better. Better still, dozens of independents now producing excellent-value white wines, and a renaissance—or gold rush—is underway.

BUSSIÈRES

Pocketsized, between Pierreclos and La Roche Vineuse; alongside Serrières, Bussières forms part of the so-called Golden Triangle of the Mâconnais. This area nurtures both fine white and good red wines. Philippe Trébignaud's **Domaine de la Sarazinière** (Tel: 03 85 37 76 04 or 06 11 96 85 27, philippe.trebignaud@wanadoo.fr, by appointment) stands out for excellent reds and remarkable whites, and routinely runs out of both. Les Devants, a vineyard, has grapevines eighty years old; they yield tiny quantities of highest-quality grapes. *Best wines:* Mâcon-Bussières Les Devants Vieilles Vignes (red), Mâcon-Bussières Cuvée Claude Seigneuret Vieilles Vignes (white).

Some of Jean-Marie Pidault's vineyards at **Domaine de la Tour Vayon** (Chemin Testot-Ferry/Route de Pierreclos, Tel: 03 85 35 71 78, www.latourvayon.com, by appointment) overlook the family château at Pierreclos (others are near the main road in the valley, south of Pierreclos). Pidault's wines may be tasted and purchased there. *Best wines:* Mâcon-Pierreclos de la Condemine, Saint-Véran au Grand Bussière (both white).

CHAINTRÉ

Between Mâcon and Saint-Vérand, Chaintré is Mecca to migratory bobos. **La Table de Chaintré** (Tel: 03 85 32 90 95, closed Tuesday and Wednesday, prix fixe only, very expensive), formerly a regional restaurant (in the house where Résistance heroine Lucie Aubrac was born) morphed under Gérard Alonzo into a hotspot of creative haute. Alonzo decamped, handing to Sébastien Grospellier, who's talented but also adheres to the truffles, foie gras, and edible arabesques school. The cheeses and wines are local.

On the road to Juliénas, you'll spot co-op **Cave de Chaintré** (Tel: 03 85 35 61 61, www.cavedechaintre.com, open daily without appointment, closed three weeks in August), a landmark, from 1928. One hundred winegrowers belong; the wines range from anemic to zippy. Whites are the warhorses; Beaujolais reds are quaffable. With personable staff, this is also one of few co-ops where visitors dig into cold cuts and local goat while tasting.

LA CHAPELLE DE GUINCHAY

In the Beaujolais near Romanèche Thorins, trendy restaurant La Poularde has nary a hint of *terroir*. At the tourism office, find **Maison de Pays** (Clos Méziat, Tel: 03 85 33 85 07, hours vary widely) selling, among local products, chèvres from **EARL La Chazère** (La Grange, Château, Tel: 03 85 59 32 50, open daily from March to December). Organic wine is grown in outlying Boccards-Deschamps at **GFA Château des Boccards** (Tel: 03 85 36 81 70, by appointment), where James Pelloux makes certified quaffables. Nearby is **Domaine des Gandelins** (1887 Route des Deschamps, Tel: 03 85 36 72 68, open daily without appointment). Patrick Thévenet makes good Burgundy and Beaujolais AOCs following *agriculture raisonnée*; his Chénas red is remarkable, from grapevines fifty years old. At **Domaine des Pierres** (2775 Route de Juliénas, Tel: 03 85 36 70 70, by appointment) Georges Trichard specializes in Saint Amour (red).

CHARNAY-LÈS-MÂCON

A western suburb of Mâcon, Charnay is on hills bisected by D17, the old highway to Cluny. **Domaine Jeandeau** (26 Allée du Teil, Tel: 03 85 29 20 46, by appointment) is where Madeleine and

Sylvain Jeandeau use organically grown grapes to make pleasant Mâconnais wines.

Two wineries accessible without appointment are **Cave Charney-les-Mâcon** (54 Chemin de la Cave, Tel: 03 85 34 54 24), a co-op, and **Domaine Richard Luquet** (2816 Route de Davayé, Tel: 03 85 34 41 56), with good Mâcon white and Pouilly-Fuissé.

CHASSELAS

Either Chasselas gave its name to, or was named after, the variety (in Switzerland, aka Fendant or Gutedel). Long used for wine-making (also in Pouilly-sur-Loire), it's gone out of fashion, and is now a table grape. A pity. Ironically Chasselas, the village, is in prime Chardonnay and Gamay country. New-wave organic grapegrower **Domaine Catherine et Philippe Jambon** (Tel: 03 85 35 17 57, by appointment) produces highly regarded Mâcon Fuissé (plus Beaujolais white and red and Beaujolais Villages). Look for the church and you'll find the property.

Easier to spot is turreted **Château de Chasselas** (Tel: 03 85 35 12 01, www.chateauchasselas.fr, open daily without appointment), taken over in 1999 by Jacky Martinon and Jean-Marc Veyron la Croix. They make good Beaujolais and Mâcon-Chasselas, but it's their Crémant de Bourgogne and Saint-Véran Le Clos (made in stainless steel) that stand out for typicity and excellence. No oak interferes with the nervy minerals.

CHEVAGNY-LES-CHEVRIÈRES

North of Charnay-lès-Mâcon, this village is celebrated as home to certified-organic goat's-milk cheesemakers **Jacqueline and Michel Bourdon** (Rue Porte des Jacques, Tel: 03 85 34 83 26, open daily, ring the buzzer). Follow signs marked "*Fromages de chèvre*," back of the church. It's also a modest B&B. The Bourdons have been making cheese forever. The goats spend their lives out-doors, in pastures with views of hill and dale. The cheese facility is spic 'n' span, the rest of the farm, too. Try the aged whites or blues, particularly flavorful. Visit the farm's mini-museum of winemaking tools. The Bourdons sell from a stand in nearby Igé on Saturday mornings.

CLESSÉ

Highly regarded white wines come from here. The landscape of green hills and hidden valleys looks too scenic for wine. Among fine wineries is **Domaine des Gandines** (Route de la Vigne Blanche, Tel: 03 85 36 95 16, open daily without appointment), an organic operation run by Robert and Benjamin Dananchet. The Viré-Clessé and Mâcon Villages Blanc are crisp, refreshing, and pure.

Nearby, **Cave Cooperative de Clessé** (La Vigne Blanche, Tel: 03 85 36 93 88, www.vire-clesse.com, open daily without appointment) makes good Viré-Clessé, Crémant, and Mâcon whites, at bargain prices.

More distinguished is award-winning **Domaine de la Bongran—Domaine Jean Thévent** (Quintaine, Tel: 03 85 36 94 03, www.bongran.com, by appointment). Thévent was early in making high-quality whites in Clessé, and key in raising its profile. He grows about 40,000 bottles a year of outstanding Viré-Clessé Cuvée Tradition.

For a rustic-hayseed luncheon, seat yourself at a bistro table at **L'Auberge des Chasseurs** (Place du Marché, Tel: 03 85 36 93 66, closed evenings and Sundays, extremely inexpensive), surrounded by wine barrels and tools, winegrowers, farmers, construction workers, lost tourists, and, as the name suggests, hunters bent on blasting boars and songbirds. The set menu usually includes terrines, cold cuts, salads, stewed meat or poultry, cheese, a fruit tart or mousse, a quarter-liter of the kind of wine sometimes mistaken for paint remover, and good cheer. Since smoking in public is now illegal, this auberge is possible without gas masks.

LA CROIX BLANCHE

Bordering the Mâconnais and Clunysois, footing Berzé la Ville, **Le Relais du Mâconnais** (Tel: 03 85 36 60 72, www.lannuel.com, closed Sunday dinner and Monday, and early January to early February, moderate to expensive) is a comfortable hotel-restaurant once run by Christian Lannuel and his wife. Christian handed to his son, ambitious Artaud, who promptly redecorated in global-contemporary style, revamping the menu to reflect time in famous kitchens. The artistically arranged tidbits seem out of place, and disconcertingly familiar. The menu changes seasonally. Expect a single, solitary snail lightly battered and fried tempura-style, surrounded by squirts of turnip purée. Though local lamb is wonderful, you'll probably be served delicious Pyrénées lamb, with stuffed, fried artichokes, or suckling pig and Japanese mushrooms braised and dropped skillfully into crystal. An appreciation for spirit of Burgundian place? Still partly rooted, at certain times, Lannuel deigns to offer succulent Charolais, simmered in red Mâcon, or thick filets wrapped in lard, seared with its own marrow, and finished in the oven. The chèvres are local, the vertical, seasonal desserts (salted butter-and-chocolate cream stuffed into a cigar-cookie poised atop chocolate mousse, or deconstructed strawberry millefeuille), are delicious. The wine list includes good Mâconnais. The service is more stilted than intended, the clientele blends migratory bobos and nostalgic regulars who wish Artaud would turn the clock back.

CRUZILLE EN MÂCONNAIS

In the northern Mâconnais, near Brancion, this is the cradle of organic grape-growing. The Guillot family of **Domaine des Vignes du Maynes** (Savy, Tel: 03 85 33 20 15, www.vignes-du-maynes.com, open daily without appointment) began in 1954. The founder's fragile health meant he couldn't stand pesticides. He also saw no need for chemical warfare to make wine. At the time, "modern" winemakers snorted and said "*impossible*!" The Guillots have had the last laugh. No one has ever used chemical anything at this uncontaminated, seventeenth-century winery, underpinned by Roman foundations. Wine was first made here in 922 AD, by monks from Cluny. They were drawn by the exposure, sunshine, and veins of calcium carbonate and manganese. The Guillots grow highly mineral, floral whites, and challenging reds, which connoisseurs love or hate. Grapes are hand-picked. No sulfites are used, and the Guillots don't sugar, ever. The remarkable Mâcon Cruzille Blanc Cuvée Aragonite is redolent of cinnamon and ripe pears. Made entirely with Gamay, Mâcon Cruzille Rouge Cuvée Manganite is spicy and shot through with liquid manganese that electrifies the tongue.

Cousins in the village at **Domaine Guillot-Broux** (Tel: 03 85 33 29 74, domaine.guillotbroux@wanadoo.fr, by appointment) are also certified organic since 1990 and make outstanding, flowery, fruity Mâcon Cruzille Blanc La Croix that marries ripe plums and acacia, and peppery Mâcon Cruzille Rouge red, made with Pinot Noir and Gamay. Guillot-Broux is preferred by many connoisseurs. The reds are rough diamonds, needing many years to mellow.

DAVAYÉ

Amid prime vineyards west of Mâcon, near Solutré, two miles from Fuissé, Davayé is known for its school of oenology, offering short courses and fully accredited degrees in winemaking, grape-growing, wine-waiting and wine commerce.

Near the square and bakery, outstanding biodynamic wine-grower **Domaine Denis Jeandeau** (Les Durandys, Tel: 03 85 40 97 55 or 06 80 98 18 73, denisjeandeau@yahoo.fr, by appointment) respects *terroir*. He hand-works the soil, hand-picks and selects only perfect grapes, uses only native yeasts, and ages his wines on the lees for up to a year. The trouble is, he doesn't make enough. Though based in Davayé and Fuissé, his best wine is Viré-Clessé.

FUISSÉ

Fuissé and Pouilly, Solutré, Davayé and others nearby, appear to be joined at the hip. Their vineyards overlap, and the picture-puzzle is confusing. The confusion is heightened because names and wines are double-barreled, the most famous example of which is Pouilly-Fuissé. The village restaurant in Fuissé follows suit: **Au Pouilly-Fuissé** (Tel: 03 85 35 60 68, closed dinner Sunday through Tuesday, Wednesday, and three weeks in January, very inexpensive to expensive). Long the fief of flamboyant Didier Jeannin, this sunny, upscale restaurant with contemporary décor and an outdoor terrace under a sycamore, currently serves good traditional French and Burgundian food, and is a favorite of winegrowers and business people. The wine list features dozens of locals, some available by the glass.

Long regarded as the area's best winery, handsome, family-run **Château de Fuissé** (Le Plan, Tel: 03 85 35 61 44, www.chateau-fuisse.fr, open weekdays without appointment, weekends by appointment only, closed holidays and one week mid August) been in the Vincent clan since 1852. Elder scion Jean-Jacques Vincent took over in 1966, was innovative and dynamic, and earned the château its reputation for buttery, oaked bottlings. It routinely sells nine in ten for export, notably to the U.S. Cheerful "JJ," now the *eminence grise*, encourages his son Antoine and daughter Bénédicte to do the heavy lifting. They're also innovators, have embraced *agriculture raisonnée*, and grassy vineyards, but, though tastes are evolving away from oak, have stuck to fat wines assembled from premium parcels. The Pouilly-Fuissé Vieilles Vignes comes from vines eighty years old; the gigantic results are worthy of the Côte de Beaune. The château's single-vineyard bottlings, and its regional AOCs, are leaner, showcasing the mineral qualities of the soil. *Best wines:* Bourgogne AOC "JJ," Pouilly-Fuissés Tête de Cru, Les Brûlés, Les Combettes.

LEYNES

Ten miles southwest of Mâcon, on the square find **Le Bec Fin** (Place de la Mairie, Tel: 03 85 35 11 77, closed Sunday dinner and Monday, Thursday dinner in low season, the first half of January, two weeks from late July to early August, and one week

Domaine Corsin (Les Plantés, Tel: 03 85 35 83 69, www.domaine-corsin.com, by appointment). Note: this thirty-acre estate practices *agriculture raisonnée*; grapes are hand-picked and wines are made on the lees in big tanks and then lightly oaked. *Best wines:* Pouilly-Fuissé, Saint-Véran.

Domaine de la Croix Senaillet–GAEC Richard et Stéphane Martin (En Coland, Tel: 03 85 35 82 83, www.domainecroixsenaillet.com, open weekdays for retail sales, tastings, and visits by appointment only). Note: this sixty-two-acre estate is organic. *Best wines:* Mâcon Blanc Vigne aux Mésanges, Saint-Vérans Les Rochets, La Grande Bruyère, Les Buis.

Domaine Frédéric Curis–Château de Chailloux (Tel: 03 85 35 88 02, f.curis@terre-net.fr, by appointment). *Best wine:* Saint-Véran Terre-Noire (a Vieilles Vignes from eighty-year-old vines).

Domaine des Deux Roches (Route de Fuissé, Tel: 03 85 35 86 51, by appointment). Note: *Best wines:* Saint-Vérans Vieilles Vignes, Les Chailloux, and Rives de Longsault.

Domaine de la Denante (Les Gravières, Tel: 03 85 35 82 88, martin.denante@wanadoo.fr, open weekdays and Saturday without appointment, Sunday by appointment). Note: the wines are big and made to last. *Best wines:* Mâcon-Davayé, Saint-Véran.

Domaine Gaillard (Les Plantés, Tel: 03 85 35 83 31, domaine.gaillard@wanadoo.fr, by appointment). *Best wines:* Pouilly-Fuissé, Saint-Véran.

Domaine Pascale Renoud Grappin (Les Plantés, Tel: 03 85 35 81 35, by appointment). *Best wine:* Saint-Véran.

❧ OTHER WINERIES ❧
IN OR NEAR FUISSÉ

Oenothèque Georges Burrier (Le Plan, Tel: 03 85 32 90 48, by appointment). Note: Burrier is a long-established winegrowing family and at this newish *oenothèque* sells its wines made from half a dozen local AOCs. It stocks old vintages. The wines tend to be New World style. *Best wine:* Mâcon-Fuissé.

Christophe Cordier · Cordier Père et Fils (Les Molards, Tel: 03 85 35 62 89, domaine.cordier@wanadoo.fr, by appointment only). Note: this highly regarded small winery makes whites and often sells out. *Best wines:* Mâcon-Fuissé, Mâcon-Villages Clos de la Maison, Mâcon-Milly Lamartine Clos du Four.

Domaine Denis Dutron · Château Vitallis (Tel: 03 85 35 64 42, open Monday to Saturday without appointment, Sunday morning by appointment, closed Sunday afternoon and the first eighteen days in August). *Best wine:* Mâcon-Fuissé.

Domaine Jean-Yves Éloy (Le Plan, Tel: 03 85 35 67 03, by appointment). *Best wine:* Saint-Véran. *Best wines:* Mâcon-Fuissé, Saint-Véran.

Domaine Ferret-Lorton (Le Plan, Tel: 03 85 35 61 56, earlferretlorton@terre-net.fr, by appointment). *Best wines:* Pouilly-Fuissés Le Clos and Les Ménétrières.

Domaine de Fussiacus (Tel: 03 85 27 01 06, fussiacus@wanadoo.fr, open daily by appointment only, closed Sunday afternoon). *Best wines:* Pouilly-Vinzelles, Saint-Véran.

Domaine La Source des Fées (Route de Chaintré, Tel: 03 85 35 67 02, www.lasourcedesfees.com, open daily without appointment). Note: also a B&B in a restored, 1500s building. *Best wines:* Mâcon-Fuissé, Pouilly-Fuissé Cep Éternel, Saint-Véran.

Domaine Roger Luquet (Tel: 03 85 35 60 91, by appointment). *Best wine:* Pouilly-Fuissé Cuvée Terroir.

Domaine Daniel Pollier (Tel: 03 85 35 66 85, www.domainedanielpollier.com, open daily without appointment, closed at Christmastide). *Best wines:* Mâcon-Chaintré, Mâcon-Fuissé.

Domaine Thibert Père et Fils (Tel: 03 85 27 02 66, domthibe@wanadoo.fr, open weekdays without appointment, weekends and holidays by appointment). *Best wines:* Pouilly-Fuissé Vignes Blanches, Mâcon-Fuissé.

....

in November, very inexpensive to expensive). Cozy, with rustic-Baroque décor, this ambitious eatery attempts to turn *terroir* into *cuisine gastronomique* plated with naïf artistry. The wine list features dozens of local independedents.

For a quiet B&B that's also a good winery, head uphill to **Le Bois de Leynes** and **Chambres-d'Hôtes-Domaine du Prieuré** (Tel: 03 85 35 11 56 or 06 62 37 11 56, http://jeandeau.suivezlagrappe .com, bruno.jeandeau@wanadoo.fr, by appointment). Bruno and Nadine Jeandeau will happily ply you with their Mâcon-Fuissé, Crémant, Saint-Véran, Pouilly-Fuissé, and Beaujolais. These other nearby wineries are worth a visit if you have the time: **Domaine Château des Correaux-Jean Bernard** (Les Correaux, Tel: 03 85 35 11 59, bernardleynes@yahoo.fr, open daily without appointment). Note: Correaux oaks some of his wines for up to a year, adding to their natural fatness, but somewhat diminishing trueness to type. *Best wine*: Saint-Véran Les Spires. **Domaine des Crais** (Les Pasquiers, Tel: 03 85 35 10 31, open daily without appointment, closed Sunday afternoon). *Best wines*: Mâcon-Fuissé, Saint-Véran. **Domaine La Maison** (Tel: 03 85 35 10 16, domain. la.maison@free.fr, open daily without appointment). Note: Jean and Françoise Chagny hand-pick their grapes and do not use oak. *Best wine*: Saint-Véran and Saint-Véran Clos La Maison Vieilles Vignes.

LOCHÉ

Known for its TGV train station, Loché is a handsome village on hills groomed with fine vineyards. Winegrowers **Céline et Laurent Tripoz** (Place de la Mairie, Tel: 03 85 35 66 09, cltripoz@free.fr, by appointment), near the village hall (*la mairie*), are organic, and produce true-to-type Mâcon-Loché (white), Pouilly-Loché (white), Mâcon-Vinzelles (white), Aligoté, and a rough-and-ready Mâcon Rouge (red).

Another good independent, on the back road to Fuissé, is **Domaine Alain Delaye** (429 Route de Fuissé, Les Mures, Tel: 03 85 35 61 63, michele.delaye@wanadoo.fr, closed Thurday afternoon, Sunday by appointment, open the rest of the week without appointment). *Best wine:* Pouilly-Loché Les Mures.

LUGNY

Between Montbellet and the prehistoric grottoes (and medieval houses, and umpteen self-styled *artisans d'art*) of Blanot, Lugny foots winegrowing hills where two-lane highways D82 and D103 meet. Insiders flock to butcher **Aubertin** (Rue Église, Tel: 03 85 33

22 46, closed Sunday afternoon and Monday) to buy meat, terrines, jambon persillé, ham, and salami. The village also has a modest bakery, should you want to throw together a picnic. Lugny is home to enormous co-op **Cave de Lugny** (Rue des Charmes, Tel: 03 85 33 22 85, www.cave-lugny.com, open daily without appointment), with 2,500 acres, a leading regional player. It's easy to visit and makes many good regional and village AOC whites. The co-op's real claim to fame is its Crémant. Note: this winery has outlets in Chardonnay, and Saint-Gengoux-de-Scissé, on the road to Azé.

Driving south toward Péronne, visit Hubert Laferrère of **Domaine Hubert Laferrère-Domaine Saint Denis** (Route de Péronne, Tel: 03 85 33 24 33, domaine.saintdenis@free.fr, by appointment). Some of the vines were planted in the 1940s, and their yield is low and extremely high quality. Grapes are hand-picked when over-ripe, and no oak is used, allowing *terroir* to shine. *Best wines:* Mâcon-Chardonnay, Mâcon-Lugny.

MÂCON

Mâcon's symbol is eleventh-century Pont Saint-Laurent across the Saône, linking Burgundy to Bresse. Like many provincial cities, Mâcon is struggling to keep its historic downtown alive. The suburban strip malls and big-box stores are huge, because two autoroutes meet outside town. Also, Mâcon is traditionally a transit point between the Mediterranean (via Lyon) and North-ern Europe.

Central Mâcon is compact and partly pedestrianized, bounded to the west by Place de la Barre, to the east by Place Poisson-nière and the river, to the south by the train station, and to the north by Place Gardon. The main east-west pedestrian road is Rue du Pont, which changes name to Rue Philibert Laguiche and Rue de la Barre. Branching off it are Rue Sigorgne and Rue Lamartine. The main north-south road, one in from the quayside, is Rue Carnot.

Visit for the atmosphere and local history: **Musée Lamartine** (Hôtel Sénécé, 41 Rue Sigorgne, Tel: 03 85 39 90 38, closed Sun-day morning, Monday and holidays), and **Musée des Ursulines** (Allée de Matisco and 5 Rue des Ursulines, same phone and hours as Musée Lamartine). The unusual Vieux Saint-Vincent church, near the Prefecture, is a hodgepodge. The oldest house in town, wooden La Maison du Bois, from the late 1400s, is on the south-east corner of Place des Herbes (and houses a pub-café).

Mâcon's Saturday morning market features over 150 stands and spreads along Quai Lamartine, also called Esplanade

Lamartine, along the river. Each second and fourth Thursday of the month, the esplanade hosts Le Marché Bio—a sizeable organic-foods market (Tel: 06 21 07 74 88). Dozens of stands sell chèvres (Fromagerie Fermière de la Petite Guye in Chevagny-sur-Guye), fresh dairy products, terrines, flour, seed oils, fruits and vegetables, honey, essential oils—all organic.

Places to eat and drink

Michelin-starred **Pierre** (7–9 Rue Dufour, Tel: 03 85 38 14 23, www.restaurant-pierre.com, closed Sunday dinner, Tuesday lunch, and Monday, first two weeks in July and two in February, moderate to very expensive), near the corner of Rue Carnot, remains tops after years of service. The *terroir* element is light and elegant. Christian Gaulin's heart lies in the realm of lobster nage and Guanaja chocolate lingots with crunchy praline and fresh vanilla sauce. The establishment is conservatively chic (exception made for the dauber's naïf mural), and the upholstered chairs are a comfortable perch. The wine list is one of Burgundy's heaviest.

Restaurant **L'Amandier** (74 Rue Dufour, Tel: 03 85 39 82 00, closed Saturday lunch, Sunday dinner, and Monday, second half of August and two weeks in February, inexpensive to expensive) is on the same street, has an outdoor terrace, and serves *terroir* and updated traditional, seasonal food. The décor is summery and pastel-hued, the atmosphere relaxed. Florent Segain likes spices and herbs and has a light touch with the snails, frog's legs, and pike-perch (daring concoctions also abound). Desserts are classic; the wine list features regional bottlings.

L'Ethym'Sel (10 Rue Gambetta, Tel: 03 85 39 48 84, closed Sunday and Tuesday dinner, and Wednesday, from September to July; closed Sunday and Monday in July and August, prix fixe menu inexpensive, à la carte inexpensive to moderate) faces the chamber of commerce 200 yards from the banks of the river. Laurence and Patrick Chantemesse run this neo-bistro where locals eat amazingly affordable lunch prix fixe menus. The interior is done in off-white and tan, and features comfortable banquettes and large mirrors on the walls. White butcher paper tops the tablecloths at lunch, but few blue collars are found tucking into the carefully plated snails, veal kidneys in mustard sauce, filet mignon of pork slow-cooked with red wine with shallots, or Charolais with green pepper sauce. The desserts are excellent and seasonal (sablé cookie sandwich with whipped cream and fresh strawberries, baked apples with hot chocolate sauce). Wines include well-chosen locals; the service is friendly and professional. A winner.

Mâcon's cafés are interchangeable. Those on Place des Herbes near the Maison du Bois have quiet, leafy terraces. The riverside drive is breezier but noisy. On the latter, **Le Café Français** (154 Quai Lamartine, Tel: 03 85 38 84 18, open daily) is comfortable, though the daily lunch specials can be bizarre.

Gourmet shops and food artisans

The city's pastry, chocolate, and ice cream kings, **Noyerie** (39 Rue de la Barre, Tel: 03 85 38 31 11, open nonstop 7:30am to 7:30pm, closed Monday and afternoons on Sunday and holidays), faces Place de la Barre. The Idéal Mâconnais—almond-meringue pastry with crushed hazelnut nougatine and buttery cream—was invented here by award-winning *pâtissier* Joël Noyerie. The frozen Idéal is a raspberry sorbet with a mini waffle. Of the dozens of wildly good ice cream-pastries, don't miss Le Solutré (caramel, vanilla ice cream, and a crushed hazelnut biscuit base). There are dozens of fine housemade chocolates and classic pastries.

Nearby and new to the Mâcon scene is outstanding, Cluny-based chocolate, pastry, and ice cream shop **Germain** (10 Rue de la Barre, Tel: 03 85 29 05 66, www.chocolaterie-germain.fr, open daily, see Cluny for details).

Long-established, luxurious **Au Palet d'Or** (11–13 Rue Sigorgne, Tel: 03 85 38 00 23, open nonstop 8am to 7pm, closed Monday and the first half of August), on a fork in the same street, after the Lamartine Museum. Martine Berthet is proud of her skill displaying the excellent pastries and chocolates her husband makes. Try the almond croissants, bursting with cream and coated with almonds, Tigré (tiger-striped, round and spongy, with soft chocolate in the center), chocolatey Métis à la crème brûlée, or another of the twenty treats. Classic chocolates run the gamut—filled, solid, bars. There are usually thirty different varieties.

Mâcon's longest-established, most traditional *pâtisserie* is **Claude Poissonnet** (54 Rue Victor Hugo, Tel: 03 85 38 47 31, closed Monday), near the train station. Also made are delicious chocolates, housemade ice creams (summer), and crunchy Florentins, nougats, macarons, and butter cookies.

Recent **Chocolats & Tasses de Thé** (184 Quai Lamartine, Tel: 03 85 39 07 75, open nonstop 9am to 7pm, closed Sunday morning and Monday), south of Place Poissonnière, has a terrace on the riverside drive, and a salon wherein you enjoy delicious pastries, crêpes, light meals, good coffee and tea.

For artisanally roasted coffee, tea, espresso machines, teapots, and accessories: **La Brûlerie** (214 Rue Carnot, Tel: 03 85 38 01 07, open Tuesday to Saturday, Thursday and Friday nonstop, closed Sunday and Monday). The four pure-Arabica blends, roasted daily, are excellent (Délice is mildest); each contains six to eight varieties (La Brûlerie's second outlet, north of Place de la Barre, is at 11 Rue de l'Héritan).

La Maison du Pain (90 Rue Chatillon, Tel: 03 85 38 08 70, www.maisondupain.fr, open Tuesday through Friday 6:30am to 7:30pm nonstop, Saturday until 6:30pm, closed Sunday and Monday), fifty yards east of the Prefecture, is where idealistic Jean-Pierre Averoux bakes the city's best, organic-certified bread. A former wineseller and social worker, he sees breadmaking as therapeutic, and trains troubled youths to bake. Averoux restored an 1890s bakery and its original wood-burning oven. His country loaf is leavened twice and baked exactly as it would have been a century ago. The wholegrain sourdough loaf could've been baked in Caesar's Matisco. This is outstanding stuff. Also made are delicious, equally wholesome, rustic pastries: apple pies, chocolate or walnut cakes, shortbread cookies, breakfast pastries, and savory tarts. Don't miss it.

Two of Mâcon's best sources for cold cuts, hams, and cheeses, are near Place de la Barre. Across from Noyerie, find tempting, upscale **Guy Lebeau Traiteur** (40 Rue de la Barre, Tel: 03 85 38 02 29, closed Sunday afternoon and Monday). Buy everything from lobster bavarois or puréed, housemade foie fras with figs, to earthy, layered puff-pastries with veal sweetbreads and morel mushrooms, terrines, pâtés, game in season, local goat, Époisses, Chaource, and other cheeses. Around the corner at less swank **Boucherie Charcuterie Lamartine** (7 Rue Lamartine, Tel: 03 85 38 31 30, closed Sunday and Monday), find rustic ham in layered puff pastry, and snails packed with butter, parsley and garlic, classic pâtés, delicious rabbit terrine with mirabelle plums.

Wine shops and wine bar

Mâcon has surprisingly few wine shops. Most locals buy direct. However, **La Carte des Vins** (10 Rue Saint Nizier, Tel: 03 85 31 89 29, closed Sunday and Monday mornings), facing the side entrance of unremarkable Saint Pierre church, is a spotlit, independent boutique with helpful staff, and a fine selection of Beaujolais and Mâconnais at reasonable prices.

A mile north of central Mâcon, **La Maison Mâconnaise des Vins** (484 Avenue De-Lattre de Tassigny, Tel: 03 85 22 91 11, www.maison-des-vins.com, wine shop open daily 9am to 7pm, restaurant open daily 11am to 10pm) is a showcase for Mâconnais co-ops and independents, with two dozen AOCs from the Côte Chalonnaise south, plus the northern Beaujolais. The opening hours are convenient, and the bistro-style restaurant serves good regional classics and daily specials. Founded in 1958, distinguished chef Michel Rigaud took over in 2004 and has brought new dynamism. Tastings are inexpensive and informative. Also stocked are corkscrews, glassware, and accessories.

PÉRONNE

West of Viré and Clessé on highway D15, Péronne produces remarkable whites. Three good wineries are accessible: **Domaine des Terres de Châtenay** (Les Picards, Tel: 03 85 36 94 01, janinmojc@wanadoo.fr, open Monday through Saturday without appointment), where Jean-Claude and Marie-Odile Janin make fine Mâcon-Péronne and Viré-Clessé; highly regarded **Domaine du Bicheron** (St Pierre de Lanques, Tel: 03 85 36 94 53, domainedubicheron@wanadoo.fr, by appointment, closed Sunday afternoon), owned by the Rousset family, makers of excellent Péronne Cuvée Vieilles Vignes, Bourgogne AOC (red), and Crémant Blanc de blancs; **Domaine Papillon** (St Pierre de Lanques, Tel: 03 85 23 95 70, www.domainepapillon.com, open daily without appointment) is where Catherine and Robert Papillon grow very good Mâcon-Péronne.

PIERRECLOS

On a rise above the narrow valley where Pierreclos nestles amid vineyards, **Château de Pierreclos** (Tel: 03 85 35 73 73, www.chateaudepierreclos.com, closed Sunday and holidays, and weekends in winter, entrance fee required) is what irreverent visitors might call a picture-postcard pile. Crowned with glistening glazed-tiles, with the requisite towers and turrets, the belltower and apse of a Romanesque chapel loom in the garden. The Pidault family's other wineries in the area produce well-regarded wines. Lamartine, the galavanting poetaster, is at the heart of a salacious tale involving this château, its lord, and above all its lady. His memory is duly honored. The château is a house-museum, a popular wedding venue. The vast medieval kitchen boasts a waxwork boar that fools many a visitor. In the twelfth-century, barrel-vaulted cellar is the enterprising Pidaults' tasting room and boutique. Sample the château's and, happily, many other wines, particularly of the Mâconnais. **Domaine Marc Jambon et Fils** (La Roche, Tel: 03 85 35 73 15, marc.jambon@free.fr, by appointment). Note: Pierre-Antoine Jambon took over from his father at this premium independent, and makes true-to-type wines using native yeasts; he also produces oaky Fût de Chêne white for lovers of butterscotch. *Best wines:* Mâcon-Pierreclos Cuvée Classique (red), Mâcon-Pierreclos Vendanges de la Saint-Martin (white). **Domaine Maurice Lapalus & Fils-Domaine des Bruyères** (Les Bruyères, Tel: 03 85 35 71 90, open daily without appointment). Note: this ultra-modern winery has a distinctly New World feel. *Best wines:* Mâcon-Pierreclos (white), Aligoté. **Vignobles Jean-Claude Thévenet** (Tel: 03 85 35 72 21, vignoblethevenet.jeanclaude@wanadoo.fr, open weekdays without appointment, weekends by appointment). Thévenet is visitor-friendly and good value. *Best wines:* Beaujolais (red), Mâcon-Villages (white).

POUILLY

See Solutré and Fuissé.

PRISSÉ

Brin de Sel (Place Église, Tel: 03 85 37 60 83, closed Sunday, Monday, and Wednesday afternoon). Françoise and Jean-Louis Gachet run this upscale gourmet food shop and take-out deli, abutting a homely church. Check the chalkboards for a changing list of cheeses, hams, cold cuts, take-out dishes, and wines.

If you have problems with sulphites found even in most organic wines, visit **Domaine Combier** (Rue de l'Ancien Presbytère, Tel: 06 19 39 64 72, arnaud.combier@club-internet.fr, by appointment), where Arnaud Combier makes pleasant Saint-Véran without any sulphites.

Easy access, wide choice, hand-picked grapes, and stainless steel, are reasons to seek out third-generation **Domaine de La Feuillarde** (La Feuillarde, Tel: 03 85 34 54 45, www.domaine-feuillarde.com, open daily without appointment). Lucien Thomas happily receives visitors. The winery makes many wines; the best is true-to-type Saint-Véran Vieilles Vignes from old vines: no oak, pure *terroir*.

Domaine Nicolas Rousset (Chemin de Mont, Chevigne, Tel: 03 85 35 89 62, domaine.rousset@wanadoo.fr, by appointment), getting organic certification, makes good Mâcon-Prissé, Pouilly-Fuissé, and Saint-Véran.

Vignerons des Terres Secretes-Chai de Prissé (Les Grandes Vignes, Tel: 03 85 37 64 90, www.terres-secretes.com, open daily without appointment). Formerly Cave de Prissé, the marketing men have been busy. This major co-op (with wineries in Sologny and Verzé, and a shop on Cluny's main street) is a remarkable crowd-pleaser. Its good wines: Mâcon Rouge Cuvée Prestige Vieilles Vignes (red), Saint-Véran.

LA ROCHE VINEUSE

"Wine-rock" is an apt name. La Roche Vineuse, on scenic highway D17, belongs to both Clunysois and Mâconnais. Fine bread is baked on the main square: **Le P'tit Fournil** (Place du Chaucher, Tel: 03 85 37 70 88, gilles.westrich@wanadoo.fr, closed Monday). The housemade chocolates, ice cream cakes, special breads (some organic), and classic pastries (strawberry or lemon-custard tarts, extravagant chocolate confections) are outstanding.

Based here and glad to share his wines with serious clients by appointment only is up-and-coming **Alain Normand** (Chemin de la Grange-du-Dîme, Tel: 03 85 36 61 69, domaine.alain.nor-mand@wanadoo.fr). Drive uphill from the bakery toward the Romanesque chapel, then follow signs to La Grange-du-Dîme, once a customs house on the Roman road. Alain and his wife will uncork red Bourgogne AOC, unusual because made with Pinot Noir (the red grape hereabouts is Gamay). After macerating for three weeks, it comes out strong on red fruit and blackberry. The simple whites are best: Mâcon-La Roche Vineuse is pleasant, clean, crisp, with a citrus quality, and amazingly affordable. A winery to watch.

Also near the church is **Domaine du Vieux Saint-Sorlin–Olivier Merlin** (Tel: 03 85 36 62 09, merlin.vins@wanadoo.fr, by appointment). Olivier and wife Corinne grow but also buy grapes, and are known for big wines that walk the line between oaky fat (Saint-Véran Le Grand Bussière) and authentic, *terroir* nerve. You'll find butterscotch, pears, and under-growth in many. The best are Pouilly-Fuissés Terroir de Fuissé and Clos des Quarts, a fine but woody Clessé-Viré Terroir de Clessé, and an outstanding Mâcon-La Roche Vineuse Les Cras. The excellent-value Mâcon La Roche Vineuse red, made in stainless steel, is wonderfully grapey, easily taken for a top Beaujolais Cru.

The vineyards atop the hill belong to **Domaine Perraud** (Nancelle, Tel: 03 85 34 59 22, by appointment), where Jean-Christophe Perraud—still in his twenties—makes pleasant wines using *agriculture raisonnée*. Perraud is third generation, trained at Davayé, worked at the co-op in Prissé, and broke away in 2005. Nine in ten of his wines are white; the red is typical. The Saint-Véran, though oaked and muscular, is good. His truest-to-*terroir* bottling is Mâcon-La Roche Vineuse, redolent of honeysuckle and white flowers, with hints of peach and apricot. Another winery to watch.

No need to phone to visit friendly **Domaine Chêne** (Tel: 03 85 37 65 30, gaecchene@aol.com, open daily, closed noon to 2:30pm), in the valley, on the road to Milly-Lamartine. In an oak-filled tasting room you discover wines which, happily, are not oaky, despite the name (*chêne* = oak). The Mâcon-Milly is a winner: grapey, with a flinty quality and zippy citrus scents.

ROMANÈCHE THORINS

On Burgundy's southern border, many wineries here make Burgundian and Beaujolais AOCs. There's a museum of wood-working, and a wild animal park. In keeping, this is the fief of

Maison Georges Duboeuf. The winery is part of **Le Hameau du Vin** (La Gare, Tel: 03 85 35 34 20 and 03 85 35 22 22, www.hameauduvin.com, open daily except Christmas). If you thought it impossible to turn winemaking into a theme park for infants—toddlers to centenarians—think again. In the former train station of Mainstreet France are waxworks and automata that act out the Four Seasons of winegrowing and more. Much more. The fun chugs along, like the vintage rolling stock also on hand. Naturally, there's a boutique, and an eatery, **Café des Deux Orologes**, should you swoon from low blood sugar. Duboeuf is too famous to need introduction, and too skilled at introducing himself for anyone to do him justice. He's from the Mâconnais, and makes lakes of drinkable Beaujolais, better-than-average Saint-Véran, and wantonly oaky Pouilly-Fuissé.

For authenticity, seek out **Domaine Fumet Dutrève** (Les Fargets, Tel: 03 85 36 51 48, by appointment), a micro-winery run by Bernard and Jean Fumet, makers of true-to-type Pouilly-Vinzelles, Pouilly-Fuissé, and red and white Beaujolais.

Make time to visit **Château Portier—Denys Chastel-Sauzet** (Le Moulin à Vent, Tel: 03 85 35 59 39 and 03 85 35 58 91, moulinavent@wanadoo.fr, open daily without appointment June to late September, on weekends in April, May, October, and November), from the mid 1800s, incorporating the famous fifteenth-century windmill that gave a name to the appellation Moulin à Vent, one of the top Beaujolais crus, ironic, given it's in Burgundy. The property rides two regions; the best wines are red Chénas Château Portier, Bourgogne AOC, Beaujolais red and white. The fresh grape juice is thirst-quenching. Phone ahead to visit the property and cellars, and reserve a tasty *machon beaujolais*—a winegrower's snack (bread, cold cuts or terrine).

Easy to visit, **Domaine Jean-Pierre Mortet** (Tel: 03 85 35 55 51, jean.mortet@free.fr, open weekdays without appointment, weekends by appointment) makes good Moulin à Vent and Beaujolais Villages reds.

SAINT-AMOUR-BELLEVUE

Bordering the Beaujolais, and home to romantic bide-a-wee hotel-restaurant **L'Auberge du Paradis** (Le Plâtre-Durand, Tel: 03 85 37 10 26, www.aubergeduparadis.fr, closed Sunday dinner, Monday, Tuesday, Friday lunch, and January, inexpensive to expensive), this is indeed a paradise—of trendy, spicy world cuisine. Utterly anti-*terroir*, perhaps, but the wine list is outstanding, with dozens of local independents.

There's not much else worth your trouble, unless you'd like to choose your lobster from a tank and watch the chef flambée it at similarly non-*terroir* **Chez Jean Pierre** (Le Plâtre-Durand, Tel: 03 85 37 41 26, closed dinner Sunday and Wednesday, Thursday, and late December to mid January, inexpensive to expensive). These nearby wineries are worth a visit if you have the time: **Domaine de l'Ancien Relais** (Les Chamonards, Tel: 03 85 37 16 05, earlandrepoitevin@wanadoo.fr, by appointment). Note: landmark cellars date to the turn of the fifteenth century; extremely old vines, the wines derived from them are powerful. Most bottlings sell out. *Best wines:* Saint-Amour Vieilles Vignes, Beaujolais (white). **Domaine du Clos des Carrières** (Le Clos des Carrières, Tel: 03 85 37 19 70, by appointment). *Best wine:* Saint-Amour (red). **Domaine Jean-Yves Cognard-Domaine de Savy** (Le Clos des Carrières, Tel: 03 85 37 19 07, domaindesavy@ wanadoo.fr, open Monday through Saturday without appointment, Sunday by appointment). *Best wine:* Beaujolais (white). **Domaine des Duc** (La Piat, Tel: 03 85 37 10 08, domainedes-duc@free.fr, open daily except Sunday without appointment). *Best wine:* Saint-Amour.

SAINT-VÉRAND

Wrapped around a Romanesque church, the village ends with a silent "d"; for marketing purposes, the wines are Saint-Véran, no "d." Saint-Vérand is known for its big, flowery whites, produced throughout the extensive AOC. Few AOCs are more confusing. Saint-Véran is the name of the wine; the village is Saint-Vérand. Covering 1,250 acres—vast for Burgundy, a tenth of the Mâconnais's total—Saint-Véran is theoretically a prestige cru. In reality it ranges from sublime to ridiculously hyped. Boosters call it "Southern Burgundy's White Gold." Maybe. It's produced in six communes, from Prissé in the north, near the RN79 expressway, to Davayé several miles south; the AOC leapfrogs Solutré, Pouilly, and Fuissé—the Pouilly-Fuissé AOC—and starts up again at Chasselas, then goes south to Leynes, Saint-Vérand, and Chânes. Though limestone (atop a granitic and volcanic base) characterizes the sub-soil, the exposure, micro-climates, and top soils vary widely, with bottomlands fattened by a mixture of sand, siliceous rocks and clay, and steeper slopes that are rocky and lean. Mechanized harvesting is widespread; only the best, and often the smallest, estates hand-pick grapes. Responding to New World demands, many winegrowers drown the minerals in butter by over-oaking. There are excellent Saint-Vérans, but some lesser

Mâcon-Villages made within the AOC are as good or better, and cost half as much.

In a reconverted watermill, **Auberge du Saint-Véran** (La Roche, Tel; 03 85 23 90 90, www.auberge-saint-veran.com, closed Monday and Tuesday in fall and winter, and from late December to end January, inexpensive to moderate) offers *terroir* meals (and has eleven comfortable rooms). The old-fashioned dining room gives onto a back terrace.

SOLOGNY

See Prissé, for Vignerons des Terres Secretes.

SOLUTRÉ

Sunny and dry, with fine soil and drainage, the stone-built villages of Solutré, Pouilly, and Fuissé are within hailing distance of each other, clinging to the bowl of vineyards south of soaring limestone hogback La Roche de Solutré. It was a favorite hunting ground during Flintstone times, which is why Solutré gave its name to the Solutrian Phase of the Upper Paleolithic. Worth visiting for the views and didactic displays (bones, bows, arrowheads, scrapers), and sometimes-fascinating temporary exhibitions, is **Musée Départemental de Préhistoire** (Roche de Solutré, Tel: 03 85 35 85 24, www.musees-bourgogne.org, open daily yearround, hours vary), built into the cliff's base, where hundreds of thousands of bones—mostly of wild horses—were discovered in the 1800s. Climb to the top for the panorama, literally breathtaking. François Mitterrand made a yearly pilgrimage here, by helicopter, preceded and followed by tame journalists.

Should the hike induce hunger and thirst, try **Le Pichet de Solutré** (Tel: 03 85 35 80 73, closed Sunday dinner and Monday, very inexpensive to inexpensive), in the village, near the church. Trees shade the terrace, and the dining room is cozy. No surprises, but good *terroir* food, with remarkable coq au vin (made with Saint-Véran), and local wines, some by the pitcher or glass. Simple rooms await upstairs, in case you'd like to hike up again at midnight or dawn.

On a crest due west bordering the Beaujolais, at La Grange du Bois, find **La Ferme du Prieuré** (Tel: 03 85 35 80 27 and 03 85 35 85 28, www.la-grange-du-bois.com, farm closed Sunday afternoon, B&B always open). Reinvented Swedish IKEA manager Karin Gribenski operates the B&B while her partner, farmer Guy Favier, makes organic chèvres. Given the opportunity, loquacious Favier, whose family has been here at least 500 years, will teach

you everything you never wanted to know about chèvre, from nipple to curd, whether fresh and white, rock-hard and yellow, or blue with mold. Cheeses air-dry in a tiger-sized cage in the rough-and-ready farmyard. Idealistic yet down-to-earth, the couple will take you on nature walks, introduce you to neo-Druids, and cater dinner if you stay at the tidy, comfortable B&B, whose rooms boast stupendous views.

VERGISSON

The "other" bluff, lesser-known but as spectacular as that of nearby Solutré, Vergisson is a hogback outcrop and a winegrowing village. Among excellent wineries, a handful stand out. **Jacques et**

Nathalie Saumaize (Les Bruyères, Tel: 03 85 35 82 14, nathalie.saumaize@wanadoo.fr, by appointment) have scattered vineyards. Among their outstanding wines—all white—the Mâcon-Bussières Montbrison is a bruiser, clocking in at thirteen percent alcohol. It's balanced nonetheless, fat and not flabby, with a vein of minerals. Also remarkable is Saint-Véran La Vieille Vigne des Créches, which smells of honey and buddleia blossoms, has surprising structure, and a long, slow finish. The Pouilly-Fuissé Les Courtelongs comes from a vineyard with eastern exposure, on the Roche de Solutré, and spends about ten months aging, a fifth on new oak.

It's easy to confuse Nathalie and Jacques with the village's other fine winegrowing Saumaizes, Roger and Christine. They identify their winery as **Saumaize-Michelin** (Le Martelet, Tel: 03 85 35 84 05, saumaize-michelin@wanadoo.fr, by appointment). They, too, make outstanding Saint-Vérans, the best Fleur, Vieilles Vignes, and Les Créches. They also make excellent Pouilly-Fuissés, one from Les Courtelongs vineyard (astonishingly complex, with a mineral backbone). Fresher and lighter is Pouilly-Fuissé Clos sur la Roche, while Les Ronchevats has punch, fruit, and nuts. All grapes are grown organically, and the vineyards will soon be biodynamic. Phone ahead, or check the website before visiting: the winery is expanding, and may have a new address. These other nearby wineries are worth a visit if you have the time: **Domaine Corinne et Thierry Drouin** (Le Grand Pré, Tel: 03 85 35 84 36, corinneetthierrydrouin@wanadoo.fr, by appointment). *Best wine:* Pouilly-Fuissé Maréchaude. **Domaine Roger Lassarat** (Le Martelet, Tel: 03 85 35 84 28, by appointment). Note: Lassarat is big, with thirty-seven acres, and generously oaks his wines. They're fatter than many. *Best wines:* Pouilly-Fuissés Cuvée R, Racines, Close de France. **Domaine Sangouard-Guyot** (Chez Marcel Lemonier, Carmentrant, Tel: 03 85 35 89 45, pekty@wanadoo.fr, by appointment). *Best wines:* Mâcon-Vergisson, Pouilly-Fuissé. **Domaine Simonin** (Tel: 03 85 35 84 72, domsimonin.ja@wanadoo.fr, by appointment). Note: The soil of the Simonins' vineyards is chock-full of minerals. Their oldest grapevines are from the 1950s. *Best wines:* Pouilly-Fuissés Vieilles Vignes, Cuvée des Roches, and Les Ammonites.

VERZÉ

Little more than a crossroads, Verzé to insiders is home of **Le Petit Bouchon—Chez la Martine** (Tel: 03 85 33 35 75, closed Monday, lunch served Tuesday to Friday, dinner by reservation only on Sunday in fall and winter, or for groups of ten or more). Heavy-smoking, wry, and with strong opinions, Martine is colorful. She also knows how to cook. Hers is the village's only café, tobacco shop, and restaurant, the essence of nitty-gritty. At lunchtime, winegrowers, farmers, hunters, and blue-collar workers chow cheek by jowl at wooden tables: tasty pot roasts, oxtail stews, roast chickens, grilled pig's trotters and suchlike, washed down with local wine. In hunting season, Martine makes dinner on Sunday night (or by reservation, for groups); you'll find wild boar stew, venison, pheasant, and whatever the hunters bring in. The specialty here is *brechets de poulet*—chicken wishbones—which Martine gets from Bresse, and cooks up in the style of frog's legs, with butter, garlic, and parsley. An experience.

VINZELLES

West of Mâcon and surrounded by prized vineyards, brothers Jean-Guillaume and Jean-Philippe Bret of **La Soufrandière–Bret Brothers** (Tel: 03 85 35 67 72, www.bretbrothers.com, by appointment, closed Sunday) took over their grandfather's winery in 2000 and turned things upside down. Now ranked among the district's best, they've switched to organic grapegrowing and also buy from other organic growers, producing over a dozen excellent whites. The Vieilles Vignes come from vines over seventy years old. Both the Brets apprenticed themselves to marquee oenologists and worked in wineries such as Domaine des Comtes Lafon in Meursault, or Baron Philippe de Rothschild in Médoc, and at Loach and Ridge. They know the tricks of the trade, but have opted for typicity over butterscotch. Their luscious, mineral-rich Pouilly-Vinzelles Les Quarts comes from antique vines; the Pouilly-Loché La Colonge is as meaty as an excellent Charolais steak and yet flinty. *Best wines* (all whites): Pouilly-Vinzelles Les Quarts, Viré-Clessé sous Les Plantes, Viré-Clessé La Verchère, Pouilly-Loché La Colonge.

VIRÉ

In scenic hills between Mâcon and Tournus, Viré is a top winegrowing village and gastro-pilgrimage site, thanks to the reconverted village café, an unusual Parisian bistro-Venetian *caffè-gastronomique* hostelry: **Le Relais de Montmartre** (Place André Lagrange, Tel: 03 85 33 10 72, closed Monday yearround, Sunday dinner November to mid March, mid to end January, and the second week of July, moderate to very expensive). Frédéric Carrion worked at Paris's Tour d'Argent, and with Paul Bocuse and Pierre Orsi in Lyon, which explains the professionalism. *Terroir* isn't the thing; however, amid the arabesques you'll find pike-perch dumplings and Charolais beef (long-simmered or in the form of steaks), duck breast flavored with honey from the region, and good regional cheeses and wines. The hotel next door, owned by Carrion, is a temple of luxury, opened in spring 2009.

Domaine André Bonhomme (Rue Jean-Large, Tel: 03 85 27 93 93, open daily without appointment), now run by Bonhomme's son-in-law Éric Palthey, battled for decades to upgrade Mâconnais wines and is credited with inspiring the current renaissance. His Viré-Clessé Cuvée Hors Classe is fat yet crisp, fresh, and lemony.

Also producing muscular whites is award-winning **Domaine les Grands Crays—Dominique Terrier** (Rue du Champ-Cholet,

Cray, Tel: 06 12 15 49 12, by appointment only). Their best—for those who like honey-and-citrus scents and flavors—is Viré-Clessé Vieilles Vignes (5,000 bottles are produced and disappear overnight).

At **Domaine de la Verpaille**, officially **EARL Baptiste et Estelle Philippe** (Buc, Tel: 03 85 33 14 47, www.domainedela verpaille.com, open without appointment afternoons Monday to Saturday, by appointment the rest of the time), friendly organic winegrowers Baptiste and Estelle Philippe make crisp, fresh Mâcon Villages whites, Viré-Clessé, and Crémant. Their best is a fat, citrus-perfumed Mâcon Villages Vieilles Vignes white.

Cave de Viré (Vercheron, Tel: 03 85 32 25 50, www.cavedevire -bourgogne.com, open daily without appointment) is huge but makes several good, award-winning wines: Viré-Clessé Cuvée Spéciale, Viré-Clessé Viré d'Or, and Viré-Clessé Vieilles Vignes. For these top bottlings, the grapes are hand-picked and -selected, aged up to a year and a half, and lightly oaked (ten percent, in new barrels, assembled with the rest).

CLUNY and CLUNYSOIS

*Includes: Ameugny, Azé, Berzé-le-Chatel and Berzé-la-Ville,
Bourgvilain, Chapaize, Cluny, Cormatin, Cortevaix-Mont,
Igé, Lys, Massilly, Mazille, Milly-Lamartine, Prayes,
Serrières, Salornay-sur-Guye, Tramayes*

CENTERED AROUND CLUNY, SITE OF THE LARGEST,
MOST POWERFUL MEDIEVAL MONASTIC COMPLEX
outside Rome, the Clunysois sub-region reaches as far
north as Cormatin, east to Igé, Berzé la Ville, and Serrières,

south to Tramayes, and west to the Butte de Suin—one of the area's tallest peaks, bordering the Charollais. Particularly lovely, the Clunysois is dotted with remarkable Romanesque churches, spinoffs from Cluny Abbey, and merges the scenic beauty of cattle and wine country. Note that "Clunysois" is also sometimes spelled "Clunisois."

AMEUGNY

Ten miles north of Cluny, on winding D981, at the junction of D14, **Aux Berges de la Grosne** (Le Bois Dernier, Tel: 03 85 50 17 68, closed Sunday dinner and Monday, inexpensive) has tables not on the riverside, as the name suggests, but on the edge of the Voie Verte, a bike path. The reason to stop is to eat before or after touring the Château de Cormatin, less than a mile north. "Aux Berges" plays on words, meaning "on the riverbanks," but sounds like "auberge." The menu follows suit. Dishes have silly names, and many make for silly eating. "Kermit sur la Voie Verte" is a waffle of frog's legs, presumably flattened by cyclists ("Sesame Street" is still broadcast in France). Stick to simple dishes: tomato and chèvre tarte, grilled pork ribs, steaks, seasonal fruit tarts. Didier Masy and wife Anne are professional enough to keep clients smiling. Good, affordably priced local wines by the carafe or glass are on chalkboards. The dining room has plank floors, armoires, and heavy furniture. Aux Berges is the best restaurant near Cormatin; you'll be glad you skipped those fronting the château.

AZÉ

Between Cluny and Mâcon, Azé is famed for its grottoes (and cave-bear bones), but should also be visited for the honeys made by beekeeper **René Lafoy** (Tel: 03 85 33 33 36, phone ahead). A good co-op is here: **Cave d'Azé** (Tarroux, Tel: 03 85 33 30 92, www.caveaze.com, open daily March through December without appointment, closed on Sunday in January and February). With about 700 acres owned by forty winegrowers, the choice of bottlings is vast: Mâcon Villages, AOC Bourgogne white and (less successful) red, Aligoté, and Crémant.

Independent Frédéric Lenormand of **Domaine de la Boffeline** (Fourgeau, Tel: 03 85 33 33 82, frederic.lenormand@wanadoo.fr, open daily except Sunday without appointment) routinely wins medals for his Crémant, and also makes quaffable Bourgogne AOC white and Mâcon-Azé.

BERZÉ-LE-CHATEL AND
BERZÉ-LA-VILLE

Edging the Clunysois and surrounded by vineyards and forests, Berzé is two hillside hamlets a mile apart. Berzé-le-Chatel boasts a tenth-century château with thirteen towers and three rings of walls (Tel: 03 85 36 60 83, visit the grounds only). Berzé-la-Ville, formerly the summertime residence of the Abbot of Cluny, is celebrated for **La Chapelle des Moines** (Monk's Chapel, Tel: 03 85 36 66 52, open daily April through October), with looming eleventh-century frescoes in excellent condition. In the village is casual café-restaurant **Le Moustier** (Tel: 03 85 37 77 41, closed Sunday dinner and Wednesday year-round except June to September, when closed only Wednesday; September to June lunch daily except Wednesday, dinner Friday and Saturday only, closed Christmastide, inexpensive to moderate). Despite its complicated hours of opening, this village hangout fills with winemakers, commuters who work in Mâcon, and visitors. An umbrella-like horse chestnut shades the court; the rustic-elegant dining room has timbers and stone walls. The good-value prix fixe menus often include housemade terrines, fresh salad with garlicky snails, classic frog's legs, roast chicken with thyme, pressé de boeuf with asparagus (in season), roast veal with wild mushrooms, or rump-steak with tarragon. There's a cheese platter; the fruit tarts and seasonal desserts are delicious. Stick to good, local bottlings.

BOURGVILAIN

Near the château of Saint Point, eight miles south of Cluny, Bourgvilain isn't *villain*, it's pretty. The auberge on the main square looks tempting, but chefs have come and gone too many times of late. Put on your driving gloves and follow coiling D212 toward Pierreclos, up 1,000 vertical feet to the pass, Col des Enceints, and reliable **L'Auberge de la Pierre Sauvage** (Tel: 03 85 35 70 03, in July and August open daily for lunch and dinner, in winter from Friday to Sunday only, the rest of the year closed Sunday dinner and Monday, also closed early January to early February, very inexpensive to moderate). Wonderfully baba cool and Zen, the owner looks like an aging flower child. His postmodern wife stays behind the scenes, cooking up seasonal delights with *terroir* roots, and house classics. Summer is best: the stone-paved terrace and its pergola are open, with keyhole views. The dining room is authentically antique, with contemporary décor; in cold weather, a fire crackles. Pierre Sauvage appears preserved in amber: delicious cassolette of snails and wild mushrooms, housemade terrines, hearty stews or roasts, local cheeses, and luscious housemade desserts (the fig semifreddo with gingerbread sauce and fruit tarts are memorable). Wines are from Pierreclos, Bussières, and Milly-Lamartine.

CHAPAIZE

On scenic highway D14 (east of Cormatin), the striking Romanesque Saint Martin church has a graceful belltower and is hemmed by winegrowers' houses from centuries past (summertime concerts are held here, Tel: 03 85 50 70 75, www.chapaize .org). **Café Saint Martin** (Tel: 03 85 50 13 08, opening hours vary widely, inexpensive to moderate) fronting it, is good for stylishly served coffee, snacks, light meals or dessert. Run by laid-back Swiss gentlemen, the menu is eclectic—Italian-Mediterranean-French-Swiss—with fresh salads, ravioli, and luscious chocolate cake. The espresso is excellent, the shaded terrace pleasant, and the contemporary chic interior cool and comfortable. Business hours are at the whim of the owners; the service can be painfully slow.

CLUNY

Handsome and lively with 5,000 inhabitants, Cluny spills cobbled streets down a slope toward the Grosne River fifteen miles northwest of Mâcon. The medieval houses, churches, and street layout, little changed for 1,000 years, hint at the site's history. This was the largest, most powerful monastic complex in Christendom, housing 10,000 monks. The main church was over 400 feet long. Much of it disappeared, quarried in the early 1800s. Still standing are the right transept, several towers, a cellar-granary, the cloister, a pilgrim's hostel, and sections of perimeter wall.

Founded in 910, Cluny was the Vatican's right arm, run by abbots later made saints. At its zenith in 1109, Cluny controlled 1,100 monasteries in Europe and England. About 250 of Southern Burgundy's Romanesque churches were built by Clunysian monks. Visit **Le Musée Ochier-Palais Jean de Bourbon** (Tel: 03 85 59 12 79, www.monuments-nationaux.fr) for the art and architectural treasures, and a 3-D scale replica of Cluny circa 1100 AD. The ruined abbey is moody, with pitted dirt floors. Don't miss the medieval mill tower and granary (upstairs are remarkable, eleventh-century capitals, and a ribbed wooden ceiling). The **Tour des Fromages** (6 Rue Mercière), a watchtower, is accessed via the tourism office (Tel: 03 85 59 05 34, www.cluny-tourisme

.com), and affords inspiring views. Cluny celebrates its 1,100th anniversary in 2010; expect fireworks.

Cluny's National Stud Farm (Tel: 03 85 59 85 12, Cell: 06 22 94 52 69, www.haras-nationaux.fr) draws the equine set. Competitions and shows are held year-round.

Traditional food lovers will be well served, often at a leisurely pace, at Cluny's longtime, likeable gourmet restaurant, **Hôtel de Bourgogne** (Place de l'Abbaye, Tel: 03 85 59 00 58, www.hotel -cluny.com, closed Tuesday, Wednesday, and in January and February, prix fixe moderate to expensive, à la carte expensive). Built in the 1800s with the abbey's stones, it sits atop the former nave, and is the kind of provincial establishment some dream of, while others avoid, because of its hushed, slightly airless atmosphere. Coffered and stone-paved, the comfortable dining room has antique furniture, wall sconces, old prints, and silver candlesticks. The ghost of poet-politician Alphonse Prat de Lamartine, a habitué, flits among the penguin-suited staff; imagine him smiling as the silver domes come off diners' oversized plates. Some of Frédéric Carazon's dishes are almost daring: earthy snails in puff pastry with asparagus tips; succulent rabbit fricasséed with blackcurrant mustard; thick Charolais filet with coarsely mashed potatoes, wild mushrooms, and (unnecessary) truffle oil. The Terroir prix fixe menu offers delicious, beautifully presented classics (particularly good oeufs en meurette with bacon, mushrooms, onions, and rich wine reduction sauce). The cheeses are local; desserts include housemade sorbets, fresh confections with berries and fruit, rich double-chocolate delights. The Mâconnais wines are reasonably priced. There's a leafy courtyard open in summer.

Auberge du Cheval Blanc (1 Rue Porte-de-Mâcon, Tel: 03 85 59 01 13, closed Friday dinner, Saturday, and dinner in November and the second half of March; also closed December to mid March, and ten days in the first half of July, inexpensive to moderate) is less cushy than Hôtel de Bourgogne, the service less polished, the dining room anodyne, though daubed with a naïf mural whose Brueghelesque elements are unappetizing. Never mind. Run by the third generation of the Bouillon family, who do a serious job, the auberge serves tasty food that is archly traditional: fresh frog's legs in cream, impeccable beef bourguignon and coq au vin, Charolais filet with wild mushrooms, roast pigeon, laudable cheeses, and luscious, old-fashioned desserts. Wines are good value.

In style, price, and substance, **Hostellerie d'Héloïse** (Pont de l'Etang, Tel: 03 85 59 05 65, www.hostelleriedheloise.com, closed for dinner on Sunday and Tuesday, and Wednesday, moderate to expensive) is halfway between Cheval Blanc and Hôtel de Bourgogne. It's on Cluny's eastern edge, facing the former train station on the highway to Mâcon. The comfortable dining room extends into an enclosed riverside terrace. A curiosity: François Mitterrand ate here regularly (his widow Danielle is from Cluny); nostalgics continue to seek his table. The management and décor have changed since. The prix fixe menus—Marché and Terroir— are fine value; on the latter: a dozen snails, tender, flavorful rump steak cooked in a red wine sauce with shallots, fresh farmstead cheese with cream (or regional cheeses), and house chocolate mousse (high-quality chocolate). Seasonal menus always include classics (antebellum Ile Flottante). The wine list has many local bottlings, the service is friendly and professional, the clientele regulars and tourists.

Of the casual places near the abbey for coffee, drinks, or daily specials, salads, steaks and fries, the best are **La Nation** (21 Rue Lamartine, Tel: 03 85 59 05 45, open daily from 8am, closed mid December to mid January), on the main drag; and rustic **La Halte de l'Abbaye** (3 Rue Porte-des-Prés, Tel: 03 85 59 28 49, lunch only, closed Wednesday, inexpensive), facing the National Stud farm. Both have shaded outdoor terraces; La Nation is chic, has better coffee (from Café Monika), good wines (Château de Fuissé, Michel Sarrazin, Émile Juillot) and the food—guinea fowl fricassée with gingerbread—is more ambitious, though not always sterling (the pike-perch is frozen, the mustard comes in plastic packets).

By the old train station Hostellerie d'Héloïse, is organic food emporium **Patio Nature** (Le Pont de l'Etang, Tel: 03 85 59 24 50, open daily June to September, closed Sunday afternoon and Thursday the rest of the year), with a simple café-restaurant serving innovative snacks and daily specials, excellent organic coffee, a bakery (**Le Pain sur la Table**) with exceptionally good organic bread, including rustic Pain des Moines sourdough; and a boutique (**Epicerie Bionali**, closed Wednesday morning and Sunday) stocking organic foods (excellent jams, essential oils, honey from Jacques Desroches, fruits and vegetables). The tables in the courtyard are a joy. Chummy and well meaning, the staff are laid back; seek elsewhere if in a rush.

Cluny has one of the region's more charming Saturday morning open markets, facing the abbey on Place de l'Abbaye and abutting streets. Among dozens of stands selling grandfather clocks, baskets, jams, hams and salamis, fruit and vegetables,

poultry, baked goods, plants and flowers, cheeses and wines, seek out: Jean-Paul Le Du (on Place du Marché), with outstanding organic chèvres. Next door is beekeeper–deer rancher Mikkael Rebandet of **La Ferme de l'Apicerf** (Le Plaisir, Tel: 03 85 59 32 54, www.apicerf.fr, phone ahead), on the outskirts of Cluny; his acacia honey and gingerbread, terrines, and rillettes of venison and pork, are excellent. One stand over is **Ferme de Blanchizet** (Saint-Point, Tel: 03 85 50 56 06, call ahead), makers of duck, quail, pheasant, and pigeon pâtés, and foie gras. At the back of the market square, find organic vegetables and breads at **Domaine de Saint Laurent** (Saint Laurent, Château, Tel: 03 85 59 05 92, phone ahead). At a tiny stand, David Delbelle sells delicious honeys, gingerbreads, chocolates, and old-fashioned brittle (**Le Rucher de Donzy**, Donzy-le-National, Tel: 03 85 59 62 33, phone ahead). Facing the ATM machine on the main street, jam-maker Yvon Dubois of Au Jardin d'Eden, from Suin, transforms ripe, home-grown fruit (berries, apricots, peaches) into high-fruit, low-sugar jams. On the same side, find chèvre cheese-maker **GAEC Bonin-Gauthier** (Charnay, Saint-Martin-de-Salencey, Tel: 03 85 24 52 09, phone ahead); friendly Monsieur Gauthier makes delicious classics (and raises poultry).

Among Burgundy's best wine shops, **Le Cellier de l'Abbaye** (13 Rue Municipale and Rue du 11 Âout, Tel: 03 85 59 04 00, closed Sunday afternoon and Monday) has an entrance facing the market, another behind, facing the abbey. Under high ceilings with thick timbers are fine vintages from top producers, starting with local, easy-to-drink Mâconnais (from Domaine Perraud of La Roche Vineuse, among others). The empyrean includes Domaine de la Romanée Conti and dozens of Côte d'Or greats. Transplanted American Alice Brinton, and local oenologist Sonia Blondeau, make Le Cellier de l'Abbaye an excellent resource on winemakers and trends. Taste wines at a bar in the back, and, by arrangement, organize horizontal or vertical tastings. Brinton and Blondeau promote premium organic and biodynamic wines; among those from Burgundy find Bret Brothers-La Soufrandière and Domaine des Comtes Lafon. Also stocked are liqueurs (vintage Marc de Bourgogne from Jacoulet or Jacques Cartron); gourmet foods (outstanding jams from Cadole des Douceurs); housemade vinegar; and accessories— glasses, carafes, corkscrews. See Top Burgundian Winesellers' Favorites, page 61, for their picks.

On Cluny's main street, find century-old, sparkling **Germain-Au Péché Mignon** (25 Rue Lamartine, Tel: 03 85 59 11 21, www

.chocolaterie-germain.fr, open daily). Displayed like fine jewelry are exquisite handmade chocolates, pastries, and cakes. Denise and Daniel Germain, flanked by son Nicolas, have run it since 1978. Excellent originals include Truffes du Moine (chocolate-gianduja truffles), toasted almonds and candied orange peels coated with chocolate, Les Blanc Cassis (white chocolate with creamy blackcurrant), chocolate brittle with hazelnuts, jams and fruit preserved in alcohol. The café is next door; try a luscious housemade ice cream.

Directly facing is gourmet shop and coffee roaster **Archi Bon** (36 Rue Lamartine, Tel: 03 85 59 80 02, closed Sunday), with artless displays, but fine Arabicas, roasted daily in small batches, teas, jams from Peché-Sucré, oils and vinegars from Leblanc, nougatine-chocolate Croquettes from Christian Leiser, canned pâtés and terrines, and hard candies.

Rue Lamartine changes to Rue Filaterie. On the right side, near Société Générale bank, is Cluny's best butcher, **Yves Roux** (15 Rue Filaterie, Tel: 03 85 59 08 10, closed Monday and two weeks in July), an upscale shop with picture windows and great picnic supplies (including housemade ham and jambon persillé). A few shopfronts further is top *charcutier* **Bruno Dupaquier** (3 Rue Filaterie, Tel: 03 85 59 23 10, closed Sunday afternoon, Monday, and the last week of August to mid September). Look for the nineteenth-century wooden shopfront with painted, mirrored-glass panels. Dupaquier's ham, jambon persillé, salads, and housemade salted lard, are exceptional.

CORMATIN

Cormatin is a must for its château (see page 367), which draws 60,000 visitors yearly. The coffee in Cormatin won't do permanent damage; you're better off eating elsewhere. Snack on

CHÂTEAU DE CORMATIN
AND
FRANCE'S FIRST
MODERN COOKBOOK

NOT A WINERY, CHÂTEAU DE CORMATIN (Tel: 03 85 50 16 55, www.chateaude cormatin.com, open 10am to noon and 2pm to 3pm, closed mid November to Easter; interior open by guided tour only) is an early-1600s castle atop twelfth-century foundations. It boasts the country's best-preserved Louis XIII interiors, and also happens to be where, in 1651, François Pierre de la Varenne (1618 to 1678) wrote groundbreaking *Le cuisinier françois*. The manual ushered France out of the culinary Dark Ages. Presumably, de la Varenne tested his buttery, garlicky mushrooms duxelles and other recipes in the kitchen he directed, which is on the charming tour. If you visit only one château in Burgundy, let it be exquisitely gilt and painted Cormatin. The Grosne River provides a natural moat doubled by one dug by the mushroom-loving Du Blé d'Huxelles family, originally military governors, then courtiers in Versailles. Don't miss the fortified outbuildings, which house a lovely café (hot and cold drinks, simple pastries), open daily in July and August, or the *potager* kitchen garden. In the entry, the château sells good organic wines.

. . . .

delicious croissants or quiches at **Boulangerie Pâtisserie Aux Delices de Cormatin** (Grande Rue, Tel: 03 85 50 14 03, www .aux-delices-de-cormatin.com, closed Wednesday); they supply the château's tearoom. **Caveau du Figuier** (Rue Principale, Tel: 03 85 50 10 16, caveaudufiguier@hotmail.fr, open daily April to November, the rest of the year open Friday, Saturday, and Sunday morning, closed February), fronting the château, stocks good local wines (including Domaine de l'Echelette, domaine.echelette@ wanadoo.fr, makers of a fine late-harvest white from old vines) and gourmet items (jams from La Cadole aux Douceurs). Owners Evelyne and Dominique Lagrange are helpful. For groceries, wines, roast chickens, or house-roasted coffee, try Robert Berger at **Rotisserie Torrefaction Artisanale** (Grande Rue, Tel: 03 85 50 12 25, closed Sunday afternoon and Monday), on the main drag. You'll spot the chickens turning, like the heretics of old. Pottery and crafts lovers should hit the cavernous, dusty chambers of **Galerie Artisanal et Gourmande de la Filaterie** (Rue de la Filaterie, Tel: 03 85 50 35 34, www.galerie-artisanale-et -gourmande.fr, open daily in July and August; out of season, hours vary widely), in a reconverted yarn factory 200 yards north of the château. Sixty self-styled artist-artisans sell their sublime-to-ridiculous creations; thirty regional foods are also sold (honeys, jams, cherries in liqueur, terrines and confits, wines not readily found elsewhere, often for good reason).

CORTEVAIX-MONT

Between Salornay-sur-Guye and Cormatin, far above the TGV line, drive into scenic hills with oak, hazelnut, hornbeam, and black pine—ideal for Burgundy truffles—and stop at truffle, saffron, and heirloom peach farmer Olivier Devevre's **Le Cos-Piguet** (Mont, Tel: 03 85 59 99 72, devevre@yahoo.com, by appointment). For a fee, Devevre takes you on truffle-hunts (late September to late January), and teaches you about *Tuber uncinatum*, from the botanical history to regional recipes. Buy fresh truffles in season at his boutique. Also sold is the saffron he collects from 15,000 mauve crocuses planted in 2003. It takes 160,000 *crocus sativus Linnae* flowers—480,000 pistils—to produce 2.2 pounds of saffron, hence the cost, and widespread fraud. Here you get the real thing. Devevre's third cash crop is heirloom *pêches de vigne*, small, thick-skinned, intensely flavorful, the essence of peach. Devevre's are white-fleshed or blood (*sanguines*), grown without chemical fertilizers or pesticides (available early August to mid September).

IGÉ

Between Mâcon and Cluny, at the crossroads of scenic highways D85 and D134, Igé is unremarkable, but its château, from 1235, is gorgeous, and houses luxury hotel-restaurant **Château d'Igé** (Route du Château, Tel: 03 85 33 33 99, www.chateaudige.com, closed Monday, Tuesday, Sunday night in winter, Wednesday in early November, and from end November to end February, expensive to very expensive). Turreted, in landscaped grounds with towering trees and a fountain, this authentic feudal castle belongs to the Germond family, currently represented by affable Françoise Faucon Lieury. The guest rooms have canopy beds and frescoed vaulting; the dining rooms are a lordly match, with walls a yard thick, massive timbers, giant fireplaces, and Louis XIII-style furniture. The classic haute and lightened, nicely presented *terroir* dishes are crafted by Olivier Pons. The entry-level prix fixe features snails and fricasséed mixed mushrooms, bacon bits, and mild garlic; braised Charolais; old-fashioned fromage blanc à la crème; and luscious desserts. Other good-value menus offer frog's legs, classic snails, Bresse chicken (the thigh with foie gras, the breast with unneeded truffle oil), or Charolais filet with Béarnaise. The cheeses are excellent, the desserts gorgeous, the service professional yet friendly, and the wine list weighty.

There's an open market in the village on Saturday mornings; among stands seek out organic cheese-makers Jacqueline and Michel Bourdon from Chevagny-les-Chevrières.

LYS

If another potter, weaver, or "artist" moves into this twee hamlet, it will burst its landmark timbers. A mile from Prayes, two miles from Cormatin and Chapaize, you'll have no difficulty finding Lys. Follow signs out and uphill on a one-lane road to **Chèvrerie de la Trufière** (Tel: 03 85 50 15 26, open 9am to noon and 4pm to 6pm daily from March to November), where many varieties of goat are made; visit the barn, designed for children and curious adults to have a look-see.

MASSILLY

Nine miles north of Cluny on highway D981, look for signs to Ronzières and **Ferme des Coteaux** (Tel: 03 85 50 07 96, phone ahead). Like the best chèvre-makers, this farm's animals roam free. Ferme des Coteaux regularly wins awards at the Mâcon agricultural fair—high recognition. Rightly: the cheeses are remarkable.

MAZILLE

On ridge-top highway D17 three miles south of Cluny, Mazille is home to **Ferme du Paradis** (Le Paradis, Mazille, Tel: 03 85 50 80  92, phone ahead). Buy livestock, fresh pork, chickens, lamb, and, for picnics, outstanding jambon persillé, terrines, salami, sausages, and headcheese. Butcher Yves Desroches and family have owned the farm for umpteen generations. Everything is processed or cooked on site, or at the **Desroches** butcher shop south of Mâcon in Crèches-sur-Saône (Rue Brancionne, Tel: 03 85 23 04 25, closed Sunday afternoon). You can also buy Ferme du Paradis goods from their itinerant truck, in Igé on Wednesday, La Roche Vineuse on Thursday, Sainte-Cécile on Friday morning, in Charnay-lès-Mâcon on Friday afternoon, and in Davayé on Saturday morning.

MILLY-LAMARTINE

The charming manor (and winery) of poetaster Alphonse Prat de Lamartine lures many to this pocketsized hamlet perched amid vineyards between Cluny and Mâcon. Eat at popular café-restaurant **L'Auberge de Jack** (Tel: 03 85 36 63 72, open for lunch only Tuesday, Wednesday, and Thursday, for lunch and dinner Friday and Saturday, closed Sunday dinner and Monday, inexpensive to moderate). Skilled Jack and extremely hospitable Sylvie Bouschet, from Mâcon, took over in 1981 and have been booked ever since. Done in tasteful style, with wooden chairs and tables, chalkboards, old posters and knickknacks, this authentically antique auberge feels like a Lyonnais *bouchon*. The food: classic wild, Burgundy snails (*Helix Pomatia*), housemade pâté, huge Lyonnais salad with poached egg and bacon, tripe sausage with mustard sauce, veal kidneys in cream sauce, sausage in flavorful red-wine reduction sauce, excellent rib-eye steak, huge platters of thick, perfect french fries. The desserts are luscious (the Marquise with caramel and chocolate is to die for). Wines include many fine locals (Olivier Merlin, for one), listed or chalked up, at reasonable prices. Pink Floyd on the sound system? Indeed. Jack's an aging rocker; his lively, likeable hangout draws aging hipster-boomers, winemakers, road workers, and the local gentry.

PRAYES

Three miles west of Cormatin, straddling scenic highway D187, find likeable **Auberge du Grison** (Prayes, Chissey-lès-Mâcon, Tel: 03 85 50 18 31, www.auberge-du-grison.com, closed Monday dinner and Wednesday, inexpensive), a casual hotel-restaurant with simple rooms. The Grison, a creek, runs behind. The frogs whose legs you feast upon don't come from it, but rather Indonesia. Cold cuts, salads, omelettes, served at any time of day, are good, and classic regional dishes more than edible. Sarah and Jean-Pierre Large have done up the dining room in retro style, with wooden tables, chairs, farm tools, a bar, a grandfather clock, and a terrace out front. Overhead fans spin lazily. A good place to chill out between Romanesque churches, wineries, and the prehistoric caves of Blanot and Azé, nearby.

SERRIÈRES

In the eastern Clunysois, where it merges with the Mâconnais, due south of Pierreclos, a creek runs through lovely Serrières. On it find insiders' hangout, café, and restaurant **Le Serrières** (La Croix, Tel: 03 85 35 71 49, closed Tuesday dinner and Wednesday, inexpensive). Winemakers, truckers, and farmers come for the frog's legs, terrines, pot roast, and steaks, cooked with gusto and served with a wry smile. There's a cheerful little dining room, and a big terrace. Not *gastronomique*, but solid and fun.

Young, welcoming winegrowers and B&B hosts Martine and Patrick Ferret of **Domaine de Monterrain** (Les Monterrains, Tel: 03 85 35 73 47, phone ahead) make a sprightly, quaffable white

Clos de Monterrain, typical of sandy Serrières, and also sell the goat's-milk cheeses of a cousin and neighbor. The B&B is attractive and comfortable.

SALORNAY-SUR-GUYE

On D980 eight miles north of Cluny, Salornay has two medieval bridges and one excellent butcher-*charcutier* on the main drag (in from the highway): **Xavier et Véronique Balon** (32 Grande Rue, Tel: 03 85 59 44 59, closed Sunday afternoon and Monday). Xavier makes nearly everything in-house, from pheasant or pork terrine and fresh salted bacon, to outstanding jambon persillé. His beef is chosen on the hoof locally. Also pick up picnic supplies: salads, simple desserts, goat's-milk cheeses from Saint-Vincent or Saint-Martin, and local wines.

TRAMAYES

Ten miles south of Cluny, close to the Beaujolais, this large village part-way up one of Burgundy's highest mountains, La Mère Boitier, doesn't have a great restaurant scene, so it may seem a long way for the 360-degree views reaching to Switzerland on a clear day. On the peak is rustic, certified-organic farmstead eatery **Ferme-Auberge de La Mère Boitier** (Chemin de La Mère Boitier, Champvent, Tel: 03 85 50 59 83, ebriday@aol. com, open from Easter to November on weekends and holidays only, or by appointment, very inexpensive to inexpensive). In a sylvan setting, hale and hardy Elisabeth Briday and family regale guests with salads, terrines, headcheese, chicken rillettes, salami, chicken simmered in cream or beef bourguignon, goat's-milk cheeses and simple desserts—everything housemade and almost all of it homegrown. On Saturday mornings they sell direct on the farm.

CHAROLLES and CHAROLLAIS

....

Includes: Amanzé, Bourbon-Lancy, Charolles,
Châteauneuf, Châtenay-Lavaux, Chevagny-sur-Guye,
La Clayette, Collonges-en-Charollais, Cray, Digoin, Iguerande,
Mailly, Matour, Montmelard, Nochize, Oyé, Paray-le-Monial,
Perrecy-les-Forges, Poisson, Saint-Bonnet-de-Joux,
Saint-Christophe-en-Brionnais, Saint-Julien-de-Jonzy,
Saint-Martin-de-Salencey,
Saint-Laurent-en-Brionnais, Saint-Vincent-Bragny, Suin

THE CHAROLLAIS OFFICIALLY DISAPPEARED WITH OTHER *ANCIEN RÉGIME* MEDIEVAL REGIONS, A result of the French Revolution. The southwesternmost portion of the Saône et Loire, it overlaps with—or comprises—the equally ancient, sleepy, officially defunct Brionnais sub-region.

AMANZÉ

Ten miles south of Charolles, northeast of La Clayette, find **Ferme-Auberge des Collines** (Tel: 03 85 70 66 34, philippe. paperin@wanadoo.fr). From highway D985, follow signs toward Château de Chaumont. Philippe and Marie-Christine Paperin serve homemade terrines, salads, the farm's free-range chicken simmered in heavy cream, Charolais pot roast, apple meringue pie, or strawberry or raspberry sorbet. Rusticity is writ large: tables are built from carts and wine presses. The opening hours pose a challenge, and you must reserve ahead; most tables are shared. This is a popular venue. Easter to November, the farm opens on Saturday and holidays (dinner), and Sunday (lunch and dinner; theoretically without reservations, but you won't find room). In July and August, dinner is daily by reservation. One way around the challenge is to spend the night, and include dinner. The *ferme* was formerly part of a château torched by French Revolutionaries. Stay the night and see how comfortable the better sort of peasant could be during the Ancien Régime.

BOURBON-LANCY

An atmospheric—read moody—Second Empire thermal spa of 6,000 inhabitants, with a glitzy casino, artificial lake, campground, and decent if unexciting hotels and restaurants, Bourbon-Lancy is a typical victim of an outsized suburban mall which has killed off most family-run businesses, especially those in the upper, feudal citadel. The Gauls and Romans came for the hot springs, view, and strategic position a mile from the Loire River. See fascinating ancient and medieval artefacts, plus colorful 1800s canvases, at Musée Saint-Nazaire. A market brings animation on Saturday morning to the squares fronting homely Sacré Coeur and town hall. Here and on nearby Rue du Docteur Pain—no joke—Rue du Commerce, and Rue du 8 Mai, you'll find holdouts (a butcher, selling picnic supplies, several bakeries). Bourbon-Lancy's famed pastry shop, and longest-established, independent chocolate shop, were going out of business as this guidebook went to press, and so are not included.

Authentic, traditional hotel-restaurant **Villa du Vieux Puits** (Tel: 03 85 89 04 04, 7 Rue Bel-Air, closed Sunday dinner and Monday, and mid February to mid March, prix fixe inexpensive to moderate, à la carte moderate to expensive) is also for sale. Its owners are retiring after forty-five years. Since much real estate is for sale, it may take years before the establishment closes. In the lower part of town, past the main spa hotels, the *vieux puits* in the name refers to a medieval well on the hotel's grounds. The kitchen garden is where Hubert Perraudin grows herbs and the produce he cooks. Enjoy premodern specialties amid knickknacks from yesteryear in a cozy setting—caned chairs, timbers, tiles, wall sconces, copper pots, and superior motel art. Everything is delicious, housemade, old-fashioned, from exquisite chicken liver terrine, to pike-perch dumplings with crayfish sauce, piquant chicken cooked with vinegar and sage (or heavy cream and morel mushrooms), and satisfying, Titanic-era desserts. Ginette, your hostess, is larger than life.

Cluttered with kitsch and farm tools, frequented by busloads and wise-cracking locals, and run by a self-adoring gentleman, **La Grignotte du Vieux Bourbon** (12 Rue de l'Horloge, Tel: 03 85 89 06 53, inexpensive to moderate, closed at Christmastime), on an alley in upper Bourbon-Lancy, is fine for coffee, drinks, or unambitious meals (salads, stews, steaks). There's a summer terrace near a splashing fountain. Next door is the wine bar; taste by the glass or bottle, and buy regional wines.

What passes for the top table, **Le Manoir de Sornat** (Allée Sornat, Tel: 03 85 89 17 39, closed for lunch Monday and Tuesday, Sunday dinner except in July and August and on holidays, and January 2 to the second week in February, expensive to very expensive), lies in quiet, landscaped parklands at the end of a tree-lined alley off the main highway, west of the Fiat-IVECO diesel motor assembly plant. Executives from the plant (and the guests they seek to wow) are habitués. The décor, service, and cooking are luxurious, mannered, and flowery; the food might feature on similar menus in Paris, Marseille, London, or New York.

CHAROLLES

A farm town of 3,000 astride irrigation canals and the meandering Arconce River, Charolles is nicknamed "the Venice of Burgundy." Mosquitoes are common to both. The Arconce's deposits have created ideal pasturelands so fertile that locals say they grow *herbe violente*—"violent grass." Waddling through it are giant cows and bulls seemingly lifted from Gary Larson's *The Far Side*.

On a knoll in the midst of Charolles rises the Tour du Téméraire, a reminder of the town's feudal past. View flower-patterned local ceramics at the history museum, **Musée du Prieuré**, or buy them at **Fayences du Pays** (15 Place de l'Église). Worth a look is **La Maison du Charolais** (see page 376).

✦ INSTITUTE ✦

L'INSTITUT CHAROLAIS (ROUTE DE MÂCON, Tel: 03 85 88 24 00, www.maisonducharolais.com, open daily except holidays, 10am to 6pm; restaurant open for lunch only, very inexpensive), a publicly funded research institution, think tank, lobbying organization, "ecology museum," and grill-style, casual restaurant, serves good steak and goat's-milk cheeses. Its headquarters flank the expressway. Rejecting claims by rivals in Dijon that Charolais are descended from Marguerite of Flanders' cattle (1390s), the institute demonstrates how historians have traced the breed's origins to the ninth century (other historians reach back to Gallo-Roman times or prehistory). That boeuf bourguignon, deprived of its winey base, is a lot like the *stamppot* stew of the Netherlands, is too disconcerting to be openly discussed.

The institute is also spearheading the drive to win Appellation d'Origine Controlée (AOC) status for Charolais born and raised in the Charollais region. AOC status is associated with premium wines; relatively few food products and, so far, no cattle breeds, have it.

Wine tasting has lent some of its vocabulary to the emerging world of Charolais beef tasting, one of the institute's pet projects. By request, a tour can include samplings of local beef, and an initiation into the tasters' vocabulary. It supposedly helps tasters express their sensations. Like sommeliers, beef experts gauge color and nose raw and cooked. Regarding *goût* (taste) they focus on tenderness, juiciness, texture, and flavor. The type and amount of fat is key. It should be woven between muscle fibers, not concentrated on the outside, and average three to five percent by weight. The density and degree of marbled fat is expressed by the term *persillé* ("parsleyed," a bastardization of *parsemé*, "scattered"). Single-word associations include "silky," "herby," "vinous," "caramel," "floral," and "hazelnut." Take the course and, when next you sip a Vosne-Romanée, perhaps you'll describe it as "beefy."

✤ HERE'S THE BEEF ✤

FOR CENTURIES, CHAROLAIS OXEN HAULED lumber and wine to Paris, a seventeen-day, 300-mile trek. Paris butchers noticed Charolais made for good eating. In 1747, Charolles-area rancher Émilien Mathieu began breeding, fattening, and herding Charolais north for slaughter. The muscles inherited from the original draft animals give Charolais their taste and help them thrive in divergent conditions, and so have not been bred out.

What Charolais eat matters. The Charollais area's grasslands merge wild grasses with dandelions, alfalfa, clover, wheat, and barley. Wine grown here is not distinguished; but experts refer to the land and its beef as Grand Cru, comparing them to the Côte d'Or's greatest. Soil, flora, humidity, and microclimates are as important to the flavor of beef as they are to that of wine. Charolais are fattened for the last three to six months on cereals, grains, and the dry residues of beets and oilseeds, particularly linseed, which appear to impart a nutty, rich flavor to the meat.

Contrary to expectations, the most mouthwateringly delicious, uniformly marbled Charolais meat comes from mature cows and not eighteen-month to three-year-old heifers or steers with pink, mild meat (preferred by most big-city consumers). A combination of naturally occurring female hormones, and the aging process, appears to explain this fact. Mature bulls are too tough for prime cuts and most wind up as long-cooked beef bourguignon, pot roast or, alternatively, hamburger meat. Sadly, only one butcher remains in Charolles; others have been driven out by competition from supermarkets. The annual Festival du Boeuf, with food and livestock displays, is held the first weekend in December.

....

For its beef, Charolles has been designated a site of gastro-nomical pilgrimage by the Conseil National des Arts Culinaires, an organization that inventories what it deems to be national food-related treasures.

Charolles's cafés are **Café du Siècle** and **Le Cru du Beaujolais**, both on the main square fronting the church; neither has remarkable food or coffee. The weekly outdoor market in the church square on Wednesday mornings brings animation to an increasingly quiet place. The local chestnut fair (the second-to-last weekend in November) is an excuse to wolf sausages and steaks, and swill Beaujolais Nouveau.

Facing the church is family-run Charolles institution **Hôtel de la Poste-Restaurant Daniel et Frédéric Doucet** (2 Avenue de la Libération-Place de l'Église, Tel: 03 85 24 11 32, www.la-poste-hotel.com, closed Sunday dinner, Monday, Thursday dinner, last two weeks of November, and first two weeks of February, inexpensive to very expensive). After training with marquee chefs, Frédéric Doucet took over from his father Daniel in 2000, and redecorated in fall 2008, transforming the dining room from authentic French provincial into could-be-anywhere contemporary. The menu now includes the predictable artistically plated, globalized food. Doucet still serves locally raised Label Rouge Charolais, dry-hung for three weeks. He's known for his thick, delicious rib steaks, pan-fried in sweet butter with coarse sea salt.

Charolles's outstanding butcher is **Jean-Paul Courtois** (10 Rue du Générale Leclerc, Tel: 03 85 24 00 09, closed Sunday afternoon and Monday). He visits local ranchers' farms, selecting animals on the hoof, and posts the origin, age, sex, and date of slaughter of each side of beef sold. Courtois also makes remarkable terrines and salads, and sells fine hams and salami.

Seated at a pink table, enjoy pastries and chocolates with good tea (ten types) or coffee two blocks east at **Pâtisserie Le Téméraire · Daniel Brocard** (3 Rue Gambetta, Tel: 03 85 24 01 85, closed Monday). Brocard makes Le Téméraire (meringue, pastry cream, hazelnut nougatine, almonds), chocolate truffles, classic fruit or custard tartelettes, and filled chocolates. The housemade ice creams are excellent.

Rival **Pâtisserie Thierry Hubér** (3 Rue Baudinot, Tel: 03 85 24 05 98, closed Sunday afternoon and Monday), on the main, semi-pedestrianized street to the château, specializes in walnut cakes and pastries and is also good.

❧ DRY-AGED CHAROLAIS ❧

DRY HANGING MEANS AGING BEEF IN A refrigerated room at just above freezing. The process allows natural moisture to evaporate. This concentrates flavor; it also causes weight loss and discoloration of exposed surfaces. Consequently, dry-hung beef is expensive. By contrast, so-called "wet-aged beef" is not aged at all; the term is misleading. It is beef packed in shrink-wrap plastic which, it is claimed, "matures" in the time it takes to transport it from the packing plant to the supermarket or restaurant kitchen, with no weight loss or discoloration. In truth it doesn't mature, which explains why it's pale, tough, and lacking in flavor when compared to old-fashioned, dry-aged beef.

. . . .

CHÂTEAUNEUF

Many French villages—several in Burgundy—are called Châteauneuf. This specimen is unremarkable, four miles west of far-flung Chauffailles on highway D8. Its claim to fame is a handful of antiques shops, a roadside café, and popular gourmet restaurant **La Fontaine** (Tel: 03 85 26 26 87, closed Monday, Tuesday, Sunday dinner September to June, mid January to mid February, a week mid November, prix fixe inexpensive to expensive, à la carte moderate to expensive). Yves Jury and wife converted a former textile mill (on the slope as you enter the village from the north), adding mosaics to the walls, and decorating the dining room and "winter garden" in vaguely 1920s—'30s style. Jury did time with top chefs, and is recognized for his skill in lightening regional specialties, from Bresse chicken breast with a pistachio cream sauce, to innovative Charolais tasting menus with select cuts of local meat cooked in three different ways. The grilled freshwater fish is excellent. Cheeses and desserts are high quality. On the wine list are many affordable locals, and enough big-ticket bottles to please the well-heeled locals and savvy gourmet travelers, many foreign, who eat here.

CHÂTENAY-LAVAUX

East of La Clayette six miles on highway D987, a mile or so north of Châtenay, is attractive, upscale **Ferme-Auberge de Lavaux** (Tel: 03 85 28 08 48, ferme-auberge-lavaux@wanadoo.fr, closed mid November to Easter, by reservation only, inexpensive), a B&B and restaurant in a reconverted farmstead. This is a real working farm, producing many of the foods served, including the poultry; how the hard-working but elegant owners and their friendly staff keep the grounds spotless and odor-free is a mystery. You wouldn't guess the skillfully built faux medieval tower is from the 1990s. Take a table on the covered terrace, or inside the cozy, stone-walled dining room with communal tables, where cheerful visitors and locals out for a lark—chicken, actually—feast and roar. Poultry is the specialty; pre-order the chicken liver gâteau, more a loaf than a terrine, and a meal in itself. Freshly picked home- or locally grown lettuce and greens, local hams and cold cuts, succulent oven-roasted chicken, luscious chicken with farmstead cream, are followed by fresh chèvre (from Jean-Paul Morin, down the road), with a dollop of farmstead cream. Or top the cheese with honey from bee-keeper Didier Chatelain at **La Grande Combe** in Ozolles. The aged chèvres come from Alain Auclair and Monique Gillette of **Ferme des Avoinneries** in Gibles (Tel: 03 85 84 50 54, phone ahead). The farm's tasty housemade desserts follow the seasons (fruit tarts and French classics). Among wines, local Brionnais-Charollais bottlings are worth trying, plus reliable regional wines, at low prices. Surprising given the setting, the service is swift, the atmosphere thoroughly enjoyable. Don't miss it.

CHEVAGNY-SUR-GUYE

Northeast of Saint-Bonnet-de-Joux six miles, one mile north of Saint-Martin-de-Salencey, on highway D983 find organic goat's- and cow's-milk cheese-makers **Fromagerie Fermière de la Petite Guye** (Tel: 03 85 24 50 45, open daily, mornings only). The goats are up the road at Les Landes, and lope in idyllic pasturelands or lounge in an airy barn, nibbling organic wild grasses or fodder. The cows receive the same humane treatment. Cheeses come in classic Burgundian shapes and sizes, plus small, flat round tomes not often available elsewhere. These cheeses are also sold at markets in Chalon-sur-Saône on Wednesday, Givry on Thursday, second Thursdays at the organic market in Mâcon, and first and third Tuesdays in Saint-Gengoux-le-National.

LA CLAYETTE

Pronounced "lah-klet," this likeable town south of Charolles thirteen miles boasts a turreted château on a dreamy lake and one of France's finest chocolate makers, **Bernard Dufoux** (32 Rue Centrale, Tel: 03 85 28 08 10, www.chocolatsdufoux.com, open daily). Dufoux, past retirement age, still shakes his scepter and spoons, flanked by heir Pierre-Yves Dufoux. Dufoux

senior is charming, a gentleman of the old school. Be-toqued and quaking with pleasure, he adores making chocolates and teaching others how to taste cocoa beans, sugar, and spice, and turn them into wonderfully nice chocolates. Full-immersion courses are the first Wednesday of each month (by reservation, for a fee). You make and sample chocolates, and come away with Dufoux recipes. Every day at 3pm, tour the facilities and do guided chocolate tastings. The shop is dazzling—a vision of Las Vegas, also selling glitzy accessories. Never mind. The scent alone makes a trip worthwhile. Dufoux et al handmake chocolates from the bean up. Bars contain varying intensities of cacao (plain, with candied or dried fruit, ginger, nuts). The filled or solid chocolates include classics (chocolate-coated candied orange peel) and luscious ganaches, while novelties feature spices, liqueurs, caramel, and salted butter. Found here only are sixteen apéritif chocolates to accompany whisky, Pouilly Fuissé, and other white or red Burgundies. The lightness and pure flavors of Dufoux chocolates are exceptional. Dufoux also has a boutique in Lyon, where he trained, in the 1950s, with France's other great chocolatier, Bernachon.

For local cheeses, housemade sausages, baked bone-in ham, terrific terrines, silken goose rillettes, and refreshing salads, head to **H. Tacher** (8 Rue du Château, Tel: 03 85 28 21 13, closed Sunday afternoon and Monday, and three weeks in September), an old-fashioned *charcuterie-traiteur* near the château and the best picnic supplier in town.

The tourist office, flanking the château, shares space with **Le Centre du Goût** (3 Route de Charolles, Tel: 03 85 28 18 09, open daily late June to late September), a threatening name for a modest shop promoting local gourmet products. This is a good place to buy and, occasionally, to taste, regional specialties and wines from fledgling wineries.

La Clayette's lake-front drive boasts interchangeable cafés offering nice views and edible food. Two restaurants in town are on a par in quality (good), décor (ultra-classic), and price (inexpensive to moderate): **Hôtel de Bourgogne** (9 Route de Charolles, Tel: 03 85 28 90 50, closed Wednesday), is run by Laurence and Clovis Danière, who pride themselves on serving straightforward, traditional French and local foods (snails, frog's legs, Charolais steaks, creamy cheeses, rich desserts), near the tourist office; facing the train station is **Hôtel de la Gare-Restaurant Le Valclair** (Avenue de la Gare, Tel: 03 85 28 01 65, closed Sunday dinner and Monday), where Monika and Eric Pignot serve please-all dishes and local specialties.

More contemporary is **Lesclette Restaurant** (Rue Lamartine, Tel: 03 85 28 28 60, prix fixe inexpensive to expensive, closed Wednesday September to June), in a new, somewhat charmless chalet-style building above the lake and highway on the northern end of town. The views from the terrace are lovely. On offer: updated, creatively plated regional food (frog's legs boned and nestled in puff pastry with creamy herb sauce; Charolais beef from tail and hoof to snout; lavish desserts). The wine list is strong on reasonable regional bottlings. In summer, reserve ahead.

About five miles out of town, **Château de Drée** (Curbigny, Tel: 03 85 26 84 80, www.chateau-de-dree.com, opening hours vary widely, seasonally), a private residence, is owned by Ghislain and Isabelle Prouvost, textile and finance magnates. They've spent millions restoring this 1620 château, purchased in 1995 from its last aristocratic owners, les Princes de Croÿ. The layout resembles Château de Cormatin. So does the story of corrosive decline: furnishings sold, gardens gone to seed. The Rococo Salon and Salon Louis XVI are again wall-to-wall with treasures, from the carpet (90,000 knots per square yard), to the Baccarat chandeliers. The boxwood embroidery facing the mock-Versailles fountains comprises 26,000 plants; the gardener needs three weeks to trim it. The château sells picnics, including local products, among them, the Charolais beef terrines of **Ferme de la Barbarandière** (Route de Charolles, Tel: 03 85 84 55 71, www.la-barbarandiere.com, daily by appointment).

COLLONGES-EN-CHAROLLAIS

On the extreme northern edge of the Charollais, north of Mont-Saint-Vincent and east of the Côte Chalonnaise winegrowing area, this hamlet is home to an old-fashioned country eatery of the most authentic kind, **Restaurant La Gladie** (Montvoisin, Tel:

03 85 79 80 91, inexpensive to moderate, reserve ahead). Don't expect culinary fireworks. Locals from miles around drive over for the authentic, housemade food, especially the Charolais steaks.

CRAY

At the junction of highways D980 and D983, between Charolles and Saint-Gengoux-le-National, find insiders' address **L'Etape Charollaise** (Croisée de Cray, Saint-Marcelin-de-Cray, Tel: 03 85 96 24 50, closed Monday and Tuesday dinner and Wednesday, inexpensive), with a pink façade. Forget the non-setting. This is a very good, reliable, unpretentious place to stop for a classic rabbit terrine, frog's legs, steak, or a full meal from egg to apple tart at unbeatable prices, prepared and served by an affable couple; he cooked for the Doucets at fancy Hôtel de la Poste in Charolles in the good old days, before it went global. There's a terrace for summer dining.

DIGOIN

Many farmtowns have a similar look and feel—flat, sun-baked, vaguely dusty, and scented by livestock, with long straightaways and canals (usually for irrigation) and, perhaps, a railway line and agro-industrial district with grain elevators to add authenticity. Digoin has all of the above, and a tiny medieval section with narrow streets, not to mention the Loire, Arroux, and Bourbince rivers, the Canal du Centre, the Canal latéral à la Loire, and Canal de Roanne à Digoin. The biggest of the three canals—du Centre—flies over the Loire on a spectacular canal-bridge, an engineering feat of the 1830s. Digoin is a major port for pleasure craft and riverboats, with a well-equipped harbor (Port Guichard-Campionnet, Tel: 03 85 88 97 26). There's a glitzy museum of waterways facing the canal-bridge, dedicated to the Loire (L'Observaloire, Tel: 03 85 53 75 71). There's even a museum of ceramics—the local specialty—from Roman times to the present, alongside the tourist office (8 Rue Guilleminot, Tel: 03 85 53 00 81, www.digoin-tourisme.com). It would be rash to incite anyone to drive or navigate out of the way to visit Digoin—a place plucked from Steinbeck, it doesn't easily seduce. However, if you're passing through, get a good, traditional meal at comfortable **Hotel-Restaurant Le Merle Blanc** (36 Route de Gueugnon, Tel: 03 85 53 17 13, closed Sunday dinner and Monday lunch, inexpensive to moderate). Stay elsewhere: the location, a mile north, on the road to industrious Gueugnon, is not felicitous. The efficient service and high-quality steaks, freshwater fish dishes, local cheeses, and big, creamy desserts, lubricated by good wines, will help you forget the surroundings.

Downtown, snack or lunch light at any of the hotel-restaurants or cafés, particularly those near the canal-bridge; all get plenty of customers. The good bakeries and butcher shop—delis in town are interchangeable. After all, this is the birthplace of local hero Alexandre Dumain, spiritual master of chefs from Bernard Loiseau to Jean Ducloux. On Rue Nationale, near the church, is the plaque marking Dumain's family house. That he made his fortune elsewhere is something visitors must never mention.

If in Digoin on the first weekend (and Monday) in August, you won't be able to avoid La Fête de l'Escargot (www.fete-escargot .org), a hayseed feeding frenzy excogitated in 1989 to celebrate the bicentennial of the French Revolution. A success, it has been repeated annually. Expect music live and canned, a flea market (Place de la République), fireworks and, naturally, the gleeful sacrifice of millions of gastropods and other creatures. If it seems too warm in August to devour truckloads of garlicky snails, try the other specialties: putatively light canalou (freshwater fish, poached and sauced) or epogne aux grattons (a savory brioche studded with pork cracklings).

IGUERANDE

On highway D982 in the Loire Valley, in the southernmost Brionnais, the lower village compensates for a lack of scenic charm with historic oil mill **Huilerie Artisanale J. Leblanc et fils** (Le Bas, Tel: 03 85 84 07 83, www.huile-leblanc.com, open daily 8am to 7pm), a national treasure. Founded in 1878 and run by the same family, in the same spot, using the original equipment, this is a living museum of the oil-maker's art of 130 years ago. Thick canvas belts whirl, clockwork gears engage, and a granite mill-stone turns in the dark, Dickensian workshop, quietly crushing seeds or nuts. The pastes are scooped by hand and gently heated in a cauldron, imparting toasty flavors and easing extraction. (Luckily, oilseeds and nuts aren't delicate olives.) The hot nut- or seed-pastes are transferred to antique hydraulic presses, and out comes the oil. Some raw materials are regional, others imported, all are high quality. Jean-Charles Leblanc, current scion, makes a dozen types: hazelnut, walnut, rapeseed, pistachio, pine nut, almond, pecan, sesame, peanut, pumpkin seed, grapeseed, and wild plum pit. Chefs at Lameloise or Grand Véfour in Paris use Leblanc's oils (on everything from terrines to scallops). Easy going yet passionate Jean-Charles has overseen expansion of the retail business—to Paris, London, Barcelona, New York, Sydney, Tokyo—but has refused to modernize. Flanking the workshop is the rustic-chic boutique. Lining shelves and display cabinets are oils, Leblanc-branded olive oil from Italy, flavored vinegars, perfumed soaps, and Fallot mustard. The Leblanc outlet in Paris is at 6 Rue Jacob, in the sixth arrondissement. Leblanc packages make perfect gifts. Don't miss it.

MAILLY

On a ridge between Saint-Julien-de-Jonzy and the Loire Valley, on scenic highway D9, **Cave Coopérative de Mailly** (Tel: 03 85 84 19 21, open 9am to noon Saturday or by appointment), also known as Les Coteaux du Brionnais, is a revival winery with local curiosities. A few miles north at Les Chavannes, at independent **Vins des Fossiles** (Tel: 03 85 84 01 23, closed Sunday and open Saturday 2pm to 7pm September to July; in July and August, open 3pm to 8pm Monday through Saturday), Jean Claude Berthillot is getting certified organic, and respects *terroir*, producing drinkable wines from Auxerrois, Sauvignon Gris, Chardonnay, Gamay, and even Pinot Noir. His unusual Pinot Gris-Sauvignon Gris blend, Cuvée Marie Constance, stands out. Pale straw to the eye, it's redolent of candied fruit, quinces, and pears, and is refreshing. These are "fossil" wines, because the clay and limestone is studded with fossilized seashells from the Jurassic, when the world-sea covered the area. A discovery.

MATOUR

Isolated in gorgeous hills edging the Charollais, Clunysois, Mâconnais, and Beaujolais, Matour feels like the back of beyond. There's a compelling reason to detour here: **Christophe Clément** (Place de l'Église, Tel: 03 85 59 74 80, closed Sunday dinner and Monday year-round, mid December to mid January, and weekday dinner from October to May, inexpensive to moderate). Isolation explains the challenging business hours. In everything but high season and on weekends, only dinner is served. Yet lunch is best, because, unless you're staying at a B&B nearby, you'll have a long, winding drive after your sumptuous meal, washed down with wines from Burgundy and the Beaujolais. You can't miss the address, facing the church, with a rooster on the façade, and countless cocks of various substances around the premises. As the symbol of France, known for its pluckiness, the rooster explains the proprietor's good-natured strut; a proud Gaul, native son, and master of poultry, from eggs en meurette to coq au vin, and fluffy

eggwhite meringue. There's also boeuf bourguignon, and an unusual interpretation of the unavoidable tripe sausage, andouillette du père Clément, flanked by fricasséed frog's legs.

MONTMELARD

On the heavily wooded mountainsides separating the Charollais from the Mâconnais, above Montmelard rises Mont Saint Cyr, with panoramas from 2,400 feet. Pleasant hotel-restaurant **Le Saint Cyr** (Tel: 03 85 50 20 76, www.lesaintcyr.fr, closed Monday dinner, Tuesday, the second half of February, and at other times, phone ahead) is comfortable, with tidy guest rooms and a dining room whose main attraction—beyond the food—is the view, seen through picture windows. Frédéric Bonnetain is local, his wife Nelly from farther away; the cooking merges lightened classics with a few Creole dishes. Try crisp puff pastry with oxtails and foie gras, Charolais steak with wine sauce, slow-cooked rabbit, and fricasséed chicken. Some creative dishes—chèvre with marinated salmon, or cod with bacon and peanut-oil vinaigrette—may be skipped. Bonnetain worked for top chefs; his food is presented on outsized white china, his desserts almost too pretty—some might say fussy—to eat.

In the village, find **La Maison de Joseph** (Tel: 03 85 50 24 61, closed Sunday), an organic grocery with everything from food and cleaning products to paint.

Near highway D41, at **Ferme de la Boisette** (Le Tronchat, Montmelard, Tel: 03 85 50 90 37, open daily except Sunday, 4:30pm to 7pm), shy Monsieur and Madame Gelin make good raw-milk chèvres in classic shapes, sizes, and ages. The cheeses have a fine texture, and the desired natural taste.

Charmont is off highway D41 between Dompierre-les-Ormes and Montmelard. Here idealistic Sylvie Bricard bakes organic, sourdough breads in a wood-burning oven at **Côté Pain** (Charmont, Montmelard, Tel: 03 85 50 29 10, phone ahead). The flour comes from local Moulin Gribory; the salt travels far—from Guérande. She usually sells from a delivery truck, at markets, and grocery stores, but opens her bakery twice weekly (Tuesday and Friday, 3pm to 7pm).

NOCHIZE

No cheese, perhaps, but Nochize is crawling with snails. Escargot experts Emmanuel and Nathalie Porcu at **La Ferme du Troncy** (Le Troncy, Tel: 03 85 24 01 13, cell: 06 87 77 53 18, by reservation only) raise free-range snails of the delectable variety *Helix*

Aspersa maxima, a plump sub-species nicknamed *Gros Gris*—Big Gray. Spoiled, they feed on clover, cabbage, and radishes. The Porcus will show you around and, for a fee, prepare a snail tasting menu; take-out snails are sold frozen or bottled. Croquilles à la Bourguignonne have butter, garlic, shallots, parsley, salt, pepper, and come in a crispy "shell" popped whole in the mouth. Grenouillette, a mini casserole of snails and de-boned frog's legs, with cognac-flavored cream, is most unusual. The farm is off highway D10, south of Nochize, east of Poisson, seven miles south by southeast of Paray-le-Monial. The squeamish need not apply.

OYÉ

Cradle of the Charolais race, Oyé is ten miles south of Charolles, edging the Arconce Valley. The encircling, scenic tuck 'n' roll pastures allowed pioneering breeder Émilien Mathieu to fatten his livestock in under three months, a feat in the mid-1700s. Mathieu's son Claude expanded the ranch in 1773 from Oyé to the Nivernais, closer to demand in Paris; that's why Charolais are also called Nivernais.

There's still a Fête de l'Entrecôte—a beef barbecue with live music, the first Sunday in August, fronting the village château. Narcoleptic Oyé's single, dusky café is **Le Chaumont** (Tel: 03 85 25 86 55, lunch only, inexpensive), haunted by locals, The real capital of Charolais is Saint-Christophe-en-Brionnais.

PARAY-LE-MONIAL

Architectural historians confirm that the basilica of Paray-le-Monial is a miniature Cluny in its third incarnation (Cluny was rebuilt and enlarged several times). You'll find an odd mix of souvenir-sellers and mediocre eateries, pious busloads, many with glazed eyes. The basilica is a must, the town fronting it skippable. It does host several good bakeries and butcher shop-delis on the main drag, and the handsome Place Guignault, where you'll find small but praiseworthy chocolate shop **Les Chocolats de la Tour** (Tel: 03 85 81 57 40, closed Sunday and Monday). Sold but, alas, not served, are excellent, artisanally roasted coffees from Montceau-les-Mines, and chocolates handmade for it by a fine chocolatier (whose identity is a closely guarded secret). Eat elsewhere—at Restaurant de la Poste-La Reconce, in Poisson (seven miles south) or, if you're feeling adventurous, and aren't in a rush, a few miles north in pastureland at **L'Auberge de Vigny**, at the crossroads in Vigny-les-Paray (Tel: 03 85 81 10 13, aubergedevigny213@wanadoo.fr, closed Monday, Tuesday, January, and the second half of

October, inexpensive to moderate). Nathalie and Christophe Lagarde restored and expanded a farmstead, adding a backyard terrace. The yawning dining room has polished stone floors, North African ethnic or medieval-style furniture, bistro chairs, and tables draped with rough cotton. In one corner stands an antique deep-diver's helmet. Like the décor, the cooking ranges far and wide, with spices shaken in, and much rolling and stuffing of fine ingredients which might be more delicious if left unmolested. The desserts are complicated, lovely, and irresistible. The wine list is thick. In high season, the service can slow to an escargot's pace.

PERRECY-LES-FORGES

Ten miles southwest of Montceau-les-Mines on D60, Perrecy's ironworks were famous. The ancient Roman road ran through town. On its path you'll now find medieval streets, an antiques dealer or two, several cafés, and one of the region's best-preserved Romanesque churches, with a narthex, mini-museum of sculptures, and evocative carved capitals. Perrecy is also worth detouring to for casual, traditional **Le Cheval Blanc** (28 Grande Rue, 03 85 79 34 77, closed mid July to mid August), just what you'd expect. Look for the red awnings on the main road, facing the butcher shop and bakery (good for picnic supplies), and the names Véronique and Henri Dutreuil, writ large. Discover old wooden tables, an antique bar with stools, cane chairs, timbers, lace on the windows, and food to match: frog's legs, salad with chèvre cheese and smoked goose, steaks, stews, veal filet, and the ubiquitous tripe sausage. Enjoy the chummy atmosphere.

POISSON

The Arconce River runs by Poisson, equidistant—ten miles—from Charolles and Saint-Christophe-en-Brionnais. The name means "fish" and seems unlikely in cattle country, but the fish farms were created by Clunysian monks 1,000 years ago. For beef lovers, Poisson spells Charolais. **Restaurant de la Poste–Hôtel La Reconce** (Tel: 03 85 81 10 72, www.hotel-lareconce.com, closed Monday and Tuesday, first half of October, February and first week of March, inexpensive to expensive) has a comfortable, white-and-beige dining room and sunny terrace abutting the Arconce (and guest rooms next door). Jean-Noël Dauvergne, slim and quiet, offers Charolais cooked in many ways. Most beef eaters demand prime cuts, the main reason flavorful flanks, shanks, butts, shoulders, jowls, and variety meats, no longer popular, often wind up as industrial canned beef or dog food. Dauvergne delights in bringing back old-fashioned recipes and reintroducing the public to them. He buys local, top-quality sides of mature cows and dry-ages them several weeks. His filet is remarkably tender and silky, his rib-eye steaks satisfying and buttery. But don't miss the slow-braised beef jowl baked in a flaky piecrust—luscious, irresistible—and the stews or variety meats. Dauvergne also excels with fresh-water fish. Expect to dine with savvy locals—Poisson isn't on any beaten path.

SAINT-BONNET-DE-JOUX

Sizeable and ten miles northeast of Charolles near Butte de Suin and its panoramic point, Saint-Bonnet doesn't win beauty contests. A tiny market is held in summer (usually on Sunday). One of the region's top butchers, **Robert Touillon** (Place Champ de Foire, Tel: 03 85 24 71 55, closed Sunday afternoon and Monday), and family, on the main square, buy neighborhood cattle on the hoof, run them through the local slaughterhouse, and dry-age them in-house for at least two weeks. Also on the square is a good bakery and several cafés, one in a hotel-restaurant where, if you're dying of hunger, you can safely eat a daily special or steak.

On the road to Suin, near another perfectly good bakery, is soft-spoken *charcutier* **Michel Morant** (Tel: 03 85 24 71 13, closed Sunday afternoon and Monday), from the Ardennes. Morant makes Burgundian classics—boiled beef in aspic, terrines, pâté en croûte—but also giant loaves of saucisson brioché—sausage terrine in a brioche—and handmade salamis. Connoisseurs flock here to buy Morant's house-cured hams, air-dried in the hallway flanking the shop for nine months. A minor drawback: you have to buy a whole ham.

Second-generation ironworker **Jean-Yves Bouillot–Ferronier d'art** (73 Rue Pépinière, Tel: 03 85 24 79 65, open weekdays 7am to noon and 1pm to 4pm, until 3pm Friday) is known nationwide for his traditional, corkscrew-shaped, wrought-iron candlestick holders, *rats de cave*—cellar rats—for centuries used by wine-makers to shed light on their barrels. Buy them here or at Le Cellier de l'Abbaye in Cluny.

SAINT-CHRISTOPHE-EN-BRIONNAIS

Every Wednesday afternoon, Charolais professionals and hard-core beef-aficionados converge on the cattle market in this handsome village in "violently rich" grazing land southwest of

Charolles. An average 600 head of cattle stand in rows under the marketplace on the main drag. Farmers, buyers, and inspectors move deftly, prodding and pinching livestock. When sales open, they shout, their hands flying into the air. These rituals—sans loudspeakers—go back to 1488, when the market began. This is France's biggest market for Label Rouge, organic, and other certified premium beef, nearly all of it Charolais. Numbers declined from 100,000 head in the 1970s to 31,000 in 2004, but have rebounded to about 35,000. Trends and prices are still set here. Take a free, guided tour with a municipal official before sales begin (go to town hall and ask for a *visite guidée*, Tel: 03 85 25 82 16).

Longtime regulars hunch over paper place settings at the pair of authentic, rustic café-restaurants facing the marketplace. They're interchangeable and inexpensive: **Hôtel-Restaurant La Tour d'Auvergne** (Grande Allée de Tenay, Tel: 03 85 25 82 23, open daily for breakfast and lunch, closed dinner Wednesday yearround; in winter, dinner served only Friday, Saturday, and Sunday) and **Mur d'Argent** (Place Belle Air les Foires, Tel: 03 85 25 81 31, closed Monday, Tuesday, and Friday). Don't be surprised if, for breakfast, locals order braised calf's head, steak, or pot roast—the Holy Trinity hereabouts—served from dawn onwards.

Two equally fine butchers, with great picnic supplies, are **Didier Voisin** (Place Halles, Tel: 03 85 25 82 17) and **Sébastien Chabanon** (Grande Allée de Tenay, Tel: 03 85 25 95 52), both closed Sunday afternoon and Monday. Both practice "old-fashioned" buying, butchering, and dry-hanging. For bread and simple pastries: **Jean-Michel Gonnot** (Grande Allée de Tenay, Tel: 03 85 25 85 44, closed Sunday afternoon and Monday).

SAINT-JULIEN-DE-JONZY

On the Brionnais's southern edge, six miles east of Marcigny, Saint-Julien splays itself across a ridge, with gorgeous views. The Romanesque church has a handsome belltower—and bells that ring through the night. You'll hear them at likeable **Le Relais de Saint-Julien** (Tel: 03 85 84 01 95, closed Monday, inexpensive to moderate), where Audrey and Franck Lesaige took over from legendary starred chef Bernard Pont. The décor and skilled cooking merge classic and globalized contemporary. Stick to the fresh, very well-prepared, seasonal market dishes. The service is friendly, there's a nice terrace, and a good wine list with local and bigger bottlings.

For a traditional, tasty home-cooked French meal, and a quiet night—except for the tinkling church bells—in a handsome manorhouse, surrounded by antiques and with lovely views, reserve at **Chambre d'Hôtes La Paillalire** (Tel: 03 85 84 11 67, mag_aubry@yahoo.fr, inexpensive, by reservation only), 200 yards west of the church. Look for the giant sequoias. Aubry Magali, your gracious hostess, doesn't want to compete with Le Relais, but will gladly whip up something simple, as the market dictates. This is convenient on Monday nights, when the restaurant is closed. Aubry's homemade jams are exceptional, made from homegrown raspberries, blackberries, figs, and pears.

SAINT-LAURENT-EN-BRIONNAIS

A few miles southwest of La Clayette, half a mile west of the village on the road to Saint-Christophe-en-Brionnais, find young honey-maker **Patrick Fayard** (34 Route de Saint-Christophe, Tel: 03 85 28 06 54, cell: 06 50 49 32 21, fpfayard@aol.com, phone or email ahead). His acacia, forest, millefleurs honeys are prized by local gourmets.

On the village's southern edge **GAEC des Monts** (Les Monts, 30 Route de Vauban, Tel: 03 85 28 04 89, closed Sunday, open Monday to Thursday 10am to noon, Friday and Saturday 10am to noon and 2:30pm to 5pm) is where Celine and Jean-Bernard Gaillard encourage their forty goats to nibble on the greenery that gives their cheeses a delicious freshness. The Gaillards still milk by hand, less stressful for animal and cheese-maker (though a workout). The quality reflects a premodern, manual touch. This farm embodies *terroir* and the antique dictum, "If it ain't broke, don't fix it."

SAINT-MARTIN-DE-SALENCEY

Five miles north of Saint-Bonnet-de-Joux, turn east at Charnay and follow signs a hundred yards to **GAEC Bonin-Gautier** (Tel: 03 85 24 52 09, phone ahead if possible, closed Sunday), run by a pair of affable chèvre cheese-makers and poultry farmers. Bonin-Gautier also sells at local markets, from Cluny to Montceau-les-Mines, and through *charcutier* Xavier Balon in Salornay-sur-Guye.

SAINT-VINCENT-BRAGNY

Five miles north of Paray-le-Monial, sleepy Champeaux is home to top chèvre cheese-makers Denis, Marie-Pierre, and François Mathieu of **GAEC Ferme Chevalier** (Champeaux, Tel: 03 85 70 40 88, 06 99 12 71 56, call ahead). They run fifty free-range goats, and do everything by hand, from milking to ladling and shaping the cheeses. Don't miss the Charollais AOC and tome—saucer-sized rounds. Taste Mathieu cheeses at L'Institut Charolais-Maison du Charolais in Charolles.

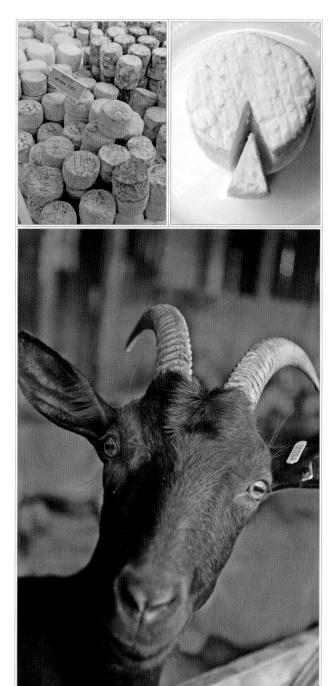

SUIN

Fifteen miles west of Cluny, east of Charolles, magical Suin's boulder-strewn, 2,000-foot summit overlooks dreamy farmland and forests. The Romans built a fortress atop a sacred Gallic site, and Cluny Abbey built a Romanesque church atop the fortress. On a clear day you can see the Alps, and spot sixty-four steeples. **Au Jardin d'Eden** (Tel: 03 85 24 85 27, call ahead), in the village, makes fine jams from ripe, often home-grown fruit—berries, apricots, peaches, plus unusual piquant green tomato jam with organic lemon zest, raisins, and Marc de Bourgogne. Buy them at the Saturday morning market in Cluny.

Harder to find but worth it are excellent cheese-makers **Jean-Paul et Bernadette Le Du** (Les Bois de Vaux, Tel: 03 85 24 75 08, call ahead, they bring back the goats around 6pm). Isolated, in a fold, on the northeastern side of Butte de Suin, follow signs from the narrow road to Saint-Bonnet-de-Joux. On an even narrower, perilously steep, slaloming road, once in the deep, dark woods, turn right. Affable but retiring, the couple are getting organic certification. Their free-ranging Alpine Chamoisée goats nibble on meadow grass. Four types of cheese are available, from fresh to extra moldy; connoisseurs prefer the kind with "skin" that peels. Outstanding, these are among the best, most flavorful chèvres in Burgundy. If you can't find the farm, buy Le Du cheeses on Saturday at Cluny market.

CHAPTER 5

WESTERN BURGUNDY

Département: Nièvre.

Population: 222,000.

Population density: 33 inhabitants/sq. km

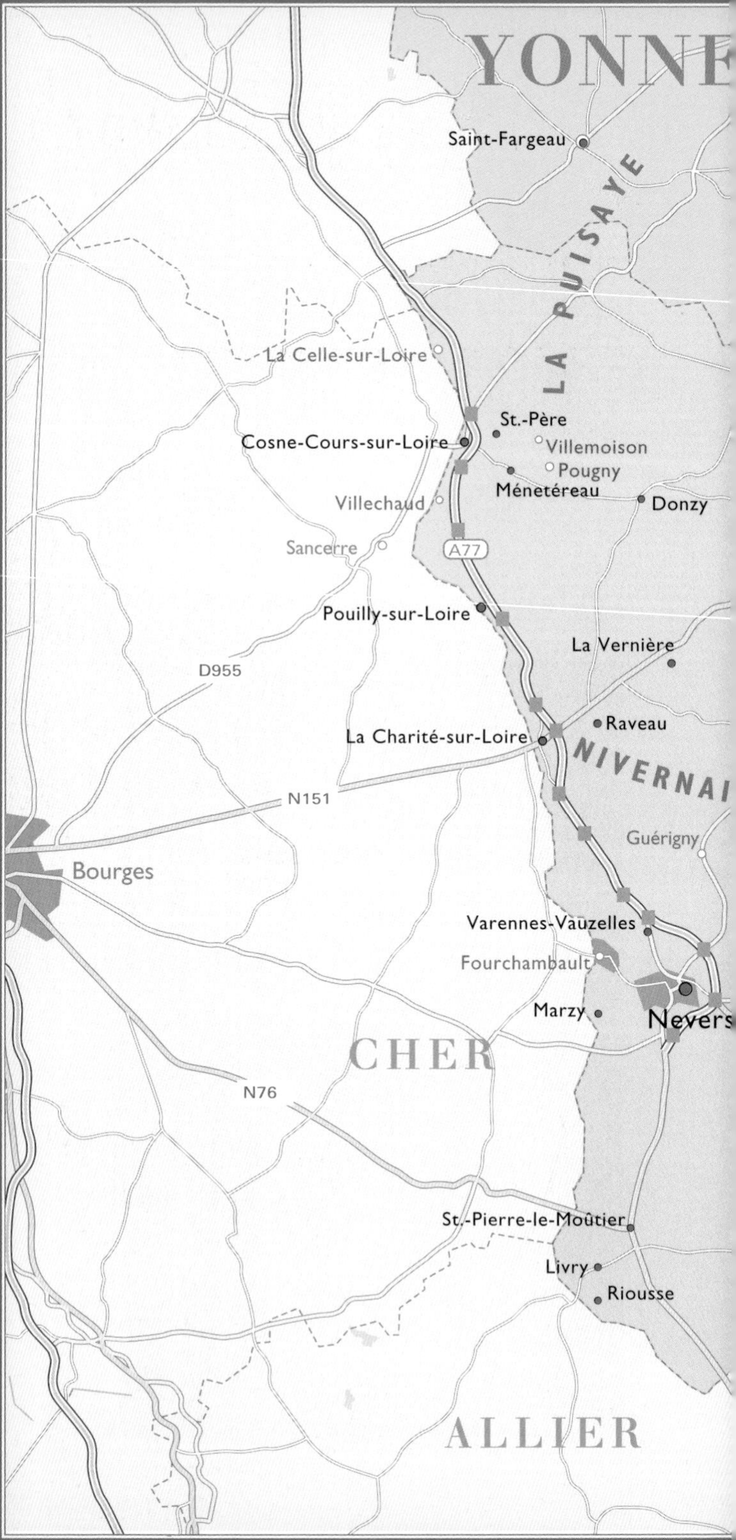
YONNE
Saint-Fargeau
LA PUISAYE
La Celle-sur-Loire
St.-Père
Cosne-Cours-sur-Loire
Villemoison
Pougny
Ménetéreau
Donzy
Villechaud
Sancerre
A77
Pouilly-sur-Loire
La Vernière
D955
Raveau
La Charité-sur-Loire
NIVERNAI
N151
Guérigny
Bourges
Varennes-Vauzelles
Fourchambault
Marzy
Nevers
CHER
N76
St.-Pierre-le-Moûtier
Livry
Riousse
ALLIER

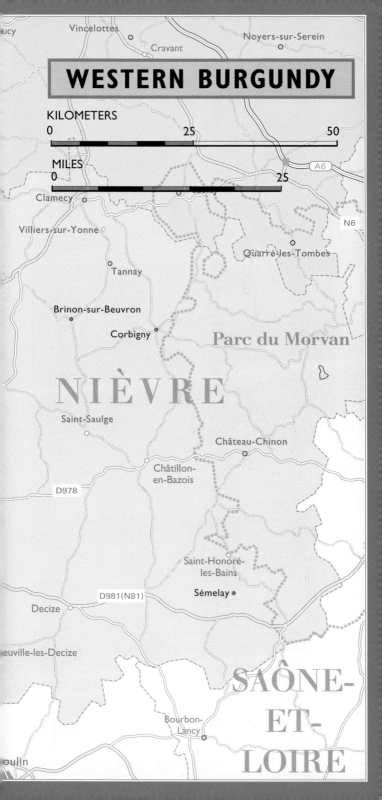

WESTERN BURGUNDY

KILOMETERS
0   25   50

MILES
0   25

ucy

Vincelottes

Cravant

Noyers-sur-Serein

A6

N6

Clamecy

Villiers-sur-Yonne

Quarré-les-Tombes

Tannay

Brinon-sur-Beuvron

Corbigny

Parc du Morvan

NIÈVRE

Saint-Saulge

Château-Chinon

Châtillon-
en-Bazois

D978

Saint-Honoré-
les-Bains

D981(N81)

Sémelay

Decize

euville-les-Decize

SAÔNE-
ET-
LOIRE

Bourbon-
Lancy

oulin

NEVERS and NIVERNAIS,
LA PUISAYE

....

Includes: Brinon-sur-Beuvron, La Charité-sur-Loire,
Corbigny, Cosne-Cours-sur-Loire, Donzy,
Livry, Marzy, Nevers,
Pouilly-sur-Loire, Raveau, Riousse,
Saint-Fargeau, Saint-Père,
Saint-Pierre-le-Moûtier, Varennes-Vauzelles

NEVER SAY NEVERS. ALWAYS SAY NEVER—*NEVH-AIR*
—WITH A SILENT "S." NEVERS, CAPITAL OF THE
Nièvre, is a soulful city of 38,000 (50,000 counting the
suburbs). Chalky white against the gray-blue skies of the Loire
Valley, it rises on the river's western bank, the extreme western
border of Burgundy. Long an independent duchy ruled by the
Hispano-Mantuan Gonzaga clan, most Burgundians and many
Nivernais don't think of this as Burgundy. The wines—Pouilly-
Fumé, Pouilly-sur-Loire, Coteaux du Charitois, and Coteaux du
Giennois—belong to the Centre and Loire winegrowing regions.
You'll rarely find them listed as Burgundies, though grown and

bottled *en Bourgogne*. (For a complete listing of wineries, and information on the AOCs and VDTs, visit www.vins-centre -loire.com). The food is that of the Loire and Burgundy, with emphasis on Morvan specialties, largely because many Nivernais are economic refugees from the Morvan. Locals call Charolais beef Nivernais. Even chèvre cheese is different in name, size, and density: AOC Crottin de Chavignol, typical of the Loire. It's often eaten warm and partly melted, on toast or salad.

The Nivernais is typical of the Val de Loire, Berry, and Bourbonais: watery, flat or lazily rolling, open, with few hedgerows. The second-most extensive forest in France is east of Nevers. Factory farming is widespread; villages are few. The architecture merges stone and half-timbering. With the exception of the Loire River basin, the Nièvre is sparsely populated; mining and river transportation, which made it rich in centuries past, have disappeared.

The eastern part of the *département* becomes mountainous and merges with Le Morvan, which lies between the Nivernais and the dynamic eastern side of Burgundy. Dijon, the regional capital, is a four-hour drive from Nevers. The geography and road network are two reasons Nevers looks toward Bourges—an hour by car—or Paris—two hours.

The inhabitants of Nevers—also called Nivernais—don't exactly have a chip on the shoulder, rather they view themselves as citizens of an independent duchy, glued for administrative reasons into the Burgundian puzzle during the French Revolution.

Northwestern Burgundy—sandwiched between the Nièvre and the Centre—is La Puisaye, and belongs to the Yonne. The Puisaye is lightly populated, with fields, pastures, forests, and marshlands. Its main town is Saint-Fargeau, with an impressive château and a mere 1,800 inhabitants.

BRINON-SUR-BEUVRON

On the Nivernais's western edge, on corkscrew highways D34 and D23, lunch or dine from Easter to mid December at **Ferme-Auberge La Bèlerie** (La Bèlerie, Tel: 03 86 29 64 73, very inexpensive, by reservation only), an old stone farmstead run by Brigitte and Bernard Blondeau. It's so spic 'n' span you'll be hard-pressed to believe it's a real working farm, until you see the cows, sheep, pigs, and big kitchen garden. The food is authentic—from farmyard to table—and includes housemade terrines, braised duck, coq au vin, and delicious fruit tarts. Unless you have a GPS, when you call to reserve, also ask for directions.

LA CHARITÉ-SUR-LOIRE

On the Compostella pilgrimage route from Vézelay to Spain, with a many-arched bridge spanning the Loire, handsome La Charité, as locals call it, is itself a pilgrimage site. The partly ruined medieval church near the river, footing the steep main street, was built by Clunysian monks and resembles Cluny Abbey during its twelfth-century apex. Restorations are ongoing. Take time to visit the cloisters and church, which houses the tourism office (5 Place Sainte-Croix, Tel: 03 86 70 15 06, www.lacharitesurloire -tourisme.com, open daily in spring and summer, closed Sunday and Monday the rest of the year).

La Charité calls itself *La Ville du Livre*; book lovers will delight in the secondhand bookshops, and regular book-related events. For info, check the tourism office or www.ville-du-livre .info.

Places to eat and drink

La Charité is compact, with many landmarks, and has about 5,500 inhabitants. There are several good restaurants, many mediocre ones, and cafés with outdoor terraces serving undistinguished food. The most authentic and best *terroir* restaurant is **L'Auberge de Seyr** (4 Grande Rue, Tel: 03 86 70 03 51, closed Sunday dinner, Monday, one week in February or March, and two to three weeks from mid August to early September, very inexpensive to moderate), on the main street, near the abbey. Look for the blue-gray shopfront with lattice windows, and two narrow dining rooms with lots of wood. Calf's head, which the chef makes from scratch, is the specialty. Everything is housemade from scratch, following the market and seasons: terrines, salads and soups, thick veal pavé or sweetbreads (with wild mushrooms in fall), pan-fried steaks, local pike-perch filet in luscious beurre blanc, local cheeses, and desserts such as fresh fruit tarts. The wine list includes good local bottlings. The service is professional and courteous. Townsfolk eat here when they don't want to crack the piggy bank.

Up the scale though still affordable, with a sunny dining room in a landmark early twentieth-century addition (to a seventeenth-century townhouse), with views through picture windows of the Loire and bridge, is **Le Grand Monarque** (33 Quai Clemenceau, Tel: 03 86 70 21 73, www.le-grand-monarque .fr, open daily, closed mid February to mid March, very inexpensive to expensive). James Grennerat cooks updated creative and authentic *terroir* dishes, from oeufs en meurette to boeuf bourguignon—an A-to-Z of Burgundy, artistically plated and professionally served. The very inexpensive weekday lunch prix fixe is a deal. There are 200 wines on the list. In summer, choose the terrace (with a view); upstairs are comfortable guest rooms.

Two good fallbacks serving *terroir* food in casual settings, both very inexpensive to moderate, are **Hôtel Le Bon Laboureur** (Quai Roman Mollot, Tel: 03 86 70 22 85, www.lebonlaboureur .com, closed Monday and late November to mid December), on the western bank of the island, reached by Pont de Pierre; and **La Pomme d'Or** (8 Avenue Gambetta, Tel: 03 86 70 34 82, www .lapommedor.net, closed Tuesday except in July and August), at the top of the main street, overlooking a parking lot (Place du Glui), with an outdoor terrace.

Gourmet shops and food artisans

La Charité has an excellent coffee roasting house, in the same hardworking family since 1946: **Brûlerie des Ponteaux-Huillier**

Torréfacteur en Café (5 Rue des Ponteaux, Tel: 03 86 70 05 53, closed Sunday and Monday). Founded by Maurice Huillier, it's now run by his widow Susanne and son François. Follow your nose. Scented with delicious perfumes broadcasting throughout the town, the boutique is on a backstreet parallel to the main drag. The Arabica blends, and monovarietals, are roasted several times a week. Accessories and gourmet items are also sold (Champagne, wine, cookies, chocolates, artisanal oils).

Many gourmet foods are stocked northeast of Place de Gaulle, La Charité's main square, on the main street at **Le Gaulois Gourmand** (34 Rue Camille Barrère, Tel: 03 86 70 18 82, closed Sunday and Monday). Affable Nicolas Roicomte, a chef, ferrets out the best terrines, foie gras, chocolates, honey, jams, cookies, artisanal liqueurs, wines, tea, and more, from Burgundy, the Loire, and further afield.

Downhill and opposite, a good source for local specialty Les Croquets —light, crispy meringue-almond cookies—is **Le Palais Gourmand** (47 Grande Rue, Tel: 03 86 70 23 11, closed Sunday afternoon and Monday). The main street changes name to Grande Rue, and descends to the ruined abbey and Place des Pêcheurs. On the square, find two outstanding shops. **La Confiserie du Prieuré** (#11, Tel: 03 86 70 01 81, lechocolat.charpentier@laposte.net, closed Monday), a 1930s landmark, is where Jean-Claude Charpentier and wife Houdé make exceptionally excellent chocolates, and serve them with snacks and treats in their cozy tea salon (in summer, the flower-filled patio is open). Charpentier took over in 2006, after years under chocolate-makers in France, and a stint in Tunisia, where he married and returned laden with spices. A founder of the French Confrerie des Chocolatiers, the lavishly moutachioed maestro is among Burgundy's great practitioners.

The base chocolate is Olivier de Loisy's 73-percent cocoa from Java. Charpentier makes dozens of seasonal, stylish, filled chocolates with lavender, jasmine, gingerbread, cinnamon, star anise, and more. The filling of long, slender "Moi" is forty percent crushed almonds, forty percent sugar, and twenty percent peanut butter, and is possibly the best peanut-butter chocolate anywhere, period. Blackcurrant lovers should taste Perle au Cassis, filled with blackcurrant liqueur paste. Charpentier also makes old house specialty Le Charitois (soft-centered caramel with a firm chocolate or coffee shell).

Directly across, don't miss wine boutique **Le Vin** (#7, Tel: 03 86 70 21 30, closed Sunday and Monday), where equally dashing, also mustachioed (and bearded) Jean-Paul Quenault, a retired chef, sells the best of Pouilly-Fumé, Pouilly-sur-Loire, Coteaux Charitois, and Sancerre (and other fine Burgundies). Chatty and well-informed, Quenault is the ambassador of reborn Coteaux Charitois. A VDT, it grows Chardonnay, Pinot Noir, Pinot Gris (Pinot Beurrot), and Sauvignon Blanc. Quenault will uncork a bottle or three—provided you're serious about buying, and not just tasting—and walk you through the minute details of his favorite wines, with background on the region's winegrowers. Discover Alphonse Mellot of Domaine des Pénitents, maker of excellent, organic Chardonnay and Pinot Noir, and the rich Pinot Gris and Pouillys of Serge Dagueneau & Filles. A must. See Top Burgundian Winesellers' Favorites, page 62, for Quenault's picks.

CORBIGNY

Edging Le Morvan, each Tuesday afternoon, and second Tuesday of the month, this farmtown (with a major slaughterhouse) hosts an important cattle fair and market. It reaches from Place de l'Hôtel de Ville to Place Saint-Jean and Champ de Foire. Each Friday morning you'll find the smaller outdoor market in Grande Rue, a street lined by shops, including bakeries, a cheese shop, several good *charcuteries*, and many cafés and restaurants. For info on the markets: Office de Tourisme du Pays Corbigeois (8 Rue de l'Abbaye, Tel: 03 86 20 02 53, www.corbigny.org). Among the dozens of stands seek out La Maison des Escargots, selling fresh and conserved snails.

Eat good *terroir* food—avoid the creative fare—at traditional **Restaurant Le Cépage-Hôtel de l'Europe** (7 Grande Rue, Tel: 03 86 20 09 87, www.hoteleuropelecepage.com, open daily in July and August, closed dinner Sunday and Wednesday, Thursday, and Christmastide, very inexpensive to moderate), on the main drag.

COSNE-COURS-SUR-LOIRE

The "s" in Cosne (and Cours) is silent; say the whole name, other-wise "Cosne" sounds like "jerk" (or worse), which may be why the town merged with abutting Cours. Formerly a Loire River port with railyards, quarries, mines, and wine, Cosne-Cours-sur-Loire is sizeable, with 11,000 inhabitants, in the northwesternmost Nivernais. Surrounding it are Val de Loire and Vallée de Nohain (along the Nohain River).

Cosne's industry and shipping are gone; farming and wine-making have survived. Unlike other rust-belt towns, Cosne pros-pers, and is appealing, with historic buildings, a long riverside greenbelt, fine bakeries, pastry shops, butcher shops, cheese shops, and restaurants. The Wednesday and Sunday morning markets, in the center of town around city hall, are animated and include many local cheese, honey and winemakers, some organic. It's a real place, with little tourism. The Coteaux du Giennois winegrowing district wraps the town; the best vineyards (in the Burgundian sector) lie beyond the highway in abutting Saint-Père and Pougnes.

The Coteaux du Giennois AOC was created in 1998, though wines have been made here since at least the second century AD. Winegrowing took off during the Middle Ages around Saint-Père. The appellation comprises 400 independent winegrowers, five co-ops, and thirty-five *négociant*-growers with a total of 500 acres in fourteen villages, from Gien (not in Burgundy), via Lavau (in the Puisaye), south to Cosne-Cours-sur-Loire and southeast to Pougny. Total production is 1.2 million bottles. The soil contains limestone and flint, best suited for growing Sauvignon Blanc, and, for the reds and rosés, a blend of Pinot Noir and Gamay. Expect flint, pears, and quinces, in the nose and flavor of the whites; red fruits and mild pepper in the reds; and mild spices or peach in the rosés. These are light, easy-to-drink wines not meant to be laid down. They rarely cause experts to swoon, but can be excel-lent value, the perfect match to the freshwater fish, poultry, and cheeses of the area. For an exhaustive list of winegrowers in the AOC: www.vins-centre-loire.com.

On the main drag downtown, near the bridge and Nohain River (fronting city hall), look for **Le Vieux Relais** (11 Rue Sainte Agnan, Tel: 03 86 28 20 21, www.le-vieux-relais.fr, closed lunch Saturday, dinner Friday, Sunday from mid September to June, and from late December to mid January, inexpensive to moderate). This coaching inn with an ivy-draped courtyard and stone or half-timbered salons from the 1500s, is a comfortable, tidy traveler's hotel and restaurant. The dining room—timbers, floral drapes—matches the remarkably good, authentic cooking. Jean-Paul Carlier excels at *cuisine bourgeoise*, following the seasons, and offers a good-value *terroir* menu: Burgundy snails in a flavorful frothy nage, oeufs en meurette, tripe sausage with mustard, housemade pike-perch dumplings with (delicious but unnecessary) Époisses sauce, a thick slab of Charolais with dense, reduced Coteaux du Giennois red wine sauce, local cheeses, gingerbread millefeuille, or creamy toasted hazelnut pudding. Wines include the best of the Giennois, Pouilly, Sancerre, the Loire, and Burgundy. Wife Françoise Carlier runs the dining room with affable aplomb.

Good local favorites downtown serving generous portions of *terroir* food are **Le Grain d'Orge** (18 Rue du Général De Gaulle, Tel: 03 86 28 01 05, closed Tuesday dinner, Wednesday, and the second half of July), on the main east-west street; on the north side, **Hôtel du Point du Jour** (47 Rue Maréchal Leclerc, Tel: 03 86 28 08 78, closed dinner Friday and Sunday, Monday, and late April to early May); both are very inexpensive to moderate.

An excellent cheese shop near the main church is **Fromagerie Saint Jacques** (18 Rue Saint Jacques, Tel: 03 86 26 36 75, closed Sunday afternoon and Monday), where you'll discover the cheeses of Burgundy and Loire, from local Crottin de Chauvignol to Époisses, and a Chaource Nivernais from **Ferme de Neuftables** (Luthenay-Uxeloup, Tel: 03 86 58 13 26, ferme-neuftables@aol.com, closed Sunday). Also sold are fine wines from the Coteaux du Giennois (including organic Domaine Alain Paulat) and Pouilly-Fumé.

Of the many good bakeries and pastry shops, among the best is **Pain et Sucre** (7 Rue Anatole France, Tel: 03 86 28 19 15, closed Monday and Tuesday), on the pedestrianized street behind the main church. Expect French and Burgundian or Centre classics, plus delicious, fresh chocolates. Another is **Le Petit Duc** (28 Rue du Commerce, Tel: 03 86 28 07 72, closed Sunday afternoon and Monday, and two weeks in February), also downtown, on the main shopping street. More a pastry shop-chocolate shop and ice creamery, Le Petit Duc makes Merlettes de Cosne (dark chocolates with ganache, candied orange peel, and Cointreau). The ice creams are delicious and made from scratch with milk, cream, fresh fruit, or housemade caramel and chocolate.

For gourmet foods and wines, also downtown, near Hôtel du Point du Jour, try **Le Bois Fleury** (30 Rue Maréchal Leclerc, Tel:

03 86 26 79 76, closed Sunday afternoon and Monday). Sold are terrines and tinned specialties, from foie gras up, cookies, teas, hundreds of liqueurs, whiskeys, regional and other wines, jams, and local cheeses.

In the southern outskirts, 300 yards east of the riverside park past the rail-bridge now used by "Cyclorail," is chèvre factory and regional foods emporium **Ferme du Port Aubry** (Port Aubry, Tel: 03 86 26 63 61, e.melet@wanadoo.fr, open daily except Christmas and New Year's). Emmanuel and Marguerite Melet and Bernard Robin keep about 400 she-goats, and use a computer-assisted, merry-go-round milking machine to extract the milk. With it they make dense, compact Crottins de Chavignol and other chèvres, most of which have the texture of moist chalk, and are very popular with locals. Next door is an old-fashioned country grocery, where farmstead products from Burgundy and the Centre are stocked (dry beans and lentils, honeys, jams, eggs, fruits and fruit juices, beer from Sancerre, flour, walnut oil, duck terrines, foie gras, wine, chocolate, and cookies).

In suburban Saint-Agnan, seek out certified-organic beekeeper and honey-maker **Christian Perreau** (102 Rue des Rivières, Tel: 03 86 26 71 20, phone ahead). If you're in Cosne for the Sunday market, you'll see his stand. He also sells organic bread and wine, beeswax, honey candies, and very good gingerbread.

DONZY

The Nohain and Talvanne rivers, if such they may be called, meet in medieval Donzy, twenty miles east-by-southeast from Cosne-Cours-sur-Loire on old highway D33 to Clamecy. Half-timbered buildings, bridges over the waterways, decent bakeries, hardware stores, florists, three cafés, a newspaper shop, and a very pleasant hotel-restaurant, another hotel, and three food artisans, make a detour worthwhile. A lively Saturday morning market, on the main square, features cheese-makers and organic winemakers and farmers.

Flanking the outsized Gothic church, with its skyscraper of a belltower, find **Hôtel-Restaurant Le Grand Monarque** (10 Rue de l'Étape, Tel: 03 86 39 35 44, monarque.jacquet@laposte.net, closed Sunday dinner and Monday in winter, and from January to mid February, very inexpensive to moderate). Anne-Marie and Marc Mercier, he a native, took over in January 2008, and began redecorating this 500-year-old inn with a landmark spiraling stone staircase (leading to comfortable rooms). In the bar area, locals and Elmer Fudds meet. The bistro occupies what was the

These wineries make Coteaux du Giennois unless otherwise noted; a few are in distant hamlets.

Emmanuel Charrier (L'Épineau, Paillot, Saint-Martin-sur-Nohain, Tel: 03 86 26 13 11, emmanuel. charrier58@free.fr, open daily without appointment). Note: Charrier makes fine whites.

Domaine Couet (Croquant, Tel: 03 86 28 14 80, e-couet@hotmail.fr, open daily without appointment nonstop 8am to 8pm). Note: Emmanuel Couet's reds are particularly good.

Domaine Alain Paulat (3 Rue des Bougiers, Villemoison, Tel: 03 86 26 75 57, by appointment). Note: organic winegrower Alain Paulat makes fresh, quaffable, true-to-type red, white, and rosé.

Hubert Veneau · Domaine des Ormousseaux (Les Ormousseaux, Tel: 03 86 28 01 17, hubert.veneau@ wanadoo.fr, open daily without appointment). Note: Veneau's reds are complex; he also makes fine Pouilly-Fumé.

Domaine de Villargeau (Villargeau, Pougny, Tel: 03 86 28 23 24, fthibault@wanadoo.fr, open daily except Sunday without appointment). Note: the Thibault brothers (and associates) make surprisingly complex white and red wines.

Domaine de Villegeai-Quintin Frères (Villegeai, Tel: 03 86 28 31 77, quintin.francois@wanadoo.fr, by appointment). Note: the whites are outstanding.

....

kitchen—with a nineteenth-century coal-fired stove. There's also a spacious dining room. Mercier prepped food here back when the coal-burner still worked; it's no phony retro invention. He also did time in big kitchens, and was chef of the European Union Football Association (hence the photos of Mercier and Platini). Mercier loves *terroir*, simple and unaffected. For lunch opt to eat with blue collars and farmers in the bistro (the delicious, generously served "worker's menu" includes soup or salad, roast beef or pork, cheese or housemade dessert, for an absurdly low price). Forgive the naïf mural in the dining room, and the dentist-office music. The food, service, and wine list are remarkable: oeufs en meurette or snail turnovers with herbs and garlicky butter, daily *terroir* dishes, boeuf bourguignon, or braised bone-in ham with tarragon-mustard cream sauce. Cheeses come from the village or Cosne; the desserts are housemade—chocolate mousse with crispy Croquets de Donzy cookies—or sweet *Crapiau aux pommes fruits* (caramelized apples in a thick, rustic pancake). Among wines by the glass, Chablis from William Fèvre, les Coteaux des Moines AOC white or Château de Souzy, from Bouchard Père & Fils, and Coteaux du Giennois from Les Tuileries.

On the main road south is landmark **Huilerie du Moulin de l'Ile** (14 Rue de l'Eminence, Tel: 03 86 39 31 48, in theory closed Saturday afternoon and Sunday, in practice always open, except at lunchtime). Thérèse Pradalier is the third generation of the family since 1850 to own and operate this walnut- and hazelnut-oil mill. Little has changed. The mill, still driven by water, uses a modern electric turbine, instead of a wooden water-wheel. The two-ton millstone, cast-iron machinery, even the canvas belts and premodern tools, are original and in working order. Pradalier, whose diamond-point eyes and wryness are startling, is formidable, and refuses to allow her age to appear in print. It's commonly said she was born before Hemingway wrote *The Sun Also Rises*, or Mussolini marched on Rome. The walnuts and hazelnuts are local, brought in by families who have always used the mill. The oil is extracted from freshly crushed nuts, gently heated, and then pressed. Pradalier claims that, unlike olive oil, heating preserves and improves walnut and hazelnut oils. She's won enough medals to make her point. Don't miss it.

On Donzy's opposite side, near the supermarket that has driven most merchants out of business, find signs to Saint-Loup and **Chèvrerie des Brosses** (La Grande Brosse, Tel: 03 86 26 29 02, open daily 5pm to 7:30pm or by appointment). Here Jean-François Vavon crafts excellent goat's-milk cheeses, from fresh to firm, including AOC Crottin de Chavignol. This is some of the best Crottin made; the goats range free, nibbling on grasses, instead of hay, straw, and industrial fodder. Taste these cheeses at Le Grand Monarch in Donzy.

South, off the road to La Charité-sur-Loire, Frédéric Coudray-Ozbolt of award-winning **Les Oies du Pré** (Donzy le Pré, Tel: 03 86 39 47 65, open Monday through Saturday year-round, Sunday by appointment) is among the region's top artisanal makers of foie gras and terrines—with hazelnuts, wild mushrooms, or sour cherries—and rich rillettes of goose and duck. He'll show you around, and might even convince you that the famished fowls, treated humanely, don't suffer from force-feeding. They're not forced—they demand their corn and grains, like junk food addicts. Luckily, the fowl eat better.

LIVRY

Pintsized Livry's stonebuilt houses stand a few miles from the Loire, fifteen miles south of Nevers. Near Livry are barely perceptible hills replanted with vineyards. Facing the church cheerful, veteran chef Jean-Pierre Duchassin of **l'Escapade des Gourmets** (Tel: 03 86 37 28 40, http://perso.orange.fr/escapade-gourmets, jean-pierre.duchassin@orange.fr, closed Wednesday and Thursday, very inexpensive to inexpensive, reserve ahead) is known for his calf's head with gribiche sauce. Duchassin strokes his moustaches and grows loquacious when asked about long-time customers and calf's head, consumed whether it's below zero or 100 degrees Fahrenheit. Also on the short menu: local goat's-milk-cheese salads, cheese turnovers, oxtail terrine with ravigote sauce, meltingly tender beef cheeks cooked in local red wine, steaks, sautéed breast of guinea fowl, and simple, classic desserts. Everything is fresh and housemade from scratch. This is a fine place to taste—no need to do much more—the fledgling wines of Livry, Riousse, and, better, Tannay (in Le Morvan). Also available is excellent Saint-Roman from Alain Gras, outstanding Gevrey-Chambertin from Frédéric Magnien. The décor isn't—spartan is too large a word. In summer, sit on the shady terrace.

Behind the church and *mairie* (with a museum of winemaking, and impossible opening hours), winegrower and Charolais cattle farmer Fabrice Barle, son of the mayor, produces what is probably the best wine of this unsung *vignoble*. **Domaine de la Perrine** (Tel: 03 86 37 46 76 or 06 18 91 20 52, open Saturday afternoon or by appointment), is in a restored medieval farmstead, with a handsome round tower and duck pond. Barle's vins de pays du Val de Loire come in red (Pinot Noir) and white (Chardonnay). The 7.5-acre estate was planted in 2001; the vines are too young to be up to much (the first vintage is 2004). Barle does many things right—respects the soil, hand-picks and sorts, and makes two versions of his wines, oaked and not-oaked. The latter are drinkable, and doubtless will improve as the years go by.

MARZY

West of Nevers three miles, almost on the Loire, find authentic organic dairy farm **La Ferme du Chasnay** (Tel: 03 86 60 84 44, open daily except Sunday from 5pm to 7pm or by appointment), where Bénédicte, Émilie, and Basile Dequiedt make cow's-milk cottage cheeses, semi-soft mild rounds, fresh cream, and yogurt. (This is not Chasnay, the winegrowing hamlet near La Charité-sur-Loire.)

NEVERS

Mist often billows up from the Loire, covering Nevers, and it's in the mists of antiquity that locals set the legendary birth of this, the westernmost stronghold of the fierce Aedui tribe, dubbed Noviodunum Aeduorum by invading Romans. Anyone who has read Caesar's *The Conquest of Gaul* will recall it was hereabouts that the Aedui butchered Caesar's men and burned their outpost. According to Gaul-boosters, the tide of war almost changed. This glorious rebellion lives on in the spirited Gallicism of the Nivernais, known as plucky. Nevers was a stronghold of the Résistance, and in 1944 stood between retreating Nazis and safety in Germany. The city was also strategic, on the Loire. For these reasons, the Allies bombed it, WW II scars remain, and postwar eyesores sprout between hard-driven landmarks.

Downtown Nevers is compact; food- or wine-related addresses are within a quarter-mile radius of the much-restored cathedral and Ducal Palace, with its duncecaps and leafy esplanade. The main tourist office (2 Avenue Saint-Juste, Tel: 03 86 36 39 80, www.nevers-tourisme.com) is in a subterranean complex flanking the palace. Pick up free city maps there.

The main car-free shopping street, formerly Rue du Commerce, is Rue François Mitterrand, the main square Place Carnot. Here you'll find Nevers's principal covered market (closed Sunday and Monday). Though charmless, the marketplace boasts many fine shops, including organic growers Denis Revel and Séverine Kovachiche of **GAEC du Rebout**, and, on Saturday, organic cow's- and ewe's-milk cheese-maker Christian Jorand of **Ferme du Creuset** (Tel: 03 86 50 64 35, open daily except Sunday 3pm to 6pm, or by appointment). A huge outdoor market is held all day Saturday in Parc Roger-Salengro (west one block); each first Saturday of the month (except in May) this market extends into Place Carnot and Rue Saint Martin, a shopping street off the square. Another, smaller covered market is on the Rue de Nièvre/Rue Saint-Arigle (closed Sunday and Monday). Summertime markets are on Wednesday afternoons in the park. Avenue Général de Gaulle, Nevers's main thoroughfare, links Place Carnot to the train station.

Nevers is known for its painted ceramics and tableware. The **Faiencerie d'Art de Nevers Jean-Pierre Georges** (11 Avenue Colbert, Tel: 03 86 61 09 12, closed Sunday and Monday) is one of a handful of family-run workshops where plates and decorative items are still made and painted by hand.

Places to eat and drink

Nevers has several good restaurants; few offer *terroir* cooking. By far the best restaurant downtown is chic, timbers-and-stone, Michelin-starred **Jean-Michel Couron** (21 Rue Saint-Étienne, Tel: 03 86 61 19 28, www.jm-couron.com, closed Sunday dinner, Monday, and Tuesday lunch, and mid July to the second week in August, inexpensive to very expensive). *Terroir* is expressed in the ingredients: freshwater fish, Charolais (or Nivernais) beef, and locally grown and bought produce, a long wine list with premium regional bottlings. The cooking style is creative and global (beef jowls with onions, honey and black olives; beef roasted with wasabi, etc.). Don't miss the soldier-of-God, Romanesque church of Saint-Étienne, around the corner.

The best casual spot for *terroir* food is **Le Gambrinus** (37 Avenue Général de Gaulle, Tel: 03 86 57 19 48, closed Sunday, lunch on Monday and Saturday, and the first three weeks in August, very inexpensive to inexpensive), near the train station. Local shopkeepers, blue and white collars, and savvy travelers, eat oeufs en meurette, jambon persillé, chèvre salads, Charolais steaks and the like in a bistro-auberge setting, with lots of wood, yellow tablecloths, and globe lights. The desserts are classic, the wine list limited, with a few good locals.

A hundred yards closer to Place Carnot is contemporary chic **Le Bistrot de Chloé** (25 Avenue Général de Gaulle, Tel: 03 86 36 72 70, www.le-bistrot-de-chloe.com, closed Sunday and Monday, Christmastide, and the first three weeks in August, very inexpensive to moderate). Handsome, this bistro could be anywhere, including Paris or Milan (many pasta dishes are available). *Terroir* is not flaunted; the ingredients are fresh, however, and follow the seasons, and the food is good. Vegetarians take note: the millefeuille of fresh vegetables is delicious. The desserts are too; the coffee is Illy, and possibly the best in town.

La Botte de Nevers (Rue du Petit Château, Tel: 03 86 61 16 93, closed Sunday dinner, Monday, Tuesday lunch, inexpensive to very expensive), conveniently behind the Ducal Palace, with kitsch medieval theme décor, is frequented by tourists and business people, but serves good *terroir* food, from egg to apple, including pheasant terrine with foie gras, coq au vin, and grilled mutton. The wine list includes local bottlings (Pouilly-Fumé from Château de Nozet). Disregard the Gothic candlesticks and scarlet cushions, and tune out the dentist-office music, and you'll be fine.

For tea, coffee (good Lavazza espresso), ice cream, crêpes, and deliciously rustic housemade pastries—fruit tarts—regulars perch at unusual **Le Balcon** (Rue de Rémigny/Place Maurice Ravel, Tel: 03 86 57 00 85, open 2pm to 7pm Tuesday through Saturday, closed Sunday and Monday). It's one story above Place Maurice Ravel, at the top-end of the pedestrian street, and its décor has not changed since 1975. Think white plastic buckets, orange or yellow tablecloths, white globe lights with paper shades, and carpeting. Also unusual, the tables merge with a furniture showroom.

Gourmet shops and food artisans

Across from the small covered market on Rue de Nièvre, seek out **L'Epicerie** (66 Rue de Nièvre, Tel: 03 86 59 04 04, closed Sunday and Monday, open daily in December). Jean-Philippe Demizieux was in the restaurant business, and knows his gourmet specialties. Small and narrow, under the spotlights of this upscale boutique discover dozens of best-quality delicacies, from canned snail caviar (*Hélix Escargotière*), to wines and liqueurs from the Coteaux du Giennois (award-winning Domaine Michel Langlois), cookies, pâtés, plus delights from Spain to Scotland.

Aux Gourmets (13 Avenue Général de Gaulle, Tel: 03 86 57 26 99, closed Monday) is north of the train station on the main drag, an old-fashioned, appealing gourmet foods boutique with a green shopfront and 1950s décor, run by Jérôme Leclerc. It carries the Hédiard line, Champagne, truffles, and foie gras, plus eaux de vie from Joseph Cartron or Domaine Michel Langlois, crunchy Craquants du Val de Loire from Christian Leiser, outstanding honey from Les Ruchers du Morvan, Pouilly-Fumé from Ladoucette-Château de Nozet, Langlois's award-winning Coteaux du Giennois reds and whites, and Nougatines de Nevers.

Caramel lovers: don't miss **Au Négus** (96 Rue François Mitterrand, Tel: 03 86 61 06 85, closed Sunday, and Monday morn-

ing). Alain Hiriart is the fourth generation to run this landmark from 1893. On the pedestrian street, Au Négus is named for a dark, eye-shaped, double caramel invented—and registered—in 1902, to mark the visit of Menelik, Emperor of Abyssinia. The recipe and handsome round tin haven't changed; neither has the Art Nouveau décor.

Across is **Édé** (75 Rue François Mitterrand, Tel: 03 86 61 02 97, closed Sunday afternoon and Monday). Nougatine—toasted, crushed, candied hazelnuts—is rarely better than what you'll taste in Nevers, specifically at this landmark chocolate and candies shop, where everything is still handmade and hand-packaged, under the guidance of Nicole Édé. Nougatines de

Nevers have *glace royale* (orange candy coating), and a pedigree dating to 1843, when the shop's founder perfected the recipe.

The candy's fame spread after Napoleon III and Eugénie visited in 1862 (the empress packed a gross of the bonbons, which became a staple of the court). The filled chocolates and Pavés Nivernais (sugar-dusted almond chocolates made to resemble meringues) are very good.

Newcomers, in 2007 Christophe and Carole Ragueneau opened **Ragueneau Chocolatier** (5 Rue du Doyenné, Tel: 03 86 59 47 45, closed Monday), a chic chocolate boutique between the cathedral and Place Carnot. This is the city's best and boldest. Christophe worked with top chocolatiers elsewhere before returning home; Carole is a skilled chocolate artisan in her own right. They use Valrhona 70-percent cocoa base to make handsome, decorated, filled chocolates using fresh ingredients, flavored with mint or spices (the vanilla is exquisite: the Ragueneaus import fresh vanilla beans). Found here and nowhere else are Les Trésors de Gonzague (chocolate marbles dusted with gold), and edible chocolate artworks (chess pieces, Buddha miniatures, reproduction Nevers faience, masks, plaques of solid chocolate with white cocoa-butter filigree-like drawings, and more).

Artisanal coffee roaster **Au Bon Café** (14 Place Saint Sébastien, Tel: 03 86 36 41 14, closed Sunday and Monday), near the pedestrian street, has outstanding pure-Arabica blends, particularly the Italian espresso. Also sold are artisanal jams and other treats.

POUILLY-SUR-LOIRE

Where La Charité is charming, picturesque, and fascinating, Pouilly, ten miles north, is no-nonsense. Don't expect anything as attractive as you'd find on the Côte de Beaune: Pouilly is a working town on the Loire, with a dusty, rural feel. It has a few old buildings around the main square, equipped with a standard-issue, vintage church, a riverside drive with old sycamores, and a few good food-related addresses. The old highway—RN7, renumbered as D243—bisects it. The real draw is wine. In May, July, and August the municipality organizes Caves Ouvertes—open wineries—three Saturdays of each month. Wine is poured liberally, and you'll learn more than you ever thought necessary about local drink.

The tourist office on the riverbank provides maps of vineyards with wineries; on the same premises, visit temporary exhibits related to the Loire (Pavillon du Milieu de Loire, 17 Quai Jules Pabiot, Tel: 03 86 39 54 54, www.pavillon-pouilly.com, open daily April through October, closed Tuesday the rest of the year, and from January to April). Note: The tourism office is not in the middle of the river. Sold are gourmet delicacies, including crunchy, nutty cookies made by Christian Leiser of **Les Craquants du Val de Loire** (the cookie factory is in the southeastern outskirts, near the autoroute, on D184-Route de Châteauneuf, Les Bardebouts, Tel: 03 86 39 09 67, closed Sunday).

The weekly Friday-morning market faces the church and a remarkably good bakery with a wood-burning oven: **Le Cadran Solaire** (9 Place des Frères Mollet, Tel: 03 86 39 18 43, closed Tuesday afternoon and Wednesday). Beyond the many excellent sourdough, specialty loaves with corn, bacon, walnuts, raisins, and so forth, the house pastry is a classic, light, crispy meringue.

For authentic *terroir* in a homey setting, on the main drag, facing winery Domaine Masson-Blondelet, lunch or dine at **Chez Mémère** (72 Rue Waldeck-Rousseau, Tel: 03 86 39 02 43, closed Sunday dinner and Monday, very inexpensive to inexpensive). Locals chow down on good housemade jambon persillé, snails in an earthy stew, terrines, pan-fried pike-perch, Charolais steaks, stews, and simple desserts. The décor isn't "décor" (think pink tablecloths, timbers, and knickknacks), the atmosphere cheerful. Reserve ahead; Chez Mémère is often packed.

Nearby and in a similar vein (with basic rooms upstairs, and a bar) is **L'Ecu de France** (64 Rue Waldeck-Rousseau, Tel: 03 86 39 10 97, in winter closed Sunday and Monday, very inexpensive to inexpensive). L'Ecu has its regulars, and serves good housemade terrines, tête de veau, coq au vin, and classics.

Up the scale, south, on the old highway facing the co-op, hostelry **Hôtel-Restaurant Le Coq Hardi** (42 Avenue de la Tuilerie, Tel: 03 86 39 12 99, www.lerelaisfleuri.fr, closed Tuesday and Wednesday in low season, Wednesday in summer, and from mid December to mid January, moderate to very expensive) was taken over in April 2008 by Dominique Fonseca, latterly of Le Ritz in Paris, and his wife Françoise. This comfortable property has a sloping, landscaped garden reaching to the Loire, a pleasant terrace, and a fuddy-duddy dining room (bourgeois French with torero-red tablecloths and mock Louis XIII chairs). Though this is clearly a *gastronomique* address, with certain pretensions, and a tank of live lobsters in the lobby, it deigns to offer a few of the former chef's favorites (crispy fry of Loire River minnows, and delicious Charolais with shallots and marrow, hearty torpedo fish stew). The rest of the menu you'd find at the Ritz. The wines include some inexpensive locals, the service is efficient if stylized, in keeping with the atmosphere.

South two miles on the riverbank is local hangout **Le Relais de Pouilly** (Quai de Loire, Tel: 03 86 39 03 00, www.relaisdepouilly .com, open daily year-round, inexpensive to moderate). The freeway runs on one side. Happily, the other side is quiet (anyone reserving a guest room should insist on a riverside room). There's a children's playground, and the Loire slips greenly by the spacious garden terrace, where regulars and tourists enjoy grilled meats—Charolais beef or Bourbonais lamb—salmon, seafood, and classics from the French repertoire. The atmosphere and service are casual; the wine list boasts affordable bottlings. Don't expect culinary fireworks.

Wineries

Wines were made here in antiquity. Documents from the fifth century AD attest to vineyards owned by religious orders and called *Pauliacum super fluvium ligerim*. Superfluous? What the monks meant was, above the riverbank—*fluvium*, as in effluvium. The twin AOCs of Pouilly-sur-Loire, made from Chasselas grapes, and Pouilly-Fumé, originally from Chasselas but postphylloxera from Sauvignon Blanc, were created in 1937. They reached their apex in the 1980s, dropped out for several decades, and are making a comeback. Pouilly-Fumé covers 3,100 acres (and produces 10 million bottles per year), dwarfing Pouilly-sur-Loire's ninety acres and 260,000 annual bottles. Dry, flinty, often redolent of citrus, Pouilly-Fumé is considered the premium wine of the pair, often aged on oak, which encourages fat, and the scent and flavor of ripe pineapples or passion fruit. Its original name was Blanc-Fumé de Pouilly, because of the noble rot that often attacked and improved Chasselas, giving it a gray, smoky appearance. Pouilly-sur-Loire AOC, a softer, more authentically Burgundian wine, still made with Chasselas, has nutty, honey-and-flowers scents and flavors, sometimes highly nuanced and short-lived. Of the hundred-plus winegrowers in the two AOCs, several good ones are in town; most are scattered around other villages and hamlets: Tracy-sur-Loire, Les Cornets, Les Loges, Nozet, Le Bouchot, and Les Berthiers, part of Saint-Andelain, the most sought-after growing area.

Among the best is **Jean-Claude Châtelain** (Les Berthiers, Saint-Andelain, Tel: 03 86 39 01 13, www.domaine-chatelain.fr, jean-claude.chatelain@wanadoo.fr, open weekdays without appointment, weekends by appointment, closed Christmastide). Though Jean-Claude and his son Vincent continue to machine harvest, they're selective. The Pouilly-Fumé Les Chailloux and Cuvée Prestige are balanced, muscular, the latter grown on Kimmeridgian oyster shells like those of Chablis, providing a mineral backbone.

☙ OTHER WINERIES ☙
IN OR NEAR POUILLY-SUR-LOIRE
OPEN TO THE PUBLIC

These wineries make Pouilly-Fumé and/or Pouilly-sur-Loire, their best wines (unless otherwise noted).

Domaine de Bel Air (6 Rue Waldeck Rousseau, Le Bouchot, Tel: 03 86 39 15 85, mauroygauliez@aol.com, open Monday through Saturday without appointment, Sunday by appointment). Note: organic winegrowers Katia Mauroy-Gauliez and partners welcome visitors.

Domaine du Bouchot (Le Bouchot, Tel: 03 86 39 13 95, www.domaine-du-bouchot.com, by appointment). Note: organic winegrowers Pascal and Rachel Kerbiquet make several remarkable wines, including Pouilly-Fumé Cuvée Regain (6,000 bottles) and Pouilly-sur-Loire.

Caves de Pouilly-sur-Loire (39 Avenue de la Tuilerie, Les Moulins à Vent, Tel: 03 86 39 10 99, www.caves pouillysurloire.com, open daily without appointment). Note: a co-op founded in 1948, with 100 member-growers, it makes award-winning wines, and faces hotel-restaurant Le Coq Hardi, on the southern edge of town; among wines are good Coteaux du Giennois.

Maison de Ladoucette · Château de Nozet (Château de Nozet, Tel: 03 86 39 18 33, open daily without appointment from Easter to November, open weekdays the rest of the year). Note: this huge winery in a fairytale white turreted castle is off the autoroute north of town and is the area's biggest producer, also making Sancerre. It has been in the Ladoucette and Comte Lafond families for over 200 years.

Domaine Masson Blondelet (1 Rue de Paris, Tel: 03 86 39 00 34, www.masson-blondelet.com, open daily without appointment). Note: in town, this multi-generational winery makes reliably very good wines.

Domaine Guy Saget (La Castille, Tel: 03 86 39 57 75, www.guy-saget.com, open weekdays without appointment, weekends by appointment, closed Christ-mastide). Note: this large, upscale, eighth-generation winery is easy to visit; cuvées Les Logères and Les Genièvres are outstanding.

....

Bigger, premium winery **Serge Dagueneau & Filles** (Les Berthiers, Saint-Andelain, Tel: 03 86 39 11 18, www .s-dagueneau-filles.fr, dagueneau@s-dagueneau-filles.fr, open weekdays without appointment, Saturday by appointment, closed Sunday), makes fine Pouilly-Fumé, exceptional Pouilly-sur-Loire from 100-year-old vines, and quaffable Montées de Saint-Lay red (Pinot Noir). A curiosity, the fifty-acre estate, also on chalky, Kimmeridgian soil called Terres Blanches, has a few rows of humidity-and-noble-rot-loving Pinot Gris (Pinot Beurrot), with which Dagueneau makes a few precious bottles. All grapes are hand-picked and -selected. The AOC whites are fresh and crisp, redolent of citrus or hazelnuts, and surprisingly plump.

Sometimes difficult to visit, because the wines sell out, is Benoît Chaveau's **Domaine Chaveau** (Les Cassiers, Saint-Andelain, Tel: 03 86 39 15 42, pouillychaveau@aol.com, by appointment only), a medium-sized estate, with thirty acres, and a well-earned reputation for fat, flowery, fruity Pouilly-Fumés. In particular, La Charmette, Sainte-Clélie, and Croqloups cuvées are regular award-winners.

RAVEAU

Four miles east of La Charité-sur-Loire, on the edge of La Fôret des Bertranges (France's second-largest), Raveau attracts hunters, hikers, mushroom-pickers, and vacationers. There's a roadside café-auberge, and a humble bakery on the square, **Boulangerie Sébastien Lainé** (Tel: 03 86 70 03 08, closed Monday). Beyond good bread and croissants, the bakery also sells excellent honey from **Jean-Pierre Vaurs** (444 Route des Bertranges, Tel: 03 86 70 14 28, phone ahead). Try the earthy, powerful *miel des fôrets* Bertranges or more delicate *miel de printemps*.

Enfolded by the forest, south of Raveau, at Fontaine de la Vache, is **Le Comptoir des Bertranges** (Tel: 03 86 70 13 96, hours vary widely). Sit under a towering sycamore, near a former mill-forge complex, and have coffee or drinks; local farm produce and foods are also sold when available.

Next door is ostensibly luxurious, sui generis B&B–*table d'hôtes–chambres d'hôtes* **Domaine des Forges de la Vache** (Chemin de la Fontaine de la Vache, Tel: 03 86 70 22 96, www .domaine-des-forges-dela-vache.com, closed Tuesday in winter, meals inexpensive to moderate). Shabby chic, this reconverted forge complex dates to the 1700s. Formidable Madame Claudine Muller, very French, is a countrified ex-city dweller. Her lodge attracts migratory Parisians, and hunters with designer camouflage. The vast rooms are tastefully decorated; holding ponds and streams beautify the garden, and there's a funky glassed-in terrace. The dining room is cozy, with built-ins and wooden furniture. Overnight guests dine on market-based cooking whipped up by budding cooks, usually using garden-grown or forest-plucked ingredients, from snails and lettuce to wild mushrooms. Some good local wines are on the list (Pouilly-sur-Loire, Pouilly-Fumé, and Pinot Beurrot whites and a Montée Saint-Lay Pays red from Serge Dagueneau).

More authentically Nivernais is seasonal *chambres d'hôtes* **Le Bois Dieu** (Le Bois Dieu, Tel: 03 86 69 60 02, www.leboisdieu .com, leboidieu@wanadoo.fr, closed mid November to April, meals [not served on Sunday night] inexpensive, including wine). Also edging the forest, less than a mile from the village, at Le Bois Dieu, this ivy-clad B&B—*table d'hôtes* is in a handsome farmhouse of centuries past, with a leafy garden shaded by an old cedar. Most of the food is raised on the farm by Dominique and Jean Mellet-Mandard. Expect Burgundian and Loire specialties, following the seasons, from fresh salads with chèvre cheese or terrines to grilled, roasted, or stewed chicken and lamb—perhaps the ones you saw in the courtyard and abutting pastures.

RIOUSSE

In pastureland south of Livry, near the Loire, winemakers are attempting to revive lost traditions. On a hillock spread **Clos de Riousse** and **Cave Le Rioussat** (Tel: 06 11 33 31 60 or 03 86 90 80 46, www.lerioussat.com, vignoble.riousse@yahoo.fr, open daily afternoons only or by appointment). This co-op, founded in 1991, has 37.5 acres and makes table wines—red and white—from Gamay, Pinot Noir, and Chardonnay. Recently, a new oenologist has improved the estate's fortunes. For now, these wines have curiosity value.

SAINT-FARGEAU

The sub-regional capital of the watery Puisaye, in the Yonne, Saint-Fargeau is a surprisingly attractive stop on highway D965, between Auxerre and the Loire. It was long famed for wealth from timber, mining, and pottery. The château—the main tourist attraction—is where the formidable cousin of Louis XIV, Louise d'Orléans, alias **La Grande Mademoiselle** (Tel: 03 86 74 05 67, www.chateau-de-st-fargeau.com, closed mid November to April) took refuge. Of the restaurants and hotels catering to vacationers and travelers, try cozy, archly traditional **Auberge la Demoiselle** (1 Place de la République, Tel: 03 86 74 10 58, open daily in summer, closed dinner Sunday and Wednesday, Monday, and from Christmastide to February, inexpensive to moderate). The regional and classic French food is good; visible is the château, out front.

In the reconverted train station find the city outlet of working farm **L'Auberge Les Perriaux** (Tel: 03 86 74 16 45, www .lesperriaux.com, open daily year-round, very inexpensive to moderate). The farm produces much of what you eat, from apple cider, foie gras, rich terrines of waterfowl, to nicely presented duck magret or confit, roasted or stewed chicken, and housemade seasonal desserts (cheeses are locally made). The sunny dining room is in the refurbished waiting rooms and entrance; in summer, tables are set up on a terrace. Also in summer, or on weekends, you may opt to eat two miles away at the farmhouse, in a rustic dining room with a fireplace (Champignelles, Tel: 03 86 74 13 22, same website, prices, and food, by reservation only).

SAINT-PÈRE

A few miles east of Cosne in gently rolling hills, Saint-Père has been growing wine since the Middle Ages. The local festival, Foué Avaloue, is held the second weekend in September. In outlying Croquant, look for **Chambres d'hôtes–table d'hôtes L'Orée des Vignes** (Tel: 03 86 28 12 50, www.loreedesvignes.com, open daily year-round, meals inexpensive and for overnight guests only, reserve ahead). At this quiet, comfortable, family-owned B&B you dine on garden-grown lettuces, vegetables, and farm produce, prepared and served with flair by Marie-Noëlle and Michel Kandin. Foie gras is the house specialty (you can learn to make it, in winter). The farmstead is centuries old; guest rooms nest under mansard roofs. The dining room is furnished with authentic, highly polished antiques. A bread oven is part of the sitting room décor. In summer, the garden is open for breakfast, lunch, lounging, and snacking.

Due east in Pougny is one of the AOC's best, most professional wineries and distilleries: **Domaine Michel Langlois** (Tel: 03 86 28 47 08, catmi-langlois@wanadoo.fr or catmi-langlois@orange .fr, open daily without appointment, Sunday afternoon by appointment only). Michel and Catherine Langlois took over the family business in 1996, expanded and remodeled. They produce true-to-type reds and whites in stainless steel, and several ambitious wines (Le Champ Galant red and Chardonnay, a *vin de table*) that spend a considerable time on new oak. They also produce uncommonly fat Pouilly-Fumé, from the Domaine des Granges estate, which they took over in 2004. Affable, the couple are celebrated for their fruit liqueurs and eaux de vie, notably wild blackberry and bilberry (both local, hand-picked), and Cassis (blackcurrants come from a grower). They produce local aperitifs Bourguignon (blackberry and red wine) and Myro (bilberry and rosé), plus Kir.

SAINT-PIERRE-LE-MOÛTIER

Near the fledgling vineyards of Riousse and Livry, this ungentrified village famous because Joan of Arc battled the English here, now abuts the recently completed N7/A77 expressway-autoroute, and is therefore convenient for lunch or dinner. On the freeway's east side, find long-established **Restaurant La Vigne** (Route de Decize, Tel: 03 86 37 41 66, closed Sunday dinner and Monday, the second half of November, and the second half of February). Wrapped in leafy grounds, with a shaded terrace, this old-fashioned, country restaurant in a turn-of-the-nineteenth-century building resembles a chalet (with guest rooms in mini-chalets). It has been in the same family since 1932. The décor and menu haven't changed a great deal (knotty pine, copper pots, Nevers china plates, white tablecloths on well-spaced tables), nor has the pleasant, Titanic-era atmosphere. Expect housemade terrine forestière with hazelnuts and Muscat jelly, Bourbonais chicken breast with cream and mushrooms, Loire pike-perch with a creamy tarragon sauce, local cheeses, and simple but delicious housemade desserts. The wine list includes locals and big Burgundies.

VARENNES-VAUZELLES

Only drive here if you're willing to interpret *terroir* liberally: **Restaurant Le Bengy** (25 Route de Paris, Tel: 03 86 38 02 84, www.le-bengy-restaurant.com, closed Sunday and Monday, end July to late August, the first week in January, and late February to mid March, inexpensive to moderate) has *gastronomique* writ large. Upscale gourmets from Nevers dine here on artfully served, creative haute—which makes the setting all the more improbable. The restaurant is tastefully decorated, elegant, and comfortable, with a garden patio, but it's at the north end of an interminable strip mall north of Nevers, near the #33 autoroute exit. Dominique Gérard belongs to the Toques Nivernaises group of gourmet restaurateurs. Like many, he uses local ingredients (pike-perch from the Loire) but largely shuns tradition. Like all too few chefs, he also makes everything from scratch, and runs a tight ship. Gérard is equally recognized as a wine expert; his list is long and deep.

✤ MARKET DAYS IN BURGUNDY ✤

Arnay-le-Duc Thursday *124*

Autun Wednesday and Friday *126*

Auxerre Tuesday and Friday *72*

Avallon Saturday *131*

Beaune Wednesday and Saturday *223*

Bourbon-Lancy Saturday *374*

Brancion and **Martailly-lès-Brancion** first and third
        Sundays of the month *277*

Buxy Thursday *277*

Chablis Sunday *96*

Chagny Sunday *278*

Chalon-sur-Saône various locations daily except
        Monday *280, 283*

Charolles Wednesday *378*

Clamecy Saturday *138*

Cluny Saturday *363*

Coeuzon Sunday *139*

Corbigny Tuesday *409*

Cosne-Cours-sur-Loire Wednesday and Sunday *410*

Le Creusot Saturday *294*

Dijon Tuesday, Thursday, Friday, Saturday *181*

Donzy Saturday *412*

Givry Thursday *295*

Igé Saturday *369*

Joigny Saturday (under Saint Aubin sur Yonne) *80*

Louhans Monday *319*

Mâcon Saturday, second and fourth Thursdays of the
        month *341*

Meursault Friday *243*

Nevers Saturday *417*

Nolay Monday *252*

Noyers Wednesday *110*

Planchez Friday *146*

Pouilly-en-Auxois Friday *175*

Pouilly-sur-Loire Friday *423*

Quarre-les-Tombes Sunday *147*

Saint Florentin Saturday *82*

Saint-Bonnet-de-Joux Sunday in summer *393*

Saint-Christophe-en-Brionnais Wednesday (cattle) *393*

Saint-Gengoux-le-National Tuesday, first and third
        Thursday of the month, some Saturdays *304*

Saulieu Saturday *155*

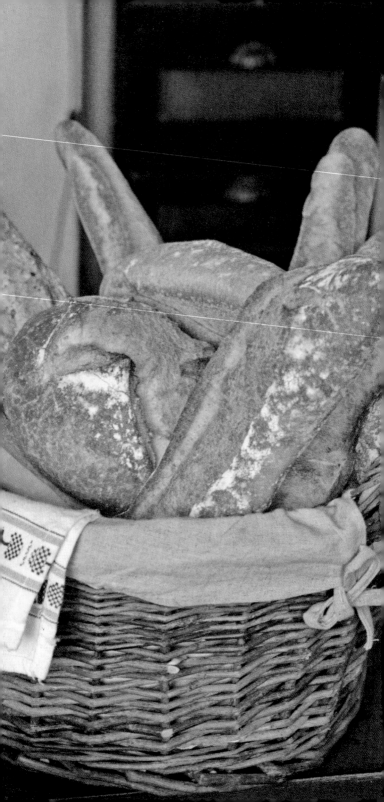

FOOD & WINE GLOSSARY

....

affinage (*affiner, affineur*): aging (usually of cheese), cheesemonger who ages cheese

andouillette: peppery tripe sausage; a specialty of Chablis (and other towns)

anis de Flavigny: candied aniseed, made at the Abbey of Flavigny (Côte d'Or)

AOC/AOP: *Appellation d'Origine Contrôlée/Protégée*; product (usually wine) whose origin is controlled/protected by a governmental entity (in France, INAO)

arrachage: uprooting (also *défonçage*), usually of grapevines

bâtonnage: weekly stirring of white wine lees

bouchon, bouchage, bouché: cork, stoppers/corking, corked (defective)

bourgeon: bud (*débourgeonnage* or *ébourgeonnage*, or removing excess buds from vines)

bûchettes Sénonaises: log-shaped candies from Sens (*bûchettes* are also log-shaped filled chocolates from Central Burgundy)

buttage: mounding, covering of grapevine base with soil

capsule à vis: screwtop

caviste: wineseller, wine merchant

cépage: grape variety

Climat: particular Cru (usually Grand Cru or 1er Cru) or *terroir* with micro-climate and peculiar characteristics

clos (*de vigne*): vineyard (often part of estate name)

corniotte: pastry with triangular shortbread base turned up at the corners, topped by a sweet, miniature puff pastry (typical of the Bresse Bourguignonne)

côte: hill, slope, coastline (in wine, steep vineyard slope, wine country, winegrowing district)

coteaux: mildly sloping hillside (lesser winegrowing district)

courtier: trader (wholesaler of grapes or wines)

crapiaud: rustic Morvan crêpe filled with everything from bacon and cheese to snails

Cru: in wine, literally "growth," a measure of the quality of a vineyard and hence of the wine produced from it; in food, raw, uncooked *cuvée*: vintage, year, or batch of wine (*cuve* = tank, vat; *cuverie* = tank room in winery; *cuvaison* = tanking, initial making of wine in tank or vat, usually for maceration and alcoholic fermentation)

débourbage: decanting and settling of pressed juice

débuttage: uncovering of (removal of soil from) grapevine base

désherbage: removing grass from vineyard

écrevisse: crayfish

élaboration/élaborer: making of wine (turning of bottles, *manipuler*), usually sparkling (Crémant)

élevage: aging (of wine); ranching, farming, husbandry (of cattle, sheep, etc.)

éleveur: farmer, rancher (also winemaker, specifically one who ages wine)

enherbement: allowing grass to grow (between rows of vines)

épamprages: removing excess branches (*pampres*) from vines

escargot: snail

faisselle(s): fresh cottage or farmstead cheese (often plural)

fermier: farm-raised, farmhouse (also farmer, rancher)

feuillette: an oak cask holding 132 liters

fouler: to crush grapes (lightly)

fût: cask or barrel (of oak)

gougère: Burgundian cheese puff, served with aperitifs

grappe: bunch (of grapes; *égrappage* or *éraflage* = detaching grapes from stems)

jambon: ham (*jambon persillé* = in parsley aspic; *sur l'os* = bone-in; *cru* = raw, air-dried)

Marc de Bourgogne: distillate or eau de vie made from grape leavings, vinous dregs, and/or wine residues (brandy)

matelote: freshwater fish stew (see *pocheuse*)

mildiou: mildew, fungal pest (also *rouille* = vine rust, *oïdium* = powdery mildew)

millésime: vintage (from *mille*, 1000); logically, since 2000, the term should be *deux-millésime*

négociant: wine merchant, wholesaler; winemaker who buys grapes from others; (same as *maison de négoce*)

nonnettes: silver-dollar-sized, half-inch-thick sweets flavored with honey and spices

oeufs en meurette: eggs poached in a winey sauce made with bacon, onions or shallots and thickened with flour (***meurette*** = a wine sauce in which rabbit, hare, beef, lamb, poultry were once cooked)

omble chevalier: char, *Salvelinus alpinus*, related to salmon and trout

parcelle: vineyard plot

pets-de-nonne: sugar-dusted fritters

phylloxera: pest of the aphid family, *Phylloxera Daktulosphaira vitifoliae*, saps the life from grapevines

pêche de vigne: heirloom vineyard peach, small, firm and often purple-fleshed

pigeage: pushing down the mass of crushed grapes floating on top of the vat during maceration or alcoholic fermentation (the opposite is remontage, pulling up the mass)

pocheuse (***paucheuse, pauchouse***): freshwater fish stew, originally from Verdun-sur-le-Doubs, also ***matelote***

pot-au-feu: pot roast

pourriture: rot (***pourriture noble*** = noble rot)

pressurage: pressing out juice

raisin: grape

rochers de Sens: chocolate-coated caramelized almond clusters from Sens

rosette: rustic salami, sometimes flavored with garlic and white wine

taille: pruning (style of pruning) of grapevine

tête de cuvée: best wine of vintage (best of the vat, select batch)

tonneau: large barrel (of oak)

treffe (***treuffe***): potato

truffe: truffle (Burgundy truffle = *Tuber uncinatum*)

vendanges: grape harvest (***vendanges tardives*** = late harvest)

véraison: the coloring of green, immature grapes into semi-mature, red or purple grapes (Pinot Noir, Gamay)

vigne: grapevine

vigneron: grape-grower, winemaker, winegrower (also producteur)

vignoble: wine-growing district, vineyard area, vineyard (rare)

INDEX

....

B

D

E

I

N

Q

R

T

U

V

X

Y

ABOUT THE AUTHOR

....

David Downie is an American author and journalist who divides his time between France and Italy. For the last 20 years he has been writing about European food, culture and travel for magazines and newspapers worldwide. His books include *Enchanted Liguria: A Celebration of the Culture, Lifestyle and Food of the Italian Riviera*; *Cooking the Roman Way: Authentic Recipes from the Home Cooks and Trattorias of Rome*; *The Irreverent Guide to Amsterdam*; and *Paris, Paris: Journey into the City of Light*. Downie's first Terroir Guide, *Food Wine The Italian Riviera & Genoa*, came out in November 2008. His political thriller, *Paris City of Night*, was published in 2009, as was his second Terroir Guide, this one to Rome. Please visit David Downie's website at www.davidddownie.com.

ABOUT THE PHOTOGRAPHER

....

Alison Harris lives in Paris and travels extensively taking photos for travel books, cookbooks, advertising campaigns, newspapers, and magazines. Her latest books, *Markets of Paris*, *The Pâtisseries of Paris*, and *Chic Shopping Paris*, are published by The Little Bookroom. She has also photographed two other Terroir Guides: *Food Wine Rome* and *Food Wine The Italian Riviera & Genoa*. Please visit Alison Harris' website at www.alisonharris.com

Other titles in The Terroir Guides *series*

FOOD WINE ROME

by David Downie • Photographs by Alison Harris

". . . an invaluable key to the city's authentic quaffs and cuisines. Eschewing eateries that are likely to be visited by the typical bus-group turiste, Downie walks readers through bountiful food markets, into artisanal-food shops and to the front doors of Rome's temples of food and drink. The reviews in this highly informative restaurant guide, accompanied by Alison Harris's photographs, also celebrate the people, customs and tastes that tempt so many travelers to eat as discriminating Romans do." —*Town & Country*

ISBN 978-1-892145-71-0

FOOD WINE THE ITALIAN RIVIERA & GENOA

by David Downie • Photographs by Alison Harris

"Outside of general guidebooks to Italy, few individual regions have had single volumes dedicated to their gastronomy, and this, one of a series of 'Terroir Guides,' is both thorough in its listings of places to eat and drink, from ristoranti and focaccerie to pasticcerie and chocolate shops, as it is a well-written depiction of what makes Liguria so very special—and heretofore underrated—as a territory for wonderful food and wine, with its rippling, seafood-rich coastline, its famous basil that goes into making pesto, and its ties to the cooking of Southern France. Excellent, evocative photos too." —John Mariani

ISBN 978-1-892145-64-2

FOOD WINE BUDAPEST

by Carolyn Bánfalvi • Photographs by George Konkoly-Thege

"It is, quite simply, the best guide available today to the culinary renaissance of the city and region in the post-communist era. Banfalvi profiles some of the best restaurants and wine bars in Budapest, but also includes cafes, pastry shops, specialty food shops and markets, as well as the traditions behind their offerings. Helpfully, she includes extensive translations for the names of wines, foods and cooking methods as well. This is the first book in a new series called Terroir Guides, which promises to explore cities or regions, focusing on the way local influences are reflected in food and wine. The Budapest guide sets a high standard for those that follow." —Laszlo Buhasz, *The Globe and Mail*

ISBN 978-1-892145-56-7

FOOD SAKE TOKYO

by Yukari Sakamoto • Photographs by Takuya Suzuki

Yukari Sakamoto—a Japanese-American chef, sommelier, journalist, and restaurant consultant—leads the reader to the best food in Tokyo, de-mystifying the ingredients, dishes, and culinary culture of this fascinating city.

ISBN 978-1-892145-74-1

• • •

To see all of The Little Bookroom's *guidebooks, please go to* www.littlebookroom.com